D1202311

Gateway to the Northern Plains

Gateway to the Northern Plains

Railroads and the
Birth of Fargo and Moorhead

CARROLL ENGELHARDT

University of Minnesota Press
Minneapolis · London

An earlier version of chapter 1 appeared as "The Incorporation of America: The Northern Pacific, the Lake Superior and Puget Sound Company, and the Founding of Fargo–Moorhead," *North Dakota History* 68, no. 4 (2001): 26–38; reprinted with permission. Part of chapter 2 appeared as "Henry A. Bruns, Failed Frontier Entrepreneur," *Minnesota History* 58 (summer 2002): 92–104; reprinted with permission from Minnesota Historical Society Press.

Published by the University of Minnesota Press
111 Third Avenue South, Suite 290
Minneapolis, MN 55401-2520
http://www.upress.umn.edu

Library of Congress Cataloging-in-Publication Data

Engelhardt, Carroll L.
  Gateway to the northern plains : railroads and the birth of Fargo and Moorhead /
Carroll Engelhardt.
      p. cm.
  Includes bibliographical references and index.
  ISBN-13: 978-0-8166-4956-3 (hc/j: alk. paper) — ISBN-10: 0-8166-4956-1 (hc/j: alk. paper)
  1. Fargo (N.D.)—History—19th century. 2. Moorhead (Minn.)—History—19th century.
3. Fargo (N.D.)—Economic conditions—19th century. 4. Moorhead (Minn.)—Economic con-
ditions—19th century. 5. Northern Pacific Railway Company—History. 6. Great Northern
Railway Company (U.S.)—History. I. Title.
  F644.F2E54   2007
  978.4'1301—dc22

                                                                                    2006103291

Printed in the United States of America on acid-free paper

The University of Minnesota is an equal-opportunity educator and employer.

15 14 13 12 11 10 09 08 07   10 9 8 7 6 5 4 3 2 1

For those other fraternal twins
grandchildren Cecilia Ruby and Gus Nathaniel Gerlach
and Oscar Paul and Annalise Caroline Gerlach

Contents

Acknowledgments

RESEARCH AND WRITING ARE BY NATURE SOLITARY ACTIVITIES. YET neither can take place without the support of many individuals and institutions. Together these comprise the community that all scholarship requires. This project began with my participation in a National Endowment for the Humanities Summer Seminar at the University of Virginia in 1992. I am grateful for the encouragement provided at that time by its director, Olivier Zunz.

During the book's prolonged gestation, Concordia College awarded me two semester-long sabbaticals and a summer research grant. College librarians efficiently processed countless interlibrary loan requests. An energetic departmental secretary afforded cheerful and extensive clerical assistance. Historian colleagues from Concordia and North Dakota State University gave important aid. Hiram Drache shared newspaper research notes and the example of his own local history publications. Computer literate Vince Arnold rendered invaluable technical help in preparing the manuscript for the press. Rick Chapman, Joy Lintelman, David Danbom, and Claire Strom read and commented extensively on a primitive early draft. Don Hofsommer at St. Cloud State University and Paul Groth at the University of California, Berkeley, read and critiqued a later version. I have discovered that readers' comments are greater than the sum of their parts. Their questions and suggestions often triggered more substantive changes than they may have intended. Hence, I alone am responsible for all errors and confusions in the present account.

Reference librarians at many institutions near and far have given courteous assistance. During one summer, I visited the McCormick Harvester Machine Company Collection at the Wisconsin State Historical Society in Madison; R. G. Dun and Company Collections at the Harvard Business School Baker Library in Cambridge; the Ada Louise Comstock Notestein Papers in the Schlesinger Library at Radcliffe College in Cambridge; and the Thomas Hawley Canfield Papers at the Vermont Historical Library in Montpelier and the University of Vermont Library in Burlington. Closer to home, many librarians at the Minnesota Historical Society aided my research with the Northern Pacific Railway Company Papers, the Great Northern Railway Records, and several other collections. I used the James J. Hill Papers at the James J. Hill Library in St. Paul, the Roy P. Johnson/Louis Pfaller Collection at the State Historical Society of North Dakota Archives in Bismarck, and the Lily Snyder Haynes Collection at Montana State University in Bozeman.

I am most indebted to Moorhead and Fargo libraries and librarians. I began my research at the Northwest Minnesota Historical Center at Minnesota State University Moorhead. Archivist Terry Shoptaugh's talk of "early metropolitan dreams" encouraged and stimulated me. Archivist Mark Peihl at the Clay County Historical Society helped me search his collections, answered my many questions from his detailed knowledge, and shared his own research materials on Moorhead prostitution. He also assisted in selecting and scanning images. The Institute for Regional Studies at North Dakota State University provided newspapers, collections, and other materials on Fargo's history. John Bye, John Hallberg, and Mike Robinson answered questions, retrieved sources, made suggestions, and assisted in so many ways. I am grateful to editor Pieter Martin and others at the University of Minnesota Press for their assistance in developing and producing this book.

Last and most important, I thank my life partner, Jo Engelhardt. She lived with this book for years. She joined in the journeys and, as always, helped with the work.

Abbreviations

AFL	American Federation of Labor
AOUW	Ancient Order of United Workmen
ARU	American Railway Union
BFA	Better Farming Association
GAR	Grand Army of the Republic
IOOF	Independent Order of Odd Fellows
LS&PS	Lake Superior and Puget Sound
NDAC	North Dakota Agricultural College
OES	Order of the Eastern Star
SPM&M	St. Paul, Minneapolis and Manitoba
TLPU	Trades and Labor Protective Union
WCTU	Woman's Christian Temperance Union
WRC	Woman's Relief Corps
YMCA	Young Men's Christian Association

Introduction

J. A. JOHNSON DIED QUIETLY AT HIS FARGO HOME ON THE MORN-ing of June 14, 1907. His passing marked the end of an era and cast a pall over the city he had helped transform from a small town. His grieving widow, five children, and three grandchildren received sympathy resolutions from the Old Settlers Association, the Commercial Club, the North Dakota Municipal League, and several fraternal bodies. Many workers paid their respects, testifying to the popularity of the deceased with the "tin-pail brigade." The Reverend R. A. Beard of the First Congregational Church presided at the Christian funeral service; after that the Knights Templar conducted a Masonic rite. A lengthy procession accompanied the casket to the Great Northern depot and an eastbound train carried it for burial near Stillwater, Minnesota.[1]

Johnson, a lifelong Republican, had taken keen interest in his community. In his fifth mayoral term at the time of death, he previously held seats on the school board and city council. More than a half century earlier, this native of Sweden had immigrated to Minnesota with his parents. He came to Fargo via the Northern

Fargo mayor J. A. Johnson served his community as a civic and business leader. Photograph from *Hon. J. A. Johnson: A Partial Copy of His Letters, Travels and Addresses*, edited by Alice E. Chester and Laura A. Johnson (Fargo: privately printed, 1908).

Pacific in 1879 to establish a farm machinery branch office. Seymour, Sabin & Company hoped to profit from the new Bonanza wheat farms created by the railroad corporation to advertise its fertile federal land grant.[2]

The coming of the Northern Pacific in 1871 created Moorhead and Fargo where the tracks spanned the Red River. During the next three decades the Northern Pacific and other railroads shaped the two cities economically, socially, and politically. The railroads brought wheat farmers who settled the hinterland and created opportunities for businessmen such as J. A. Johnson. Trains carried the materials for constructing homes, businesses, churches, schools, and urban improvements. They brought the goods for establishing genteel culture. They transported harvest hands and purveyors of vice that challenged middle-class moral order. They connected civic leaders with eastern technologies and methods for creating good municipal government.

A Northern Pacific work train constructing the first railroad bridge into Dakota Territory in 1872 after corporate managers determined "the crossing" and the location of Moorhead and Fargo. Courtesy Minnesota Historical Society.

They restricted the newer and smaller twin cities of the Red River Valley to economic dependence on the older and larger Twin Cities of Minneapolis and St. Paul.[3] While distant railroad corporations and allied companies initiated settlement and fostered growth of Fargo and Moorhead, local small businessmen formed an uneasy partnership with corporate managers. Each partner needed the other to attain wealth. Sometimes they cooperated and at other times they conflicted in their mutual pursuit of profits.

Boosters and entrepreneurs in Fargo and Moorhead aspired to make their city the "Gateway to the Northern Plains." Although neither city realized its dream, Fargo attained more success than its Minnesota rival. From their beginning, booster-minded editors often referred to Moorhead and Fargo collectively as "the Crossing," "the Dual City," or "the Twin Cities." The latter perhaps better conveys their shared history as fraternal twins. Although firstborn Moorhead hoped to build upon an early size advantage, Fargo soon surpassed it. As the towns grew, they experienced sibling rivalry but at times achieved fraternal accord. Indeed, observers deprecated conflict as harmful and urged cooperation as more conducive to growth. The *Fargo Evening Republican* warned in 1882: "The interests of the two cities are identical as far as they can be under two different governments and it is suicidal folly to stir up . . . differences." To be sure, the *Republican* also disparaged the jealousy and copying exhibited by its smaller rival and archly stated: "God and nature have ordained that Moorhead will always be inferior to Fargo." Despite frequent slurs of this kind by editors on both sides of the river, boosters at times cooperated in promoting growth by hosting editors, state officials, and additional visitors. The Twin City Ministers' Association and other religious-minded folk met periodically to advance religion and moral order in both cities. Energetic businessmen with a vision of shared prosperity occasionally nurtured common ties as they advertised both towns.[4]

Geography and climate of the northern plains determined that the twin cities would be small places. Temperature extremes, limited rainfall, and a short growing season discouraged many settlers, potential and actual. Although the region's subhumid grasslands could not sustain large numbers, the soil yielded bumper wheat crops, which provided the principal earnings for the farmers who populated the plains. Dependence on wheat monoculture, however, placed farmers at an economic disadvantage. Profits fluctuated widely, giving them a lower-than-average per capita income in good times and bad. Additionally, the region's remote location from the largest U.S. cities dictated high transportation costs to principal markets, preventing the development of manufacturing. This lack made the area even more dependent on the railroads, grain elevators, flour mills, and banks of

St. Paul and Minneapolis. It did not serve these corporate interests to permit an urban rival on the northern plains.[5]

Fargo and Moorhead competed to become the gateway city for the region in the same way that Omaha and Kansas City struggled against nearby towns for dominance of the central plains. The geographic isolation of the twin cities, however, prevented them from attaining the population and economic power of these southern gateways. Omaha's population reached just over 140,000 by 1890, while that of Kansas City climbed to more than 132,000. They served hinterlands in Nebraska and Kansas with more than three to four times as many people as North Dakota. Excellent connections to Chicago and other metropolitan areas made them major rail centers and attracted eastern capital, which established packinghouses and stockyards. Kansas City shipped most of the nation's livestock. New York and Boston firms established insurance and mercantile companies there. As the headquarters of the Union Pacific Railroad, Omaha controlled the jobbing trade for Nebraska and became "the Gate City."[6]

Based on the U.S. Census category for urban, it can be objected that neither Moorhead nor Fargo qualified as cities during most of the period examined by my study. Not until the 1890s did Moorhead permanently surpass 2,500 people—the lowest and arguably too small threshold established by the first federal census. Later in that same decade, Fargo exceeded eight thousand residents, the minimum set by the federal census in 1860 for inclusion among urban categories. Despite their small size, Moorhead and Fargo performed the functions of cities. Like colonial Boston and New York, they served as commercial "centers for the surrounding countryside and as points of contact for the outside world." Additionally, from their birth they viewed themselves as cities. Both shared a "metropolitan dream" of becoming places typified by industry, commerce, and, after 1880, the full array of urban services—electric lights, waterworks, streetcars, and daily newspapers. In calling Moorhead and Fargo cities, I have accepted their functional role, cultural self-definition, and metropolitan dreams rather than the statistical definitions offered by the U.S. Census.[7]

Historians have long stressed the importance of cities to the development of the United States. As Carl Bridenbaugh observed, urban factors have governed much of American life from "the earliest settlement on American soil." Similarly, Richard Wade argued that cities played a fundamental role in the westward expansion of the United States in the early nineteenth century. According to Wade, "cities represented the more aggressive and dynamic force. By spreading their economic power over the entire region . . . they speeded up the transformation of the West." More recently, Diane Shaw contends that the commercially minded consciously created frontier cities for profit. The founders built urban structures and spaces that projected an "image of economic vitality and bourgeois gentility." They viewed "cities as vehicles of improvement" that enhanced economic productivity and carried civilization westward.[8]

In the late nineteenth century, Fargo and Moorhead played a similar role in the settlement and economic advance of the Red River Valley. Hence, both are worthy of study as small cities founded at a time when the United States expanded westward, built a national railroad network, underwent rapid industrialization, and created a corporate economy. Small cities are numerous, have a large population collectively, and have made a significant contribution to urban culture. Scholars have long noted the need for more information about small cities in order to better understand their significant contribution to American society. More specifically, according to Carroll Van West in his fine history of Billings and the Yellowstone Valley, little attention has been paid to the development of particular cities on the northern plains in the late nineteenth century, although superior studies by John Hudson and Paula Nelson have examined early-twentieth-century town growth in North and South Dakota, respectively.[9]

To help fill this scholarly void, I have written an analytical urban biography of Fargo and Moorhead, showing how the railroad shaped their growth. While tracing the changes brought by the impersonal forces of industrialization and incorporation, I describe the development of their local community cultures. Whether or not these municipalities were distinctive is difficult to assess. I see them as most likely similar to many other urban places. As Sam Bass Warner Jr. suggested in his classic study of Philadelphia, "The tradition of privatism is . . . the most important element of our culture for understanding the development of cities." Men seeking wealth created families and the communities of Fargo and Moorhead. Small businesses predominated. Commercial-oriented civic leaders controlled municipal government. They kept peace among profit-seeking families and aimed at preserving opportunities for all to prosper, thus determining the twin cities' success. Urban historian Lawrence Larsen has argued that western cities "were carbon copies of those constructed earlier in the older parts of the country." Taking on Warner's thesis, Larsen asserts: "Uncontrolled capitalism led to disorderly development that reflected the abilities of individual entrepreneurs rather than most other factors." New cities of the West transplanted technology, urban services, public schools, and churches. They shared similar ethnic composition, boosterism, and street grids with cities of the East.[10]

Although Fargo and Moorhead defined themselves in opposition to "the other" during their frequent bouts of intercity rivalry, this did not create the distinctive civic identities that Mary Lethert Wingerd has uncovered in her excellent study of St. Paul, Minnesota. In contrast to Minneapolis, a city dominated by Yankee capitalists and industrial corporations, St. Paul became a transportation and distribution center in which business negotiated settlements with labor mediated by the Irish Catholic church. As a consequence, St. Paul developed an intensely local outlook and a distinctive civic identification with place.[11] In contrast, similarities in commercial economy, ethnic composition, and religious affiliations led Moorhead and Fargo to develop a common culture dominated by a shared commitment to entrepreneurial boosterism and to middle-class social and moral order.

Part I begins with the coming of the railroad and the founding of each town. It examines the expansion of corporate institutions and values into the rural hinterland and the response of middle-class residents who had designs and dreams of their own. Railroad managers and local businessmen at times competed, often cooperated, and always negotiated in promoting the economic development of each city and the agricultural hinterland. At the same time, steel rails linked the twin cities and their hinterland to the expanding metropolitan economy of such places as Minneapolis, St. Paul, and Chicago. Although these connections created opportunities for local businessmen, they also increased the high risks of town building and other western enterprise. Failure might thwart local dreams of opportunity and success. Moorhead entrepreneur Henry A. Bruns suffered business ruin as he failed to make Moorhead the key city of the valley at the same time that Fargo succeeded in becoming the "Gateway City" to North Dakota. Yet the bigger Twin Cities to the south forever prevented Fargo from realizing its dream of becoming the "Gateway to the Northern Plains."

Part II examines "the search for moral order." As Northern Pacific advertisements throughout Europe and the eastern United States attracted prospective settlers to the region, dual city boosters and businessmen soon perceived the connection between rural settlement, urban population growth, and their own economic success. Hence, they welcomed most immigrants and their families of whatever cultural and religious background as being vital to their respective cities. American- and European-born joined in creating churches, lodges, schools, and other institutions that fostered the hegemony of middle-class values in the twin cities. Saloons, brothels, and gambling dens, however, served the single men who congregated during the wheat harvest season. These vices offended the respectable middle class, who struggled to contain or eliminate their pernicious effects on the moral order. Bourgeois difficulties in distinguishing between the tramps they loathed and the harvest laborers they required complicated middle-class efforts at reform. Organized labor similarly challenged middle-class hegemony. Workers participated in the bourgeois moral ethos when they organized and acted like fraternal lodges. However, when these behaved like labor unions, adopted the strike as a weapon, and engaged in violence against property, they undermined the middle-class moral order.

Part II also examines government, tracing its evolution from "booster politics" to "service cities" financed more responsibly. Boosters and businessmen dominated civic administration. They bridged the Red River and established rudimentary urban services to attract settlers and to promote economic development. Financial excesses and vice provoked middle-class reformers and businessmen to demand better government. Reformers called for mayors and aldermen who promoted fiscal responsibility, moral rectitude, and services that protected as well as promoted the physical comforts of residents. By 1900, progressives and their reforms had enabled Fargo and Moorhead to achieve an institutional maturity that provides an appropriate place to end this study. Fargo had become the distribution center for the settled valley and region. Well-established urban services,

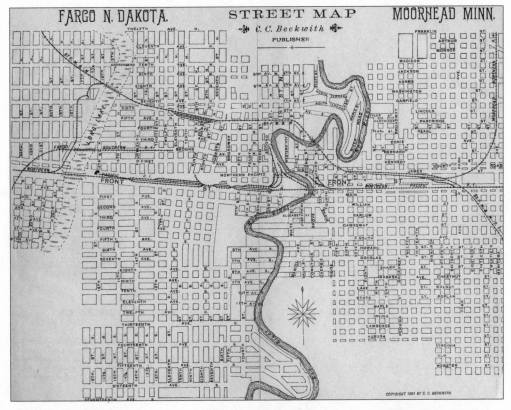

A street map from 1891 indicates the Fargo and Moorhead grid pattern initially established by the Northern Pacific and the LS&PS companies. From *Fargo and Moorhead City Directory* (Fargo: C. C. Beckwith, 1891).

civic organizations, schools, and churches supported the middle-class moral order that pervaded both communities and contained lower-class vice and disorder.

Mayor J. A. Johnson personified these political achievements. He stressed the advantages of strictly enforced prohibition for Fargo. He spearheaded the drive for good government by participating in state and national municipal leagues. He helped secure new state legislation that permitted the assessment of railroad properties for municipal tax purposes as well as special assessments of other property owners to pay for paved streets and an improved sewerage system. He advocated municipal ownership of water and electricity. He worked with businessmen as well as the railroads to promote Fargo and commercial development by attracting new businesses and numerous conventions. Moorhead mirrored several of these trends. By 1900, the twin cities had attained a maturity that charted their course and sustained their growth in the twentieth century.

PART I

Railroads at Red River

At the Crossing

I hope to get the crossing at Red River established & the place for the town designated before we leave. I have much trouble with my town matters in consequence of changing lines by the Directors—I hope however this is last time the line will be changed & that I shall have no more trouble from that source.

—Thomas Hawley Canfield to
Carrie Canfield, August 19, 1871

The object of the [Northern Pacific] Land Department is to get as much as possible for the lands, as rapidly as possible, with the least possible expense. . . . Bear in mind that the best interests of the company & purchaser are identical.

—Frederick Billings to
George Wright, April 19, 1872

MANY NINETEENTH-CENTURY AMERICANS BELIEVED THAT WHERE railroads crossed rivers, great cities might arise. As the Northern Pacific built west to the Red River Valley in the summer of 1871, speculators gathered at Georgetown, Oakport, and elsewhere to claim land at the crossing. Others patrolled the river's edge, watching for activity. To prevent their success, Thomas Hawley Canfield—president of the Lake Superior and Puget Sound (LS&PS) Company charged with creating railroad town sites—utilized secrecy and duplicity. In addition to the original route surveyed to where the Elm River entered the Red north of Georgetown, surveyors ran one fake line to Oakport—later called Bogusville—and another to the mouth of the Wild Rice River. Meanwhile, Canfield secured the actual crossing at a high point to avoid flooding. After one of his agents purchased the site on the eastern shore from a homesteader, a small party—led by surveyor George Beardsley, disguised as "Farmer Brown"—crossed the river and claimed three thousand acres. Because Canfield's men had entered unsurveyed Indian Territory, they estimated the placement of their markers from survey lines already run on the Minnesota side. At the Pembina Public Land Office, Canfield then deposited fifty thousand dollars in Sioux scrip—government-issued vouchers used to hold unsurveyed ground. Three Norwegian "settlers" hired to hold the claims later surrendered their rights to the LS&PS Company for payments ranging from three hundred dollars to fifteen hundred dollars.[1]

At a meeting in Georgetown on August 21, Northern Pacific directors approved the crossing. They also ordered the construction of a railroad bridge and headquarters building on the west bank. A few days later, Canfield informed his wife: "[I spent yesterday] . . . traveling [in] the brush, weeds and mosquitoes . . . looking for a place for the railroad bridge." At a subsequent meeting in New York City, the directors named the new towns for two board members, William G. Moorhead (a brother-in-law and banking partner of Jay Cooke) and William G. Fargo (a founder of Wells-Fargo Express).[2]

This story reveals how capitalism and the Northern Pacific Railway Company created the twin cities. In conjunction with the St. Paul, Minneapolis and Manitoba (SPM&M) that arrived a decade later, the Northern Pacific promoted the settlement of the Red River Valley and northern Dakota Territory. Iron rails thus bound the cities and region to Minneapolis and St. Paul as well to Chicago by lake steamers via Duluth. These metropolitan areas marketed and milled Dakota wheat and in return offered investment capital and finished products. Dependent from their start on corporations for transportation, capital, and processing, Fargo and Moorhead thus shared in the dependence of the American West on eastern and European capitalists. Additionally, the initial incorporation of America by the railroads affected the twin cities. Railroads pioneered corporate organization by hiring numerous full-time managers to coordinate widely scattered units and activities. Federal land grants transformed transcontinental railroads into private colonizers who incorporated western lands, cities, and resources into the eastern industrial system. By creating a national market on a continental scale and linking it to an expanding global economy, railroads created networks of dependent localities. As a consequence, spreading corporate values and control made American society more tightly structured.[3]

How did the Moorhead and Fargo populace respond to policies of incorporation first implemented by railroad managers? Records of the Northern Pacific Railway Company and its LS&PS subsidiary suggest that the corporations never attained total control. The Northern Pacific often lacked the coherent policies or means to dominate completely settlers who had designs of their own. The Northern Pacific created towns, but geography, climate,

products, and people limited its capacity to create wealth. Residents contested the location of tracks and facilities. They fought higher rates. They
imposed taxes. Negotiations entailed complex exchanges between the railroad and its auxiliary on the one hand and citizens of two contending cities
on the other. Locals attempted to obtain advantageous terms and at times
succeeded.[4]

NATIVE AMERICANS, FURS, AND THE RED RIVER TRADE

Red River Valley abundance attracted humans long before Thomas Canfield
and other Europeans competed for the crossing. For several millennia, native peoples occupied the flat land of the vanished glacial Lake Agassiz. Lush
prairie grasses, wetlands, and winding rivers sustained plentiful bison, elk,
sturgeon, geese, and ducks as well as fur-bearing beaver, mink, muskrat,
and marten. Numerous prehistoric communities lived along the forested
Red River and its tributaries. During the last millennium, these peoples
hunted bison, made pottery, and planted gardens of maize and other plants.
Projectile points, pottery styles, Knife River flint, and obsidian from the
Rocky Mountains suggest long-distance trade networks and persistent contact between Minnesota Woodland and Plains cultures. Both peoples used
the basin simultaneously. Some visited seasonally; others stayed longer.
Many groups after the thirteenth century briefly lived in the valley before
later arrivals pushed them westward onto the Great Plains.[5]

The expanding European fur trade displaced many tribes. British and
French traders recruited native allies to extract furs from the northern forests and prairies during the seventeenth century. Indian middlemen brought
Red River furs to the French on the St. Lawrence River and the British at
Hudson's Bay before 1700. French traders entered the valley in the 1730s
and three decades later British merchants reached Saskatchewan. By century's end, the recently founded North West Company established posts at
Pembina and elsewhere. The Hudson's Bay Company matched these efforts,
soon defeated its rival, and merged the two firms under its name.[6]

Meanwhile Hudson's Bay stockholders approved a humanitarian proposal
by Thomas Douglas, the Fifth Earl of Selkirk, for settling poor Scotsmen at
"the Forks" of the Red and Assiniboine rivers. This site became Fort Garry
and eventually present-day Winnipeg. The unskilled, ill-equipped colonists
faced a daunting task. Both the North West and Hudson's Bay traders actively opposed farmers as a threat to their livelihoods. Low yields, grass-
hoppers, and severe floods afforded additional discouragement. Despite
the loss of as many as five hundred migrants southward in the 1820s, the
colony survived partly through U.S. commerce. Americans drove herds of

cattle northward and merchants at "the Forks" traded freely in other goods until the mid-1830s when the sixth Earl of Selkirk returned his Canadian lands to the Hudson's Bay Company. The Red River Settlement at that time numbered more than three thousand residents of varied ethnicity and religion scattered along riverbanks near the fort.[7]

The Hudson's Bay Company attempted to stop illegal trade by imposing import duties, licensing traders, seizing goods, and summoning British regulars. Trader Norman W. Kittson, who in 1843 relocated from Big Stone Lake to Pembina, derailed these efforts. He consolidated commerce between the Red and Mississippi rivers. He helped the Métis destroy the Hudson's Bay monopoly. The Métis were mixed-blood offspring of "marriages of the country" between Indian women and European traders. They practiced a subsistence household economy based on small-scale farming, daily labor for the Hudson's Bay Company, and hunting buffalo. They processed buffalo hides as well as meat for pemmican that fed Arctic-based fur posts. They dramatically expanded the annual Red River Hunt after Kittson gave them access to American goods. As more abandoned subsistence farming and embraced the capitalistic production of robes, buffalo in the region disappeared by the 1860s. Métis hunters and their families then relocated more than five hundred miles westward to continue the trade.[8]

In 1844, Kittson sent six carts south to St. Paul, each filled with eight hundred pounds of buffalo hides, tongue, pemmican, and furs in exchange for tea, coffee, sugar, tobacco, alcohol, clothing, and hardware. From that small amount valued at $1,400, the Red River trade had expanded by 1857 to five hundred carts with furs and hides valued at more than $145,000. Even with competition from freight wagons and steamboats by the late 1860s, the Red River trade still employed between a thousand and 1,500 carts. The sound of coin in merchants' coffers compensated for the inhuman squeal of ungreased wooden wheels on the streets of St. Paul, which claimed to be the second leading fur market after St. Louis.[9]

American influence moved northward as trade expanded, stimulating the interest of speculators and settlers in the Red River Valley. Not until 1823 had soldiers led by Major Stephen H. Long marked the new boundary at the forty-ninth parallel. After Minnesota became a territory, its politicians promoted both international trade and civilian authority on the border. An 1849 military expedition examined the valley and recommended sites for a fort. After a decade-long disagreement about the proposed locations, Congress finally authorized construction of Fort Abercrombie. In the meantime, a U.S. post office and customs official had been placed at Pembina, and the Hudson's Bay Company had obtained U.S. permission to bring its goods duty-free through St. Paul. It established a post at Georgetown,

Métis hunters from the Red River Settlement supplied the buffalo robes carried by these Pembina oxcarts and drivers camped on St. Anthony Hill near St. Paul in 1858. Courtesy Benjamin Franklin Upton, Minnesota Historical Society.

situated on the Red River forty-five miles north of the fort. Only ten miles farther upstream from the garrison, St. Paul merchants had recently platted Breckenridge, Minnesota, at what they optimistically assumed to be the head of steam navigation.[10]

Although St. Paul merchants had talked of Red River steamboats as early as 1849, they did not offer a prize for the purpose until a decade later. Accordingly, Captain Anson Northrup steamed north from Breckenridge on June 6, reaching Fort Garry on June 10, 1859. His return voyage required eight days. The captain then abandoned ship and rushed to collect his prize in St. Paul. Meanwhile, the Burbank Brothers' Minnesota Stage Company, which moved mail and passengers from St. Cloud to Fort Abercrombie, extended its line northward through the Moorhead site to the Hudson's Bay post at Georgetown. The Burbanks also contracted to transport Hudson's Bay freight overland between these points. The commodities then moved northward from the post to Fort Garry on the refitted *Anson Northrup*. The Burbanks compiled a rather dismal record that first year. When the freight wagons could travel on dry roads, the steamboat could not on the low river.

Nonetheless, the trade continued until interrupted by the Dakota War in 1862. Families of Hudson's Bay employees sought shelter at Fort Garry as American settlers took refuge at Fort Abercrombie, which the Dakota briefly besieged.[11]

Rapidly encroaching settlement in southern Minnesota caused the war. Similar pressures earlier led to treaty negotiations that cleared the way for Euro-American occupation of the Red River Valley. An 1851 treaty with the Dakota arranged purchase of valley lands east of the Red and south of the Wild Rice River. Not until 1863—when they were pressured by the hostile Euro-American feelings generated by the Dakota War—did the Red Lake Ojibwe vacate the Moorhead site by ceding the area from the Canadian border south to the Wild Rice River on the east and the Sheyenne River on the west. Not until June 19, 1873, after the Sisseton, Yanktonai, and Wahpeton Dakota had relinquished the Red River west bank south of the Sheyenne River, did Fargo open officially for settlement.[12]

Although dispossessed from the valley, the Ojibwe left behind the river's name. According to Warren Upham, it derives from the native word for Red Lake, conveying the reflection of sunlight on the water. Misunderstanding the Indian convention of naming sections, Euro-Americans applied this name for a single part to the entire river.[13] This mistake added insult to the injury of displacing Indians from the valley. However different their respective cultures, the newcomers shared experiences with the natives they replaced. Both peoples had been drawn by the region's resources or had been compelled westward by forces beyond their control. Both became tied economically to national and international markets. For Indians, the fur trade fostered ecological change that reduced the viability of their communities. Similarly, Euro-American farmers transformed the prairie into wheat fields, subjecting themselves and their communities to disruptions from world markets.

The Red River trade not only displaced Indians and made St. Paul an early commercial center, it contributed directly to railroad construction. As the Hudson's Bay Company committed to the southern trade route and as supplies flowed west to new forts erected to control Indians in northern Dakota, volume and profits increased, attracting railroad entrepreneurs. The St. Paul and Pacific Railway built north to meet carts at St. Cloud in 1866 and west to meet them at Breckenridge in 1871. Convinced of the valley's potential riches by his decade-long participation in the trade, James J. Hill and his associates later acquired the bankrupt St. Paul and Pacific and extended it northward to Canada. Similarly, the region's proven wealth convinced banker Jay Cooke about the soundness of financing the transcontinental Northern Pacific.[14]

JAY COOKE, THE NORTHERN PACIFIC, AND
ITS TOWN-SITE AUXILIARY

After Jay Cooke and Company committed to funding the Northern Pacific, the always critical *Philadelphia Ledger* called it a "wild scheme to build a railroad from nowhere through no man's land to no place." The projected two thousand-mile route from Lake Superior to Puget Sound ran through arid lands of dubious value, Indian Territory, and country without any European settlements. How could such a road yield earnings? Furthermore, the glutted railroad security market discouraged investors. No wonder lack of capital delayed construction until February 1870 even though Congress had chartered the Northern Pacific in July 1864. Cooke exercised caution initially by only agreeing to raise $5 million in thirty days for building to the Red River Valley. He hoped revenues from the profitable Red River trade might assure nervous investors. Although Congress never awarded the generous government loans for each mile constructed as it had done with the Union Pacific, it permitted the Northern Pacific to issue first mortgage bonds on its substantial federal land grant, track laid, and other assets.[15]

What impelled a reputable banker to back a seemingly foolhardy venture? Cooke, an enterprising, pious optimist, thought big. Having bankrolled Northern victory in the Civil War by aggressively selling U.S. bonds, Cooke now looked to the Northwest for new worlds to conquer. After investing in Iowa, Wisconsin, and Minnesota lands for almost two decades, he acquired nineteen thousand acres of pine forest near Duluth, which he visited in 1868. Its natural harbor impressed him, and he envisioned a great city developing there. He invested in Duluth real estate, the Lake Superior and Mississippi Railroad, and its subsidiary, the Western Land Association. He hoped that financing the Northern Pacific would enhance the profitability of these properties. In addition, Cooke imagined a great northwestern empire joined by the Northern Pacific and other railroads.[16]

After the Lake Superior and Mississippi arrived at St. Paul, Cooke gained stock control of the St. Paul and Pacific Railroad, which had reached the Red River at Breckenridge by 1871 and the next year pushed northward toward the border. By connecting Canada to Duluth and St. Paul, Cooke's railroads might realize the dreams of Minnesota newspaperman James W. Taylor, Senator Alexander Ramsey, and Representative Ignatius Donnelly, who called for annexing central Canada. This compelling vision faced daunting reality. Committed to Duluth, Cooke did not see Minneapolis and St. Paul as more logical termini for the Northern Pacific. Furthermore, Cooke's costly entanglement with other lines contributed to his eventual failure.[17]

The visionary financier hoped to overcome these difficulties with largesse

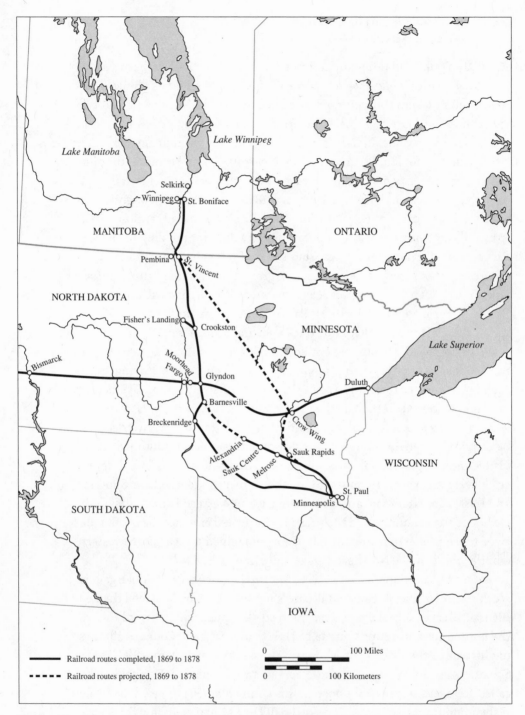

Railroad building in the Red River area, 1869–78. From Stanley N. Murray, *The Valley Comes of Age* (Fargo: North Dakota Institute for Regional Studies, 1967); redrawn by Patti Isaacs, Parrot Graphics.

from selling the largest land grant awarded to a transcontinental, profits from founding town sites, and astute management. None of these fulfilled his expectations. Although the operations of the Northern Pacific Railway Company and its town site auxiliary brought corporate structures and values to the northern plains, its bureaucracy proved inadequate for containing speculation and profit seeking by too many of its managers. Such behavior afforded another cause of Cooke's collapse and the railroad's bankruptcy.

The land grant and government survey of public lands gave Cooke significant potential capital. The St. Paul and Pacific received odd-numbered sections for ten miles on both sides of its main line to Canada. The Northern Pacific acquired odd-numbered sections for twenty miles on each side of its track in Minnesota and for forty miles on each side in Dakota Territory. Together the two companies gained 1.5 million acres in the Red River Valley. Land came packaged for sale. The 1785 Land Ordinance provided for surveying in a grid pattern of townships six miles square. Each contained thirty-six sections of 640 acres, one mile square. Largely an idea of Thomas Jefferson, who chaired the congressional drafting committee, this Enlightenment model of geometrical rationalism made it easy to locate and sell any parcel by its section, township, and range numbers. These rational procedures facilitated the corporation's converting its land grant into cash. Thus federal and corporate bureaucracies spread capitalism to the valley in the forms of real-estate speculation and commercial farming. As we shall see, railroad managers similarly mapped and marketed towns.[18]

From the outset, Cooke and Land Committee chair Frederick Billings urged a coordinated effort that sold land, recruited settlers, and promoted emigration. They wanted income from land transactions and freight shipments, which only rapid settlement could provide. The Land Department undertook to map, plat, appraise, and clear titles, while the Immigration Bureau advertised extensively for emigrants in Europe and the eastern United States. Cooke enlisted the support of the press, as he had often done, by sending free cigars to editors and offering them passes to see the new Eden of northern Minnesota and Dakota. Managers arranged cheaper fares with the principal steamship lines. They waived train tickets west of Duluth for purchasers of at least forty acres and reduced prices for prospecting parties. Land agents sold at an average of $5.50 an acre. They worked to expand sales, giving discounts on cash purchases, allowing seven-to-ten-year credit arrangements and selling large blocks to groups. Hence, colonies settled on large holdings at Wadena, Detroit Lake, Hawley, and Glyndon. This campaign, unfortunately, did not yield enough revenue in time to ward off bankruptcy.[19]

To reap profits from founding towns, Cooke's original contract specified a town site company. Both he and Billings expected it would serve their well-coordinated plan for rapid settlement. The Northern Pacific created the LS&PS Company to monopolize town sites by excluding private competitors from all good spots on even-numbered sections of public land between the Great Lakes and the Pacific Coast. By 1872, LS&PS president Thomas Hawley Canfield claimed to have located thirteen towns in Minnesota, four in Dakota, and seven in Washington Territory. Because the two companies shared stockholders, directors, and land agents, their finances became closely intertwined as well. Although pledged to work amicably, the railroad did not directly control the subsidiary.[20]

Almost immediately, settlers, editors, and politicians criticized both Canfield and his company for monopolistic practices that precluded speculation by private individuals. The public also condemned the company's secrecy, speculative windfalls for insiders, and high lot prices. This bad publicity disturbed Cooke, who believed it slowed settlement and hindered his sales of railroad securities. Personally, Cooke disliked how Canfield laid out the towns with small lots, high prices, and inadequate alleys, which kept away businessmen. Billings warned that secret selections of choice town sites and Canfield's private speculations hurt the Northern Pacific.[21]

Canfield's activities made credible the public charges. By June 1872, he had applied for more than five thousand acres located one to three miles from several Minnesota town sites. At the same time, he had not accounted for conflicting applications by the LS&PS Company for another twelve thousand acres. Meanwhile, conflicts developed with the Land Department colonies. Colonists, who wanted to profit from organizing their own towns, became angry when thwarted by LS&PS ownership. The Land Department requested control of the lands in question. Northern Pacific managers agreed and proposed canceling LS&PS contracts to satisfy the colonists. Emigration commissioner George Hibbard reported the widespread dissatisfaction with LS&PS policies in August 1873: "Towns along the line are far behind what they would have been had the right course been pursued; the settlers . . . are . . . finding fault with the policy pursued by that company." He added that many Northern Pacific officials wanted a policy change.[22]

The collapse of Jay Cooke & Co. on September 18, 1873, and the ensuing bankruptcy of the Northern Pacific increased the determination of railroad managers to eliminate the LS&PS Company. Indeed, termination had been long considered. Billings had assured Cooke as early as November 1871 that "the Puget Sound Divorce" would soon be completed. Opposition by LS&PS stockholders probably derailed this and a second purchase attempt. During the third effort in May 1873, Canfield assured Billings, "I will be glad to cooperate in carrying out any plans which will be for the interest of all parties." Reporting to LS&PS directors and stockholders in early September, Canfield stated that Northern Pacific directors had decided to eliminate the company because it hindered railroad success. Although the public condemned LS&PS operations "as a kind of Crédit Mobilier," Canfield denied any fraudulent acts. The directors and stockholders approved his recommendations for the sale, his resignation, and the dismissal of all salaried employees to reduce expenses. Although the purchase agreement had been completed in 1874, it took much longer to resolve all the issues involving individual land titles, fair compensation for unsold lands, and railroad construction on LS&PS lands. LS&PS stock valued at two hundred thousand dollars at last became available to the Northern Pacific in April 1890.[23]

Because Cooke's expectation of large profits from town site development had not been realized, he blamed that company for the railroad's downfall. The auxiliary had performed poorly, but Cooke overstated its importance. The company had never paid dividends, according to an 1878 report by LS&PS president George Stark. No "inside ring" had profited, but "injudicious purchases and management with taxes, expenses and losses" had nullified earnings. Private parties had received about five dollars an acre for forty-eight thousand acres scattered throughout northern Minnesota, Dakota Territory, and western Washington Territory.[24]

It is significant, however, that public rumors of an "inside ring" gave the Northern Pacific management a bad reputation at a time when the Crédit Mobilier Construction Company scandal aroused public suspicions of the Union Pacific and all other western railroads. These negative perceptions hindered Cooke's sale of Northern Pacific bonds to wary investors. For example, he allocated $30 million worth of 7.3 percent bonds for Holland, but probably sold none. Widely circulated stories about Northern Pacific mismanagement made more cautious a Dutch market already inundated with St. Paul and Pacific securities. In this regard, the inefficiency of Canfield and his LS&PS cronies formed only a small part of a larger problem. Inspector A. B. Nettleton reported shoddy construction of the line and had warned Billings about the excessive cost of the Duluth, Brainerd, and Glyndon Reception Houses for Immigrants. Cooke dreaded this kind of bad news and tried to keep it from the newspapers and already nervous investors.[25]

That the Northern Pacific built from Duluth to Bismarck at the cost of just over fifty-four thousand dollars per mile, considerably above the thirty-eight thousand dollars originally estimated, suggests that President J. Gregory Smith and his associates had not built economically or honestly. After corrupt managers squandered millions, Cooke also made ethically dubious decisions. He covered shortages by using funds from his own bank and the deposits of others. He misled investors about the potential value of

Northern Pacific lands. He promised that these would be sold rapidly to secure investments, but this proved excessively optimistic and may have discouraged wary financiers. As a banker, Cooke needlessly assumed excessive responsibility for the construction and promotion of a railroad that had no immediate prospects of revenue from its operation. His acquisition of the St. Paul and Pacific and the Lake Superior and Mississippi railroads added burdens to the Northern Pacific and his bank.[26]

Even if J. Gregory Smith and Thomas Hawley Canfield had managed their respective companies more responsibly, the entire enterprise may have been doomed from the start. Too much of the nation's wealth had become invested in overexpanded and unproductive western railroads. With much of its assets frozen in the Northern Pacific, Jay Cooke & Co. closed. The Panic of 1873 resulted. It triggered the longest depression on record; investors lost heavily and became more cautious about even sound railroad securities. Perceived unfavorable long-term investment prospects prevented recovery through 1877. This is not to say that Canfield and Smith did not engage in questionable activities. They did not act alone, however. Many railroad officials—from surveyor Thomas L. Rosser to Land Committee chair Frederick Billings and financier Jay Cooke—used inside information to speculate in railroad lands. They misled the public and investors about company finances and operations. Their actions show the complex way that managers combined bureaucratic order with irregular profit seeking, as historian Olivier Zunz has observed. Land speculation furthered western railroad expansion. It attracted talent and capital to the corporation. It lured private individuals to settle along the line. When public criticism of "inside speculators" damaged the corporate interests of the road, men like Cooke and Billings extended bureaucratic control over their firms in an effort to curb speculation and to manage them more efficiently.[27]

Although much criticized for corruption and inefficiency, the LS&PS Company usefully surveyed town sites and prepared them for commercial development. As Americans moved westward after the Civil War, some railroads assumed the primary responsibility for town founding. Canfield did not invent the poor design of which Cooke complained. He followed standard procedures for platting railroad towns that geographer John Hudson and historian John Reps have described. Projecting its towns as successful trade centers for farmers, the Northern Pacific followed a strategy similar to that of other western railroads. Managers valued the long-term profits from traffic volume generated by businesses even more than the prized immediate profits from real-estate sales. Railroad towns had advantages in transportation costs that enabled them to attract merchants from scattered locales and to strangle any nearby competitors. Created as part of an urban system and hierarchy, Fargo and Moorhead limited villages dependent on them just as more centrally located Minneapolis and St. Paul restricted the dual city in turn.[28]

The Northern Pacific Land Department laid out Fargo in the same way that the LS&PS Company laid out Moorhead. Corporate managers platted both symmetrically with the railroad track located between two principal business streets—Northern Pacific Avenue and Front Street in Fargo and Front and Main streets in Moorhead. Elevators, lumberyards, and other companies needing direct rail access used the railroad right-of-way between the major streets. Distances tended to be standardized in what the *Red River Gazette* called "invariable grooves."[29] Surveyors divided the town sites into three hundred-foot square blocks. They parceled each half block into either six fifty-foot-wide and 140-foot-deep residential lots, or twelve twenty-five-foot-wide and 140-foot-deep business lots, all backed by twenty-foot alleys. They kept commercial parcels small, hoping to attract numerous merchants. This gridiron pattern defined railroad towns: platting them primarily as real estate rather than communal space facilitated the sale of property and commercial development controlled by the railroad for profit.[30]

THOMAS HAWLEY CANFIELD, THE LS&PS COMPANY, AND MOORHEAD DEVELOPMENT

Railroad towns originated in New England and New York. Yankees such as the Vermont-born Thomas Hawley Canfield brought such towns to the northern plains. Reared on a farm and educated at Burr Seminary, Troy Episcopal Institute, and Union College, Canfield saw his schooling end with his father's death. He soon abandoned farming for the retail and wholesale trade, which involved him in Vermont's first railroads. At the end of the Civil War, he became principal promoter for the Northern Pacific Railway Company. Perceived as "a man of . . . wonderful vitality and energy," Canfield probably persuaded many. Perhaps stung by public condemnation of his inefficiency and speculation, he often stressed publicly his integrity, managerial skill, and service to the Northern Pacific. Nonetheless, he extracted every personal advantage he could from the railroad. Near the end of his life, his real-estate holdings, valued at four hundred thousand dollars, included nearly ten thousand acres of agricultural land as well as 270 acres and nearly three hundred town lots distributed along the line in Washington, North Dakota, and Minnesota. He appears to have been rich in lands but starved for cash. An active Episcopalian, he participated extensively in the lyceum and temperance reforms of the day. He fostered such values in Moorhead and other towns. "Roughs" and liquor dealers taking root before the "respectable element" alarmed him. He hoped that newly organized localities would soon ban liquor.[31]

As we have seen, Moorhead's story began with Canfield outwitting private speculators at the crossing. At his behest, Andrew Holes purchased the site for the princely sum of two thousand dollars from Joab Smith, who had homesteaded 173 acres in 1869. Holes—a New York native, descended from English immigrant farmers—had been a farmer, fur trapper, gold miner, and public surveyor before Jay Cooke and others employed him to locate lands for them. He became a lifelong resident, successful real-estate dealer, county commissioner, school trustee, and promoter. Reserving twenty-four acres for his home and speculative purposes, Holes subsequently deeded the remainder to Canfield on August 28, 1871. According to the *Red River Gazette*, surveyors began laying out the original 149-acre town site on September 29. On October 11, Canfield reported, "We have Moorhead laid out—411 lots sold & two hotels up." Consternated by this news, Bogusville residents—Henry A. Bruns, Henry Finkle, Jasper B. Chapin, John E. Haggart, and others destined to be prominent citizens of the new twin cities—quickly relocated. About two hundred people therefore greeted the first train on January 4, 1872.[32]

Pioneer druggist Benjamin F. Mackall described early Moorhead as "not encouraging." He added: "It was a paper town, frame buildings covered with tar paper to keep out the cold, only it didn't." Flooded prairies made muddy streets. Residents put down single planks for crossings and double planks for sidewalks. The Reverend Oscar H. Elmer, an early Presbyterian missionary who arrived by buggy from Alexandria, gave two reasons for his lack of emotion in seeing it for the first time: "First, Moorhead broke upon my view many miles away and . . . it was almost as difficult to reach as a mirage. Second, . . . on that day the driving dust over the burndt prairies filled my eyes and the wind blew . . . emotions to 'tatters.'"[33]

To envision a moral community arising from such rude conditions required considerable imagination and hunger

Thomas Hawley Canfield, president of LS&PS, directed Moorhead development in the early 1870s. Courtesy Institute for Regional Studies, North Dakota State University, Fargo (51.127.1).

for profit on Canfield's part. He boosted the crude settlement in order to sell the lots owned by his company. As he wrote Holes, "You know I have never doubted for a moment that the Red River City would be at Moorhead—it is the best location on the River and all that may be done by the railroad company at Fargo will not stop it." Here Canfield referred to the Northern Pacific establishing its division headquarters in Fargo. A month later, Canfield urged LS&PS agent Lyman P. White: "You must encourage them to go ahead and get well established before Fargo can get started." Canfield maintained that Moorhead had two advantages over Fargo: it occupied the high ground and it enjoyed the protection of Minnesota law, in contrast to the unsettled law of Dakota Territory. Consequently, "all titles in Fargo are in doubt" and without the benefit of law "all good people will prefer to live in Minnesota under the present state of affairs."[34]

Canfield's Yankee ideas about law, religion, and morality are evident in his plans to build a moral community. Reporting to the directors, Canfield recommended donating lands to "different religious denominations . . . for the establishment of churches, schools and benevolent institutions." Already in 1872, Congregational, Presbyterian, Catholic, and Methodist agents negotiated for lots. By 1874, Norwegian Lutherans and Episcopalians joined the talks. Canfield occasionally recruited ministers. In 1875, he reported to his wife that he hoped to persuade a Minneapolis minister to come and build up a church in Moorhead. The company readily gave land for churches, although not always where the denominations requested. Although the company refused to grant choice business sites, it tried to be accommodating in order to prevent any church from moving to Fargo. As a consequence of these negotiations, several located south of the railroad track on "Angel Avenue."[35]

The LS&PS Company made other concessions with an eye to boosting lot sales by improving the moral order and enabling local citizens to work for civic goals. Toward these ends, the company provided land for public education at the request of the school trustees. It set aside two acres on the south side for a cemetery provided that residents formed an association to maintain it. It proposed planting trees for a windbreak along the southern, southeastern, and eastern boundaries. The trees not only added beauty but had the utility of overcoming buyers' fears about living on the open prairie.[36]

The LS&PS Company also furthered civic development by deeding land for a county jail and courthouse. Canfield wanted the courthouse south of the track, sufficiently far out to accommodate growth. This did not satisfy local sentiment. Fearing removal of the county seat, Canfield ordered Lyman White to settle the matter. He located the structure near downtown. Eventually, local brickmaker John Bergquist donated two blocks for a new courthouse, sited conveniently near his brickyard. Residents, who had rejected Canfield's original proposal, showed that they shared his booster dreams by placing the building on the north side about one mile from the business center. When the county wanted to withdraw the condition on LS&PS land in 1886, White requested payment of five hundred dollars in county warrants.[37]

For a town-site promoter such as Canfield—and for Yankees generally—morality and profits coincided. Indeed, he expected that sober and industrious businessmen would become the pillars of congregations and the foundations of communal moral order—hence his policy of twenty-five-foot business lots, which favored many small shops and boosted numbers. Still, promoters struggled with attracting people with capital who were willing to invest in the town's future. As Lyman White suggested: "There is more bustle than money in Moorhead. Nevertheless loose cash is on the increase." Meanwhile, cash-starved citizens asked for LS&PS assistance. Canfield offered assurance: "You can rely upon cooperation of this company in any enterprise which extends . . . the town."[38]

Canfield's correspondence reveals the ways that he attempted to meet Northern Pacific requirements, attract businessmen, and promote commercial development. He responded to inquiries, provided services, and attempted to locate businesses favorably, ensuring their success, stimulating town growth, and boosting LS&PS profits. To secure the Northern Pacific right-of-way, Canfield wired John W. Taylor: "Half blocks on each side of the railroad track are not for sale." Apparently, agents did not obey this order. Northern Pacific vice president T. F. Oakes later complained that the LS&PS had sold such lots. The Northern Pacific did not release its claim to these private holdings on its right-of-way until 1890.[39]

After establishing the passenger depot and freight house on Fourth Street, the LS&PS Company did not sell properties east of that street for several years, attempting to concentrate businesses and residences near the Red River. Meanwhile, Canfield located the Douglas Lumber Yard close to the track, but he placed the brickyard that supplied local construction outside the city limits on the north side. He attempted to secure the booming Manitoba steamboat trade for Moorhead by situating the landing where it served Fargo and yet connected by road to the depot. It alarmed LS&PS agents when the Northern Pacific laid track to the river in Fargo, but the company reassured them by placing rails on the east bank. This encouraged the recently formed Red River Transportation Company to put its office in Moorhead.[40]

After entrepreneur Henry A. Bruns requested land on which to build a mill in 1874, Canfield readily agreed. He suggested a site south of the track near the river. Seeking to encourage Bruns, he wrote: "I am very glad to hear of this . . . You must . . . be sure to have your grist mill ready for the wheat [crop] of 1874—That is all important." Canfield relied on Bruns for other services. He built a brewery for someone with limited capital and he provided the land for a tannery to be established by a Swedish immigrant. At the end of the decade, the LS&PS Company deeded two blocks for one dollar to D. M. Sabin, a large farm implement company, for erecting a warehouse. An overjoyed Lyman White—expecting lot sales to soar, as the town became a distribution center—boasted, "[The Sabin Company's] location . . . will be the biggest lift ever experienced at Moorhead."[41]

Another important negotiation involved grain elevators. Although White—thinking it "would be beneficial to the town site"—supported a proposal by Bruns and Finkle, LS&PS president and Northern Pacific vice president George Stark refused to act. He wanted a single storage facility with sufficient capacity to accommodate all grain. He informed Bruns and Finkle about company talks with Grandin Bonanza Farms, which would probably invite them to join in the enterprise. Stark argued that one structure would stimulate growth in both cities if large wheat deposits became available as working capital. Meanwhile, the two merchants solicited trade for their community by negotiating a ten thousand-bushel shipment from the Grandin Brothers. By 1878, the Northern Pacific had more grain than anticipated and discovered that local capitalists could not agree on a single facility. The railroad then permitted Bruns and Finkle to build Elevator A in Moorhead.[42]

This four-way exchange reveals much about the incorporation of America. First, the railroad corporation had limited power and capital with which to impose its will on the twin cities. Second, the Northern Pacific lacked a unified policy. The LS&PS agent preferred a different approach but in this instance deferred to his corporate superiors. Third, managers of both companies relied on residents and their capital for developing the dual city and the valley. Fourth, inhabitants divided into competing cities, each seeking railroad favors to promote its growth at the expense of the other. Thus, the Northern Pacific only advanced incorporation by negotiations with local middle-class businessmen and their sometimes working together, each for their mutual advantage. As historian Olivier Zunz has said, incorporating American life followed varied paths; it "was not simply imposed from the top down by a corporate elite."[43]

Canfield and his agents relied on local editors for publicity that promoted growth. The LS&PS Company therefore donated two lots to W. B. Nickles for establishing the *Red River Star*. Nickles began publication on July 6, 1872, describing Moorhead as "the Chief Business Centre of the Valley." It

had everything prospective settlers might desire: "healthy climate," "rich and varied resources," and favorable commercial position as a Hudson's Bay Company depot on the Red River and a Northern Pacific connection to Lake Superior. Nickles claimed that four hundred had arrived within two months of laying out the town and that lot sales currently boomed. An aspiring editor required such booster spirit if he expected his newspaper to succeed.[44]

In early 1872, Canfield placed an article extolling Moorhead in eastern newspapers. He had copies of the *Red River Star* sent to Ohio and Pennsylvania businesses and individuals. The following year, he thanked Nickles for "your attention to my suggestions, as well as for your refusal to insert articles [into the *Star*] complaining of the company." Canfield instructed Nickles expressly not to publish his long letter. Yet he wanted it understood that the "Company would do all it can for Moorhead." LS&PS agent Andrew Holes also regularly placed advertisements in the *Star*. These assured readers that "Moorhead [is the] Liveliest Town on the Northern Pacific! . . . Head of Uninterrupted Steamboat Navigation! . . . Beautifully situated on . . . highest ground along the river. Perfectly sheltered on North and West."[45]

Whatever benefits Nickles received from the town-site company did not prevent his editorial criticism of the Northern Pacific for favoring Fargo. Nickles initially accepted the company's claim that it "proposes to exercise the strictest neutrality." As businesses relocated across the river, however, he denounced the road. He then proudly trumpeted the development of Moorhead into an orderly community in the face of railroad opposition. In addition, Nickles's career reveals the risks for editors involved in town-site promotion. Delinquent on his taxes by 1874, he requested lots to sell for cash, but Canfield refused. Nickles then sold the *Star*, although he remained as editor until July 1876, when he resigned and returned to Wisconsin. Booster until the end, Nickles asserted he had aided Moorhead's prosperity and success.[46]

Corporate managers and local businessmen, who believed that new cities needed to be seen as profitable opportunities, used images for publicity. Photographer F. Jay Haynes arrived in the city on September 7, 1876. By the following year, he had published *Stereoscopic Views of the Northern Pacific*, including thirty-one scenes of Moorhead, Fargo, and the Red River of the North. His photographs recorded the proud deeds of Henry Bruns and other entrepreneurs as they completed new brick buildings and blocks. Popular lithograph city views also advertised the towns. Resident artist Ralph DeCamp completed one of Moorhead in 1880. The *Clay County Advocate*—the renamed *Red River Star*—urged merchants to order the scene for their letterheads. The *Second Annual Report of the Chamber of Commerce* reproduced an 1879 Fargo scene as its frontispiece. Both city views revealed pride in place and an optimism similar to that later displayed by Soviet realism, because the views portrayed what locals hoped their new society would become. Indeed, the *Advocate* argued that inhabitants would transform reality when they saw how much better their property looked in the lithograph. City scenes suggested commercial possibilities by stressing the railroad, grain elevators, flour mills, and steamboats on the Red River. They displayed an orderly urban landscape organized in a gridiron pattern of tree-lined streets. They thus marked what the middle class considered civilized progress, economically and culturally.[47]

Despite its community-building efforts, the LS&PS Company still faced criticism for its high prices that hindered development. After Canfield's visit to Moorhead in summer 1873, the *Red River Star* praised him for appointing resident Andrew Holes as town-site agent. The next week, the *Star* announced reduced rates on house lots to $75 north of the track and $50 south of it. Business lots dropped to $250 and $200 for corner and inside parcels, respectively. These changes aimed at preventing flight to Fargo, now legally open to settlement under the recently approved Dakota Treaty. Although the *Star* asked for more cuts in the future, Canfield resisted. "After giving

Moorhead boosters advertised with this lithograph city view in 1882. Courtesy Minnesota Historical Society.

land for churches, mills, court houses, school houses, brick yards," he replied, "we cannot afford to give the owners . . . lands for their houses also." Furthermore, if the company set prices too low, it would depreciate property values in the entire town. After all, "those who own lots are interested in having them worth something." Nonetheless, he said that the company would be reasonable. Meanwhile, Canfield urged Lyman White to review prices, being careful not to check expansion. The subsequent willingness of White and Holes to sell at discounts and with minimal down payments demonstrates the care they took in promoting growth.[48]

This exchange reveals crucial differences among town inhabitants, townsite promoters, and railroad managers: locals wanted low prices when purchasing but high prices when selling lots; the LS&PS Company wanted high prices to maximize profits from town lot sales; and the Northern Pacific wanted prices that promoted rapid settlement of towns and agricultural lands. No price set by Canfield and other LS&PS managers satisfied the disparate needs of the three groups. Moreover, the LS&PS always negotiated terms subject to the prevailing market. Agents sold land as rapidly as they could for the best terms they could get.

Canfield's personal diplomacy in Moorhead is only one instance of how the managers of the railroad and town-site companies attempted to deflect public criticism. George B. Wright, general agent of the Northern Pacific Land Department, responded in a letter to the St. Paul press that the *Red River Gazette* reprinted. Wright denied rumors that town sites had been disposed of in advance or that the LS&PS Company acquired its holdings without cost from the railroad. He defended company prices and regulations, saying that the managers wanted to build attractive towns. Hence, arrangements had been made for churches, graded streets, parks, and trees. At the time he published this statement, Wright privately wrote to Canfield, reporting on tensions between railroad managers and those of its town-site auxiliary. He had been criticized for land speculation and being in league with the LS&PS Company. Charged with opposing Northern Pacific interests, he had resigned.[49]

During their community-building and diplomatic effort, LS&PS managers pursued profits in the face of contrary pressures from the public, local governments, and the Northern Pacific. Canfield often defended the economic self-interest of his company in his correspondence, which contrasted with his public-spirited encouragement of locals. He lobbied for locating the railroad headquarters in Moorhead because he feared a rush of squatters to the west bank. Placing the headquarters on the east bank served LS&PS interests in two ways. First, it enabled the company to sell its Moorhead holdings more quickly. Second, it allowed time for surveying and establishing a stronger legal claim to the Fargo site with the public land office. He hoped thereby to avoid endless litigation with squatters. Failing to reverse the decision by Northern Pacific directors, Canfield then ordered rapid liquidation of Moorhead properties. He wanted to extract as much cash as possible from the unreliable "movable class" of people who came first to new towns. He advised granting discounts to those who paid cash because "it was best to sell when you can." He said the company need not secure lots for the future growth, since Moorhead would be smaller than other sites on the line.[50]

LS&PS managers followed these policies even after Canfield resigned. A few years later, Lyman White offered entire blocks for prices ranging from five hundred to one thousand dollars, depending on their location. He held those closest to the railroad for the even higher prices brought by growth. More rapid north-side expansion determined White's accepting $1,200 for three blocks to the southeast. His receipts for April 1878, which totaled $2,055 with $915 paid, suggest the likely ratio of cash to sales. Although the company no longer purchased lands at this time, it still needed cash to pay taxes on its unsold properties. Taxation, therefore, became another area of negotiation between corporate managers and local governments.[51]

The LS&PS Company struggled with tax payments throughout the decade. In August 1874, the company owed $1,028 on 608 unsold lots while it put its extra cash into the Bismarck town site. Clay County charged 24 percent interest until 1876, when it lowered rates to 18 percent on delinquent fees. Managers worked to reduce levies. They succeeded, leading White to report: "our taxes are more reasonable than in former years." Higher sales receipts left the company in better position to pay, but income did not suffice to settle all duties at the same time. Its Minnesota assessments in 1877 totaled $5,500, which included $1,143 for Clay County and Moorhead. By 1881, local taxes dropped to $314 on forty-six lots.[52]

Despite local hopes, the Northern Pacific acquisition of the LS&PS Company did not lower fees. When residents still grumbled about excessive charges, Lyman White explained that easy terms and buying on time increased costs. Despite his discounts for cash purchases, he continued to sell on long-term contracts with small down payments. This should not surprise; western business transactions typically involved credit. In addition, speculation by leading citizens drove prices higher at this time.[53]

Even after Moorhead grievances against the town-site company seemingly had been settled, its complaints about the Northern Pacific's favoritism for Fargo continued. Specific issues included inadequate depot and freight facilities, lack of telegraph service, rate discrimination, and Mud

Moorhead city fathers contended with Northern Pacific managers about Mud Creek, an open sewer and an eyesore in 1879. Courtesy Clay County Historical Society.

Creek—a filthy pool of stagnant water located on Fourth Street near the track. In June 1878, the Moorhead council accepted the company's terms for Mud Creek: the Northern Pacific would fill it with gravel if the city constructed a culvert. Later that summer, the telegraph office finally opened. After the Northern Pacific further alienated residents by its 1879 decision to build a new round house in Fargo, general manager Homer E. Sargent arrived bearing gifts. He announced that washouts would be filled; larger yards for lumber and freight with additional sidetracks would be created; a new and larger freight house would be built in a better location; and the passenger depot would be enlarged and moved eastward from Fourth to Eighth Street. Citizens hoped that this would finally develop the east side that Canfield's company had declared off limits. They also hoped to realize their own speculative dreams on lands they had claimed outside the original town site. That the Northern Pacific did not resolve freight rate differentials enabled Fargo to grow more rapidly, while Moorhead protests persisted.[54]

JAMES B. POWER, THE NORTHERN PACIFIC LAND DEPARTMENT, AND FOUNDING FARGO

The New York–born and Massachusetts-educated James B. Power learned corporate ways by working for the New York & Erie and the St. Louis & Pacific railroads. He joined the Northern Pacific Land Department in 1871. An efficient and capable employee, he survived staff cuts and won promotion to land commissioner. When Power initially viewed "barren" Dakota lands, he thought them "hopeless" to sell. Yet the soil brought the Northern Pacific back from bankruptcy after it failed to secure congressional relief. In August 1874, a homesteader marketed his wheat crop from forty acres and earned two thousand dollars. Word went out that he had struck gold. Power advised using large Dakota farms to publicize fertility, speed settlement, and generate revenues. The company exchanged large blocks of land at the discounted rate of four dollars an acre for bonds at par value on condition that 25 percent of the purchase be broken and cultivated each year. Northern Pacific president George W. Cass and director Benjamin P. Cheney hired manager Oliver Dalrymple and started the original Bonanza farm of 13,440 acres near Casselton.[55]

Northern Pacific land commissioner James B. Power shaped the growth of Fargo and Red River Valley Bonanza wheat farms during the late 1870s. Courtesy Institute for Regional Studies, North Dakota State University, Fargo (129.3.3).

This photograph of the Dalrymple Farm, taken by F. Jay Haynes in 1877, displayed the mechanization of wheat agriculture. Courtesy Institute for Regional Studies, North Dakota State University, Fargo (2029.11.2).

Power publicized the Dakota bonanza with letters to the *Country Gentleman,* the *St. Paul Pioneer Press,* the *New York Tribune,* and other publications. He emphasized the corporate and managerial achievements of the "Boss" wheat farms, which operated with admirable efficiency: "The management is perfect and the most complete system seems to govern. Every thing moves forward with perfect regularity." The Bonanza farms proved "that large capital can be engaged . . . successfully in the cultivation of wheat on an extensive scale." Power also attacked Major John Wesley Powell for including the Red River Valley in the arid section of the Great Plains. To the contrary, settlers as far west as Bismarck had demonstrated conclusively the region's suitability for agriculture. In 1876 Power asserted: "Work of the land department is beginning to tell for the future prosperity of the road." Dramatically increased immigration and growing wheat production gave the railroad a profitable carrying trade eastward. Two years later, Power reported "a fine class of settlers . . . going into the Red River Valley." They had purchased railroad lands as far west as Jamestown. According to the *Fargo Times,* the Northern Pacific had sold all its Cass County lands by 1879.[56]

Meanwhile, a three-way struggle complicated Fargo's founding. Power's Northern Pacific Land Department, Canfield's LS&PS Company, and homesteaders battled for title to lands not yet vacated by the Wahpeton and Sisseton Dakota. Once the Northern Pacific established its line, the railroad received section 7, located mostly south of the track along the Red River, as part of its federal land grant. Canfield filed fifty thousand dollars in Sioux scrip on three thousand acres situated on both sides of the line. Settlers attempted to preempt these lands. Already in April 1871, several Norwegians had staked out adjoining claims on the west bank. They served Canfield's purpose by forcing others from the best sites he hoped to hold for his company. Andrew McHench, Henry Back, and Jacob Lowell, concluding that "Farmer Brown" worked for Canfield, decided to locate "right there." A stampede for the property followed because the LS&PS Company had no certain title until a legal survey had been made and filed.[57]

The contending parties did not settle their disputes until after 1874. At that time, the Northern Pacific Land Department filed the original townsite plat on 240 acres of the north half of section 7. Federal land commissioner Willis Drummond already had ordered settlers to vacate railroad lands. He also ruled that Sioux scrip filed before the Indian title had been extinguished did not establish ownership. Faced with this adverse ruling, hostile local opinion and Land Department opposition, Canfield concluded that he could not win a legal battle and saved litigation costs by abandoning the LS&PS claim.[58]

Section 6 adjoined Northern Pacific Avenue on the north side. It became the city's business district. By mid-decade, homesteaders owned its four quarters: Samuel G. Roberts, Patrick Devitt and Gordon J. Keeney, A. J. Harwood, and Harriet Young. Charles A. Roberts, who had homesteaded the southwest quarter of section 7, purchased that property from the railroad for $1,600 in 1878. The company had already sold the southeast quarter. Early urban development took place on these two sections, bounded by the Red River on the east, Thirteenth Street on the west, Thirteenth Avenue South, and Twelfth Avenue North. Samuel Roberts, Keeney and Devitt, and Charles Roberts made the first additions to the city. Urban growth did transform the Back, Lowell, and McHench claims on sections 14 and 18 into real estate until the city expanded to the south and west many years later.[59]

"Urban life" began on September 26, 1871. Construction engineer Thomas L. Rosser laid out the railroad camp in military fashion over a five-block area along the southern side of present-day Main Street. As Rosser barred settlers from what was called "Fargo on the Prairie," a more disorderly collection of tent hotels, saloons, and bordellos known as "Fargo in the Timber" established itself due east on the riverbank. It probably numbered fifty before winter began, but likely did not grow to the six hundred generously estimated by one of its inhabitants. These included tracklayers, outlaws, prostitutes, and many future residents hoping for lower lot prices. Northern Pacific managers regarded them as rabble and squatters on company property. Canfield acknowledged "that the woods on the west side of the river will be a resort for the low and vile but for the present it is better for them to remain there until we can perfect the title." Canfield planned to plat the new city immediately. He sent George B. Wright to arrange for surveys at Yankton, Dakota Territory. He and the railroad wanted to avoid contested claims and to protect valuable timber from destruction on unmarked lands. Still, Frederick Billings delayed the survey until Congress finalized the treaty transferring Indian title.[60]

In the meantime, a federal order directed the U.S. marshal of Dakota Territory to remove trespassers as well as to arrest those cutting government timber and selling liquor on an Indian reservation. A raid conducted by Deputy Marshal H. E. Luther, aided by Captain William Stanley and twelve troopers from Fort Abercrombie, detained fifteen on February 17, 1872. The marshal confiscated all cigars, liquor, and saloon fixtures; he arraigned several prisoners and bound them over for trial in Pembina. Luther ordered others to leave; he threatened to arrest them and burn their property upon his return. Most refused, but the lawman did not act. Henry Back and Jacob Lowell—lawyers as well as "farmers"—sought the assistance of their acquaintance, Minnesota governor Horace Austin. Others appealed to Senators William Windom and Alexander Ramsey. These worthies contacted the U.S. attorney general, who permitted settlers to remain while negotiators completed the treaty.[61]

An angry debate between the two sides raged for many months in letters submitted to the St. Paul press. Federal officials, harshly criticized for making the arrests, defended themselves. Some residents appealed to Major General Winfield S. Hancock, military commander of Dakota Territory. Hancock reprimanded the Fort Abercrombie commander for his injudicious action. Knowing the deplorable reputation of Canfield and his company, most "Fargo in the Timber" residents blamed him for the raid. A much-irritated Jay Cooke demanded that a new treaty be negotiated at once. Not until June 19, 1873, did the federal government officially proclaim the Sisseton and Wahpeton agreement to cede their land. The chief justice of Dakota Territory meanwhile quashed the liquor cases and recognized the territorial residency of those arrested. His decision and the treaty finally resolved this dispute. As late as March 1874, authorities still arrested and arraigned settlers for cutting timber, however.[62]

On June 6, 1872, the first locomotive chugged over the just-completed bridge into Fargo, a settlement of about fifty residents and a few wooden buildings. It "was a sort of canvasback town, the most of its residents living in tents," steamboat captain Fred Adelbert Bill later recalled. Many newcomers remembered it as a dreary, windswept, treeless village wallowing in mud. Early Fargo's drab appearance did not prevent local newspapers from predicting brisk lot sales. Residents wanted the site to be developed by the Northern Pacific Land Department and not by the LS&PS Company. News that the railroad company proposed purchasing its auxiliary pleased locals. The Land Department platted only 240 acres in September 1873 and had sold the first lots by October. It opened adjoining lands to private speculation as an inducement to settlement. This contrasted markedly with the original vision of the LS&PS town-site monopoly. The fledgling town at last grew more rapidly after the Land Department filed the plat in January 1874 and the Federal Land Office moved from Pembina to Fargo in September.[63]

Despite expectations for prices lower than those charged by the LS&PS Company, initial Land Department charges were comparable. It advertised business lots for $200 to $300 and house lots for $50 to $100 paid in four installments on condition that lots were improved. When these fees did not generate sales, Power reduced prices and, after September 1875, removed the requirement that buyers contract to build a home or business. The potential competition from private landholders outside the original town site likely affected these decisions. According to contracts for the period from 1874 to 1878, business lots ranged from $110 to $160. Residence parcels sold at between $35 and $80. Purchasers acquired them on installment at 7½ percent interest. Under these more favorable terms, sales totaled $5,830 for the year ending September 1, 1878. During the next ten months, they reached $8,885. They spiked at $28,965 in June 1880 at the height of the Dakota Boom. By then, the Land Department had sold most of its lots.[64]

Power and the railroad nurtured Fargo much as Canfield and the land company did Moorhead. The Northern Pacific awarded passes to ministers and agents of the American Sunday School Union. According to one grateful recipient, these were used for "scattering seeds of kindness and . . . truth for our master's kingdom in the West." Corporate managers deeded land for a courthouse and sold other lots at nominal prices to those who established churches and schools in reasonable time. The railroad erected the Headquarters, the first major building, which served as company offices until April 1873 when the road converted it into a hotel. The hotel, which long served as the depot, made an ideal community gateway. Civic leaders regarded it as an attractive symbol of Fargo's future for more than two decades.[65]

In addition, the Northern Pacific contracted with G. S. Barnes and Company to erect an elevator, established a roundhouse and machine shop, and built stockyards west of town. It thus became the largest urban builder. It favored Fargo with lower freight and passenger rates. It granted rebates on lumber shipped to Fargo dealer William H. White, giving him an advantage

Both hotel and depot in 1879, the Headquarters served as Fargo's gateway to the world for more than two decades. Courtesy Institute for Regional Studies, North Dakota State University, Fargo (2029.8.1).

over his Moorhead competitor Henry Finkle. Contracts for delivering mail from Duluth and St. Paul to Fargo and Bismarck benefited the city more than the railroad. The corporation received almost twenty-four thousand dollars per annum between 1875 and 1879. Although this amount did not cover the cost of keeping the line open between Duluth and Bismarck during the winter months, Fargo retained reduced passenger and freight service that otherwise might have been canceled. Postal contracts, favorable rates, and construction gave Fargo ascendancy. According to the 1880 census, it outnumbered its rival by a two-to-one margin of 2,795 to 1,400 people.[66]

Power convinced the Northern Pacific to favor Fargo in yet another way by the grant of Island Park. Red River floods that filled the encircling marshes gave the area its name. Even though Jacob Lowell and Evan S. Tyler claimed to have originated the idea, Power later said he set "the Island" aside because he had early recognized its beauty. Frederick Billings opposed giving away so many valuable acres already platted into lots, but President

Cass overruled him. Marshy ground, which may have made the locale difficult to sell, possibly prompted the gift from these profit-minded corporate managers. The municipal government bestowed only minimal care on Island Park for many years. The council immediately ordered private buildings removed. Voluntary contributions rather poorly maintained it. The mayor appointed Tyler, who had an interest in civic beauty, to clear underbrush and trim trees. He increased the park by selling the city two additional blocks along the northern edge. The council ordered the weeds mowed and appropriated three hundred dollars for road construction. Attempting to lure settlers with amenities by 1881, city boosters boasted about the fifty acres of wooded parkland encircled by a drive.[67]

As mounting wheat production increased rail traffic, twin cities residents and corporate managers contested elevator and roundhouse locations. These conflicts show that corporations did not impose their will on residents. Responding to the Bruns and Finkle Elevator A across the river, Fargo businessman Evan S. Tyler and forty-three others petitioned the Northern Pacific to redress their city's inadequate grain storage. Aware that

A Fargo businessmen's petition in 1880 spurred construction of the Union Elevator. Courtesy Institute for Regional Studies, North Dakota State University, Fargo (2029.8.36).

the growing volume of wheat dictated action, the Northern Pacific authorized G. S. Barnes and Company to build the Union Elevator. It also permitted Barnes to establish seven other grain-handling facilities along its line. When the 1880 harvest ended, the elevator had received more than eight hundred thousand bushels by rail and river.[68]

In the roundhouse competition, attorney Solomon G. Comstock and Thomas Hawley Canfield lobbied on behalf of Moorhead, which offered four thousand dollars, bricks for construction, and forty-five acres near the right-of-way. Northern Pacific land agent W. A. Kindred charged treachery, saying the money could not be raised. He pointed out that larger Fargo did four times more business and afforded greater potential for growth than its rival. General manager Homer E. Sargent agreed and accepted 12½ acres situated on the right-of-way, $2,500, and unlimited access to water from the nearby slough. Businessmen complained that the competing bid forced them into offering a bonus, which they were slow to pay.[69]

To boost Fargo, the real-estate trade, and the region, corporate managers recruited newspapers. William G. Fargo offered a bonus of five hundred dollars in early 1873 for establishment of the *Fargo Express*. Begun by A. H. Moore and continued by A. J. Harwood, it appeared on January 1, 1874. About the same time, Evan S. Tyler started the *Northern Pacific Mirror*, subsequently edited by E. D. Barker. In May 1875, E. B. Chambers, editor of Glyndon's *Red River Gazette*, purchased the *Express* and the *Mirror*; he combined and renamed them the *Fargo Times*. Chambers erected a two-story structure on Northern Pacific Avenue, then almost the only business on the north side. His newspaper dutifully boosted the city, serving not only the interests of the railroad but his own. Power arranged in 1877 to print ten thousand copies of a *Fargo Times* "special edition" devoted to attracting immigrants to the Northwest. Two years later, Chambers contract-

Enterprising Evan S. Tyler, an early settler, engaged in many commercial activities that boosted Fargo. Courtesy Institute for Regional Studies, North Dakota State University, Fargo (51.121.2).

ed with the Northern Pacific for forty thousand copies of another edition promoting "Northern Pacific Country." To publish this job, Chambers inaugurated steam power printing in the twin cities. These kinds of joint efforts by local businessmen working with railroad managers furthered the incorporation of Fargo and the United States.[70]

According to historian Sig Mickelson, editorial boosterism typically emphasized advantages of economy and climate. For example, a September 1875 issue of the *Fargo Times* included land advertisements by the Northern Pacific and St. Paul and Pacific railroads, one article on "splendid wheat lands," and another on "inducements to settlement." The companies offered more than 5 million acres at prices ranging from $2.50 to $10 an acre at 7 percent interest for seven years. The *Times* claimed the superiority of well-watered Dakota lands compared to those of Ohio and Iowa for wheat and raising livestock as well as for growing oats, barley, rye, potatoes, and garden vegetables. Chambers's special edition of 1879 began with a story about "Wheat Farming in Dakota" and included a picture titled "Threshing Scene on the Cass, Cheney and Dalrymple Farm." To counter the negative publicity about the frigid temperatures of Dakota Territory spread by competing transcontinental railroads, the *Times* assured potential settlers that the climate is "one of the most healthful in the world" and that the "bracing and tonic properties of the air work wonderful cures in lung diseases." The *Times* expected a threefold increase in immigration over the previous year, perhaps because the Northern Pacific had distributed ninety thousand copies of Chambers's "extra edition" in the English, German, Norwegian, and Swedish languages.[71]

Promotional materials appeared in the *St. Paul Pioneer Press*, the *Chicago Tribune*, and other newspapers throughout the United States, Canada, and northwestern Europe. To ensure continued favorable coverage, Northern Pacific excursion cars brought editors from Chicago and other major cities to visit along the line in Minnesota and Dakota. The Land Department also exhibited produce annually at the Minnesota State Fair. According to Mickelson, extensive advertising yielded rapid settlement and land sales in Fargo and Cass County.[72]

Bonanza farm publicity dominated Northern Pacific marketing during the mid-1870s. After construction west of the Missouri River started again in 1879, the Land and Immigration departments energetically resumed activity in Western Europe and the eastern United States. As it had before bankruptcy, the railroad company aimed at colonizing its federal land grant with small farms and towns. Promotion of Bonanza farms seemed to contradict this policy. Between 1875 and 1878, stockholders purchased more than eight hundred thousand acres and forty persons acquired nearly six

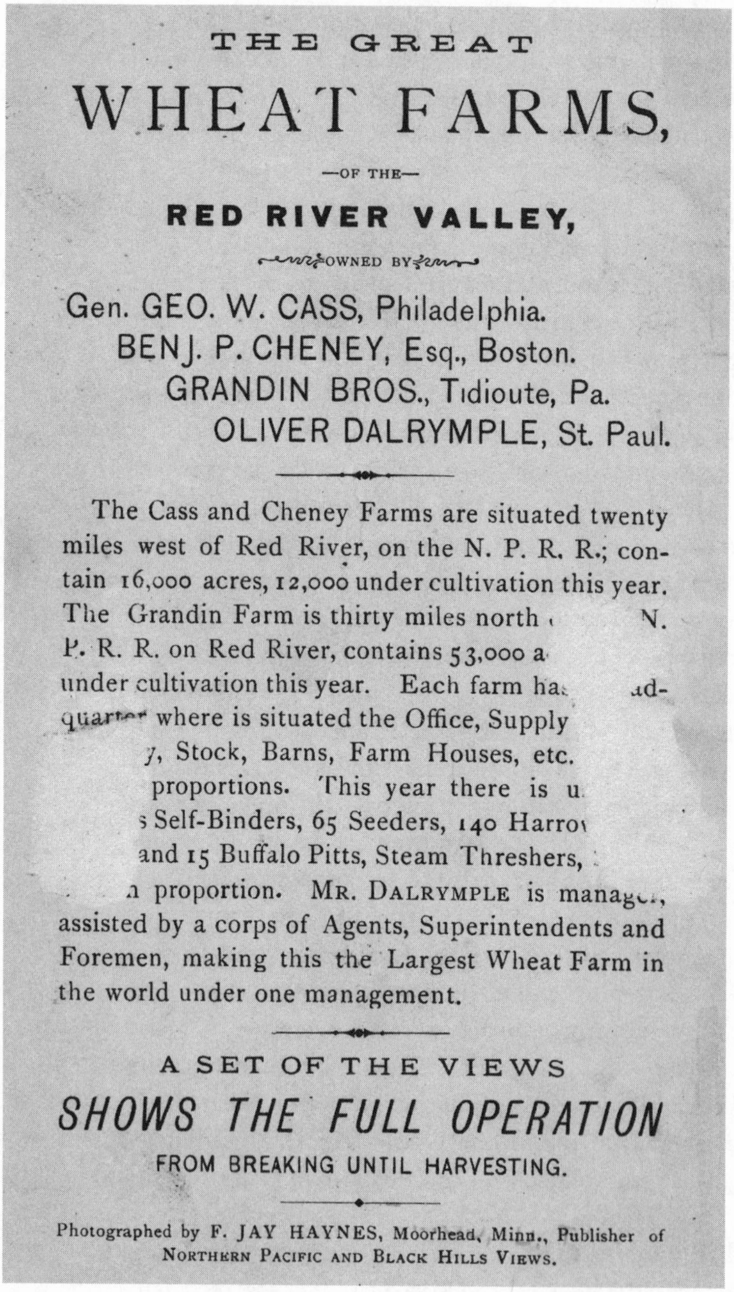

THE GREAT

WHEAT FARMS,

—OF THE—

RED RIVER VALLEY,

OWNED BY

Gen. GEO. W. CASS, Philadelphia.
BENJ. P. CHENEY, Esq., Boston.
GRANDIN BROS., Tidioute, Pa.
OLIVER DALRYMPLE, St. Paul.

The Cass and Cheney Farms are situated twenty miles west of Red River, on the N. P. R. R.; contain 16,000 acres, 12,000 under cultivation this year. The Grandin Farm is thirty miles north   N. P. R. R. on Red River, contains 53,000 a   under cultivation this year.   Each farm ha   ad-quar   where is situated the Office, Supply   y, Stock, Barns, Farm Houses, etc.   proportions.   This year there is u   s Self-Binders, 65 Seeders, 140 Harro   and 15 Buffalo Pitts, Steam Threshers,   a proportion.   MR. DALRYMPLE is manag   assisted by a corps of Agents, Superintendents and Foremen, making this the Largest Wheat Farm in the world under one management.

A SET OF THE VIEWS

SHOWS THE FULL OPERATION

FROM BREAKING UNTIL HARVESTING.

Photographed by F. JAY HAYNES, Moorhead, Minn., Publisher of NORTHERN PACIFIC AND BLACK HILLS VIEWS.

This Northern Pacific advertisement accompanied a photograph by F. Jay Haynes of threshing on a Bonanza farm. Courtesy Institute for Regional Studies, North Dakota State University, Fargo (2070.136.1).

hundred thousand acres. The need for operating capital and the desire to reduce expenses for advertising and taxation led to continued sale of large blocks of land to real-estate syndicates. Yet these lands were sold and settled quickly, as corporate managers had stipulated. The average farm size of 293 acres in eastern North Dakota in 1899 indicated that the

Bonanza farms had declined and that smaller farmers now predominated. Meanwhile, the Northern Pacific had encouraged groups from the East to settle as communities along the line at Buffalo, Tower City, Oriska, and Sanborn. By the turn of the century, the corporation had sold most of its North Dakota lands that totaled almost 11 million acres, or nearly 24 percent of the entire state.[73]

Rapid settlement of the Red River Valley and points west developed the hinterland for Fargo, enabling the city to grow and become the distribution center for farm machinery, lumber, and all other supplies used by the farmers and towns of the region. The Northern Pacific owed much of its corporate success to the policies and management of James B. Power. Although a skilled manager, Power also speculated privately in railroad properties. Indeed, the Northern Pacific investigated his department, dismissed Power, and charged him with fraud in 1881. Power called these charges malicious and maintained his innocence. It is possible that managers who wanted to charge higher prices, which Power resisted, may have engineered his removal. Power very quickly found new employment as land commissioner for the SPM&M railroad.[74]

The early history of Fargo and Moorhead demonstrates several important points about the incorporation of America. Although railroad corporations in particular altered the lives of Americans everywhere, these companies did not possess unlimited power. The Northern Pacific put Fargo and Moorhead on the map and connected them to an expanding national economy. As historian Ronald Ridgley has argued, Dakota railroads operated out of "enlightened self-interest" and recognized that corporate survival required benefiting the public. They thus opened the territory to settlement; promoted towns, businesses, and farms; and brought the essentials of civilization to the northern plains.[75]

In this chapter I have argued that residents, who had designs of their own and who resisted those unilaterally imposed by the Northern Pacific and LS&PS companies, fostered railroad enlightenment. Fortunately for both, railroad and settler interests often converged, as each recognized that the growth of one required the growth of the other. Corporate managers and local businessmen then cooperated, each in pursuit of their own advantage. They worked jointly in establishing the churches, schools, businesses, and homes that made Fargo and Moorhead viable communities. Both agreed that sober and industrious businessmen should become the pillars of the congregations and the foundation of the communal moral order.

These efforts at community building often involved complex four-way negotiations between residents of the competing cities of Moorhead and

Fargo on the one hand, and the railroad managers of the often-conflicting Northern Pacific and LS&PS companies on the other. Whatever their own disagreements, both companies often were forced to work with residents and rely on their capital to carry out their plans for developing Fargo, Moorhead, and the Red River Valley. Inhabitants of each city competed by seeking railroad favors to promote their own growth at expense of their rivals. They thus contested corporate decisions about land prices, railroad facilities, grain elevators, and the steamboat trade.

To take only one of these contests as an example, some Northern Pacific managers developed different strategies of promoting towns from that originally conceived when Jay Cooke proposed establishing a town-site company as a condition for his financing the Northern Pacific. Settler opposition to the LS&PS Company attempt to monopolize all speculation in town lots forced consideration of new strategies. As land commissioner James B. Power explained in an 1880 letter to Frederick Billings: "When taking charge of the land department work in 1873, the reputation of the [Northern Pacific] Company was suffering from the attempt to control through the LS&PS Co. the town site interests." The railroad's poor reputation retarded Dakota land sales that year after the territory was opened to settlement. To attract settlers, corporate managers promoted Bonanza farms and developed a more liberal land policy. Additionally, managers only retained 240 acres in each of three cities—Fargo, Jamestown, and Bismarck—and opened all other lands along the line to town-site speculation by private individuals. Power thought this new strategy had shown good results in North Dakota. In contrast to the LS&PS attempt to locate towns in advance of settlement, Power argued that towns could more profitably be established after the line was built.[76]

This debate about competing corporate strategies and the other contests in Fargo and Moorhead demonstrate that the incorporation of America did not simply proceed from the top down. It resulted instead from the complex and dynamic interaction of managers with each other and with local businessmen as each group sought prosperity through economic expansion.

Booster Dreams 2

HENRY BRUNS AND MOORHEAD'S COLLAPSE

*Moorhead. The Key City of the Famous Red River Valley . . . A Big
Boom Now in Progress— . . . Splendid Houses, Big Railroad Shops,
Fine Post Office, Water Works, Street Cars, and all the Paraphernalia
of a City.*

—*Daily Argonaut,* January 20, 1882

*Looking south from the Grand Pacific nowadays it is possible to see . . .
a boundless field of grain. It extends fully thirty-five miles. . . . In all
that distance . . . there is not a single rod of fence to obstruct the way.*
—*Moorhead Weekly News,* August 10, 1882

ENTREPRENEUR HENRY A. BRUNS STAKED HIS CONSIDERABLE PER-
sonal fortune on Moorhead becoming a railroad center and the "Key
City" of the Red River Valley. Settled first, the town captured the booming
steamboat trade with southern Manitoba. Although Fargo had grown larger
by the end of the decade, Bruns and other residents hoped the SPM&M
railroad might yet make their city the dominant distribution point at the
crossing. Unfortunately for Bruns, Moorhead attained only a fraction of
its projected population and Fargo became the gateway city. To a large extent, Moorhead's failed growth dictated the bankruptcy of its foremost
champion. Many blamed railroad magnate James J. Hill's broken promises
for that failure, yet Bruns charitably maintained that neither he nor Hill
foresaw how economic reality would unfold.

An 1889 biographical compendium of Red River Valley worthies had
nothing but praise for Bruns: "He has taken a leading part in every move or
enterprise . . . to build up the city or develop the surrounding country. . . . He
has done more toward making Moorhead what it is today than any other
resident." Two decades later, a Minneapolis newspaper headline summarized

Henry A. Bruns (center front) and Solomon G. Comstock (on Bruns's left), photographed with other founders in 1889, worked to make Moorhead the "Key City" of the Red River Valley. Courtesy Clay County Historical Society.

Bruns's changed circumstances: "Once Rich, Now a Cheese Clerk. Man Who Built $150,000 Hotel in Moorhead Earns $10 a Week."[1]

Bruns's story of fortune won and then lost is a familiar tale of the American West. Western historians from Frederick Jackson Turner to William Cronon have recorded how nineteenth-century Americans viewed the West as a land of opportunity. Although Cronon much revised Turner, he agreed that the "unexploited natural abundance" and "free land" of the frontier offered the potential of vast rewards for any human labor expended. To be sure, as Cronon and other historians have pointed out, the high risks of town building and other enterprise often thwarted dreams of opportunity and success. Western entrepreneurs depended on credit, faced competition from newly emerging corporations in national and international markets, and confronted a boom-and-bust business cycle.[2]

Bruns shared dreams of western opportunity and willingly accepted entrepreneurial risks. Born in 1847 to German immigrant parents, who farmed in Dubuque County, Iowa, Bruns graduated from commercial college at sixteen. He worked on his father's farm and for Dubuque stores as a clerk, bookkeeper, and traveling salesman before striking out on his own in early 1871. Learning in Brainerd that the Northern Pacific expected to build into

Dakota Territory, he returned to St. Paul and purchased a wagonload of provisions and ready-made clothes. He took them in late June to Oakport, a makeshift tent village located at one of the anticipated railroad crossings of the Red River. To pay transportation costs on his goods, he borrowed a hundred dollars from Oakport resident Henry G. Finkle, who became his partner in a newly opened tent store. When the railroad revealed the true crossing, Bruns and Finkle relocated to Moorhead at the end of September. Within two months after the arrival of the first Northern Pacific train on January 4, 1872, they joined other residents in converting their tents into wooden stores and homes.[3]

RED RIVER STEAMBOATS AND THE MANITOBA TRADE

The coming of the Northern Pacific greatly expanded steamboat traffic, fueling optimism that Moorhead would become a key distribution point. Thousands of Canadian settlers and tons of freight passed through the fledgling town, which soon became a boat-building center. When the *Selkirk* of Hill, Griggs and Company offered stiff competition to Norman W. Kittson's *International,* James J. Hill and Kittson merged in 1873. Their new Red River Transportation Company operated five boats and twenty barges. Steamboats generally carried more than a hundred tons of freight plus a number of passengers and pushed or pulled two barges; these measured about a hundred feet by twenty-four feet and had a capacity of three hundred tons. A boat left Moorhead generally every third day on a round-trip voyage to Winnipeg that netted almost twenty-four thousand dollars in profit, *International* clerk Frank M. Painter recalled many years later.[4]

Lured by profitable prospects and dissatisfied with the high rates of the Kittson–Hill monopoly, Moorhead, St. Paul, and Winnipeg businessmen in early 1875 incorporated the Merchants International Steamship Company. The firm built the elegant *Manitoba* and the less ornate *Minnesota* in the local boatyard from timbers sawed by Henry Bruns's mill. Manager James Douglas erected a warehouse, attracted more tracks as well as other improvements on the levee, and brought about rate reductions. Freight charges from St. Paul declined from $6 in 1860 to $2.25 per hundredweight in 1875. A combined train–boat passenger ticket now cost $19 compared to $35 paid earlier for the trip by boat and stagecoach. Unfortunately, the new firm lost half its business for a critical six weeks when the *Manitoba*—queen of the Red River steamboats—sank in early June after colliding with the *International.* Although the *Manitoba* returned to service by the end of July, Kittson and Hill acquired it and the *Minnesota* for assuming the debts of their nearly bankrupt rival.[5]

As slightly more than seven thousand Mennonites, their substantial baggage, and huge cargoes of other goods for the Canadian settlements passed through, newspaper editors detailed how the trade developed the city. The boatyard consumed quantities of lumber and employed numerous men in building the many steamboats, barges, and flatboats engaged in the river trade. The Northern Pacific made expensive levee improvements. Before the 1873 shipping season began, corporate managers expanded their freight depot at the river's edge, laid track to the Hudson's Bay Company warehouse, and extended rails to the steamboat landing so that the boats could be loaded directly from the cars. Two years later, railroad managers constructed a triangular system of passenger walkways from the steamboat offices on Fourth Street to the landing, along the levee to the bridge, then back to the offices. Now, the *Red River Star* insisted, the town should build a firm road to prevent wagons from sinking to their hubs in mud after hard rains.[6]

The Northern Pacific regarded the Red River Transportation Company as one of its "best feeders and allies." Railroad managers therefore respectfully considered Kittson's request for storing forty carloads of freight after a hard November freeze ended the shipping season abruptly in 1875. Kittson and Hill had 2,700 tons of Canadian Pacific iron rails and six hundred tons of flour in Moorhead and Crookston warehouses, as well as another five hundred tons of freight on boats frozen in the river. During the winter, horse-drawn wagons delivered a portion of these goods to Canada. Rebates paid by the Northern Pacific to the Red River Transportation Company on charges for shipping goods through Moorhead afford additional evidence of cooperation. Competition from the St. Paul and Pacific Railroad, however, perhaps forced these payments. That railroad moved goods to Breckenridge and thence by flatboats to Canada. It more seriously threatened the Northern Pacific's Moorhead traffic when its track reached Fisher's Landing on the Red Lake River east of Crookston. An alarmed *Red River Star* reported that Kittson's steamers planned to run to Fisher's Landing for the remainder of the 1876 season. Denying that low water had made the notorious Goose Rapids impassable, the *Star* suggested that the St. Paul and Pacific had threatened to stop its trains unless the steamboats went immediately to the new railhead.[7]

Moorhead jealously defended its interests in the river trade. The *Star* reported that the railroad and steamboats had handled more than 33 million pounds of freight in 1873. It increased to more than 76 million pounds two years later. Less than half that amount came through the city, however. The St. Paul and Pacific had shipped 10 million pounds on flatboats from Breckenridge and 30 million pounds from Fisher's Landing. Although the local trade had increased slightly over previous years, editor Nickles com-

plained that most of the increase had been lost to competitors. He blamed
the Kittson Line for breaking its promise to ship from Moorhead. He rejected as phony the company's excuse of "low water." The *Star* editor also
attacked the Northern Pacific for its wasteful construction of a sidetrack
to the river in Fargo, claiming that his city ought to retain the trade it already possessed. Whether or not Nickles realized it, railroad expansion
northward rendered fruitless his defense of the river port. Completion of
the St. Vincent extension to the border in December 1878 and its link to
Winnipeg via the Canadian Pacific Railroad signaled the steamboat's eventual demise.[8]

Residents responded to the loss of trade in two ways. Initially, they built
flatboats and continued shipping goods north. After the Canadian rail connection foreclosed that opportunity, they attracted new steamboat companies for
the growing wheat trade. The Alsop Brothers Freight Line in November 1877
contracted with the boatyard to build the steamboat *Pluck* and four barges. By
1881, they had established a two hundred-foot dock, erected a warehouse, and
built the stern-wheeler *Henry W. Alsop* and five more barges. Bad investments,

Steamboats at the busy Moorhead levee in about 1880 stimulated early growth. Courtesy Institute
for Regional Studies, North Dakota State University, Fargo (51.51.21).

low water, and competition from the SPM&M railroad forced the line's sale to Kittson and Hill in 1885. In the same period, the Grandin Brothers Bonanza Farm put up an elevator on the Fargo riverbank and contracted with the boatyard to build its own steamer and barges. In 1880, the *Grandin* carried more than 15 million pounds of freight and 281 passengers. The *Pluck* transported almost 2 million pounds of freight, 700 cords of wood and 52,000 bushels of wheat. The Alsop Brothers and the Grandin Line together provided seven months' employment each year for seventy-six men. Their steamers and barges carried freight, groceries, provisions, flour, household goods, and farm machinery downriver to Pembina or St. Vincent. They returned with cargoes of wheat, oats, and potatoes. As train service improved, this trade disappeared. At the end of the 1880s, newspapers referred only to the *Grandin* and the *Pluck* bringing wheat cargoes each spring to the twin cities.[9]

Steamboats thus proved a fragile basis for a permanently prosperous economy. Long winters and natural obstacles made uncertain the length of the shipping season. The Red River is a shallow, winding stream filled with snags. As one engineer reported: "The river is very tortuous, averaging two miles of water to one of land, being a perfect system of short bends. In some cases a distance of one mile by water will accomplish 300 feet by land." The Goose Rapids—located forty miles north of Moorhead at Caledonia and extending twenty-two miles to Frog Point—formed an impassable barrier in low water. On good years like 1873 or 1875, the shipping season might last from mid-April to early November, enabling the *Red River Star* to claim seven months of uninterrupted river navigation. However, in other years— 1876, 1878, 1879, 1883, and 1886—low water shortened the season considerably. At these times it might last only two and a half months.[10]

Moorhead did not surrender easily its dream of becoming the major Red River port city. Beginning in January 1873, the *Red River Star* called for federal appropriations to correct the problem of low water at Goose Rapids by constructing locks and dams. As a first step, Congress funded a river survey by the Corps of Engineers, which began in August. Despite repeated calls for action from the valley, three more years passed before Congress even considered a ten thousand-dollar appropriation bill that failed. Another two years transpired before two hundred men attended a Red River Improvement Convention at Breckenridge. A resolution from that body helped to obtain a twenty-five thousand-dollar congressional grant for dredging. Beginning in May 1879, the *Unser Fritz*—built at the boatyard and commanded by a Captain Wanzer—had removed sixty thousand yards of material by October, creating a three-foot channel to the mouth of the Sheyenne River. Wanzer's crew worked through the winter clearing snags as far south as McCauleyville.

The *Unser Fritz*, a U.S. government dredge, attempted to make the Red River more navigable in the early 1880s. Courtesy Clay County Historical Society.

Scouring the channel northward continued in subsequent years. A public meeting requested $240,000 from Congress for dam construction and dredging, but to no avail.[11]

Meanwhile, new schemes surfaced for a reservoir system to raise river levels during the low-water months or a Red River and Lake Superior canal, a project perhaps inspired by an 1874 report named for Minnesota senator William Windom. Advocates argued that this waterway could be constructed with forty miles of canal and 265 miles of improved river channels. The first stage called for connecting the Red River to the Minnesota River via the Bois de Sioux into Traverse Lake, a canal, and Big Stone Lake. On the eve of a Fargo convention to consider the project in January 1886, the *Moorhead Weekly News* dismissed it as impractical. Instead, the paper preferred the longer-standing Moorhead fantasy of improving the Red River from Breckenridge to Pembina. Several years later, even the *News* dismissed Red River improvement as "honest twaddle." The editor finally posed a realistic question: With two railroads paralleling the river, what chance did slow steamboats have? Thus ended hopes for boosting the Moorhead economy by capitalizing on the

Red River. These dreams persisted because many hoped that improving water routes—"nature's thoroughfares"—would create competition and lower the high rail rates that had frustrated their prosperity.[12]

BOOSTERS AND BUSINESSMEN

Several historians have observed that nineteenth-century urban expansion often depended on local entrepreneurs who promoted the growth of their city and region. According to Carl Abbott, boosters appraised their situation, articulated a program, and advertised it widely. Like their brethren elsewhere, Moorhead boosters were newspapermen, businessmen, professionals, and municipal officials elected from these groups. They also expressed similar themes. Individual prosperity depended on community and regional growth, which required joint action by active citizens. Toward that end, Carroll Van West has maintained, they formed associations for the common good and to counteract the power of corporations on the local economy. Whenever possible, they employed corporate resources for their own designs. They raised capital, rallied support, and coordinated private and public bodies to achieve their goals. They tried to verify their claims with accurate data. Yet at times they deluded themselves. Their attempt at developing economic self-sufficiency through building an iron industry failed. They did not comprehend that their own contributions to growth, though necessary, did not suffice for success. As a consequence, external factors—population, transport, and national manufacturing—often defeated their expectations.[13]

From editor W. B. Nickles of the *Red River Star* to George N. Lamphere of the *Moorhead Weekly News*, a succession of journalist boosters recognized that growth determined their success. Accordingly, newspapers published advertisements from the

Editor George Lamphere helped his newspaper by boosting Moorhead. Courtesy Institute for Regional Studies, North Dakota State University, Fargo (328.10.7).

Northern Pacific, land agents, and businessmen to supplement their income from circulation. Editors habitually reported the latest "needed improvements" from erecting new buildings to the planting of shade trees and celebrated the latest triumphs of trade. They often noted the "bright outlook" of each coming year for their municipality and region, implicitly recognizing that an expanding rural hinterland sustained the city. While editors frequently praised merchants for their "enterprising spirit" in starting new projects, they did not hesitate to point out the need for manufacturers who would "secure the town's future."[14]

An 1874 businessmen's meeting approved several initiatives. They asked the LS&PS Company for an equalization of lot prices comparable to those of neighboring towns and pledged their cooperation in developing the city. They recommended forming a joint-stock company to build a sawmill and flour mill. When they learned that five hundred thousand bricks would be manufactured during the next summer, they suggested doubling the number. They appointed one committee to take charge of the Red River wagon bridge and another to collect funds for a Scandinavian church. Although businessmen met as circumstances dictated throughout the decade, many desired an organization that convened regularly. By 1880, a board of trade formed and elected land dealer A. A. White president and newspaperman Walt W. Partridge secretary. The *Clay Country Advocate* published their timid suggestions for the public good: paint buildings, plant shade trees, and cut grass and weeds. Inactivity compelled reorganizing the board two years later after the arrival of the SPM&M railroad occasioned a boom.[15]

According to new editor George Lamphere of the renamed *Moorhead Weekly News*, businessmen formed the body "to broadcast the possibilities of the region throughout the nation." Determined to make their city the valley's great wholesale and commercial center, the group published eleven thousand copies of a promotional pamphlet, *The Valley of the Red River of the North and the City of Moorhead*. This effort followed another booklet—*Moorhead—The Key City of the Red River Valley*—printed in 1882 by the Northwestern Publishing Company of St. Paul. Instead of relying on an outside firm, the board of trade now announced that it would publicize all statistics of Moorhead growth.[16]

Frontier merchants joined editors in boosting the town. According to historian Lewis Atherton, these men replicated an earlier undifferentiated merchandizing as it evolved slowly toward economic specialization. They provided customers with manufactured goods ordered from eastern firms through traveling salesmen or on annual purchasing trips. Storekeepers opened at dawn and often did not close until ten at night. An entire farm family often arrived by horse-drawn wagon as early in the day as distance permitted, sold their produce, did their trading, and socialized in the stores. Those farther from town might not appear until evening. Desiring to return home the next day, they wanted service immediately. Merchants took up activities as circumstances dictated. They sometimes farmed, speculated in real estate, operated saw- and gristmills, and held political office. On the cash-starved frontier, they became produce merchants to acquire the necessary capital for purchasing retail merchandise and extending credit to their customers. They typically operated with one to two years' credit from their eastern wholesale suppliers. From these experiences, many eventually became bankers and leaders in developing factories for their cities. They perceived towns and farms as a single commercial system. They believed their expansion promoted the urban and rural growth that fostered their own success.[17]

Several Moorhead merchants exemplified traits identified by Atherton. Many worked from dawn until dusk. Not until the 1890s did they consider closing at seven o'clock on winter evenings and, excluding Saturday nights, at eight in the spring and summer months. During harvest, however, they remained open nightly until ten o'clock. Many—including hardware dealer James Douglas, merchant Henry Finkle, druggist Benjamin Mackall, and dress goods merchant J. H. Sharp—made annual purchasing trips eastward to Chicago, St. Paul, and other unspecified destinations. Several engaged in varied economic activities. N. K. Hubbard and Company—trading in dry goods, clothing, boots, and supplies—advertised itself in 1873 as the Bank of Moorhead. Swedish immigrant John Erickson began as a wholesale and retail dealer in supplies, dry goods, clothing, boots, shoes, groceries, meats, and ice. He soon built the Erickson House, which offered guests a good stable as well as convenient access to steamboats, trains, and stages. By 1881, he had opened the opulent Jay Cooke Hotel, owned the only brewery, and operated a large farm on which he raised the barley he used for brewing. He later served as alderman and mayor. Henry A. Bruns, however, became the foremost booster during the first two decades when he grew from merchant into entrepreneur, building a sawmill, flour mill, elevator, bank, hotel, and foundry.[18]

Operating in the two-story frame building they had erected a few months after relocating to Moorhead, Bruns and Finkle advertised a "mammoth stock" of general merchandise that included "almost everything but liquor." They ordered from Chicago and Philadelphia and cut into the St. Paul and Minneapolis wholesale trade by shipping carloads of merchandise by steamboat to Canada. Through the Canadian trade, Bruns became acquainted with James J. Hill and furthered Hill's knowledge of the region's rich agricultural potential in 1874 by sending him samples of Peerless Potatoes that had yielded three hundred bushels to the acre. Claiming to have sold $140,000 in goods in 1876, the partners constructed a two-story brick building for their growing retail trade. They enjoyed favorable ratings from R. G. Dun, which praised their character, habits, and ability and characterized their firm as "the heaviest and soundest business concern in this region." The reports stressed the good commercial ability of Bruns in particular.[19]

Bruns early displayed entrepreneurial skill and booster spirit. He purchased five hundred bushels of seed wheat in 1872 and sold it on credit to farmers in the Minnesota counties of Clay and Norman and the Dakota counties of Cass and Trail. Two years later, he led an association of eight men in organizing the Moorhead Manufacturing Company, capitalized at twenty-five thousand dollars, and established a sawmill and flour mill. He immediately requested land from the town-site company. Thomas Canfield responded affirmatively, adding that with businessmen like Bruns going forward, "Moorhead will be the chief city on Red River." Construction commenced in late May and ended in late September. According to the *Red River Star,* the mill soon ran night and day, grinding a good quality of flour. The following year, the sawmill cut timber for the *Minnesota* and the *Manitoba,* built by the Merchants International Steamship Company in which Bruns had also invested. Yet the firm's primary activity shifted from lumber to flour with bigger wheat crops.[20]

An R. G. Dun report of November 1875 noted that the flour mill did well under Bruns's energetic and efficient management. Newspaper accounts of shipments to Bismarck, Winnipeg, Mennonites in Canada, and eventually gold miners in the Black Hills confirmed this perception. Many Northern and Canadian Pacific Railroad construction workers also dined on Belle of Moorhead flour. Unable to keep up with orders, Bruns modernized in October 1880, replacing six grist stones with rollers. During that decade, his mill shipped to Fort Benton, Helena, and Cottonwood, Montana Territory; Buffalo, Washington Territory; Chicago; Boston; and Amsterdam, Holland. After Bruns increased from 175 to three hundred barrels daily in 1886, he employed fifteen men at full capacity. To sell his increased output, Bruns traveled west, searching for buyers, and organized local millers to seek eastern outlets.[21]

Although LS&PS president George Stark advised delay, Bruns and Finkle built a steam elevator with capacity for 100,000 bushels. During the 1879 harvest, it received almost 250,000 bushels of wheat delivered in more than 5,000 wagon loads hauled up to forty miles from either side of the Red River. That same year, modernizers Bruns and Finkle installed a telephone line, connecting their elevator, store, and mill.[22]

In 1879, Bruns—in partnership with local businessman Thomas C. Kurtz—

Henry Bruns and Henry Finkle built Elevator A, drawing wheat and rural trade to Moorhead by 1879. Courtesy Clay County Historical Society.

secured the supply contract for the Northern Pacific extension west from Bismarck. The following year, the *Fargo Weekly Argus* reported that Bruns's railway sales totaled three hundred thousand dollars, while his Moorhead store grossed seventy thousand dollars. The four-year contract (1879–82) paid Bruns 2 million dollars and made his fortune, according to attorney Solomon G. Comstock.[23]

In 1880, Bruns and Kurtz built the two-story, brick Merchants Bank block, housing a bank, three stores, an opera house, and offices. They opened the Merchants Bank, capitalized at $60,000, on November 1 in the Bruns and Finkle Store and moved to the bank building six weeks later. By February, after deposits totaled more than $76,000, the officers happily reported that business far exceeded "their most sanguine expectations." After two more years, the bank increased its capital stock to $100,000 and claimed to be the leading Minnesota State Bank outside St. Paul and Minneapolis. At decade's end, the Merchants Bank alleged capital totaling $125,000 and listed the First National Bank of St. Paul, Security Bank of Minneapolis, Continental National Bank of Chicago, and Chase National Bank of New York City as financial correspondents. Bruns's opera house, on the other hand, contributed significantly to community life. The annual fireman's ball as well as Jenny Lind—the "Swedish Nightingale"—and popular preachers Henry Ward Beecher and DeWitt Talmadge appeared there in the 1880s.[24]

Ten months after Bruns and Kurtz launched their venture, several leading business and professional men—Frank J. Burnham, Solomon G. Comstock, Patrick H. Lamb, Henry Finkle, John Erickson, Lewis Benedict, and others—established the First National Bank of Moorhead with capital of $50,000. Charles H. Benedict originally served as president, succeeded by Burnham. By 1896, deposits exceeded $120,000 and capital had increased to $60,000.[25]

The city early attracted professional men. Maine native Comstock and Vermonter Frank Burnham, the second and third lawyers, arrived in 1871 and 1872 respectively. Each remained for his lifetime, becoming Clay County attorneys, successful real-estate dealers, and prominent boosters. Comstock eventually served in the Minnesota state legislature as well as Congress. Dr. John Kurtz, the first to practice medicine in the county, arrived as a physician for the Northern Pacific railroad. He became both professional and merchant, forming a partnership with druggist Benjamin F. Mackall in the local drugstore. Growth attracted nine lawyers, five physicians, and one dentist by 1900.[26]

As the city followed the normal evolution of American urban construction from wood to brick, it also replicated local brick manufacture to save on transportation costs. Only later improvements in rail transport led to concentrated and mechanized production at superior clay deposits. Brothers John and Patrick Lamb in June 1874 became the first producers. Within four years they had constructed a large barn to accommodate their work and livery teams. By the early 1880s during the Moorhead boom, the city had become the Clay County brickmaking center as five firms employed 135 men and made eight and one-half million cream-colored bricks. The manufacturers shipped to Jamestown, Bismarck, and other Dakota railroad towns. Lamb Brothers and four other producers in 1887 still employed sixty-five

Lamb Brothers Brickyard was an important industry in Moorhead in 1880. Courtesy Clay County Historical Society.

men and made 5 million bricks valued at $32,500. At the turn of the century, the recently formed and newly mechanized Moorhead Brick Manufacturing Company planned to meet demand locally by more efficiently manufacturing 3 million bricks. Thereafter, exhaustion of clay deposits, use of cement blocks, and competition from national manufacturers ended local output.[27]

Expanding valley wheat crops stimulated demands for flour production. When Nels Overboe's twenty-five thousand-dollar gristmill seemed likely to open in August 1883, the *Moorhead Weekly News* proclaimed: "Moorhead is fast becoming . . . a manufacturing city of considerable magnitude" and "an entrepôt of the wheat district." Although the new mill marketed Pride of the Valley flour for a few years, it lacked a railroad siding, struggled financially, and changed proprietors several times in the next decade. Bruns's mill meanwhile remained successful in the 1880s, but faltered subsequently under new ownership. The North Dakota Milling Association purchased and refurbished the mill in 1893. It soon employed twenty men in daily producing six hundred barrels. Residents consumed ten thousand barrels an-

nually but the mill labored to sell the additional 170,000 barrels to markets
in the eastern United States, England, Scotland, and Germany. Millers complained that competition from Pillsbury and other large firms threatened
their existence.[28]

John Erickson's brewery added another manufacturing firm to the city
in 1878. He soon employed six men in producing just over eighteen hundred
barrels annually, slightly less than one-half capacity. National competition
prevented his growth. Yet the liquor trade became a major commercial activity, especially after North Dakota entered the Union as a dry state in
1889. "Two carloads of beer" sold daily in the city's forty-one saloons that
mostly served as outlets for national brewers. Major distributors ranged
from Anheuser Busch to Schlitz; all had their own cold storage houses.
Moorhead became a wholesaling center for distilled and malt liquors. The
well-patronized business generated large freight revenues for the railroads
and seventeen thousand dollars for the municipal government, which debated the relative merits of "purity versus prosperity."[29]

While boosters looked to the river trade, retail and wholesale sales, and
manufacturing as keys to growth, businessmen did not forget that their success rested on valley farmers. Indeed, Solomon Comstock, Patrick Lamb,
R. M. Probstfield, and others in 1873 formed the Clay County Agricultural and
Mechanical Society for holding fairs to encourage husbandry and the fine arts.
These annual events attracted good crowds to the city, although the *Moorhead
Advocate* said it would like to see more interest, especially from isolated farmers who would benefit socially and intellectually. Editors also reported annually on the condition of the wheat crop and the high yields per acre. They duly
noted all threats—the grasshopper hazard of the 1870s, drought, storms, and
too much rain (a more frequent problem in the valley).[30]

Many city dwellers owned farms and several—Bruns, Comstock, and
others—dealt in farm properties. Even the Presbyterian minister Oscar H.
Elmer had filed land and timber claims. He recorded in his diary that he had
deposited his wheat money totaling more than four hundred dollars in the
Merchants Bank. During the harvest of "king wheat," the city became quiet,
except on evenings when thirsty laborers arrived to imbibe. Many town
dwellers tended to their crop in the country. Busy farmers did not come
to town. Given the pervasive investment in agriculture, farm prices interested everyone. Accordingly, the *Red River Star* in 1873 began publishing the
Moorhead market reports, listing prices for wheat, oats, potatoes, and other
agricultural produce. Subsequent newspapers continued the practice, adding reports from the Chicago, Milwaukee, St. Paul, and Minneapolis grain
markets. As wheat prices declined owing to overproduction, the *Moorhead
Weekly News* in 1894 urged urban residents to cooperate with farmers in

attempting to raise the price of wheat, reduce transportation costs, and decrease taxes. From the 1880s onward—perhaps inspired by the experimentation and promotional efforts of railroaders James J. Hill and James B. Power—the *News* urged agricultural diversification as a solution, suggesting that more livestock, sugar beets, and potatoes should be raised. R. M. Probstfield, who farmed just north of the city, had shown the way to a more scientific agriculture in the 1870s by growing and selling cabbages, onions, and potatoes. In addition to the vegetables he sold to restaurants and door-to-door in Moorhead and Bismarck, Probstfield profited most from sauerkraut. Most valley farmers, nevertheless, remained fixated on wheat.[31]

The SPM&M and the Moorhead Boom

Solomon Comstock's success as the first Clay County attorney facilitated his election to the Minnesota House. Serving four terms as a Republican representative (1875–83), Comstock supported James J. Hill's battle for the bankrupt St. Paul and Pacific Railroad. He became Hill's friend, liking him—according to his daughter Ada—"better than any man in the world he knew next to his own father." Hill bested the Northern Pacific and gained control, driving a hard bargain with Dutch investors who lost heavily and cried "fraud." The U.S. Supreme Court eventually dismissed all claims. Hill's management skills proved his worth, amply rewarding all bondholders. Hill renamed his prize the SPM&M and designated Comstock his western legal agent. Because Hill would not receive federal land grants in Dakota Territory, he planned town-site development as one way to pay his construction costs. He became a silent partner with Comstock and A. A. White in the Northwest Land Company, which developed forty-five town sites in the Red River Valley and westward along the Manitoba road. Hill provided them the proposed route; assured of a sound investment, they divided lot sales evenly with him. All partners profited. Even in 1892, after four years of dry weather and poor crops, Hill's 50 percent share yielded ten thousand dollars. Comstock thus became Moorhead's wealthiest and most prominent citizen. In return for SPM&M favors, Comstock served as Hill's eyes and ears, enabling him to foil competition and solidify his hold on valley commerce.[32]

From participating in the Red River trade Hill recognized that constructing north–south lines would tap large profits in the valley. Northern Pacific managers agreed. They attempted to block Hill from the twin cities until their company controlled the region with branches built from its east–west–running main line. After Hill bested the Northern Pacific by acquiring the St. Paul and Pacific and its Minnesota land grant he built northward, connected with the Canadian Pacific, and planned additional lines in the re-

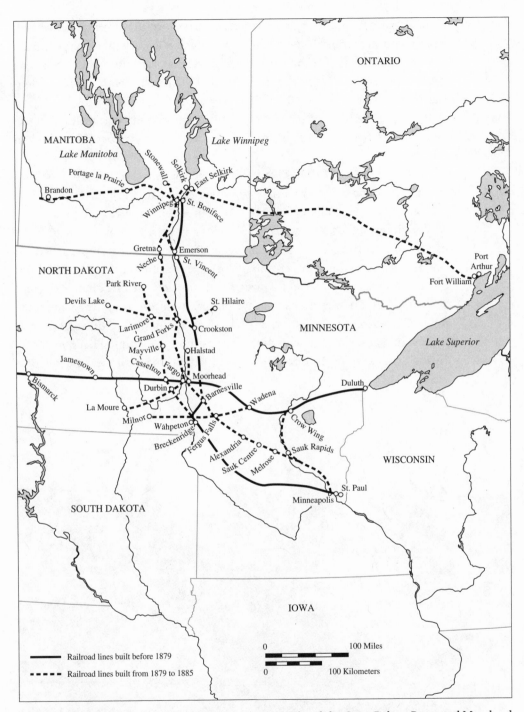

Railroad building in the Red River Valley, 1879–85, stimulated the Great Dakota Boom and Moorhead expansion. From Stanley N. Murray, *The Valley Comes of Age* (Fargo: North Dakota Institute for Regional Studies, 1967); redrawn by Patti Isaacs, Parrot Graphics.

gion. Comstock, knowing Hill's intentions, tried to lure him to Moorhead: "Can't you accomplish everything you desire with less expense and a shorter line," he asked, "by running your extension . . . here and across the river?" Assuring Hill that the "information will be as private and confidential as you desire," he added, it "will be of value to me personally," implying that he intended to profit from selling lots and acquiring right-of-way. He pledged that twin-city freight receipts would repay construction costs from Barnesville.[33]

In June 1880, the SPM&M superintendent of construction ordered Comstock: "secure by contract all the right of way you can on Minnesota side." A few months later, Comstock wrote Hill: "Before erecting any shops or other RR buildings at Red River, will you kindly give us a hint at Moorhead. We can furnish all the ground you may need." As the Manitoba approached, an injunction blocked it from crossing Northern Pacific rails on the outskirts but the courts did not stop its bridge construction. After Comstock promised Hill "you can draw on us for anything required," the Manitoba laid track down Main Street parallel to that of its rival. Residents celebrated by blowing the mill and elevator whistles, firing cannon, consuming beer, smoking cigars, and listening to Comstock thank the railroad corporation for new

This SPM&M construction crew laid track on Main Street in order to enter Moorhead in 1880. Courtesy Clay County Historical Society.

prosperity. Hill's line received permission to cross Northern Pacific tracks in December and entered Fargo early in the New Year.[34]

After beating his opponent in court, Hill began a rate war by offering free passes and 30 percent rebates. Northern Pacific resentment at the Manitoba invasion soon gave way to the pain of lost profits. It retained control of the Fargo trade only by granting 33 percent rebates, which reduced its profits by two hundred thousand dollars annually, according to Vice President Thomas F. Oakes. These losses—and their desire to keep other lines out of the region—compelled Northern Pacific managers to accept Manitoba terms for sharing the territory and pooling traffic. An executive agreement in March 1882 divided the region according to a principle previously approved in 1879. The Manitoba gained "possession of the . . . Valley . . . maintained by north south lines," while the Northern Pacific retained its "tributary country" by "east and west lines." The rivals arranged "an even pool at Moorhead and Fargo to and from Minneapolis and St. Paul and other common points, traffic rates maintained." This truce proved temporary. It collapsed the following year when Hill transformed the SPM&M into a transcontinental by building west from Devil's Lake, Dakota Territory.[35]

Dreams of fortunes in wheat and the expected coming of the SPM&M sparked the beginning of the Great Dakota Boom in 1878. Attracted by Manitoba publicity to "the Nile of the North," 42,000 immigrants came to the Red River Valley in 1882 at the boom's crest, enabling the road to sell more than 200,000 acres of its Minnesota land grant. With the railroad's arrival in Moorhead, population jumped to 2,000 in a single year, reached 3,000 in the next, and generated a boom mentality that expected a small city of 25,000 within a decade. This expectation affected many business decisions of the time, including those of the newspaper. It expanded from a weekly to become the *Moorhead Daily News*, which now published the full afternoon dispatches of the associated press, "the latest telegraphic news of the day." The newly formed publishing company justified the expense by offering an "up-to-date newspaper" to "citizens who would not be satisfied with news twelve hours old." These improvements apparently worked. The new editor reported in April 1885 that circulation had increased to a robust 744 from an anemic 193 only two years before. He credited support from "businessmen who did not want to see it die."[36]

Caught up in the speculative fever of the boom mentality and expecting the city to become a rail center, the energetic Henry Bruns moved quickly to take advantage. He had achieved considerable wealth and had established the Merchants Bank at what seemed an opportune time. He dissolved his mercantile partnership with Finkle, became a dealer in farm and town properties in Moorhead, Williston, and Billings, and invested heavily in a hotel and foundry. Having become wealthy from railroad expansion and settlement in the 1870s, Bruns now speculated on the expectation that the continued growth of Moorhead and the region ensured him an even larger fortune.[37]

To promote growth of the town and region, Bruns worked closely with Comstock in persuading Hill to build through their city. Bruns deeded land to Hill's road and helped create the Manvel and Hill additions, hoping that the Manitoba would make the city its division point and establish machine shops, roundhouse, and headquarters there. Bruns and others invested with Comstock and Hill in the Minnesota and Dakota Northern Railroad Company, which in 1883 built a Manitoba branch line northward to Halstad, and in the Northwestern Land Company from 1883 to 1886. Although these activities reveal how Hill worked fruitfully with residents to achieve his larger aims, the locals often did not attain all their expectations. The Manitoba encouraged Bruns by promising him coal cars and a warehouse to store coal for the foundry he would later build, but the company disappointed him by making Barnesville its division point. Bruns later asserted that his economic failure dated from this decision. Regarding Manitoba railroad facilities as essential to Moorhead growth, he and Comstock met with Hill in 1884 and 1888 and requested him to reconsider. Neither meeting achieved the results residents desired.[38]

Bruns's bank provided him with ready credit in a frontier economy often short of capital. He borrowed $175,000 to finance and organize three other businesses that he overbuilt for the small city Moorhead became. In November 1880, Bruns proposed a first-class hotel that the Manitoba could use as a station if it made Moorhead an eating stop. Comstock assured Hill that Bruns would "put up and maintain a house that will be a credit to your road as well as a vast improvement to our town." Hill consented. The luxurious Grand Pacific opened on November 24, 1881. Built in the Queen Anne style and furnished at the cost of $165,000, the three-story, brick-veneered structure had all the modern conveniences—steam heat, gas light in every room, twenty rooms with baths, passenger elevator, and electric bells. The almost block-long structure featured 140 rooms with capacity for 200 guests and a dining room seating 140. Located just west of the Manitoba freight depot, the hotel contained the railroad offices, two large waiting rooms, and the ticket office. Moorhead's pride, the Grand Pacific hosted many large social events during the next decade. Three hundred attended the charity dinner dance sponsored by the Ladies General Benevolent Society in 1881. An eight-course dinner for 175 guests honored legislator Solomon G. Comstock in 1887 after he secured the Normal School for Moorhead.[39]

Bruns invested in two other boom-generated ventures: the Red River Manufacturing Company and the Moorhead Foundry, Car and Agricultural

Henry A. Bruns built the luxurious Grand Pacific Hotel in Moorhead during a boom in the early 1880s. Courtesy Clay County Historical Society.

Works. Boosters thought access to the hardwood forests of northern Minnesota and low transportation costs for coal and iron delivered by competing railroads assured industrial growth. Bruns, Kurtz, Comstock, White, and other leading businessmen subscribed forty thousand dollars and founded the manufacturing company in February 1882. The firm proposed establishing the largest lumberyard in the region; employing thirty men in making doors, sashes, and blinds; and fitting and framing a large-sized house, ready to be raised and put together in two or three days.[40] The enterprise collapsed with the boom and did not reach the stage of production.

Bruns had begun negotiations with eastern capitalists for an iron foundry in January 1881. Walter M. Lenhart of Elkhart, Indiana, arrived in April of the following year. He joined Bruns and others in forming a joint-stock company capitalized at $250,000. Operations started the next year in an impressive building located several blocks east of the settled area of the city. The plant consisted of two great cupolas, each capable of melting forty thousand pounds of iron in a single heat; a molding room; a blacksmith department with six forges; and sections for making patterns, painting, and working machine steel, iron, and wood. The foundry made building columns, store-fronts, ornamental iron fence, steamboat machinery, stove castings, sleigh runners, and other items. Anticipated contracts for constructing railroad cars and the Moorhead Chief Thresher were not realized. Bruns served as president and eventually general manager of the firm when Lenhart left. He acquired extensive landholdings in this area and built cottages east of the plant for workers. He clearly anticipated rapid urban growth spurred by industrial development. Unfortunately for him, the foundry employed only one-fourth of its projected four hundred workers. Amid rumors of failure and tax abatement, Bruns unloaded his bad investment to a St. Cloud wagon maker. He lost heavily, receiving only $10,000 for his $60,000 in stock.[41]

During its first year, Anderson and Sons reported doing better business than in St. Cloud. The company made bobsleds, land rollers, harrows, and farm wagons. It did not make the threshers, tractors, and other farm machinery anticipated by boosters. Renamed Anderson Brothers in 1892, it ceased wagon making because large eastern firms such as Studebaker Brothers of South Bend, Indiana, cut prices to destroy local competitors.[42]

According to conventional booster wisdom, towns must attract railroads to become great cities. Many boomers therefore embraced railroad promotion. Newspapers regularly reported rumors of projected lines that included the Minnesota and Dakota Northern (1879), Red River Northern (1880), Moorhead, McCauleyville and Breckenridge (1881), Moorhead and Chicago, which became the Moorhead and Southeastern (1884), Fargo and Southern (1884), and the Moorhead, Leech Lake, Duluth and Northern (1887). Boomers hoped to profit from drawing wheat to the city, expanding retail trade, and speculating in real estate. They also desired to connect with and be conquered by a larger road, reaping similar rewards as Comstock did from the Manitoba. Suitors included the Chicago and North Western; the Chicago, Milwaukee and St. Paul; the Rock Island; or the Minneapolis and Pacific. James J. Hill monitored these projects carefully, relying on local intelligence supplied by Solomon Comstock. He excluded rival systems from the valley, which he preserved as the SPM&M hinterland. He directed local capital away from redundant railroad lines and toward projects that served Manitoba interests.[43]

Schemes often pitted Fargo against Moorhead. Viewing the SPM&M as a boon to its adversary, Fargo boosters sought an alternative. Comstock regularly reported their efforts to Hill. It appeared that the Hastings and Dakota division of the Chicago, Milwaukee and St. Paul would build down the Red River Valley to the city and beyond. Then stories circulated that it projected a line north from Breckenridge into Dakota Territory. A letter from a Chicago and North Western manager apparently confirmed these tales. Several months later, a newspaper listed stock subscribers for a connect-

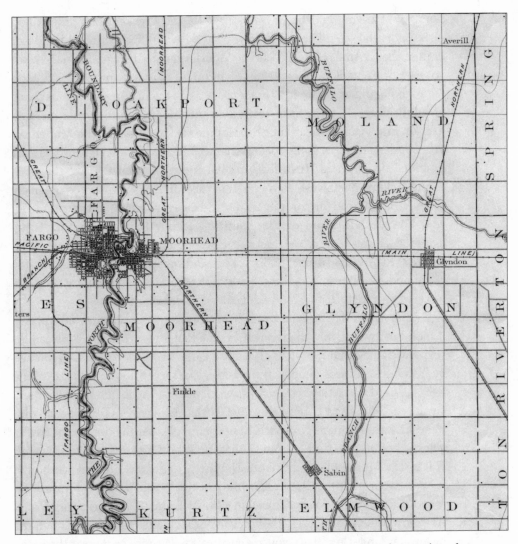

Moorhead boosters supported Clay County railroad expansion to increase their city's trade. Courtesy Institute for Regional Studies, North Dakota State University, Fargo (153).

ing link with the Milwaukee Road south of Wahpeton. Although it "might be nothing but wind," Comstock wrote, residents believed grading would soon begin. Comstock later informed Hill that twenty-five thousand ties had been purchased and shipped. Rumors became reality when the Fargo and Southern reached Ortonville, Minnesota, in 1884. Two years later, the Milwaukee Road acquired it.[44]

Then Comstock revealed Henry Finkle's scheme for a link connecting Fisher's Landing with the Northern Pacific near Moorhead. Hill checkmated this threat by invoking the 1882 branch line agreement. Comstock also reported that the Moorhead, McCauleyville and Breckenridge project had no support, but could be acquired readily if it would be useful. Hill did not act and the scheme reemerged as the Moorhead and Chicago. The backing of large landowners E. C. Sprague (sixteen thousand acres) and John Erickson (four thousand acres) made this a more serious challenge in Comstock's view. Although he offered to form a rival company, Hill ignored his suggestion and waited on further developments. In October, the Moorhead and Southeastern (as it had been renamed) began buying right-of-way for a new "Chicago" road. The *Moorhead Weekly News* reported that the Rock Island building northwest from Worthington, Minnesota, appeared the likely connecting link. After complications and "wet" country halted construction, however, Hill pounced. The Manitoba acquired the firm's right-of-way agreements and charter to construct a branch in 1887. Hill built it close to the Red River. The "driest, most direct and most improved country" lay there and a competing railroad could not come between his line and the waterway. Comstock and White developed the town sites.[45]

Comstock established two other companies to work with the Manitoba as it built northward from the twin cities. The Red River Northern Railroad incorporated in March 1880 for connecting Fargo and Grand Forks. Organized by "our best business people" from both cities, according to Comstock, the firm received no criticism. Some assumed it to be independent, but others surmised Hill's hand behind the road. After arrangements had been completed, Comstock made public the Manitoba's role. Another joint venture developed at the same time. Bruns, Comstock, White, and others invested with Hill in the Minnesota and Dakota Northern Railroad Company. Although incorporated in 1879, the branch line did not reach Halstad, Minnesota, until 1883 on right-of-way secured in 1881 by Bruns, Comstock, and White. As Comstock wrote Hill, "I know you will be delighted" as it runs through the best valley land. He added, "you are getting it in the nick of time as the Fargo Southern has considered . . . building north on the east side." Once more, the firm had been created according to Hill's wishes. After completion, the Manitoba purchased it for $510,000, the costs of construction.[46]

Hill's expansion throughout the valley aimed at capturing the steamboat-based wheat trade from the Northern Pacific elevators at Fargo. Comstock and Bruns, of course, applauded any redirection of traffic through Moorhead. Comstock negotiated with Bonanza farmers Oliver Dalrymple and J. L. Grandin, who had "an inside deal with the NP folks" and looked "on boats as a valuable auxiliary." Comstock thought the conflict could be resolved amicably, however, by running the Manitoba line to a point opposite Grandin's home farm. He had been right about "the deal." The Grandin Line received a 20 percent rebate during 1881 on 250,000 bushels shipped to Fargo.

Nevertheless, Northern Pacific managers rejected Grandin and Dalrymple's request to build a line in eastern North Dakota because the Manitoba already had.[47]

The relationship of the SPM&M and local capitalists gives insight into the impact of corporate power on a single community. The corporation stimulated the Moorhead boom and influenced many investment decisions. It produced fortunes for some and bankrupted others. Clearly, corporate manager Hill relied on Comstock, Bruns, and others to advance SPM&M interests. Similarly, residents used the railroad to boost their city and region while enhancing their personal fortunes. Now served by two railroads, capitalists expected Moorhead to become the wholesale distributing point for the thousands of settlers who flocked to the Red River Valley. Fixated by this expectation, they expended three hundred thousand dollars on new brick buildings and blocks in 1880, while real-estate values increased from 60 to 100 percent. At the end of the next year, lot prices had advanced another 60 percent, materials for the eagerly anticipated SPM&M Round House and Machine Shops arrived daily, and boosters projected the building of a hundred houses for laborers. The Webster & Richardson, Sharp & Lamb, and Holes & Davy additions to Moorhead had been platted and listed for sale. Even SPM&M assistant manager H. C. Ives caught the fever, predicting, "Moorhead will be a city of 50,000 in ten years." Dozens of new firms had opened, the imposing Syndicate Block and two others had been

FRONT ST. MOORHEAD 1884
FROM ELEVATOR   PLATEN PHOTO.,

A photograph of Front Street (present-day Center Avenue) from 1884 shows how entrepreneurs transformed Moorhead's business district from wood to brick. Courtesy Clay County Historical Society.

completed, and three more had begun. The city had transformed itself from wood to brick as it expanded.[48]

The Great Dakota Boom, which had fueled urban growth, peaked in 1883. Economic and psychological factors combined to end expansion. A downturn in the national economy slowly worsened during 1883. Prices, wages, and profits declined more sharply than production and business volume. Reduced railroad construction spread depression to related industries. Banks became reluctant to make loans. Red River Valley speculative fever cooled with falling wheat prices and slackening population increase. Land purchases and homestead entries declined. Real-estate values fell. The twin cities and other towns lost one-quarter or more of their inhabitants. As *Weekly News* editor George Lamphere later recalled, the Moorhead boom had collapsed by April 1883. Population shrank as hundreds abandoned their lands and lots that would not sell at any price. Instead of the projected twenty-five to fifty thousand, inhabitants numbered only a little more than two thousand in 1890. Those who had invested in the prospect of inflated expectations had difficulty surviving the reality of fewer residents. As a consequence, Bruns and others went bankrupt when their city failed to grow into the distribution center of the valley.[49]

BANKRUPTS AND THOSE WHO SUCCEEDED

Founding towns and establishing businesses on a capital-starved frontier required an enterprising spirit, access to credit, and willingness to take risks. Several founders—James Douglas, John Erickson, S. B. Elder, and Henry Bruns—went bankrupt. Why did they fail while others succeeded? The R. G. Dun and Company records offer clues. Their agents investigated the creditworthiness of local businessmen for potential lenders.

Scottish and Canadian immigrant James Douglas represents one type of failure. He arrived in 1871, becoming first postmaster as well as a hardware, lumber, and farm implement dealer. Initially, R. G. Dun reported him a well-liked "man of good character" and a "fine businessman" with sound habits, ability, and local credit. More negative listings followed: He is "rather slack in management," "is continuously cramped for dollars," and "is very slow to pay." After he headed the short-lived Merchants International Steamboat Company, the report said, he "tries to do too much . . . for capacity." An agent soon declared, "He is in the Sheriff's hands. Hardly enough will be realized to cover debts." The "unfortunate but . . . honest" Douglas recovered. He had placed property in his wife's name and Wilhelmina purchased his stock from the assigner. According to later accounts, "[she] appears to be doing a large and prosperous business, which is managed by her husband."

Trusting "too freely" and ignoring details, James again fell into bankruptcy. Although agents thought all claims safe, they recommend no new credit for Mrs. Douglas. James's financial struggles continued into the next decade. Hail destroyed his wheat; lightning ignited his Kragnes Elevator; and the Post Office dismissed him for a "shortfall." He and Wilhelmina sold their farmland and returned to Canada in 1889.[50]

Swedish immigrant John Erickson—who had arrived "with only the clothes on his back"—exemplified a different type of failure. Successive R. G. Dun reports characterized him vividly as "uneducated but shrewd," "energetic but ignorant & bullheaded," and "hard pushed for ready money." Although agents conceded he had good character, habits, and ability, they thought him "too much inclined to expand . . . and sooner or later [will] come to grief." Success never made him "a good pay" because he always used "money in speculation 1st." Agents recommended advancing him the goods he wanted, but said money claims should be pressed vigorously. Their assessments proved prophetic. The depression of 1893 bankrupted the chronically overextended Erickson. Old residents rejoiced in 1900, however, when he reclaimed the Columbia Hotel, saving something from the many properties that he had lost. The *Moorhead Weekly News* expressed hope that he might prosper once again.[51]

Hardware dealer S. B. Elder represented a third type. Whereas others had failed because of poor management or overexpansion, Elder's long illness that had reduced his trade bankrupted him in 1884. The community believed him to be a solvent man who would be able to arrange his affairs if given time. After his bankruptcy became public, he still retained the sympathy of a large number of friends.[52]

Henry Bruns resembled Erickson in risking and losing everything, but he lived more luxuriously while giving more to advance the city. In December 1877, he married Matilda Sharpe, a Winnipeg native, whose father emigrated from England in the 1840s at the request of the Hudson's Bay Company. Although considered a "fine looking woman" by one onlooker, photographer F. Jay Haynes described her as "a very plain acting as well as looking lady." Her wealthy husband nonetheless "thinks all the world of her . . . [and] provides the best the world affords." The couple made the Grand Pacific Hotel their residence, enjoying the most opulent accommodations on the frontier. He established an elegant, carpeted private office there as well. They lived and entertained lavishly. She wore diamond earrings that, according to one observer, "knocked your eyes out." He purchased a fine driving team and had a five hundred-dollar portrait painted. They celebrated their tenth wedding anniversary by serving 150 invited guests a sit-down dinner at heavily laden tables of oysters, ham, turkey, and ice cream. They celebrated the birth of a son and the first anniversary of the hotel's opening with another party at which guests consumed a hundred bottles of champagne. A Fargo newspaper reported: "Never before has Mr. Bruns received such an ovation and such . . . evidence of personal popularity."[53]

Unfortunately for the couple's grandiose lifestyle and his expansive business vision, the Grand Pacific lost money after the Dakota Boom crested. The economic slowdown turned into a recession, immigration slowed to Dakota Territory, and heavy traffic flows north to Manitoba declined. Optimistically estimated at 4,200 in 1883, Moorhead's population numbered 2,088 by 1890. If it had grown to the 25,000 inhabitants anticipated by Bruns, then income from his several properties might have covered his business losses and personal expenses. Insufficient growth, however, translated into insufficient cash to sustain his indebtedness. According to an April 1888 newspaper report, the hotel had enjoyed a good winter trade with full occupancy on most weekends. Nevertheless, Bruns reported losses of five thousand dollars in operating the Grand Pacific in the period from December 1, 1888, to May 1, 1889. By strict economy and his and his wife's superintending the hotel, they reduced their losses to two thousand dollars during the following winter.[54]

Although buoyed by improved prospects at the end of the decade, the fragile condition of the Merchants Bank in July 1888 compelled Bruns to borrow thirteen thousand dollars from the SPM&M railroad and slightly more than fifty-seven thousand dollars from James J. Hill. The terms stipulated 7 percent interest payable in two years with the Grand Pacific and additional Moorhead real estate as collateral. It is not known why Hill made this loan, but it is probable that he appreciated Bruns's efforts on behalf of the Manitoba and decided that the survival of Bruns's bank served the interests of the railroad. Hill had made many similar investments in agriculture and other businesses whose economic success aided the Manitoba. Moreover, Bruns and Hill shared a common economic vision. Both entrepreneurs had invested in the future growth of the Red River Valley. That the railroad had named Bruns proprietor for the town site of Williston, Dakota Territory, offered additional security for repayment of the loan.[55]

When the notes came due in 1890, however, Bruns could not pay. A financial memorandum prepared for Hill reported Bruns's difficulties. He had no credit, and paid cash on delivery for everything he needed to run the hotel and restaurant, which had deteriorated. Matilda Bruns, who now managed the hotel, loudly abused her husband in the public halls, making it disagreeable for the patrons.[56]

Compounding Bruns's financial woes, the Merchants Bank closed in February 1892. As Bruns later recalled, overextension in the valley made it difficult to call in loans. The cyclical downturn that resulted in the depression of

1893 caught Bruns and his bank. Monetary contraction worsened this crisis and delayed economic recovery. Other factors contributed: exports of crops and merchandise declined; foreigners, worried that the "free silver" campaign threatened sound currency, withdrew capital from the United States; and a chronically weak banking structure aggravated the situation.[57]

The *Moorhead Weekly News* reported that many blamed Bruns for the bank failure. Their suspicions seemed to be confirmed when the former cashier accused him of embezzling more than $80,000. Although the courts dismissed the embezzlement charges, Bruns's inability to raise additional capital from the First National Bank of St. Paul on condition that he dissolve his partnership with Kurtz further damaged his credibility. At an initial meeting of the creditors, the Merchants Bank reported liabilities of slightly more than $208,000 and assets of just over $310,000. Unfortunately, Bruns's individual notes formed a large portion of the nominal assets. He reported assets of slightly more than $264,000 and liabilities of slightly less than $122,000. His assets included the flour mill ($25,000), bills receivable ($27,000) and the Grand Pacific Hotel ($134,905). The remainder included more than two thousand undeveloped lots, mostly located north and east of the failed foundry. Creditors waited impatiently as weeks, months, and years passed while the courts untangled Bruns's complicated financial affairs. Not until 1896 did creditors receive a 10 percent dividend on the $17,000 paid by the Moorhead National Bank for the Merchants Bank block.[58]

Shortly after his bank's failure, Bruns lost a decision by the Clay County District Court, allowing Hill's foreclosure of the Grand Pacific Hotel. By agreement, Bruns and his wife occupied the building and operated the hotel until July 1893, when they were ordered to vacate. A letter from Bruns to Hill's agent described the local mood: "There is a good deal of satisfaction all around the city . . . they are all interested in the Bank but not in my private matters—and most of them would sooner see me kicked out of town hoping thereby to get Mr. Hill to . . . boom Moorhead to get his money out again."[59]

Hill now had the Grand Pacific but he did not boom Moorhead. His agents examined the hotel, reporting that the damaged roof, plumbing, and heating plant all required repair and the rooms needed repainting. Hill then offered it for sale or rent with incentives to fix the building. In 1893, John A. Baker leased it for two years, but he also failed to meet his expenses. The hotel closed after the city shut off the water in September 1895 for an unpaid bill.[60]

Comstock, the municipal government, and others did what they could to save the building. Acknowledging that the Grand Pacific had been a bad deal for Hill, Comstock told him that public opinion opposed destruction. In April 1896, the city council "resolved that destruction would be a public calamity, that James J. Hill shall refrain for two years and that assessment shall be fixed at $3,000." The council hoped its action would attract potential purchasers. Meanwhile, Comstock offered Hill information about the creditworthiness of prospective buyers. Unfortunately for the city, Hill, anxious to cut his losses, did not accept an offer of fifteen thousand dollars without substantial cash payment or security.[61]

Without an acceptable offer and thinking it useless to delay any longer, Hill reluctantly ordered the auction of hotel furniture and destruction of the building for salvage. Local opinion did not approve. "Mr. Hill is sharply criticized by all," the *Moorhead Weekly News* reported, adding that Hill displayed "the spirit of an autocrat" and "petulant spite toward the city for failing to take it off his hands." The newspaper maintained that losses on the building and loans to Bruns did not justify destruction. Moreover, if Hill had fulfilled his promises of railroad shops and other Moorhead improvements, the Grand Pacific might have been a paying investment instead of a heavy financial loss to Bruns.[62]

Meanwhile, Henry A. Bruns—pariah, poor man, and apparent failure—had left Moorhead in 1893. From a fortune earlier estimated at four hundred thousand dollars, only an estate of approximately seven hundred dollars remained. Until rumors started circulating about his impending financial collapse, Bruns had enjoyed a sterling reputation as a successful and public-spirited entrepreneur. Residents knew he had lost heavily from the collapsed boom, but they admired his uncomplaining attitude and confidence in the city's future. Admiration quickly faded with the Merchants Bank failure, for which locals blamed him. The *Moorhead Weekly News* charged that his schemes had been ill conceived. He had attempted to manufacture without raw materials and skilled labor. He had built a hotel too large and expensive for the town's size. He had hoped these enterprises would call into existence a large city that would reward his investment.[63] When Moorhead failed to grow, his misplaced hopes became evident, dooming him to bankruptcy and personal disgrace.

According to the *Minneapolis Journal,* Bruns took his loss philosophically, saying, "Some men must fail, since all cannot succeed financially." He explained his failure as a consequence of investing heavily on the expectation that his city would become a great rail center and division point with the arrival of the SPM&M. Nothing is certain, however. Neither he nor Hill could foretell the future. Bruns did not foresee that Fargo would surpass Moorhead or that other market towns would develop in the Red River Valley. The boom-and-bust cycles of the American economy and exhausted credit at a crucial time also victimized him. He lost heavily when the Moorhead Boom collapsed. His overexpansion made it difficult for him to repay loans. His bank's failure left him liable for $150,000. Although he still received ten thousand dollars in rent annually, he lost control of all his properties. The final accounting left him practically penniless. Finally, decisions of railroad executives such as Hill and the national market their corporations had created hurt Bruns. The railroads had given Bruns opportunities that he had capitalized upon. Yet high transportation costs on raw material made it difficult for Moorhead Foundry products to compete with nationally marketed finished goods delivered from the East. Nor did the anticipated SPM&M contracts for ironwork materialize. Similarly, the large Minneapolis mills that appeared in the 1880s offered increasingly stiff competition for Belle of Moorhead flour.[64]

Despite his bankruptcy, Bruns considered himself a success because he had "done a service for his country in his work as a pioneer." George Lamphere, a booster and the editor of the *Moorhead Weekly News,* had argued similarly to his probably skeptical readers at the time Bruns left town in disgrace. Although Bruns at the end had engaged in dubious practices and failed financially, Lamphere said, residents ought to be charitable because without him there would not be a Moorhead.[65]

Both Lamphere and Bruns were correct. Bruns's initial success as a frontier merchant had enabled him to become an entrepreneur who boosted Moorhead's early growth. But, as western historians have pointed out, the high risks of town building and mercantile enterprise often frustrated dreams of opportunity and success. Although, like many promoters, Bruns failed, his short-lived enterprises and theirs contributed to the settlement of Moorhead, the Red River Valley, and other areas of the American West.[66]

In contrast to Bruns and those who failed, what traits enabled others to succeed in the volatile Moorhead economy? The cases of Benjamin Mackall, John Kurtz, James H. Sharp, F. Jay Haynes, and Solomon G. Comstock offer some clues. All had good moral habits, ability, and commitments to community building. The Kurtz and Mackall drugstore did a good business and Kurtz had a fine medical practice. Sharp—"one of the best businessmen in the county"—had an excellent trade in his clothing store. The artistically gifted Haynes, a photographer, arrived in September 1876 and quickly established himself. Several months later, he wrote to his wife: "Business still keeps good and prospects for making a thousand dollars this summer are good." He received customers from "all along the line," his stereoscopic views of the twin cities and valley sold well, and, like his fellow businessmen, he advertised heavily. After he had located a place for a house, Haynes erected a fence and planted one hundred trees. All these men paid their debts promptly. Although many invested in other properties, they exercised wisdom and caution. Avoiding the speculative mania that ruined others seems to have been crucial to their success.[67]

The thrifty and hardworking Comstock emphasized similar lessons in writing to Ada—his favorite daughter—late in his long life: "Don't buy stocks and do not speculate. Buy good farm mortgages or bonds." Comstock then added as a postscript: "Better not lend to friends or relations and to no one without abundant security."[68] Comstock had not always followed his own advice, but his caution likely came from observing the fate of bankrupt contemporaries. In addition, his town-site speculations with Hill minimized risk and proved to be sound investments that produced good returns over his lifetime. In contrast, Bruns made his fortune from his Northern Pacific supply contract in only four years. He never found another investment to match that early success. Instead, he risked his wealth in speculative local enterprises that failed when the city did not attain the population he projected. Although Comstock invested some of his riches in projects that boosted the city, he neither risked nor lost as much as Bruns.

The contrast in local reactions to the bankrupt Bruns, the corporate leader Hill, and the successful Comstock reveals important tensions in the relations of small cities to newly emerging corporate America. Bruns and Comstock came to the Red River Valley prospecting for opportunities, which they both found and capitalized upon by investing in the growth of city and region. Unlike Bruns, Comstock remained successful and retained the respect of his fellow citizens. Maine-born in 1842 and a University of Michigan–educated lawyer, he arrived in Moorhead as a Northern Pacific laborer in December 1871. Stranded for the winter, he hung out his shingle. His appointment as the first Clay County attorney in April 1872 gave Comstock his first financial security since leaving Maine in 1868. According to one observer, the only capital Comstock brought to Moorhead was "a few law books, a sound mind, genial disposition, a great capacity for work and an incorruptible character." Shortly after his death in 1933, his wife—Sarah Ball Comstock—wrote: "He was as near perfect as a man could be made both mentally and physically. He could think in a flash, and his body, even in old age, remained as faultless as a child's." Thrift and hard work won him success. He opposed smoking and drinking as too expensive and celebrated his eighty-ninth birthday by working quietly in his office. His modesty is evident in an 1889 letter from Clara Gilman thanking "Cousin Sol": "It don't make a good man vain, to be thanked for his kind acts and praised for his wisdom and knowledge."[69]

In the process of assigning blame after the Moorhead Boom collapsed, the local entrepreneur Comstock fared better than the bankrupt Bruns or the corporate magnate Hill. At the boom's height the *Moorhead Weekly News* asked, "What has Comstock done for Moorhead?" And answered, "What hasn't he done?" He had used his influence to bring the Manitoba Railroad and the Pillsbury and Hulburt Elevator. He had started other railroad companies. He had invested in the Moorhead Foundry, Red River Manufacturing Company, Jay Cooke House, *Moorhead Weekly News,* and other enterprises. Residents did not blame the wealthy Comstock because he exemplified the values of the respectable middle class to which they also aspired. His reputation and fortune therefore survived the collapse.[70]

Hill did not fare as well. He represented the threatening new powers of corporate America and had not always fulfilled his promises to those Moorhead residents who had trusted in him. Populist and editor George Lamphere recognized Hill as a great railroad man who had built the Northwest. Although he praised the SPM&M when it reduced rates, he often complained about Hill and his corporation. Hill pettily withheld advertising and passes from editors who had criticized his railroad. Hill arrogantly told farmers how to farm, but resented their telling him how to run his company. The Manitoba's train schedule hurt Fargo and Moorhead hotels because trains arrived or departed too early or too late. The Manitoba's high rates and the Great Northern consolidation threatened all farmers and businessmen along the line. Lamphere's criticisms reflected middle-class unease with the corporate power Hill represented. On the other hand, farm daughter Christine Hagen Stafne remembered Jim Hill as "a friend who had taken part in our county fairs and had stopped at our homes as he traveled through the little towns along his railroad. He was one of the first to supply the ranches of ND with blooded stock." Thus Hill could be recalled fondly as a member of the middle class as well. The ambiguity of Hill's career and reactions to it symbolized the confused reactions of Americans to the transformation of the United States from a country of small towns and farms to an urban-industrial world power.[71]

Writing in 1889, editor George Lamphere again urged entrepreneurs to create more businesses and manufactories because great cities could

James J. Hill promoted settlement of the Red River Valley with his many investments and by expanding the SPM&M railroad. From *History of the Red River Valley, Past and Present* (Grand Forks: Herald Printing Office, 1909).

not depend on agriculture alone. They should organize to extend their trade by recovering commerce they had lost and by supplying the bountiful country-side.[72] Lamphere's proposals were not new. The city and its boosters had fol-lowed similar strategies without success from the start. The early steamboat trade stimulated growth but proved a fragile basis for long-term Canadian commerce. Similarly, the energetic Comstock, Bruns, and others attracted Hill and the SPM&M railroad. As a consequence, the city enjoyed a brief boom during which it attempted to build a manufacturing base and estab-lish itself as a wholesale trade center. Competition from corporations, linked by rail to national markets, eventually destroyed the city's industries—flour mills, breweries, brick manufacturers, and iron foundry. The boom collapsed, bankrupting foremost entrepreneur Bruns, who had gambled his fortune on making Moorhead the key city of the valley.

Henry Bruns's dealings with James J. Hill personified how an enterpris-ing individual might be undone in his commercial relations with corporate capitalism. They met during the steamboat era. As the SPM&M penetrated the Red River Valley, they worked together to profit from opening the new region. Both rose to wealth and influence within their respective spheres. Yet Hill died a rich and powerful man, while Bruns ended his life as "an outcast" and a widowed cheese clerk, living alone in a Minneapolis rooming house. If "ill fortune had not soured" Bruns,[73] perhaps he perceived that his own errors had as much to do with his business failure as Hill's broken promises. Certainly the case of Solomon Comstock indicated how one might win and hold a fortune while working with a railroad magnate.

The story of Seymour, Sabin & Co.—manufacturers of the Minnesota Chief thresher—typified Moorhead's inability to compete. Lured by the diplomacy of Comstock and the promise of prime riverfront property, the firm in early 1880 proposed establishing its northwestern headquarters and warehouse in the city. Local joy at this victory soon dissipated. The firm located its offices in Fargo and made J. A. Johnson the sales agent for both cities. Two decades later, Fargo numbered 9,589 people, boasted twenty-four agricultural implement dealers, possessed several wholesale houses at-tracted by more favorable railroad rates, and had become the gateway city for North Dakota. Moorhead had 3,730 people, no implement dealers, and only two wholesalers, both distributing liquor. This disparity encapsulates the story of Moorhead's failed growth. Despite the dreams and efforts of boosters and businessmen like Comstock, Bruns, Lamphere, and others, it did not become the "Key City" for the region.[74]

Boomtown on the Prairie

Wheat is king, and Fargo is its favorite resort.
— *Fargo Times,* September 30, 1880

The Red River Valley is as rich as the Nile and as healthy as the Garden of Eden.
— *Fargo Times,* January 8, 1880

Capitalists, laborers, and sightseers concur that Fargo is destined to be great.
— *Fargo Times,* August 19, 1880

FROM THE BEGINNING, FARGO PROMOTERS DREAMED OF MAKING their city the gateway to the northern plains and the Northwest. They were not alone in imagining such a future. Many places adopted the metaphor as the transcontinentals stimulated aspirations for capturing regional trade by connecting western producers and products with eastern industries. Like several other localities, Fargo assumed a central place in an urban hierarchy bound by rails that Chicago, "the gateway to the Great West," initially dominated. As wheat cultivation spread northward and westward onto the Minnesota and Dakota prairies, Minneapolis transformed itself into a flour-milling center and captured part of Chicago's hinterland. Minneapolis and St. Paul—the site of mills, grain markets, and railroad corporations—long treated North Dakota as their colony. Although rural radicals condemned Fargo as a corporate agent, the city nevertheless claimed to be the state's commercial capital and gateway. By the early twentieth century, it ranked third in farm machinery sales after Kansas City and Minneapolis. It boasted of wholesale houses for groceries, hardware, and other goods. In addition to being integrated into the national market, Fargo experienced other aspects of incorporation. Economic development of the city and region stimulated public acceptance of modern technology, scientific knowledge, and organizational forms.[1]

The patronage of three railroads enabled Fargo to best Moorhead in the gateway competition. The Northern Pacific benefited the city materially by making it a division point and publicizing the Bonanza farms. The better-drained lands west of the Red River went into wheat production more quickly than those on the eastern side. As a consequence, thousands of farmers pushed into Dakota, providing the customers that boosted urban commerce. The coming of the SPM&M in the early 1880s further fueled the Dakota Boom. Boomers created the Fargo and Southern shortly thereafter, giving the city direct access to Chicago via the Milwaukee Road. Traffic competition eventually provided the favorable rates that made Fargo a mercantile hub.

Alsop and Grandin steamboats carried wheat from the northern Red River Valley to the Northern Pacific Railroad at Fargo during the late 1870s and early 1880s. Courtesy Institute for Regional Studies, North Dakota State University, Fargo (51.51.1).

Extending rails throughout the valley destroyed the water-based commerce that had given Moorhead an early advantage. By mid-1875, Fisher's Landing near Crookston, Minnesota, had become the primary rail and boat connection. The Red River Transportation Company avoided the Goose Rapids bottleneck during the next season by shifting more trade to Fisher's Landing and Grand Forks, where it located a boatyard. These now became the principal river ports. Having long known that technologically superior railroads would replace steamboats, James J. Hill personally ended their heyday when he and his associates acquired the bankrupt St. Paul and Pacific, renamed it the SPM&M, and completed its line to Canada on December 3, 1878. For the next several years, however, the Northern Pacific utilized steamers and barges for hauling wheat to its elevator at Fargo. The volume of this trade profited the Dakota city more than its Minnesota rival.[2]

THE DAKOTA BOOM AND FARGO BOOMERS

Boosterism drove Fargo's development, as it did Moorhead and other western cities. The transcontinentals actively boosted the Great Plains because circumstances compelled transforming federal land grants into operating capital. Settlement afforded them immediate income from land sales and long-term revenues from traffic. Urban businessmen assisted corporate promotions because their own prosperity depended on community and regional growth. They formed business associations toward that end, hoping to avert corporate domination while harnessing corporate resources for their own designs. They expanded trade by fostering economic self-sufficiency. They perceived their commercial role as central to settlement. After all, they supplied farmers, marketed their crops, granted them credit, and provided them with transportation services.[3]

Promotional literature of the Dakota Boom emphasized how the city's growth depended on an expanding agricultural hinterland. The *Fargo Argus* and *Fargo Times,* according to historian Gary Anderson, created an image of bountiful nature as the foundation for metropolitan and rural opportunity. Railroad managers, real-estate agents, and farm machinery dealers advertised the region as the "Garden of Eden" and "Eden of the World." Editors echoed the garden theme, coupled it to urban commerce, and portrayed cultivators effortlessly reaping nature's rewards: "The farmer of Dakota mounts his sulky plow and turns over furrow after furrow a mile long without a break or without having his temper ruffled in the least by ugly boulders and hard heads of less favored communities. Is it any wonder that this is unanimously voted the farmer's paradise?" Editors dismissed the harsh climate as an exaggeration or exalted it as conducive to health and character. They promised that the "Dakota garden" would transform Fargo into "the Queen city of the Far West" and provide a better life for all who came. Hardworking merchants, artisans, and professionals would succeed as surely as yeomen. This echoed publicity elsewhere. American newspapers commonly used the Eden metaphor and frequently spearheaded promotion because they appeared regularly and circulated widely.[4]

To many boomers, the plentiful harvests, ample profits, and efficient management of the Bonanza farms realized the rhetorical Eden of publicists. Northern Pacific excursion trains brought notable visitors, including President and Mrs. Rutherford B. Hayes and a party of seventy-five that in 1878 toured the Cass-Cheney Farm managed by Oliver Dalrymple. Although some settlers and the *Atlantic Monthly* expressed fear that the large operations would crush small farmers, this did not happen. The Bonanzas disintegrated before the end of the century for reasons correctly predicted by the *Fargo Times*. As land values rose, the owners attained greater profits from selling their property than they could from raising wheat.[5]

The boom brought change. In just two years after 1880, Cass County inhabitants more than doubled from 8,998 to 18,566 people. The territorial governor's office relocated to Bismarck in 1883 and separate statehood followed for North Dakota in 1889. By that time, the population had increased to 182,713 from only 2,405 in 1870. During the 1880s, valley farmland expanded from 1.6 to 5.4 million acres. The percentage of cropland grew from an average of 22 percent to 65 percent. As valley wheat production increased to 16 million bushels by 1885, freight tonnage shipped from Fargo rose more than tenfold.[6]

Fargo boomed with Dakota, more than doubling from 2,693 to 7,025 residents early in the decade. The Northern Pacific expended an estimated $287,000, doubling the size of its roundhouse, machine shops, platform, and yards to handle 1,800 cars by the end of 1883. The previous year, Fargo had forwarded and received more than three times the freight tonnage shipped by Moorhead. Numerous railroad workers drew their monthly pay in the city. Boosted by this infusion of corporate capital as well as the great volume of westbound trains carrying settlers and their goods, urban real estate increased dramatically in value. Realtors sold more than $2 million and contractors erected 489 buildings in 1882. New structures included several brick business blocks, warehouses, and elegant residences designed by architects. The speculative frenzy then subsided. The *Fargo Sunday Argus* published "Words of Caution . . . From a Prominent and Much Respected Man." With high western interest rates and values shrinking throughout the country, he warned against contracting new debts. As valley farmers had low crop yields, merchants should limit their stock of goods and reduce their obligations to suppliers. No one should borrow to purchase real estate in this climate of contraction.[7]

Booms do not occur without boomers. Ellen J. Cooley, wife of an Episcopalian clergyman who served in Fargo at this time, later wrote a novel about "the western fever" that she had observed firsthand. In recounting adventures of the Bullard family from Vermont, Cooley describes the "restless characters" that packed railroad cars and the rudely built Headquarters and Continental hotels in heeding Horace Greeley's advice, "Go West!" She mocks the so-called healthy climate by depicting the painful frostbite incurred during a brief winter's day stroll down Broadway. She scorns pretensions of the social elite who gave "select teas," hosted frequent receptions, flocked to theatrical productions that always delivered less than advertised, and conducted courtships as hectic as their commerce. She ridicules gilded signs that shone conspicuously to promote "rushing" business that hardly left practitioners time to eat or sleep as they recklessly pursued dreams of "fast becoming millionaires." Exhausted by the frenetic pace and disquieted by the "sham" and "gaud" of their western life, the family returned to their more respectable Vermont existence. Not all Fargo boomers fared as well as the fictional Bullards, who escaped with their fortune intact. Few achieved the riches they sought. Many found modest success over a lifetime in business, despite temporary reverses along the way. Others went bankrupt. The stories of two Fargo founders demonstrate how their lives imitated Cooley's art.[8]

Some called Jasper B. Chapin the "Father of Fargo" for his relentless promotion of the metropolis. The Northern Pacific's offer to lease the Headquarters Hotel lured Chapin from Moorhead in April 1873. As a married man of good character and business prospects—according to R. G. Dun and Company—and as manager of the largest hotel, Chapin became Fargo's leading citizen. The New York native had roamed the American West, pursuing his fortune in both the California

As businessman and mayor, Jasper B. Chapin "boomed" Fargo in its first decade. Courtesy Institute for Regional Studies, North Dakota State University, Fargo (MSS1970.51.6).

J. B. CHAPIN.

and the Montana gold rushes. He had operated a boarding house in Leavenworth, Kansas, a freighting business in Colorado and Utah, and the Chapin House in Virginia City, Montana. He then followed the Northern Pacific construction crews westward, successively opening a tent hotel and saloon business at Oak Lake, Oakport, and finally Moorhead once the Red River crossing had been determined. When the affable Chapin transferred his well-set table to the railroad hotel the *Red River Star* predicted that Moorhead's loss would be Fargo's gain.[9]

He erected the "Chapin Block" on the corner of Broadway and Northern Pacific Avenue. It housed what became the Fargo Opera House upstairs and the Luger Furniture Company downstairs. Boomers like Chapin built "blocks" as speculative enterprises in hopes of attracting inhabitants. Chapin surrendered the hotel lease in August 1874 and established a restaurant, bar, and billiard parlor as his principal business. At the same time, he broke three hundred acres near the city and planted wheat. R. G. Dun and Company reported in February 1877 that Chapin had "several nice pieces of land near Fargo in a good state of cultivation." He may have used the rising value of his land and crops to leverage loans for acquiring seventeen city blocks and transforming them into two additions on the undeveloped north side. The *Fargo Times* credited him with stimulating construction in unoccupied areas.[10]

The opportunistic and innovative Chapin recklessly boomed the city. He and George Marselius opened a central market on Broadway in 1879 that offered customers the convenience of buying all their food in one place—fresh and salt meats, fish, game, vegetables, butter, eggs, and cheese. Chapin soon sold, announcing in October that he would break ground for "the mammoth" Continental Hotel on the corner of Second Avenue and Broadway. The three-story frame structure had ninety sleeping rooms, a dining room, a billiard room, and four parlors. Chapin later had its exterior colorfully painted in bands of red, white, and blue. The hotel opened with a grand ball. In the next day's *Argus,* Chapin expressed hope "that none of us will cease in our efforts to make Fargo the metropolis of the Red River Valley, the . . . most productive wheat region in the world."[11]

Chapin practiced what he preached. The Continental lobby became the haunt for him and other land dealers. Continuing his promotion of the north side, Chapin built four stores for two merchants. An R. G. Dun report described Peter A. Goodman and W. A. Yerxa as energetic, well-liked, "first-class" businessmen who made a strong team and would do well. In addition to helping these younger men establish themselves, Chapin furnished funds to rebuild the burned-out flour mill and to build the Northern Pacific roundhouse in the city. Colonel C. A. Morton, a prominent land dealer, later recalled Chapin as a child in business. He might have realized two hundred

Editor Alanson W. Edwards used his newspaper to promote Fargo and the Red River Valley during the 1880s and 1890s. From *History of the Great Northwest and Its Men of Progress,* edited by C. W. G. Hyde and William Stoddard (Minneapolis: *Minneapolis Journal,* 1901).

thousand dollars from his holdings in 1881, but he never sold old properties without purchasing new. His enthusiastic private investing and lavish public giving proved excessive. His bankruptcy followed the Dakota Boom's collapse and the death in 1884 of his beloved, invalid wife. He lost all his property to creditors. His suicide in 1894 aroused an outpouring of sympathy and many acknowledgments of his contributions to the city at his well-attended funeral.[12]

In contrast to Chapin's financial failure, Major Alanson W. Edwards recovered from his reverses. The Ohio native arrived from Illinois in 1878 as founder and editor of the *Fargo Republican.* He soon sold that newspaper and launched the *Argus,* which became the first daily in the city and valley. Although a genial man, he had an argumentative and savagely satirical writing style, sharpened by the editorial battles of territorial politics. A Republican stalwart, he attacked reformers of all kinds, suffered several political setbacks, and won one-cent damages in a fifty thousand-dollar libel suit against Dr. J. B. Hall, his former *Republican* partner. Despite his belligerence, he won single terms as mayor in 1886 and state legislator in 1895.[13]

Edwards always boosted his city and state during his career. He depicted the valley as an El Dorado for the ambitious. He portrayed successful residents as "self made men, who had . . . struggled into position and competence through the exercise of indomitable pluck, self denial and self reliance." He boosted through eye-catching headlines, front-page articles, and special editions that circulated widely in the United States and Europe. He crusaded for paved streets, electric lights, streetcars, gasworks and waterworks, a board of health, a fire department, and downtown brick buildings as necessary to make Fargo the commercial metropolis of North Dakota. Like editorial boosters everywhere, Edwards recognized these improvements as vital to municipal success. Additionally, he divided the paper's content between local news and "ready print," which connected readers with the national media culture.[14]

Desiring to expand with the boom, Edwards sought James J. Hill's financial assistance in purchasing a steam lithograph press, a bookbinding machine, and the *Posten,* a local Norwegian newspaper. Persuaded that Edwards could quadruple business with increased plant capacity and make the *Argus* profitable, Hill loaned him fifteen thousand dollars in 1882. Hill charged 7 percent interest with repayment in five years; he received as collateral 510 stock shares valued at fifty-one thousand dollars. The two men made natural allies. A sympathetic editor, who boosted regional growth, aided Hill's transportation enterprises. Hill's steamboats, railroad, and capital developed the valley and created readership for the editor. Unfortunately, Edwards did not repay his debts promptly. After an 1886 fire destroyed the newspaper plant, putting sixty people out of work, Edwards rebuilt immediately. When an insurance company failed to occupy rooms in the new brick building, the overextended Edwards could not repay Hill, who foreclosed. According to scholar Albro Martin, many local investments like this one ended badly for Hill.[15]

Minneapolis editor George K. Shaw took over the *Argus* from receiver Evan S. Tyler in October 1891. The popular Edwards did not long lack a newspaper. Backed by a socially and religiously diverse group of city fathers— O. J. deLendrecie, Alex Stern, Ike Herbst, John Haas, Colonel C. A. Morton, and others who shared a similar boomer mentality—Edwards immediately founded the *Forum.* Three years later, he purchased the financially troubled *Republican.* Pleased to have one less newspaper to support, locals hoped the consolidated publication might become the best evening paper in the state. After five years, Edwards had increased circulation for the weekly to 2,700 subscribers and doubled that of the daily to two thousand. Concentrating on state and local news, the *Forum* attempted to publish all viewpoints and "to be fair, open-handed and honest with . . . everyone." Despite this profession of fairness, Edwards regularly condemned Hill and his railroad for numerous sins real and imagined against Fargo and the valley. His attacks may have hardened Hill's feelings toward the city. The newly created Great Northern Railway Company often infrequently or slowly redressed local complaints.[16]

BUSINESS ASSOCIATIONS AND FURTHER INCORPORATION

Boomers Edwards and Chapin inspired others by their energy, enterprise, and expansion. They nevertheless believed that an age of incorporation required more than individual effort. Businessmen must organize to boost their city, advance commerce, combat corporate domination, harness corporate resources to their own advantage, and promote the common good.

To that end, Edwards assisted in forming the first chamber of commerce in 1879 and served on its board of directors. Intensely but briefly active, the chamber disappeared with the boom's end. A board of trade then appeared for a time before a businessmen's union succeeded it. These bodies reflected a tradition of "civic capitalism" that shaped the city's subsequent growth. Historian Carroll Van West has identified similar entrepreneurial effort for the communal well-being in Billings, Montana, and in other late-nineteenth-century American municipalities.[17]

Such efforts also furthered incorporation. In building new organizations, local businessmen followed the new middle class of corporate managers and lawyers by placing themselves within the emerging national system of an urban-industrial society, according to historian Robert Wiebe. In addition, locals promoted further railroad expansion, embraced new technologies, and created other new associations. By these actions, they learned how the scientific method could be employed to increase knowledge and improve procedures. They also participated in the rising bureaucratic ethos that stressed rules, predictability, and management techniques. While embracing the new, they incorporated the familiar virtues—frugality, punctuality, industry, and efficiency—into bureaucratic systems.[18]

The newly formed Chamber of Commerce advertised with this "bird's-eye" view of Fargo in 1882. Courtesy Institute for Regional Studies, North Dakota State University, Fargo (Folio 71.8.5).

Fargo modeled its chamber of commerce after that of St. Paul, Minnesota. The chamber published its first annual report—listing 119 businesses and describing the city's prosperity—in time for advertising the 1880 boom. Writing to a railroad manager for funds to print the one hundred-page pamphlet, Edwards declared: "The report will be a surprise to the most sanguine friends of the Northern Pacific." Embellished by a well-executed lithograph, engraved as a bird's-eye view from an F. Jay Haynes photograph, the report—according to the *Fargo Times*—would be a major benefit for the city. Haynes's photographs of the Grandin Farm operations in 1876 had already publicized the region. Indeed, the report called wheat the "backbone of Fargo . . . making the Red River Valley famous wherever wheat is bought and sold."[19]

Edwards's *Argus* Company published the *Second Annual Report of the Chamber of Commerce,* demonstrating one way that a booster might profit immediately from his own publicity. Indeed, advertisements from real-estate agents and other businesses made up almost 40 percent of the content. The second report contained all the information that journalists like Edwards often presented in special editions. It dispelled worries about weather: "The climate is healthy, bracing and . . . especially favorable for persons affected with lung diseases, or . . . consumptive tendencies." It emphasized the central role of the railroad corporations in developing the region's wheat farms. It promised that the Northern Pacific and the SPM&M assisted settlers materially. The back cover displayed land commissioner James B. Power's advertisement for Northern Pacific wheat lands. The report stressed retail and wholesale trade opportunities in Fargo, "the proud . . . Metropolis of the Red River Valley," which received "streams of wealth in golden grain . . . from the whole Northwest—the future granary of the world." Statistics on the rising values of Fargo business, grain elevator receipts, wheat farm operating costs and profits, and U.S. Land Office sales documented these assertions.[20]

The second report celebrated modern communications as essential for incorporating the city into the nation and the world. The post office provided daily mail to and from the East and West as well as from Scandinavia, Germany, France, and other countries. The postal service followed the railroads in adopting standard time in 1883. Other businesses quickly followed. Northwestern Telegraph Company wires connected Fargo with St. Paul, Minneapolis, Bismarck, and Winnipeg. During 1880, Northwestern manager J. B. Inman dispatched 14,689 messages. Each day he received bulletins from the metropolitan dailies and forwarded Fargo news in return. He also managed the Fargo and Moorhead Telephone Exchange, which strung wires linking Bonanza farms and city offices. During the 1880s, most private businesses as well as many homes acquired telephones. New poles, cables,

Erected in 1897, this new post office and government building represented improved national communications for the growing city of Fargo. Courtesy Institute for Regional Studies, North Dakota State University, Fargo (2070.276.2).

and switchboards improved service in the next decade. By 1898, residents made six thousand calls daily on 583 telephones. Telephone lines connected them to eighty-five towns in the Red River Valley and at Minneapolis to all points east and south.[21]

Most western communities actively promoted railroads at this time, according to historian Charles Glaab. Despite their relative success, each city often felt victimized by pools and high charges. Competition for trade among several lines secured favorable rates more effectively than protests. The Fargo chamber of commerce thus sought reduced fees and growth through attracting new railroad or branch extensions. Although Fargo did not become a rail and meatpacking center on the scale of Kansas City, it achieved greater importance than many places. Boomers frequently praised the Northern Pacific for its contributions to their city's growth. Yet when corporate managers refused the lower tolls conducive to boosting wholesale trade, the chamber of commerce immediately sought an additional road. Rumors about approaching lines circulated wildly, fueled by newspaper accounts. Eventually, the rumors became reality. The SPM&M arrived in February 1881 and pushed northward to Grand Forks within a few months.[22]

The new line exacerbated tensions between the dueling twin cities. Land dealer and Manitoba supporter A. J. Harwood reported these resentments to James J. Hill. Creation of the Manvel and Hill additions in Moorhead and

SPM&M advertisements that displayed Moorhead in large type and Fargo in small type, according to Harwood, had convinced residents that Hill favored their competitor and would locate his permanent shops in the Minnesota city. This perceived favoritism would cost Hill business, Harwood warned. Fargo businessmen threatened to boycott the Manitoba for one year unless they got lower rates than those offered by the Northern Pacific. Although Hill did not locate his shops in Moorhead, he did reduce charges by a third

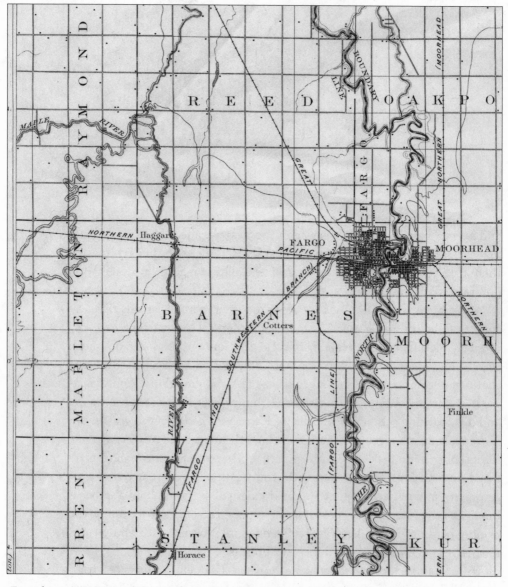

Fargo boosters promoted Cass County railroad expansion to draw trade from the countryside. Courtesy Institute for Regional Studies, North Dakota State University, Fargo (153).

in an attempt to seize Fargo traffic. Locals welcomed the ensuing rate war as well as the extension of sidetracks to the paper mill, brewery, and Fargo Car Wheel and Iron Works. Colonel Charles Tyson Yerkes—the Chicago businessman and Fargo boomer later immortalized as Frank Copperwood by novelist Theodore Dreiser's *The Financier* and *The Titan*—stated in 1883 that the SPM&M guaranteed the city's future.[23]

To check its opponent's proposed expansion west of Wahpeton, the Northern Pacific extended the Fargo and Southwestern to Lisbon in December 1882 and La Moure on the James River the following year. As contractor F. R. Delano had earlier written to Frederick Billings: "I think the Fargo & Southwestern could be so located to make them howl." To contest the Manitoba's valley trade, the Northern Pacific used the Grandin and Alsop Lines. Steamboats and barges carried wheat south from Pembina to their Fargo elevators and passengers used railroad tickets for traveling northward. Edwards applauded these arrangements as a "big boom for the metropolis." The scheme did not last long. Hill soon destroyed his competitor's water-based auxiliary by extending branch lines throughout the valley. He then used his share of the wheat traffic as collateral for financing the Manitoba's westward expansion.[24]

Additional rumors circulated about plans by the Chicago, Milwaukee and St. Paul as well as the Chicago and North Western railroad for expanding northward through the valley to Canada. Chapin and others, backed by Charles T. Yerkes, seized the initiative in mid-1881. They organized the Fargo and Southern Railroad Company to build southward, connect with either of these projected lines, and thereby secure the direct connection to Chicago they hoped would increase their city's wholesale trade. According to an *Argus* interview in late July, the excessively optimistic Chapin promised to grade and equip twenty-five miles by autumn. Although the line had been surveyed and readied for graders by late October, the threshing season created a worker shortage and delayed progress. Surveyed to Wahpeton and graded to Fort Abercrombie the following year, the Fargo and Southern stalled, unable to secure sufficient capital or favorable freight rates from its competitors. The firm reorganized in June 1883 and elected new officers. President Homer E. Sargent, former Northern Pacific general manager, general manager W. A. Kindred, and secretary Alanson W. Edwards raised funds for construction.[25]

By August of the following year, the Fargo and Southern opened for service to Ortonville, Minnesota. Prominent twin city citizens joined two hundred invited guests for a celebratory trip. Afterward, the *Moorhead Weekly News* proclaimed: "The road is well built, well equipped, well officered and deserves the support of the dual metropolis." Locating its passenger

The Milwaukee passenger depot symbolized Fargo's dreams of becoming a rail center. Courtesy Institute for Regional Studies, North Dakota State University, Fargo (2070.262.2).

depot at the corner of Second Avenue and Eleventh Street North, the firm announced plans for constructing nearby a brick freight warehouse and twelve-stall roundhouse, which would boom the west side. The Fargo and Southern Elevator Company, managed by Evan S. Tyler, erected three new elevators and planned three more along its line. Unfortunately for residents who had hoped for lower charges, the railroad announced the same rate schedule as that of the Northern Pacific and SPM&M because it could not afford a rate war. Although this locally managed company aroused considerable pride, it became part of the Milwaukee Road in 1885.[26]

Expanding railroad companies further incorporated the twin cities into the national market and urban hierarchy. Fargo became a principal commercial and financial subsidiary of Minneapolis, while Moorhead merely retailed goods and collected grain. In the 1870s, Minneapolis became the largest U.S. flour-milling center. In the next decade, it became a more important market for valley wheat than Duluth, taking three times as many bushels. As Minneapolis flour production rose from about two hundred thousand to 7 million barrels, the mills stimulated railroad expansion westward to collect Dakota and Montana wheat and market flour. Consequently, "the Mill City" became the most important center northwest of Chicago for railroads, banking, storage of grain, and distribution of farm machinery. Despite the growing independence of Minneapolis and St. Paul after 1885, Chicago still played a role in the trade of Montana and areas to the south. It also became a more important source of capital than New York and Boston. To lessen their dependence on eastern capital, Minneapolis and St. Paul businessmen expanded local banks.[27]

Fargo's ties to Minneapolis fostered rural complaints about the city being an agent for corporate exploiters. North Dakotans depended on wheat. It accounted for nearly 60 percent of agricultural production and about 80 percent of all cash income. Farmers naturally resented the exploitative practices of unfair grading, short weights, excessive dockage, and price-setting pools that state and federal investigators had confirmed. They therefore organized politically to end their dependence on the corporate interests of Minneapolis and "imperial Cass." Fargo businessmen, however, opposed all cooperative solutions urged by agrarian reformers from the Populists to the Non-Partisan League. As an alternative, they urged scientific agriculture, improved farm management, and agricultural diversification. All of these furthered the incorporation of the city and region into a national system.[28]

Established in 1890, the North Dakota Agricultural College (NDAC) and

The main building (ca. 1894) of North Dakota Agricultural College, which promoted scientific agriculture and integrated Fargo and the state into a national system. Courtesy University Archives, North Dakota State University, Fargo (Bol 2–1915.5).

Experiment Station similarly promoted integration and modernization. Its staff of scientifically trained experts embodied the new urban-industrial and professional values and attempted to transmit them to farmers. The professors struggled to win the confidence of those who stigmatized book farming, preferred radical political solutions, and distrusted any Fargo-based institution. To overcome agrarian distrust, the station emphasized research that promised immediate benefits. Although the station could not end dependence on commodity production, it did diversify commodities by investigating new plant and animal products. It thus published bulletins on potatoes, sugar beets, vegetables, sheep, and dairying, as well as wheat. Its research on fruits, trees, shrubs, and flowers promised to enrich rural life. The station popularized its work by adult education delivered through Farmers' Institutes and by building commodity-based organizations to create the new goods.[29]

The Better Farming Association (BFA) institutionalized private efforts to improve farming. Fargo and Twin City bankers as well as railroads, wholesale houses, machinery dealers, millers, lumbermen, and elevator firms created the BFA in 1911. Station scientist Henry Bolley's hypothesis about "wheat-sick soil" alarmed corporate interests. They feared it might frighten away eastern capital and thereby destroy their profitable Dakota investments. The BFA promoted improved farm management and diversified farming, which had been advocated by railroad magnate James J. Hill and James B. Power, a former Northern Pacific and Manitoba employee. After an initially favorable response, NDAC president John Henry Worst complained about BFA competition. Regulatory-minded researchers Henry Bolley and Edwin F. Ladd distrusted the BFA corporate connections. By 1920, the experiment station resolved the conflict by emphasizing strict research specialization, scientific rigor, and promotion of better farm management. Although agrarian radicals saw this as a corporate takeover, historian David Danbom argues that the station instead had become part of a national system of scientific research and maturing professional disciplines.[30]

James B. Power, a former corporate manager turned resident businessman-farmer, personified many of the trends toward further incorporation. He served as land commissioner for both the Northern Pacific and Manitoba railroads. He suggested the Bonanza farm scheme to Northern Pacific president George W. Cass. He established his own six thousand-acre cattle operation at Helendale in the Sand Hills along the Sheyenne River in 1880. More than a decade later, he became NDAC president and the experiment station director. Power thereby joined an emerging blended rural-urban elite. His correspondence reveals wide-ranging business activities. Between 1885 and 1890, Power discussed land, legal matters, banking, and payment of accounts in more than a hundred letters written to Fargo and other businessmen. Depending on the most advantageous price, he might sell cattle to the Fargo packing-house, Moorhead banker L. A. Huntoon, Chicago, St. Paul, or Minneapolis. He solicited bids on his wheat crop from Minneapolis, the Fargo mill, and the Fargo elevator. He sent samples to the experiment station, attempting to determine probable grade and dockage in advance. When he purchased live-stock from stockbreeders in Minnesota, Iowa, and Wisconsin, he negotiated the lowest possible shipping rate from the competing Milwaukee, Northern Pacific, and Chicago and North Western railroads.[31]

Power's correspondence reveals how the 1893 depression affected business. His struggles demonstrate the importance of credit locally. Writing to his son in April, Power reported unpaid miscellaneous bills totaling $2,200. He had borrowed $4,500 from Fargo banks to pay interest on his debts all over the country. Without the necessity of caring for "dead horses," Power wrote, "I would feel quite easy." Although his income had exceeded expenses, Power felt the pinch more severely by June. Without any possibility of raising money in Fargo, he could not pay his notes if called. Assuming the presidency of NDAC helped Power survive this crisis, but the economy worsened the next year. Cash shortages at the Fargo Roller Mill threatened his position. During the previous three harvests, he had sold them wheat from his Helendale and Casselton farms for higher prices than he could realize from nearby elevators or by shipping directly. If the Fargo mill could not pay cash, Power said, his son should ship to either Duluth or Minneapolis.[32]

Like James J. Hill, Power had vigorously promoted diversified agriculture since 1881. Both men widely publicized the results of livestock feeding programs on their own farms. Power corresponded extensively regarding North Dakota agricultural conditions. Although appointed president as a political maneuver to save the experiment station from the clutches of a Populist governor, Power believed in scientific agriculture and had already established cordial relations with key staff members. He continued to speak and to publish pamphlets after he left office in 1895. He argued the benefits from livestock: animals utilized every acre sown in grass, provided horses for farmwork, and produced meat for home consumption. Farmers could earn higher profits by feeding low-grade wheat to livestock and selling high-grade wheat. To this end, Power participated in the Northwestern Stock-Breeders' Association that promoted raising better-bred livestock, held conventions in Fargo, and sought to represent all stockmen of the state. He also joined a 1903 fight against Fargo politicians attempting to control agricultural board membership. The college and experiment station should not be just a local institution, but should represent all of the state's agriculturalists.[33]

While commodity producers organized for their own economic benefit,

businessmen renewed efforts to form an effective promotional association. The Fargo Board of Trade in 1891 met regularly and proposed several
growth strategies. It suggested that all destitution should be relieved from
within the state because appeals for outside aid damaged North Dakota's
reputation and discouraged immigration. It appointed a railroad committee to assist Northern Pacific construction from Fargo to Mayville, North
Dakota, and Ada, Minnesota. It met with Northern Pacific board chairman
Henry Villard and discussed building a new depot and hotel. It responded
to inquiries from manufacturers and encouraged them to relocate. It lost
the fight for a proposed Lutheran school that became Concordia College in
Moorhead.[34]

Efforts then lapsed until a businessmen's union appeared in 1895. This
functioned much like its predecessors. It recruited manufacturers and
conventions. It lobbied Hill to build a new branch line. It sent delegates
to an immigration convention called by Power. The meeting organized the
North Dakota Immigration Association and planned the North Dakota
Businessmen's Union. Both sought better ways to advertise their state
and promote its commercial development. As with previous efforts, the
union soon disappeared for lack of a full-time executive director. Early in
the twentieth century, a new set of leaders incorporated the Commercial
Club of Fargo, which became the present-day chamber of commerce in 1927.
Whatever their name, all associations from the earliest days sponsored economic growth and municipal improvement.[35]

RAILROADS, INDUSTRIAL DREAMS, AND RETAIL REALITIES

"Fargo is a business city, which has been built up by businessmen, who
founded it on business principles," *Andreas' Historical Atlas* proudly announced in 1884. Corporate railroad managers and local entrepreneurs
agreed on this point and the Fargo cityscape proclaimed it. The city grew
along the Northern Pacific track, its original link with national markets and
the dominant trade corridor. By 1901, the commercial area centered on the
southern end of Broadway and clustered north and east of the Northern
Pacific depot at Front and Seventh Street South. Twenty-two hotels, twelve
restaurants, sixteen retail grocers, six meat markets, three hardware stores,
four furniture dealers, nine dry goods stores, eight druggists, three newspapers, four banks, an opera house, and other businesses all clustered on
the southern end of Broadway and the adjacent avenues between Front
Street and Second Avenue North. Farm machinery and wholesale warehouses lined Northern Pacific Avenue from the Red River westward to Eighth
Street. Spur lines on the riverbank serviced flour, linseed oil, and feed mills,

as well as a grain elevator. Lumberyards, a meatpacking firm, an electric power plant, and other manufacturers also held trackside sites.[36]

The less developed Great Northern right-of-way reflected that carrier's smaller share of municipal commerce. It contained grain, lime, coal, wood, and oil storage facilities as well as a stock shed and cattle pens. Spur lines extended to a closed brewery, flour mill, foundry, and paper factory. Northern Broadway between Second Avenue and the Great Northern track had few businesses. Fire ruins scarred parts of the 200 block. Empty lots on both sides of the street characterized the next block. A meat market, a grocery, a cigar manufactory, and the Great Northern Hotel and Restaurant occupied the 400 block near the depot.[37]

Civic and mercantile leaders knew that their livelihoods depended on trade. As the *Forum* stated in 1907: "Fargo is rapidly growing . . . because . . . tributary to her is a large . . . thriving . . . country from which she draws her commercial life blood." Thirty-two trains arrived and departed each day on the main and branch lines of three railroads. The Milwaukee Road traversed the southern valley via Wahpeton. The Fargo & Southwestern and Casselton branch lines of the Northern Pacific opened six southeastern counties to exchange with the city. Great Northern branches to Devil's Lake through Mayville in North Dakota and to Crookston in Minnesota gave the city access to the northern valley. Such extensive rail service afforded eastern North Dakota and western Minnesota residents the advantage of shopping in Fargo. The patronage of this large farm and town hinterland fueled the growing retail trade that sustained municipal prosperity while industrial dreams often failed to materialize.[38]

Railroads worked closely with grain elevator and lumberyard owners. The former gave trackside leases and preferred shipping rates. The latter furnished vital local services, yet often channeled profits to corporate offices. The Union Elevator, built in Fargo by the Glyndon-based firm of Bonanza farmers G. S. Barnes and L. H. Tenney, shipped its grain through the Duluth port on Lake Superior to flour mills in Buffalo and Rochester, New York. After a Minneapolis group acquired an interest in 1882, the renamed Northern Pacific Elevator Company delivered its wheat to Minneapolis. Pillsbury and Hulbert, formed to serve Minneapolis millers, meanwhile had acquired 50 percent of the storage capacity along the Manitoba line. Tall, wood elevators with high central sections defined the skyline of Fargo and other prairie towns.[39]

Minneapolis lumbermen contracted with railroads for establishing yards along particular Dakota lines, supplying an area that lacked building materials. Vermont native William H. White headed one of six Fargo firms located on the Northern Pacific track in 1900. White Brothers Lumber Company for several years after its founding in 1873 had shipped as far north as Winnipeg, utilizing Red River flatboats and rafts. It erected a planing mill at the corner of Eighth Street and Northern Pacific Avenue to meet boom-generated demand in 1879. During the next two years, Fargo sales totaled six hundred thousand dollars for 25 million linear feet at prices ruled by the Minneapolis lumber market. From his Fargo headquarters in 1895, White managed the Gull Lumber Company and twenty-seven retail yards in the valley.[40]

The railroad shaped Fargo economic development in ways not fully understood by either the corporate or resident mercantile elite. It gave businessmen advantages earlier unavailable, according to geographer John Hudson.[41] It linked them to the national banking and currency system as well as to major producers and markets. It gave them access to capital, specialized goods, and name brands. It permitted long-distance transactions. It inspired dreams of

The First National Bank in Fargo, founded in 1878, expanded and proclaimed itself "the largest and safest bank in Dakota." Courtesy Institute for Regional Studies, North Dakota State University, Fargo (2029.8.10).

local self-sufficiency. Like boomers elsewhere, those in Fargo stressed manufacturing. If local firms supplied the home market and created a surplus for
export, then capital accumulated for funding more growth. Agricultural processing plants similarly yielded capital gains by making finished goods that
were more profitable than primary products. At the same time, the railroad
shattered such dreams in unforeseen ways. It subjected localities to national
panics, depressions, and competition. It created a national market, which,
combined with distance from metropolitan centers, meant that most Fargo
firms did not long remain competitive. Economies of scale enabled corporations to sell their goods more cheaply. Distance added transportation fees
for raw materials and marketing to local costs that placed small producers at
a competitive disadvantage. As boosters did not immediately perceive these
realities, they long pursued self-sufficiency.

At the height of the Dakota Boom, a promotional pamphlet recorded
Fargo's industrial progress by sketching its foremost financial, manufacturing, and mercantile institutions. It articulated a logic of commercial development: "Banks are the rock on which the . . . prosperity of a community
must always rest. . . . Solid financial institutions are the only foundations
upon which a city's industrial superstructure can be built." New towns required capital. They relied on eastern investors, local bankers, or a blend of
both. They worked to attract external capital. Banks often acted as agents
for eastern and European investors. On other occasions, outside capitalists
personally started new firms.[42]

As the 1880s began, Fargo had four lending institutions: First National
Bank, Bank of Fargo, Cass County Bank, and Red River Valley National Bank.
The federal government chartered national banks, which issued currency
secured by federal bonds and failed less frequently than state or private
banks. The First National Bank—organized by Ezra B. Eddy, Evan S. Tyler,
and other old-stock Americans in early 1878—became, it claimed, "the largest and safest bank in Dakota." The depository for many country banks, it
in turn deposited funds in the St. Paul First National Bank, the New York
City Chase National Bank, and the Chicago Commercial National Bank.
These establishments facilitated the transfer of funds and advanced loans
for expanding currency supplies during the harvest season or financial panics. The First National Bank became even more preeminent in 1906 when it
merged with the Red River Valley National Bank. At that time, the city had
ten banks, three of them national. These sustained Fargo's claim to be the
North Dakota commercial capital. It kept that position during subsequent
decades. In 1915, for example, five hundred country banks used Fargo institutions as depositories. By the 1920s, bank clearings amounted to $100
million annually.[43]

Although Fargo boosters welcomed the investment funds banks provided, they hoped to accumulate additional capital through a favorable balance of trade. Echoing an earlier mercantilism, boosters desired self-sufficiency. They hailed each new factory, claiming it confirmed their city's destiny as an industrial center. As the *Daily Republican* boasted in 1882: "Fargo will soon be independent of the rest of the world." An 1891 *Argus*-sponsored symposium on growth demanded more home industries that employed more laborers, processed more agricultural products, and supplied a larger share of the domestic market. Only in this way could Fargo become a city of twenty-five thousand people.[44]

Corporate managers, anticipating expanded traffic for the Northern Pacific, similarly promoted industry. They reported in 1882 that seven recently established Fargo plants valued at $238,000 already had produced goods worth $73,000.[45] Residents alone or in partnership with recently arrived prospectors had raised the capital for construction. Despite corporate and entrepreneurial interest, manufacturing remained a small sector of the municipal economy. Dominated by small or medium-sized firms, it focused primarily and most successfully on agricultural goods and processing of crops. Failure stalked more ambitious attempts to make other products for larger markets such as the Car Wheel and Iron Works.

The ever-growing city created a steady demand for builders and materials. Many workers found employment in construction trades that sustained several lumberyards and brickmakers. Fargo Brick and Tile, Fargo Brick and Manufacturing, and other companies mechanized to double or triple output. Their product built the new Cass County court house, Central High School, and other structures of the 1880s. Despite these achievements, brickmaking never attained the importance it did in Grand Forks. Historian Frank Vyzralik suggests two reasons why it did not. Realtors, seeking a return from their unsold lots by mining them for clay, did not commit permanently to the industry. Cheaper brick from established Moorhead and other Minnesota producers might have been adequate to meet demand.[46] If not, railroads brought brick from larger, more efficient, and more distant firms.

Other goods needed by farmers and townspeople created additional opportunities for manufacture. F. N. Whitman, whom the R. G. Dun Company regarded as a good businessman, founded Fargo Carriages in 1873. The next year, he broke ground for a factory with steam-powered machinery to make wagons and plows. The *Northern Pacific Mirror* praised him and demanded new investment in a badly needed mower factory, foundry, and machine shop. Farm machinery production never developed, despite many editorial calls for its establishment. Yet two decades later the city directory still listed four builders of buggies, carriages, and wagons. A Chicago emigrant established the Bristol Harness Shop in 1881 because he had been told that Fargo would be a good place for his business. The shop's initial location on Front Street between two saloons ensured a lively trade. After expanding into Bristol and Sweet Harness Company, the firm relocated to Broadway and became one of two wholesalers among the five harness makers in the city at the turn of the century.[47]

Two breweries, two bottlers, and a paper mill located near the SPM&M trackside in the early 1880s. The breweries sold locally and regionally. The bottlers processed Milwaukee-produced beer and other liquids. North Dakota prohibition killed these industries. J. O. Gregg relocated his paper mill from Elkhart, Indiana. The *Daily Republican* crowed: "Let the good work go on until Fargo's supremacy as a manufacturing center for the northwest is everywhere conceded." Despite supposed advantages of abundant local material, talent, capital, and demand for a factory that made construction paper from straw, it failed.[48]

Flour milling, the earliest attempt at agricultural processing in the city, enjoyed success for a long time. From a small mill erected early in 1877, Charles A. Roberts and a succession of partners expanded into the larger Fargo Roller Flour Mill built along the Red River and a sidetrack at the foot of Northern Pacific Avenue. The steam-powered mill ground 140,000 bushels of wheat and produced 28,000 barrels of flour valued at $224,000 for the year ending on June 30, 1882. Through membership in the Red River Millers Association—organized in 1885 to secure through rates to the East and expand sales—the mill shipped flour to New York as well as other eastern and European markets. It operated profitably into the next decade under new owners until it went into temporary receivership in 1896, a depression year. Although it reopened and flour comprised 45 percent of the city's total manufacturing value in 1899, its days were numbered. It could not compete with the more technologically advanced Minneapolis mills, which produced high-quality flour in high volume at low unit cost. During the 1890s, Pillsbury and Washburn-Crosby became the largest firms through mergers. By creating buying and selling networks, they further reduced costs.[49]

Looming competition from corporate giants seldom dampened booster enthusiasm permanently. When projectors proposed a linseed oil mill in 1897, the *Forum* commented: "Just . . . see the train of industries that will rapidly follow." The mill represented what boomers had long sought. It processed 1,200 bushels of locally grown flax into sixty barrels of oil daily. North Dakota lignite powered the plant, which employed twenty-five men. It sold the oil regionally, but exported the cake mostly to Antwerp, Belgium, because local farmers did not appreciate its value as cattle feed.[50]

Incorporation of the Fargo Packing and Cold Storage Company by Alex

Stern and other local capitalists provoked similar enthusiasm. Fifty prominent citizens celebrated production of the company's first sugar-cured hams
by dining on ham, summer sausage, and beer. By 1898, the firm had already
expanded regional livestock output, according to the *Forum*. It then processed monthly about 250,000 pounds of pork and 80,000 pounds of beef.
Expectations for success aroused by this promising start ignored economic
realities. Powerful Chicago firms dominated markets and prices through
their ties with railroad and stockyard companies. Packinghouses on the
northern plains typically failed because they lacked a year-round cattle supply and could not process the by-products that furnished substantial profits
for the large packers.[51]

Two years later, Armour—a large Chicago packer—opened an outlet in
Fargo. The *Forum* acknowledged the benefit to consumers, but urged buying
from the home firm. Its payroll and livestock purchases benefited the community more in the long run. Despite such sentiment, the local company
did not survive. During the 1920s, Armour established a plant near the
West Fargo station where the Northern Pacific had relocated its Sheyenne
stockyards from the city four decades earlier. The plant collected livestock
from the adjacent three-state area. It sold finished products to the municipal and regional market.[52]

Boosters also started the Fargo Car Wheel and Iron Works, their most
ambitious and ill-starred attempt at economic self-sufficiency. Walter M.
Lenhart arrived in March 1882 from Elkhart, Indiana. He offered fifty thousand dollars to establish an ironworks if residents invested an equal amount.
Chapin, Edwards, Eddy, and others at once pledged seventy-five thousand
dollars. Although Lenhart departed to organize the Moorhead foundry, his
partner, R. E. Mulcahy, invested. He became president and general manager. Mulcahy situated the factory on ten acres of donated land located just
west of Long Lake on Eighth Avenue North. The firm soon received orders
for more than a hundred tons of castings. It poured the first iron in Dakota
Territory in early June. That month it daily fashioned five tons of castings
and reported a five thousand-dollar payroll.[53]

Despite its promising start, the factory quickly faltered. The Northern
Pacific, which had promised to purchase twenty-five boxcars, did not exe-
cute a contract. Railroad managers decided that the works could not build
satisfactory cars. Insufficient credit and orders closed the plant after only
one year. During late 1885 and throughout 1886, civic leaders negotiated
with outside capitalists for reopening the works. By September, the *Argus* reported that the buyers had ordered corrugated iron roofing, paint, and other
repairs. This effort proved fruitless. A decade later, the *Forum* complained
about the lack of a foundry and suggested that a fortune awaited some iron

entrepreneur. Those who remembered the previous short-lived fiasco would not have agreed. The frequent failures should have demonstrated even to ardent boomers like Edwards that the future of the city did not lie with industry. As historian Richard White points out, small western manufacturers "thrived because of the region's isolation . . . [and] could prosper only as long as freight rates remained high enough to banish eastern competition."[54]

While entrepreneurs founded manufactories that often foundered, retailing established itself as an engine of economic growth for Fargo. Retailing grew as railroad lines enlarged the city's hinterland. At the same time, many merchandizing changes occurred. National brand names, which suggested standardized quality, became a retailing necessity. Women assumed direction of family consumption. Through purchasing stylish clothes and material goods they defined status and gentility. Their economic decision making represented a step toward female emancipation. Department stores and mail-order houses made fashionable goods available to more consumers. According to scholar Jessica Sewell, department stores were female worlds designed to seduce them with "a plethora of goods seductively displayed in luxurious settings." Small stores adapted to these changes, incorporating innovations as best they could.[55]

For a decade or more, many early Fargo merchants, like their counterparts in other western towns, engaged in a succession of unrelated businesses before achieving stability. Merchants initially created traditional general stores that sold everything one needed to establish a household, from food, crockery, and clothing to dry goods, furnishings, and furniture. Shops that specialized in the sale of particular items—groceries, boots and shoes, drugs, or confectionaries—increasingly displaced them. Most sold national name brands, with the exception of confectioners, who made their own ice cream. Few stocked products locally made. Department stores that offered a variety of elegant goods also appeared.[56]

Massachusetts-born Newton K. Hubbard and Pennsylvania native Evan S. Tyler demonstrated the fluidity of early business activity. Hubbard initially operated general stores in partnership with James W. Raymond at Brainerd, Oak Lake, Glyndon, Moorhead, and Jamestown. When this joint venture dissolved in 1873, Hubbard and Tyler formed N. K. Hubbard & Co. They soon purchased the stock of the bankrupt Mann and Maddocks store and opened E. S. Tyler & Co. in Fargo. Two years later, Hubbard merged his Moorhead business with Tyler's store. The combined firm advertised itself as general merchants, offering "dry goods, ladies and gents . . . clothing, boots and shoes, carpeting, etc." as well as a "choice stock of groceries, crockery, hardware, tin ware, etc." and a "full line of furniture." At this time, Hubbard also leased the Headquarters Hotel.[57]

Like many frontier merchants, Tyler & Co. extended credit to customers and assured them that it paid the "highest market price . . . for wheat, oats, potatoes, butter and eggs." However lenient its credit terms, the store demanded money during the fall harvest, as is evident from a notice posted in the *Northern Pacific Mirror*: "All persons indebted are requested to pay or we shall be obliged to force collection." The two men operated this store and another in Casselton until 1882. They also traded in grain and real estate. In February 1878, Hubbard and Tyler joined others as founders of the First National Bank.[58] Their evolution from merchants to hotelkeepers, bankers, and realtors indicates the volatility of early business in the city. Caught up in the whirl of wealth seeking, everyone and everything seemed in constant motion. Many came, stayed for a time, and then moved on, seeking fortunes elsewhere. Even those who remained often embarked on new business ventures, ever trying to maximize their riches.

O. J. deLendrecie exemplified those businessmen who established themselves in a particular mercantile line and expanded with the city. Originally from Canada, deLendrecie arrived as a young man by way of Paris, France, and Yazoo City, Mississippi. His department store—recognized as "one of the great institutions of Fargo"—originated in 1879 as the Chicago Dry Goods Store at 618 Front Street opposite the Northern Pacific depot and the Headquarters Hotel. At that time, women purchased yard goods for making dresses and other clothing. To do this work, fifty-three dressmakers, twenty-one tailors, and six milliners lived in the city. The store offered a large selection ranging from expensive silks imported from Japan and India to more modestly priced goods of European origin. Fashionable women from the city as well as those from the hinterland patronized the store. Although surprised by the desire of rural and village women for stylish goods, deLendrecie supplied their needs. He also sold wholesale, shipping goods north to Winnipeg, east to Brainerd, and west to Bismarck.[59]

As deLendrecie's nephew O. J. Campbell, who began work in 1906, later recalled: "We served the people outside of Fargo who had convenient train connections with the city." Shopping expeditions appealed to women on farms and small towns who wanted culture and refinement for their families. Many bought in large quantities for an entire year. They purchased clothing for confirmations, graduations, weddings, and other special occasions. They bought furniture, carpets, curtains, dishes, and additional goods that marked their homes as genteel. Female clerks, who chose this acceptable ladylike occupation in growing numbers, may have assisted them. Reassuring advertisements confirmed the wisdom of their choices: "Mr. deLendrecie is always to the front with the latest fashions, largest stock, finest assortment and at the lowest possible prices."[60]

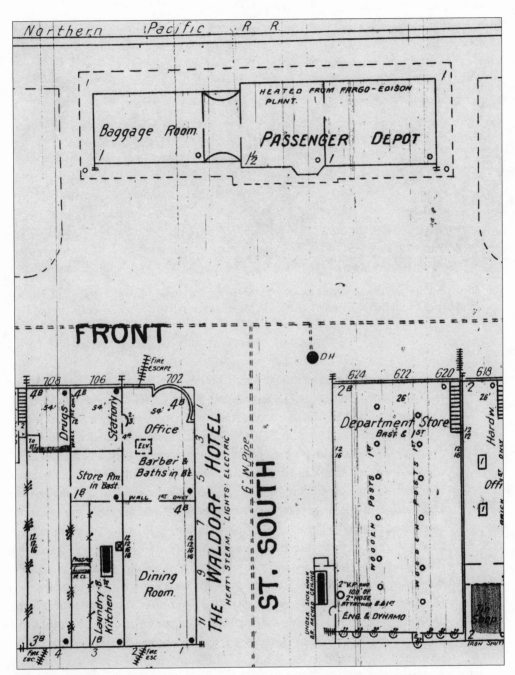

The Sanborn Fire Insurance Map of Fargo from 1901 shows the close proximity of deLendrecie's department store to the Northern Pacific depot and the Waldorf Hotel. Courtesy Institute for Regional Studies, North Dakota State University, Fargo.

The display windows of deLendrecie's Mammoth Department Store in Fargo epitomized modern merchandising. From Patricia Hull, "Pioneers in Merchandising," *Red River Valley Historian* 4–5 (1970–71): 24.

In 1894, the founder housed his "Mammoth Department Store" in a new two-story brick building at 620–624 Front Street. The *Forum* called it "A Business Palace." The front, adorned with Doric arcades and Greek pilasters, had fine plate-glass display windows "always filled with models of goods . . . arranged with a taste of design and grace of selection." Frescoes and carved deep amber oak finish decorated the interior. Polished oak and glass counters exhibited abundant merchandise. Separate departments sold Gents' and Ladies' furnishings, crockery and glassware, jewelry, furniture, boots and shoes, dry goods, draperies, carpets and oriental rugs. According to the *Forum,* surprised strangers arriving at the nearby depot favorably compared deLendrecie's with "the palaces of commerce in the capitals of the East." After the store expanded to five stories in 1909, offices occupied the top two floors. New departments and enlarged stocks filled eighty-two thousand square feet of retail space. DeLendrecie's modernized store conformed to the gentrified downtown standards of other cities. Masculine offices, sparely designed and furnished, contrasted to the feminized shopping space on the lower floors.[61]

In many American cities the business eminence of department store owners carried public responsibilities. O. J. deLendrecie similarly devoted time to the community. He held a city council seat and his suffragette wife, Helen, served on the school board. He helped employees and with Helen aided those in need. DeLendrecie made a major civic contribution in 1898 when he and a partner erected the elegant Waldorf Hotel directly across

Seventh Street from his store. The two modern brick buildings likely impressed most visitors arriving at the Northern Pacific depot. Designed in the French Renaissance style by the Hancock Brothers, a local architectural firm, this five-story structure trimmed with portage entry stone claimed to be the largest and best-equipped hotel west of St. Paul and Minneapolis. It contained 140 guest rooms, one public and two private dining rooms, a circular barbershop, and an interior finished with white oak, marble floors, and a marble stairway. Among the many city hotels, the Waldorf best embodied the metropolitan style to which all boomers aspired. It afforded convenient and comfortable accommodations for deLendrecie's wealthier customers who came from the hinterland not only to shop but also to stay several days for other business or pleasure.[62]

People from all walks of life came to Fargo for many reasons. For those who could afford it, the city offered a place to shop, enjoy theater, attend conventions, and celebrate holidays or festivals. Others came for business. They might sell grain, buy groceries, farm implements, and machinery parts, or seek bank loans. Numerous traveling salesmen secured orders for goods from retailers and wholesalers. Countless women and men from several nations sought jobs. Women worked as domestic servants or clerks.

The elegant Waldorf Hotel greeted visitors arriving in Fargo by Northern Pacific passenger trains at the nearby depot in the early 1900s. Courtesy Institute for Regional Studies, North Dakota State University, Fargo (2006.49.68).

Men toiled for the railroad, manufacturers, or contractors. Hundreds of seasonal laborers arrived each autumn for the wheat harvest. During the 1890s, scores sought divorces and fulfilled the ninety-day residence requirement by living in the city. The Metropole Hotel's fine table attracted several of these. Depending on people's needs and means, Fargo offered varied accommodations. Hotels ranged from the fashionable Waldorf and Metropole for the comparatively wealthy to the workingman's Central Hotel at 223 First Avenue North. Carpenters, painters, bricklayers, and farmers bringing grain to the nearby elevator occupied the Central's twenty-three rooms. Others with only limited means likely found lodging at two boardinghouses or the Minnesota House and the Travelers Hotel, located in the three blocks nearest the Red River on lower Front Street.[63]

By the end of the century, Fargo better embodied many of the metropolitan traits projected by boomers two decades earlier. As "the railway center of the new Northwest," it had developed substantial banking institutions. It had erected several "elegant and commodious hotels and business blocks."[64] Despite the persisting dream of economic self-sufficiency through industry, repeated failures indicated that the future belonged to mercantile activity. Indeed, businessmen such as Hubbard and Tyler, as well as businesses like White Lumber and deLendrecie's department store, had already pointed the way toward Fargo's becoming a gateway city.

NORTH DAKOTA GATEWAY: THE FARM MACHINERY AND WHOLESALE TRADE

Fargo, like United States and North American cities generally, followed a mercantile model of development strongly shaped by wholesale trade. As the only North Dakota city served by three railroads, Fargo had an advantage over potential state rivals that made it the regional wholesale center. It enjoyed superior access to information through its newspapers, post office, telegraph, telephone, and many train-borne commercial travelers. Among the several types of wholesale trade, two ruled the city. Merchant wholesalers controlled groceries, fruit, drugs, hardware, and dry goods into the twentieth century. Yet direct marketing by manufacturers of farm machinery dominated. Five wholesale grocers and the North Dakota Harness Company occupied a warehouse district in the 600 block of Northern Pacific Avenue. Stretched along that same avenue between Broadway and the Red River, implement company offices and warehouses constituted "machinery row." Intending to please their thrifty rural customers, companies designed these brick buildings plainly.[65]

Bonanza farms, the resulting Dakota Boom, and the rising demand for agricultural implements attracted many company agents to Fargo. Total sales more than quadrupled from four hundred thousand dollars in 1879 to $1.8 million by 1882. Companies initially granted franchises to dealers who often represented many firms. Barrett & Co., for example, acted as agents for Monitor seeders, DeGroat and Giddings oval steel tooth harrows, Walter A. Wood binder and harvesting machines, John Deere plows, Buffalo Pitts threshers, Cooper traction engines, and Massillon steam and horse power threshers. This changed as sales grew and manufacturers consolidated. The McCormick Harvesting Machine Company led the way. By 1885, it had replaced retailers with salaried managers and staffs. It integrated horizontally in 1902 to form the International Harvester Company that controlled 85 percent of the harvester and reaper market. After the merged companies were completely integrated in 1906, International Harvester offered a full line of agricultural machinery and became a price leader in the industry.[66]

Agricultural machinery firms furthered the incorporation of America, merging city and country into a single producing and selling system. Historian Olivier Zunz has demonstrated that farmers did not passively receive corporate-sponsored change. They willingly embraced McCormick machines to improve their own lives. Their interaction with agents affected corporate policies. Agents taught farmers how to use the new machines, provided them with technical services, extended credit, and avoided unnecessary conflict over unpaid bills. McCormick operations in Fargo confirm Zunz's analysis. As the boom began, McCormick sent general agent George F. Freudeureich from Alexandria, Minnesota, to assess the market. His report predicted that the city would become the biggest machine distribution point in the northwestern states. An immigrant flood into Dakota Territory and 250 breaking teams plowing additional acres foretold increased Red River Valley wheat production. Freudeureich expected that McCormick dealers would soon overtake the Wood and Marsh agents who led in sales.[67]

Subsequent reports informed McCormick headquarters about flawed field tests. New harvesters and self-binders did not bind properly in heavy grain. The company, which believed that prompt service ensured retailing success, immediately dispatched a technician. Newspapers eagerly reported test results. Companies widely advertised successful demonstrations by their machines. As the Fargo agency became one of its most important sales outlets, the McCormick company met its competition and subjected twine binders, one-wheel reapers, and bundle carriers to field trials. Suggested improvements comprised a voluminous correspondence between Fargo and the Chicago office. Throughout the Dakota Boom, the company met demand by diverting to the valley machines that were destined to other points. At times, the Fargo agency received the entire daily output of the Chicago factory.[68]

Freudeureich also recommended replacing an agent for failing to overtake competitors. Accordingly, J. R. McLaughlin transferred from a southern Minnesota agency to the Fargo office. His territory comprised the northern valley and along the Northern Pacific line east of Glyndon, Minnesota. Although Freudeureich thought the territory insufficiently populated, he accepted the transfer on condition that McLaughlin made a good showing.[69]

Agent McLaughlin immediately constructed a large warehouse. By increasing the number of machines in stock, he hoped to capture the Bonanza farm trade. Freudeureich agreed. Large farmers such as G. S. Barnes, Oliver Dalrymple, and the Grandin brothers presently used Wood binders because of discounts and other inducements. If their business could be secured, Freudeureich expected that small farmers would buy as well. Yet he did not depart from published prices without authorization. Agents protested they could not sell harvesters and binders without extending credit. Apparently, the corporation gave permission because agents now complained about insufficient stocks of harvesters. Marsh agents attempted to take advantage, claiming that McCormick had withdrawn because its machines had failed. McCormick at once challenged Marsh to field trials, which apparently succeeded. By August 1883, McCormick's Fargo agent claimed to have captured the Bonanza trade.[70]

The McCormick company established itself as a leading Fargo distributor. Between 1880 and 1885, sales increased from 796 to 3,259 machines. Receipts rose from $106,000 to just over $280,000. Average price dropped from $134 to $86. Extending credit expanded sales, making collections a pri-

J. R. McLaughlin advertised farm machinery with this engraving on the cover of *Farmers' Almanac and Pocket Diary, 1882.* Courtesy Institute for Regional Studies, North Dakota State University, Fargo (51.137.1).

mary preoccupation. Reports from J. D. Moulder, who gathered payments from the northern valley in the 1890s, reveal how the McCormick company adjusted to customer conditions. The company settled for what it could get from poor credit risks. It collected during the threshing season and resolved accounts as quickly as possible by making concessions. It often deducted interest payments. It gave discounts to those whose machines did not work properly even after several visits by company experts. It accepted less because it received more cash by compromise than by foreclosure.[71]

Seventy-five percent of the twenty-four agricultural implement warehouses located on machinery row in 1900 represented manufacturers. McCormick, J. I. Case, and other companies stocked numerous machines, which they sold directly to farmers or distributed to regional subagencies. Here farmers and small-town dealers acquired plows, seeders, harvesters, and large, often straw-burning, steam engines—a Buffalo-Pitts, a Gaar-Scott, or a Nichols-Shepard—for plowing their fields and powering their threshing machines. The companies and their products affected the economic development of the city from its early years to the present. In recognition of their financial importance, the *Forum* wrote in 1897: "Its machine men are its best citizens."[72]

The city sought other distributors as well. After the Civil War, wholesalers and jobbers dominated the distribution of consumer goods. Chicago became the Upper Midwest wholesaling center. As historian William Cronon has observed, each product had its own geography. Retailers of hardware or heavy machinery worried about high transportation costs and sought wholesalers nearby. Retailers of perishable goods did as well. For these reasons, Minneapolis and St. Paul displaced Chicago as the most important center for the Northwest—an area that included western Wisconsin, Minnesota, portions of Iowa, North and South Dakota, and Montana. In the same way, Fargo early assumed its place as eastern houses established representatives in the city. Their numbers continued to grow. By 1916, Fargo claimed 108 distribution agencies that included thirty-four branch houses, thirty-five wholesale houses, and thirty-nine manufacturers' jobbers. Automobiles then joined farm implements as the most important products. These firms distributed to North Dakota, northwestern Minnesota, eastern Montana, and northern South Dakota.[73]

Given their metropolitan dreams, Fargo boomers had naturally looked toward attracting wholesalers. *Argus* editor Edwards in 1881 praised several retailers who had recently expanded into the wholesale trade: Goodman & Yerxa and Raymond & Kingman in groceries; W. H. White in lumber; and deLendrecie in dry goods. By the following year, twenty-two firms had engaged, with most combining retail and wholesale business. Dakotans welcomed these trends, believing they lowered prices, developed the territory, and increased regional wealth. The *Daily Republican* hoped the continued growth of wholesaling would make Fargo the gateway to Northern Dakota Territory. By the end of 1883, the *Argus* noted that improved railroad facilities had increased the number of jobbing houses dealing in farm machinery, groceries, dry goods, drugs, books, stationary, hardware, cigars, jewelry, wine, and liquor.[74]

Residents hailed the 1887 Interstate Commerce Act. They expected it to expand wholesaling by lowering rates for goods shipped from Chicago. The *Argus* reported that freight coming directly from Chicago via the Milwaukee Road would be only $1.13 per hundredweight compared to $1.80 for that routed through St. Paul. By 1888, the city's wholesale trade totaled $1.2 million. Slightly more that 40 percent of that amount came from the Standard Oil depot established in 1887. Fargo businessmen donated land for locating the ten thousand-dollar plant north of the empty Car Wheel and Iron Works near the Manitoba tracks. The depot consisted of a large brick building and several storage tanks containing several thousand barrels of mostly fuel oil and some gasoline. It employed more than twenty men and distributed to eighteen stations in North Dakota and northern Minnesota.[75]

Fargo made large strides toward fulfilling its dream of becoming a gateway in the mid-1890s when the Northern Pacific and Milwaukee Road recognized the city as a distribution point. Both railroads granted it the same rates as St. Paul, Minneapolis, St. Louis, and Chicago. The following year, Senator John Haggart and the North Dakota Board of Railroad Commissioners managed to secure more favorable rates from James J. Hill and the Great Northern railroad. As a consequence, several new firms appeared in the city. The Fargo Mercantile Company—wholesale grocers that claimed to carry every line of groceries found in large eastern cities—established itself at Broadway and Second Avenue North. It employed ten clerks in the store and five traveling salesmen. The Clark Fruit and Produce Co. also opened that year. Will & Gleason created a jobbing house in boots and shoes. C. A. Koeppler from La Crosse, Wisconsin, erected a new building for distributing fruit on Roberts Street, attracted by the recently opened and successful Everhart Candy Factory located nearby. The factory employed twenty-four workers, shipped 110,000 pounds of candy in October, and expected much larger sales in December. The number of wholesale grocers grew to five with the initiation of the R. S. Timmins Grocery House. By the end of the decade, Bristol and Sweet Company expanded its Broadway harness factory and enlarged its territory to include Montana, Washington, and Idaho. All these developments led the *Forum* to crow: "Fargo is destined to be the great distributing point of the Northwest."[76]

Mayor J. A. Johnson's annual report, delivered in early 1900, verified how large and prosperous the city's businesses had become from their crude beginnings less than three decades earlier. It also confirmed Fargo's title as the gateway to North Dakota. The wholesale trade totaled more than $6.4 million for farm implements and $4.2 million for all other goods. Clearinghouse transactions reached almost $18 million and checking deposits in the city amounted to more than $1.7 million.[77] Perhaps only Jasper Chapin— the most optimistic of boomers, wintering in his tent hotel and saloon, warmed only by his metropolitan dreams—might have been disappointed by the substantial growth that had actually occurred.

From the beginning, Fargo depended on railroad expansion and the growth of its agricultural hinterland that boomers marketed as the "garden of the world." The Bonanza wheat farms conceived by James B. Power and the subsequent Dakota Boom made Fargo part of the hinterland of the Twin Cities and oriented local businesses toward shipping wheat to Duluth or Minneapolis markets, processing some grain and livestock locally, and distributing machinery and other goods needed by farmers. At the same time, city residents were drawn into an urban-industrial order in which scientific, professional, and corporate values competed with the older ideals of autonomous village democracy represented by agrarian radicalism or by local business attempts to control the NDAC and Experiment Station.

During the early twentieth century, Fargo businessmen consolidated the oftentimes uneven economic growth of the preceding decades. In 1899, flour millers had produced 45 percent of the city's manufacturing output and blacksmiths, wheelwrights, printers, and harness makers, tile makers, and papermakers contributed the remainder. With national economic expansion, manufacturing and assembly plants grew in importance and diminished an earlier dependence on agricultural processing. Nevertheless, retail and wholesale trade in farm machinery and other goods remained the principal economic activity. The city solidified its claim as North Dakota gateway in 1912 when the Great Northern completed the Surrey cutoff between Fargo and Minot. Solomon G. Comstock and the Fargo Commercial Club had successfully lobbied Hill for this route in order to further expand Fargo as a rail center and to develop wholesale markets in new towns. As the *Forum* argued, local distributors had a great advantage in time over their more distant competitors in Minneapolis and St. Paul. Located 250 miles nearer to North Dakota retailers, Fargo wholesalers could ship and fill orders more quickly. Although the city had not fulfilled its dreams of becoming a new Chicago or even the distribution center of the Northwest, it took considerable pride in being the gateway to a single state.[78]

PART II

In Pursuit of Vice and Moral Order

Old and New Americans

THE PEOPLE OF FARGO AND MOORHEAD

The more churches, the more people, the more people the greater the prosperity. . . . No village is complete without a church building. Nothing tempts the emigrant more than the presence of church edifices in a community.
                                        —*Red River Star*, November 8, 1873

They constitute a large and respectable portion of the Red River Valley. . . . By the arts of peace and through their industry they will establish a magnificent heritage here in the new Northwest. . . . Welcome the spirit of freedom-loving Norway and the hardy industrious Norwegians.
                                        —*Fargo Daily Republican*, May 18, 1882

MANY NATIONALITIES PEOPLED FARGO AND MOORHEAD. THESE DID not live by business alone. Old Americans and European immigrants quickly founded churches and schools for transplanting religious and moral traditions from the East and Western Europe to the frontier. This civilizing process depended on women. They joined churches in larger numbers than men. The cult of domesticity affirmed their moral superiority, which made them guardians of the home and desirable teachers in the public schools. Women thus actively shaped a Christian social order based on Victorian family values. Many families' lives centered on churches. Members worshipped; attended Sunday schools, prayer meetings, and suppers; held bazaars; and sponsored countless moral crusades. Churches disciplined members, publicized moral standards, and imposed them on the community. Churches, schools, and homes together advanced bourgeois values of individual character, moral respectability, and social progress. They transformed a raw settlement culturally by promoting literacy, musical appreciation, and intellectual growth. They attacked the disorder represented by unmarried and mobile workers by curbing their favorite vices of drunkenness, gambling, and prostitution.[1]

Twin city residents received external aid for this civilizing work. Evangelical Protestants before and after the Civil War toiled to Christianize the West. They insisted it must be saved from infidels and Catholics. They labored with railroad managers to plant churches along the lines throughout the Great Plains. Protestant denominational mission boards combined may have expended $76 million on these efforts. Lutherans and Catholics also developed elaborate home mission schemes to retain their migrating members. Despite the large numbers of unchurched in the West, churches became a leading institution for inculcating virtue.[2]

European immigrants populated western cities just as they did eastern cities. The percentage of foreign-born in 1880 ranged from 33 percent in Omaha to 45 percent in San Francisco, numbers comparable to 35 percent in Scranton and 40 percent in New York City. First- and second-generation immigrants in 1900 composed 77 percent of North Dakota's population. Therefore, it is not surprising that Fargo and Moorhead also attracted many New Americans. At that time, almost two-thirds of Fargo's 9,589 people were foreign-born (26.7 percent) or had foreign parents (36.7 percent). Among the 3,730 Moorhead residents, 46.6 percent had foreign parents and 33.6 percent were foreign-born. As Swedish-born Henry Johnson—a Moorhead Normal history professor and fourth ward alderman—recalled in his autobiography, those of English descent were Americans; they designated others collectively as foreigners and individually according to their national origin.[3]

The number and variety of Fargo and Moorhead churches reveal something of the multiplicity of peoples. Boosters welcomed all religious bodies because they believed that churches attracted immigrants and increased prosperity. In the early 1880s, Moorhead had five churches and Fargo eleven; two decades later, the number had expanded to seven and sixteen, respectively. They represented eight denominations: Baptist, Catholic, Congregational, Episcopal, Lutheran, Methodist, Presbyterian and Unitarian. Ethnic variations included two Methodist bodies—American and German; three Baptist—American, Norwegian, and Swedish; and four Lutheran—English, Norwegian, Swedish, and German. A Norwegian and Swedish mission in each city eventually became Evangelical Free churches in the twentieth century. Germans, Irish, French Canadians, Americans, and several other nationalities attended St. Mary's Catholic Church. Indeed, the "American" congregations probably had ethnic members. Swedish-born Henry Johnson, for example, belonged to Moorhead's First Congregational. Yet an orthodox Fargo Hebrew congregation established by East European Jewish immigrants in 1896 did not include the middle-class German Reformed Jews who had arrived earlier.[4]

Although there seems to have been a religious body for every theological and ethnic need, many residents did not belong. The West had the largest unchurched population among U.S. regions. According to the *Sunday Argus,* Fargo Protestant membership in 1888 ranged from "about thirty" at the German Evangelical Church to 300 at First Methodist. St. Mary's reported about 1,200 Catholics in the parish. The newspaper named seven churches and accounted for about 2,000 people. That left more than 60 percent of the population as possible nonmembers. This large group alarmed church and civic leaders, who held frequent revivals to bring them to Christianity. Even so, church influence on society always exceeded its numbers.[5]

YANKEES AND THEIR INSTITUTIONS

The first Fargo census taken on January 1, 1879, revealed that American-born constituted 69 percent of the population. New England "Yankees" and "Old Americans" from the Mid-Atlantic and Old Northwest states included many of the early businessmen and professionals of the two cities. Other groups often collectively called them "Yankees" and at times derided them for their acquisitiveness and Puritan piety. Yankees established churches and schools that civilized the frontier; they sharpened cultural boundaries with the many foreigners in their midst.[6]

Appreciating the value of churches, Northern Pacific managers issued passes to Episcopalian, Presbyterian, Congregational, Baptist, and Methodist missionaries. When the railroad overlooked the Reverend H. C. Simmons in 1884, he quickly protested. Insisting that Congregationalists had built the most churches along the line, Simmons demanded free passage for his missionary work between Fargo and Helena, Montana.[7]

The Reverend H. C. Simmons, a Congregational missionary to the West and president of Fargo College (1894–99). Courtesy Institute for Regional Studies, North Dakota State University, Fargo (2070.463.2).

Community worship for people of every affiliation began in the twin cities even before the first Northern Pacific train arrived. The Reverend Oscar H. Elmer—sent by the Presbyterian Board of Home Missions—held the first Moorhead service on October 22, 1871, in Jasper Chapin's tent hotel. The Reverend James Gurley—a Methodist circuit rider from Brainerd, Minnesota—began leading prayer and exhortation meetings in Fargo homes at about the same time. On August 28, 1872, the Reverend Joseph A. Gilfillan—an Episcopalian from Brainerd—conducted services in a passenger coach parked on a Moorhead sidetrack. The next day he led worship in the railroad's dining tent in Fargo. The next year saw many regular meetings. Elmer presided over Sunday morning worship at the Fargo Headquarters Hotel and afternoon Sunday school at a Moorhead chapel he had built. Gilfillan held services on alternate Thursday evenings at the chapel. Licensed Episcopalian lay reader and Moorhead druggist Benjamin F. Mackall conducted Sunday worship in both cities. The Reverend John Webb—a Methodist circuit rider now based in Fargo—led services at Pinkham's Hall. Methodists also created a Sunday school.[8]

Despite the drawing of denominational lines, interdenominational groups still met. Members of different churches attended annual meetings of the Cass and Clay County Bible societies. Most Protestant pastors participated in the Fargo–Moorhead Ministerial Association. Members presented papers for discussion at monthly meetings; they occasionally planned month- or weeklong community revivals, and in 1899 shared their pulpits with WCTU delegates who had stopped over on their way to the national convention in Seattle. An annual union Sunday school excursion to Detroit Lake gathered children from twin city Baptist, Congregational, Presbyterian, Episcopal, and Methodist churches. In addition, booster editors urged everyone to patronize each congregation during the winter "season for church festivals." Although Ellen Cooley ridiculed festivals in her novel about frontier Fargo, editors defended them as important communal events. Every church deserved support for preserving the moral order and thereby benefiting the community.[9]

The fourteen churches established by Old Americans in Moorhead and Fargo confirmed the denominational disintegration of American Protestantism. Divisions weakened the Protestant capacity to stand against "the runaway material progress and social fragmentation of the time," as historian Rowland Berthoff has observed. All required support of home mission societies and several toiled for years before becoming self-sustaining. Moorhead First Presbyterian struggles reveal the difficulty of founding frontier churches. First organized in May 1872, seven members worshipped in the chapel erected by the Reverend Elmer. By August 1874, he had solicited two thousand dollars from the East for a new building. Then lightning

NAME	LOCATION	FOUNDED	MEMBERS (CA. 1900)
First Presbyterian	Fifth Street and Second Avenue South, Moorhead	1872	60
Gethsemane Episcopal	204 South Ninth Street, Fargo	1872	310
First Methodist	906 First Avenue South, Fargo	1874	326
St. John the Divine Episcopal	120 South Eighth Street, Moorhead	1875	45
First Presbyterian	Eighth Street and First Avenue North, Fargo	1877	160
Grace Methodist Episcopal	Fourth Street and Second Avenue South, Moorhead	1877	47
First Baptist	Eighth Street and First Avenue South, Fargo	1879	176
First Baptist	Seventh Street and Second Avenue South, Moorhead	1879	dissolved
First Congregational	224 South Eighth Street, Fargo	1881	160
Plymouth Congregational	Broadway and Ninth Avenue North, Fargo	1884	55
St. Mark's English Lutheran	Eighth and Fourth Avenue North, Fargo	1887	100
Roberts Street Methodist	Third Avenue North and Roberts Street, Fargo	1889	100
First Unitarian Society	121 South Ninth Street, Fargo	1890	54
First Congregational	406 South Eighth Street, Moorhead	1894	85

American (Yankee) churches in Fargo and Moorhead. From *Fargo and Moorhead City Directory, 1900* (St. Paul: Pettibone Directory Company, 1900).

struck and destroyed the structure. The group quickly rebuilt, again aided by the mission board. Financial independence took many decades.[10]

Nineteenth-century Christians viewed home and church as complementary institutions that furnished the foundations of society. Family-centered church activities inculcated the Victorian moral code. Every Sabbath, families worshipped in the morning and evening and attended Sunday school. Youth and women's groups met weekly. Ministers preached sermons that sustained community moral standards, expressed spiritual devotion, attracted members, and inspired giving for home and foreign missions.[11]

Several local pastors exemplified such behavior and fulfilled parishioners' expectations by enlarging their congregations. The Reverend Edgar W. Day, who served from 1893 until 1905 at Fargo First Presbyterian, attracted many adults and youth. Membership increased to 259 and the Young People's Society became very important. Similarly, the popular Reverend Reuben A. Beard at Fargo First Congregational achieved unusual growth during his first pastorate from 1883 to 1888. Membership had grown from forty-four to 175 and the building had been enlarged by the time he departed. The Reverend G. H. Gerberding preached at St. Mark's English Lutheran from 1887 to 1894. He added only seventy members, but established a large and active Sunday school. He fraternized with clergy of all denominations. He campaigned for adopting English-language worship among Norwegian and Swedish Lutherans. He made St. Mark's widely known by his speeches and newspaper writings.[12]

All twin city Protestant churches maintained Sunday schools, demonstrating commitment to their children's religious education. In some congregations, the Sunday school preceded church organization and in others it may have overshadowed worship. After being transplanted from England to America in 1785, the Sunday school became part of the competitive denominational pattern. It played a role in birthing American public schools and spread westward in the Protestant campaign to redeem the West. The Sunday school prevailed, according to historian Martin Marty, because "it was an effective instrument of evangelical values and . . . for inculcating agreed upon virtues." Poor children were welcomed if they were "scrubbed and starched" according to middle-class standards.[13]

A Maine Congregationalist, the Reverend Francis E. Clark, founded the Christian Endeavor Society in 1881. This interdenominational youth association aimed at revitalizing Sunday schools. Young people received greater recognition. The church gained a new method for extending its influence. Nonparticipating denominations created their own fellowships for young people. A Christian Endeavor Society appeared in the twin cities during the next decade. By 1893, several Moorhead ministers objected, claiming it interfered with their own youth groups. Yet the Methodist Epworth League held a reception at the YMCA for the Fargo and Moorhead Christian Endeavor Society as well as the Young People's Baptist Union. The society remained active in Fargo for some time. It began 1896 with a social at the YMCA and sent twenty-seven delegates in June to a convention at Wahpeton, North

The members of the Moorhead First Congregational Ladies Union, shown here in 1909, helped their church. Courtesy First Congregational UCC Moorhead Archives.

Dakota. Later that summer, a member objected to Sunday baseball in Fargo. According to John Orchard, the game was "the [best] incentive to our faith for bad morals, bad companions, bad language and Sabbath breaking." Pastor Edgar Day strongly promoted Christian Endeavor participation at First Presbyterian, but Baptist, Congregational, English Lutheran, and Methodist congregations preferred to form their own fellowships. An especially active First Baptist group hosted the North Dakota Baptist Young People's Union Rally in December 1896.[14]

Each congregation relied on its Ladies Aid. At Fargo First Presbyterian, for example, it included all women and met at a member's home. It sewed clothing for the needy, called on the sick, cleaned the building, taught Sunday school, supported the youth organization, and raised money by myriad means. Women of all churches made fancy or useful articles for sale at fairs or festivals. They prepared foods for seasonal suppers or dinners. Fruit and ice cream festivals occurred in summer. Suppers that served oysters in every style—stewed, fried, boiled, roasted, or raw—took place in winter. In addition, women might recite literature, sing songs, or play musical instruments. No matter what event they sponsored, proceeds went for construction, furnishings, an organ, fuel, or salaries at their respective churches. Sometimes they donated revenues to city poor relief or other charitable causes. Denominations on occasion revealed distinctive qualities. Congregationalists held New England suppers of beans, brown bread, and pumpkin pies or maple sugar socials. Episcopalians danced or played cards at their socials, unlike other Protestants. The Unitarians supported a Woman's Free Reading Room that offered leading magazines for the use of patrons—*Atlantic, Harper's, Ladies' Home Journal, Nation,* and many others.[15]

Support for home and foreign missions—one of their most important activities—bound congregations together. In their appeals to parishioners, ministers could assume knowledge of missionary endeavors. The Fargo First Presbyterian Women's Missionary Society and most other ladies' groups promoted the cause through study, worship, offerings, and sewing. Mission work peaked in the late nineteenth century when the YMCA and the Student Volunteer Movement recruited hundreds of collegians who dreamed of evangelizing the world in their lifetimes. This demonstrated that "the Protestant churches . . . were buoyant and optimistic about the future," according to Martin Marty. Meanwhile, home missions continued among the unchurched in the West and the immigrants in the cities. The Fargo First Baptist Ladies Aid, for example, funded and conducted a mission school on lower Front Street. By early 1889, the Sunday school enrolled forty-seven and the sewing school twenty. The women made ninety-five visits and distributed twenty-five garments to the sick and poor.[16]

Twin city congregations relied on businessmen for leadership and financial aid. Banker Jay Cooke pledged $150 to Moorhead Methodists for their first church. The Northern Pacific donated lots for the Fargo Methodist and Episcopalian churches. It shipped Methodist lumber and other materials without charge. Judge Charles A. Pollock explained corporate generosity: "There is a demand for . . . the religious ideal in civic

Lumber dealer W. H. White provided leadership as a trustee and Sabbath scholar at Fargo First Methodist Church. Courtesy Institute for Regional Studies, North Dakota State University, Fargo (51.126.1).

life. Without the church no . . . city can be built and prosper." Lumber dealer William H. White typified the role played by businessmen in their respective congregations. He helped found the Methodist Sunday school in 1873. He served eight years as its superintendent, but remained a Sabbath scholar until his death. White became chair of the trustee board for the newly established church, a position he also held for a lifetime. Martin Marty has maintained that mercantile predominance in religious life during an industrial capitalist age affected Christian teachings. Evangelical ministers and theologians "progressively identified . . . with competitive individualism at the expense of the community." Clergy and laity viewed riches as a reward for rectitude and poverty as the just desert for moral failure. As Marty observes, "Ideas which ran counter to what middle-class and rich people . . . held as common property were not often expressed." Protestant churches therefore rejected state regulation, unions, and strikes.[17]

Several edifices erected in the 1890s evidenced religious success and expressed the refined, genteel taste that had become part of Christianity. The Gothic style, which recalled traditional faith in a commercial age, became popular nationally. St. Paul architect Cass Gilbert designed the best local example: Moorhead's St. John the Divine Episcopal Church. North Dakota Episcopalians also built the Gethsemane Cathedral in a Gothic Revival style with Anglo-Saxon characteristics. Although designed as a masonry building, limited funds dictated a wood structure built on a foundation of red sandstone. More dual city congregations, however, favored the Romanesque design. It featured "round arches, heavy masonry, fewer materials, simpler forms and Medieval-inspired ornament." Fargo architects George and Walter Hancock used the style for their city's First Congregational and Unitarian churches. Similar elements appeared as well in Moorhead's First Congregational. Boosters took pride in these buildings. For example, the *Fargo Forum* hailed the "asymmetrical red-brick Richardsonian-Romanesque" structure of First Methodist as a "palatial" place of worship and a "credit to the city." It contained an auditorium that seated more than three hundred; a large Sunday school room; a Ladies Aid meeting room; and a basement equipped with a kitchen, pantry, and dining room for church suppers. These made it the first in the twin cities that could host most congregational events.[18]

Evangelical Protestants relied on revivals to sustain their members, save the unconverted, and win new converts. Congregations often conducted revivals annually to renew their own parishioners. On other occasions, several congregations joined together in sponsoring a community-wide campaign to increase the membership of all churches. According to Rowland Berthoff, revivalism appealed to people experiencing economic change and social disruption. It disseminated religion nationally, but at the cost of a less

Architect Cass Gilbert's Gothic design for Moorhead's St. John the Divine Episcopal Church represented a popular style in 1898. Courtesy Clay County Historical Society.

theologically rigorous faith. It made liberation from sin in part a voluntary choice by individuals. At the same time, successful conversions enhanced church discipline. More Christians dedicated to living a godly life, revival advocates maintained, strengthened communal social order as well.[19]

In 1885, "earnest evangelists" the Reverend and Mrs. H. F. Williams conducted a monthlong gospel and temperance campaign in the twin cities. The couple sang duets and took prayers upon request before the reverend delivered his sermon. More prayers and gospel hymns followed. They performed nightly at the crowded Fargo Presbyterian Church before conducting meetings at the Methodist and Baptist churches in both cities. They shared the platform with local ministers from these denominations and directed additional prayer meetings and Bible readings during the day. The large numbers responding to the "altar call" or retiring to the inquiry room for special instruction measured the success of this campaign.[20]

Community crusades as well as congregational revivals continued into the next decade. Well-known evangelists Dwight L. Moody, William A. (Billy) Sunday, and others appeared. During a monthlong 1893 visit, the Reverend E. E. Davidson stirred enthusiasm at the Presbyterian church and an audience numbering five hundred at the Fargo Armory. He then moved across the river for meetings at an overflowing opera house, where he expected four hundred conversions. According to the *Moorhead Weekly News*, Davidson avoided "shallow sensationalism." He appealed rationally to his listeners' conscience, stressing that heaven is in one's heart and in doing good for one's neighbor.[21]

During a three-day crusade at Fargo's First Methodist Church conducted four years later, Moody attracted audiences of more than 1,200 people for morning, afternoon, and evening meetings. Assisted by Captain Burke, "the singing evangelist, whose sweet tenor voice has touched many a sinful heart," Moody delivered "clear, concise argument devoid of abstruse verbiage and flowery eloquence." He simply delivered a "logical exposition of the word of God and the path of duty." Twin city Christians also welcomed revivalists known for their "shallow sensationalism." The intensely earnest "Billy" Sunday appeared a few months before Moody at the YMCA, the Fargo Congregational Church, and a packed opera house. He delivered sermons on the topics "Baptism and the Holy Spirit," "Choosing," and "Hard Nuts for Skeptics to Crack." He returned two years later for several meetings in Moorhead during which he attacked Mayor Jacob Kiefer for running a "wide-open" city, and he condemned church members for attending the theater, card parties, and dances.[22]

Liturgical churches are not known for revivalism; Episcopalians and Roman Catholics therefore stood aloof from community campaigns. Nevertheless, they sponsored renewal. St. John's Episcopal Church in 1885 held mission meetings "to arouse the regular congregation to more earnestness and also to gain the attention of those who stand aloof from the church." Similar meetings followed at Gethsemane Episcopal Cathedral. More than five hundred Catholics attended a mission conducted by the Dominicans. The Catholic church held missions frequently to combat the desire of many

Catholic ethnics for more freedom from an Irish-dominated hierarchy as well as religious apathy and Protestant evangelism. They featured hellfire sermons aimed at conversions. The numbers that flocked to the confessionals afterward measured success. Catholic evangelism thus combated sin through the sacrament of penance. It also imposed ritual devotions and banned drunkenness, gambling, and sexual license.[23]

Protestant as well as Catholic revivalists emphasized the private religion that had characterized the nineteenth-century evangelical movement. It stressed individual salvation above all else. As Martin Marty observes, "The program of 'private Protestantism' was more appealing to middle-America for it has tended more often to approve the given social order." Evangelical Protestants therefore focused on eliminating poverty, crime, and injustice by correcting individual behavior. Toward that end they demanded public schools or Christian academies, temperance crusades, and strict enforcement of the North Dakota or Clay County prohibition laws once these were enacted.[24]

The highly mobile U.S. society of the nineteenth century, Rowland Berthoff has argued, assigned several fundamental tasks to public schools. Citizens expected schools to transmit the Western cultural heritage to thousands of new settlements; "to assume the disciplinary functions that the family, church and community had abdicated"; and to "impart a common culture to the children of every class, ethnic origin or religion." By teaching a common creed composed of the individualism, self-help, and patriotism of the middle class, schools functioned as an American established church. For example, McGuffey's readers and similar textbooks inculcated shared values. McGuffey preached religion, morality, and education to advance civilization in the West. Americans bought 100 million copies of his popular text between 1850 and 1900.[25]

Similarly, educator Catharine Beecher told female teachers to go west and civilize the frontier. She applied the cult of domesticity to public education. Classrooms extended the home; teachers, like mothers, nurtured children. Women came to dominate teaching in the West as they had in the East. Some migrated westward as part of Catharine Beecher's educational crusade to save the region from barbarism. Others viewed teaching as a career in which they could achieve independence as professionals, however poorly paid. Still others viewed it as a temporary job until they married.[26]

Twin city residents established public education as early as churches, and for similar reasons. Female teachers furthered civilization by inculcating knowledge and the American creed. Horace Mann, president of Antioch College, had educated New York–born Andrew McHench, who became the first Cass County superintendent of schools and organized Fargo School

Fargo built its impressive Central High School in 1883, demonstrating an early commitment to public education. Courtesy Institute for Regional Studies, North Dakota State University, Fargo (Folio 54.24.1).

district no. 1 on April 22, 1874. Fargo built north and south side "ward school houses" after electing William P. Burdick as first city superintendent in 1880. It completed the Central High and Grade School by mid-1883 at a cost of seventy thousand dollars. The impressive structure occupied a full block at Third Avenue and Ninth Street South. At that time the public schools enrolled 550 pupils instructed by thirteen female teachers. By 1895, steam-heated brick schools in each ward had a pole and flags for appropriate observances. Special day exercises, scientific temperance, and thorough discipline afforded additional religious, moral, and patriotic instruction. A male superintendent supervised thirty female teachers and 1,312 students now enrolled. Every spring, the community witnessed educational achievement proudly displayed at literary and rhetorical exercises, as well as high school commencement ceremonies.[27]

At that time the *Forum* editorialized: "Good schools show the stability of the community; they have a moral as well as literary aspect; the results are shown in every walk of life." Annual institutes and monthly meetings trained teachers who educated children "to become good citizens and edify . . . the communities in which they live." To that end, educators battled the pernicious effects of popular dime novels. These fostered misbehavior among boys and sowed "seeds that may blossom into crime." The board of education debated for a long time before it allowed superintendent Emerson H. Smith to purchase rattans for administering corporal punishment to the recalcitrant. Board opponents, however, preferred expulsion to beating. Indeed, expulsion and corporal punishment were methods of last resort for securing good behavior.[28]

Public educators extended the Americanizing benefits received by immigrant children to their parents at the turn of the century. The Cass County superintendent of schools and the North Dakota Federation of Women's Clubs founded Neighborhood Clubs at Washington, Longfellow, and other ward schools. When mothers became involved, they requested English instruction for themselves and a night school soon followed.[29]

Newly appointed Clay County commissioners organized the first Moorhead public school district in April 1873. Voters elected businessmen James Douglas, Andrew Holes, and James H. Sharp to the school board. The Pennsylvania-born Sharp served for thirty-three years, doing much for public education. The *Red River Star* hailed the first five-month term as "evidence of the progress of civilization." By the following May, forty-seven pupils necessitated constructing the first building on lots donated by the LS&PS Company. Overcrowding soon led to building a larger two-story brick school named for James Sharp in 1880. Although intended only as a high school, Sharp School housed lower grades until 1884, when elementary schools had been completed in the first and third wards. At some time before 1900, the board constructed the second ward Park School.[30]

As happened in many other western towns, Yankee businessmen founded Christian academies and colleges in Moorhead and Fargo. This epidemic of educational endeavor stemmed from boosters wanting to transform each place into an "Athens of the West." Desiring to save the region from barbarism, Protestant missionaries transplanted their versions of Christianity. Many of these institutions expired from the financial weakness of new towns and denominations. The struggle for survival paradoxically forced many denominational colleges into nonsectarianism. Schools also adopted coeducation as a convenient way to increase enrollments. The West thus led the nation in offering higher education to women.[31]

Editor Alanson W. Edwards wrote Northern Pacific president Frederick Billings in 1881, soliciting funds for the proposed Methodist Red River University in Fargo. He assured Billings that the trustees included banker Ezra B. Eddy, businessman Evan S. Tyler, and other prominent citizens. Despite endorsements by the Ministerial Association of the Red River District and the Minnesota Annual Conference, fund-raising efforts that continued intermittently for the next several years never raised sufficient money. Meanwhile, the efforts of W. H. Davy and R. R. Briggs to attract the Methodist college to Moorhead failed owing to the spite of Fargo, according to the *Moorhead Weekly News*. Moorhead boosters campaigned for a Presbyterian college in 1882. A meeting at Bruns Opera House donated forty acres, pledged eight thousand dollars, and created a committee to solicit additional subscriptions. Fargo boosters similarly formed a committee of notables to recruit donors, but their appeal received an underwhelming response. These twin city efforts came to naught when the Red River presbytery accepted the bid of Casselton, Dakota Territory, which offered less land but more cash.[32]

Not all of Moorhead's efforts failed. In 1882, the Reverend Thomas E. Dickey established the Bishop Whipple Academy as a school for boys. It provided English, classical, and business education. It developed manly character. Although named for an Episcopalian bishop, dedicated with Episcopalian ceremonies, and governed by an Episcopalian minister and trustees, the school was owned by a private corporation of leading businessmen. At a cost of twenty-five thousand dollars, they erected a handsome, three-story Queen Anne building that occupied two blocks donated by Solomon Comstock. Dedicated in early 1883, the building had room for sixty boarders and forty day students, but classes began with only ten residents and twenty enrolled. Dickey reported a loss of $1,400 during the first year. He announced plans to recruit boys from Montana and St. Paul with the aid of passes from the Manitoba and Northern Pacific. Numbers did not expand sufficiently to sustain the institution after June 1887. The property served as "Normal Home" for that new school until purchased by the Northwestern Lutheran College Association. It became Concordia College in 1891.[33]

Fargo College originated in a Yankee idea that Christian education perpetuated democracy. The Reverend Orville C. Clark of the new First Congregational Church and the Reverend H. C. Simmons of the Home Missionary Society called the convention that started the process for founding a Christian academy. To secure the school, Fargo offered ten thousand dollars and the old fairgrounds. The committee chose the city in 1886 but rejected the low, marshy site.[34]

The "college" opened the next September in the old Masonic hall with one professor who enrolled three students after one month. It occupied different locations in the next three years until it acquired a lovely ten-acre tract overlooking Island Park. A twenty thousand-dollar gift made possible the first building, dedicated in October 1890. The three stories of George H. Jones Memorial Hall contained dormitory rooms, chapel, library, recitation rooms, laboratories, and offices; it initially housed the college preparatory course, four-year college course, and conservatory of music. A twenty-four thousand-dollar gift from Matthew T. Dill—a Wisconsin grain merchant and North Dakota landowner—funded Dill Hall, completed in 1906. Andrew Carnegie contributed twenty thousand dollars for the Carnegie College Library that Theodore Roosevelt dedicated in 1910.[35]

Fargo College, photographed in the early 1900s, intended to transplant Congregationalism and Anglo-Saxon values to the Northwest. Courtesy Institute for Regional Studies, North Dakota State University, Fargo (2006.60.3).

The articles of incorporation specified the enrollment of students irrespective of race, sex, or creed. Twelve professorships, ambitiously designated but never staffed completely, ranged from moral philosophy to manual training. One professor facetiously described his chair as a settee because he taught philosophy, ethics, political science, and education. At the first commencement in 1896, just three college and eleven high school students graduated. Two years later, enrollment numbered thirty-three collegians, eighty-one preparatory scholars, and sixty-eight music students. Until the school closed in 1922, collegians graduated each year, with the largest class totaling twenty-six in 1916.[36]

The New York-born Reverend George Barnes initially headed Fargo College. His own education at Oberlin had been shaped by its president, well-known revivalist Charles G. Finney. Speaking at the dedication of Jones Hall, Barnes articulated the college mission in terms of the ideology of Anglo-Saxon Protestantism. According to that tradition, the United States must be kept white and Protestant in order for American evangelicals to fulfill their Christianizing world mission. Barnes cast the college as an agent for transplanting Congregationalism and Anglo-Saxon dominance to the Northwest. Both the church and the race served the broader interests of humanity and Christianity. Both were heirs to and custodians of the interconnected ideas of civil liberty and spiritual Christianity, which all peoples required in order to progress. The North Dakota governor, the superintendent of public instruction, and a large audience heard Barnes's address. The local Presbyterian pastor delivered the invocation and the Methodist minister read Scripture. Although Barnes rallied all Evangelical Protestants and northwest Europeans to the college cause, his effort did not win the Catholics and Lutherans, who composed almost 75 percent of the sixty-four thousand church members in North Dakota.[37]

Throughout its brief thirty-five-year life of financial struggle, the school defined itself as a community and nonsectarian institution. The conservatory of music staged many concerts that publicized the college. These frequently attracted large audiences to the campus and enhanced the city's culture. Although the charter specified that two-thirds of the trustees must be Congregationalists, the school did not restrict professors by affiliation. It welcomed students of every faith and nationality, striving only to make them Christian. The many Germans, German Russians, and Scandinavians who enrolled likely attended the evening classes that offered instruction in English and business.[38]

Nonsectarian and communal appeals continued during the following decade. At an 1891 public meeting called by the trustees, Episcopal and Methodist ministers called the college broadly Christian. Mayor Wilbur

Ball declared that the city should support the institution. Attorney Charles Pollack suggested that a growing school would expand the metropolis. As Methodist Alanson W. Edwards editorialized in the *Forum* a few years later: "[It is] non-sectarian in character . . . belongs to the city and state . . . and its success should be the pride of all. . . . Every individual should lend such aid . . . as is in his power." Newspaper accounts of commencement further publicized its work.[39]

Nonetheless, lack of cash always starved the college. It operated with an annual deficit and depended heavily on the largesse of eastern Congregationalists. Although President Reuben Beard in 1894 secured a $50,000 gift from Dr. D. K. Pearson of Chicago, it stipulated that residents raise $150,000 within a decade. This proved extremely difficult during an economic slump and after fire had destroyed the business district. Efforts intensified as the depression abated and the deadline approached. Congregational churches staged rallies throughout North Dakota. Finally, aided by large gifts from James J. Hill and the Congregational Education Society, the college fulfilled Pearson's conditions. It created a $200,000 endowment in 1902.[40]

Finances still remained problematic. The trustees debated dismissing President John H. Morley. The grounds included his age, inability to do the work, and, most important, "failure to secure money." Unable to solve their money problems, the trustees finally closed the college in 1922. The Great Crash of 1929 finally ended continuous fund-raising efforts by loyal alumni to reopen the school.[41]

State colleges fared better than private in the twin cities. Legislative funding, at times inadequate, proved sufficient for survival. In addition, public institutions served boosters equally well as did religious ones. The legislature founded Moorhead Normal in 1885 by passing a bill introduced by Senator Comstock. He gave the six acres that his bill promised the city would award the state. At the next session, he secured the money for erecting the main building. Next to Comstock, the first president did most in launching the school. Livingston C. Lord worked for slightly more than a decade. An excellent administrator and teacher, he imparted the moral and educational values of New England Congregationalism to the faculty, students, and community. By 1899, the Normal enrolled 285, mostly in the preparatory course. Many came from families of limited means and sacrificed to attend. Two daughters of farmer R. M. Probstfield, for example, saved boarding expenses during the depressed 1890s by driving four miles each day.[42]

Given the booster ideology embraced by Fargo promoters, it is surprising they did not more actively solicit the NDAC and Experiment Station. Residents responded indifferently to the first legislative proposal in 1883. They regarded a hospital for the insane or penitentiary as more desirable.

Others, who backed the projected Congregational institution, may have perceived an agricultural school as antithetical to that goal. Nevertheless, several Fargo men swayed the 1889 constitutional convention to locate NDAC near their municipality. Inhabitants dismissed the "cow college." Few perceived the advantages it would bring. Many farmers resented state appropriations for an alien institution located in a metropolis tied so closely to corporate wealth and power. Local opinion changed more quickly than state attitudes. When Mrs. W. H. Hays taught domestic economy in 1891, she enrolled fifty-six women, including a number from the Fargo elite. By 1896, more students perceived the chances for liberal learning. As the college course grew along with music and theater programs, the cultural advantages of the "people's college" became clear.[43]

Urban middle-class Yankees founded churches to transplant Evangelical Protestantism to the West. They established public and religious schools to transmit knowledge and civic virtue. They planned elaborate July Fourth observances for uniting an ethnically segmented population. Business and civic elites in many other cities at this time used holiday celebrations for creating an American identity and upholding social order. Independence Day commemorations drew large crowds to Moorhead and Fargo from nearby towns and the countryside. All groups honored American nationality, as the sponsors doubtless intended, but this did not prevent them from also embracing their ethnic traditions. Additionally, special group events had replaced the community-wide celebration by 1900, despite the desire to preserve the patriotic rites.[44]

The first holiday observance took place in 1873 just opposite the Headquarters Hotel. Residents enjoyed a program of music, prayer, speeches, artillery salutes, refreshments, and toasts that ended with an evening dance at the hotel. By 1879, the twin cities jointly celebrated "the Glorious Fourth." The day started at Chapin Hall. A procession headed by the Fargo Brass Band marched through the dual metropolis to Island Park for prayers and patriotic speeches. After a dinner, several hundred attended horse races at the Moorhead Driving Park. In the evening, 250 boarded the *Grandin* for a Red River excursion, returning for fireworks followed by a dance.[45]

Festivities expanded in the next decade. In 1882, the *Fargo Daily Republican* headline screamed: "In the Metropolis . . . Fourth of July Celebrated in Grand Style." A mile-long procession formed on Northern Pacific Avenue in Fargo. It included two bands, police and fire departments, two costumed theatrical companies, the Sons of Hermann (a German lodge), many business-sponsored wagons, city officials and citizens in decorated carriages. After marching through both cities, the parade ended at Island Park for prayers, speeches, and music. Father J. A. Stephan, the Catholic priest, delivered the invocation followed by lawyer Charles Pollock's reading of the Declaration of Independence. Colonel Patrick Donan's spread-eagle oration celebrated U.S. military triumphs and westward expansion. Speaking of the "Dakota garden spot" and the "Red River Eden," Donan told the audience that they held the territory's destiny in their hands. He urged them to "make it a land of God and morality, of law, order and . . . liberty." A speech in Norwegian by John C. Miller and another in German by J. H. Warnken concluded the program. After dinners at homes or picnics in the park, citizens spent the afternoon and evening in promenading, games, or dancing, which contin-ued far into the night, interrupted only by fireworks. The dual city annually held elaborate festivals for several years.[46]

The next decade saw smaller community-wide celebrations and infrequent parades. Each city now observed the holiday separately. The *Fargo Daily Argus* in 1890 reported "a very quiet 4th." The only public celebration took place at a Union Picnic sponsored by the Catholic Church Ladies in Island Park. Following the more extensive festivities of 1892, the Fargo fire limited the next year's fete. Nonetheless, several thousand people attended the Catholic picnic, which donated its proceeds to the Fire Relief Fund. Afternoon sports and evening fireworks followed a traditional patriotic program. The *Fargo Forum* called the 1894 event "the quietest celebration ever known at the cross-ing." The lack of any municipal commemoration made the next year even qui-eter. Yet an indignant *Forum* preferred such quiet to desecrating the holiday with liquor and gambling as the Moorhead saloon element did.[47]

The city's twenty-fifth anniversary in 1896 occasioned a return to more extensive festivities. Although the revelry attracted several thousand visi-tors, the *Forum* proudly reported "no accidents, no injuries, no drunken-ness . . . [and] no rioting." Fargo's peaceful patriotism contrasted starkly with the indecencies staged by Moorhead's "jag joints." By 1899, the elabo-rately staged Fargo Fire Festival had assumed such commercial importance and consumed so much municipal energy that the city fathers refused to sponsor a July Fourth community commemoration. Most businesses still closed, however. The Grand Army of the Republic (GAR), the Norwegian Baptists, and numerous other groups observed the national holiday with picnics of their own. This substitution of private for public observances marked the end to an era in the twin cities. No longer did Yankees stage community Independence Day celebrations to impart an American identity to their ethnic neighbors.[48]

Yankees resembled other frontier newcomers in lacking a common iden-tity. Like the immigrants, they formed associations to share memories and give meaning to their lives. In November 1882, they created a New England

Moorhead patriotically celebrated the Fourth of July in the early 1890s. Courtesy Clay County Historical Society.

Society in Fargo with eighty-nine members. By 1894, the Cass and Clay County Society held its first annual banquet attended by two hundred celebrants of Forefather's Day. Speakers honored the Pilgrims' landing by recounting New England contributions to the United States. Despite Puritan shortcomings of intolerance, persecution, and mistreatment of Indians, they had valued education and "had taught . . . the right . . . to self-government." They had thereby greatly influenced the "history and fortunes of this mighty Republican Empire." Such confusing of the Pilgrim and Puritan traditions in American memory typified these celebrations in Fargo and other northern communities after the Civil War.[49]

Middle-class Yankees embraced Thanksgiving as a state-sanctioned occasion for celebrating the family and the American nation. By 1900, schoolteachers had transformed the holiday into an Americanizing event. Twin city newspapers reported worship services, dinners, dances, and other commemorations. By stating that all groups, from African to Norwegian, had generally observed the day, the *Daily Republican* made its nationalism explicit. The

Forum expressed similarly thankful sentiments in 1898: "All sections had been brought together . . . into closer bonds of national purpose and identity" by the end of the Spanish-American War. Several Old American congregations annually hosted Union Thanksgiving Services. Many ethnic groups embraced the holiday. The Fargo Swedish Baptist Church, for example, held a dinner followed by worship. Like those first immigrants—the Pilgrims— Swedes and other Europeans gave thanks for the bounty of America. Food symbolized the blending of national identities as women served ethnic side dishes and desserts along with the traditional American turkey.[50]

Honorary Yankees

The booster ideology of the twin city commercial and civic elite committed them to welcoming all ethnic groups because they increased numbers and promoted economic growth. Yet boosters prized some nationalities more highly than others. For example, the Northern Pacific Land Department principally recruited Norwegians, Swedes, and Germans for settling the northern plains. Anglo-Saxons preferred these Nordic peoples in contrast to the undesirable Alpine and Mediterranean races. These northwest Europeans shared important values with middle-class Yankees. Most were Protestant, valued education, and practiced the work ethic. They subscribed to the cult of domesticity and indoctrinated their children with the Victorian values of piety, character, and respectability. These qualities made Norwegians, Swedes, and Germans honorary Yankees.[51]

The relatively rapid assimilation of immigrants aided the booster strategy for community building. Physical factors that barred groups from attaining absolute physical segregation fostered integration. Newcomers often relocated rather quickly, preventing the formation of a stable community. Rapid growth normally kept housing in short supply, forcing immigrants to live where they could. Ethnic women frequently worked as live-in domestics for American families. The relatively small urban population ensured constant face-to-face contact between groups in business and politics. Although ethnic groups formed separate cultural institutions, these functioned similarly to those of the Yankees in maintaining the communal moral order. Moreover, immigrants shared similar values of self-improvement with old-stock Americans.[52]

Immigrants glorified "the possibilities of American citizenship," as ethnic historian Jon Gjerde has observed. Instead of discarding their European culture, they developed dual and complementary loyalties to the United States and their ethnic communities. Immigrants prized America because "freedom" and "self-rule" gave them the liberty to establish communities defined by religion, language, and culture. Although the West offered the possibility of prosperity for both Americans and immigrants, European cultural leaders feared the detrimental effects of corrosive individualism. They worked to maintain corporate loyalties to church and family, often resisting assimilation that manifested itself in language, dress, political allegiance, and other behaviors. These strategies appealed more effectively to corporate-minded Dutch Calvinists, German Catholics, and Missouri Synod Lutherans than they did to pietistic Scandinavian Lutherans more readily attracted to liberal individualism.[53]

Drawn by the rich land, Norwegians arrived among the first rural settlers of the Red River Valley. By 1900, a large number had concentrated in Fargo and Moorhead. Christine Hagen, an immigrant whose family homesteaded on the Wild Rice River, later recalled her life in the Norwegian ethnic community and the attractions of Fargo for a young girl. Her confirmation in 1878 necessitated a trip to the city in order to buy shoes and the material to make her dress for the occasion. Soon she went to work at the Minnesota House, owned by Peter Johnson, a friend of the family. Timid among strangers and unaccustomed to hotel work, she left to starch men's shirts at a laundry. She worked there three consecutive winters, living at the owner's home. For enjoyment, she spent Saturday evenings at Norway Hall, the social center for Scandinavian youth. She enjoyed celebrating Norwegian Independence Day and worshipping in a real church! She married countryman Erick Stafne in 1883, after she and her mother had prepared the essentials for housekeeping. The lengthy wedding sermon stressed the religious and moral obligations of marriage.[54]

Evening entertainment in her new home often consisted of a Scandinavian newspaper from Chicago, the Lutheran *Folkebladet* from Minneapolis, the *Normanden* from Grand Forks, and the *Fargo Forum*. Her children left home for further education beyond the common school. She preferred sending them to Concordia College, which her contributions had helped build, but could only afford two winter terms for one child. Her others attended Moorhead Normal, attracted by free textbooks, low tuition, and nearby relatives with whom to board. Although she educated her offspring in English, Mrs. Stafne supported the preservation of Norwegian language and culture in the Red River Valley. She recalled fondly the leadership of Dr. Herman Fjelde for placing statues of Norwegian cultural heroes in Fargo: Bjørstjerne Bjørnson at NDAC, Henry Vergeland in Island Park, Ivar Aasen at Concordia, and Rollo at the Great Northern station. Dr. Fjelde also fostered chapters of the Sons of Norway and Daughters of Norway in Fargo and elsewhere.[55]

Scandinavian immigrants encountered prejudice and discrimination in the twin cities. Class, as much as ethnic bias, motivated these instances. Ellen Cooley's novel about the Fargo boom criticized Scandinavian servants who knew no English. One character declares: "A girl deaf, dumb, and blind would be as efficient as . . . Norwegian 'help.'" Similarly, the large homes and well-landscaped lawns of the Moorhead elite required low-paid Scandinavian domestic labor for maintenance. Workers called this neighborhood "the silk-stocking district," indicating their heightened awareness of class distinction. The *Argus* and *Times* criticized "Norwegian whiskey" and blamed foreigners for moral disorder. Two Norwegian saloonkeepers and their working-class countrymen, who at times became drunk and disorderly, prompted these attacks. In one incident, the patriotic city marshal ordered the removal of a Norwegian flag because only American flags could be displayed in the city. On another occasion, the *Argus* attacked a Norwegian candidate for municipal office by saying that dealers in vice supported him. Respectable Norwegians rejected these negative accounts as the malicious slander of good citizens. The *Moorhead Daily News* defended the veracity of its reports and denied any prejudice against Scandinavians who were "industrious, peaceful, moral, temperate and honest."[56]

At times ridiculed and treated as second-class citizens, Norwegians and other nationalities took refuge in ethnic communities. According to historian Kathleen Conzen and geographer Robert Ostergren, community building required certain elements. Ethnic groups needed sufficient numbers for a church or another institutional rallying point. A chain migration of relatives and neighbors as well as long-term persistence in an area by the first generation, their children, and their countrymen fostered concentrated settlement. Local Norwegians, Swedes, and Germans established churches that formed the core of their ethnic communities. They founded newspapers, schools, and other associations as well, but these lacked permanence.[57]

Dual city Norwegians did not create a monolithic ethnic community. The Lutherans fractured into three synods. Others became Baptists and Congregationalists or did not affiliate with any church. Middle- and working-class immigrants formed three Norwegian Lutheran congregations during the first decade of settlement. All shared pastors with nearby rural churches. All formed Sunday schools, Vacation Bible schools, and Ladies Aid societies. All struggled to build and maintain sanctuaries. All received less substantial home missionary support than Old American denominations. By the 1890s, two had affiliated with the United Norwegian Lutheran Church of America and the other with the Lutheran Free Church. Norwegian Synod members organized St. Paul's Evangelical Lutheran Church in 1903.[58]

Visits by missionary pastors prompted formation of the Norwegian Evangelical Lutheran Church at a Moorhead home in 1872. Unable to sup-

NAME	LOCATION	FOUNDED	MEMBERS (CA. 1900)
First Norwegian Lutheran	Roberts Street and Fourth Avenue North, Fargo	1872	N/A
St. Joseph's Catholic	Fourth Street and Second Avenue North, Moorhead	1873	N/A
Pontoppidan Norwegian Lutheran	Fourth Street and Fourth Avenue North, Fargo	1877	N/A
German Zion Evangelical	Tenth Street and First Avenue South, Fargo	1877	30
Bethesda Swedish Lutheran	Sixth Street and Second Avenue South, Moorhead	1880	315
St. Mary's Catholic	Broadway and Sixth Avenue North, Fargo	1880	N/A
Norwegian Trinity Lutheran	Seventh Street and Second Avenue South, Moorhead	1882	250
First Norwegian Baptist	Fourth Street and Second Avenue North, Fargo	1883	100
Scandinavian Christian Mission	Moorhead (no church building)	1883	N/A
Scandinavian Congregational	Fourth Street and Third Avenue North, Fargo	1891	N/A
Elim Swedish Lutheran	321 Ninth Street North, Fargo	1891	N/A
First Swedish Baptist	Fourth Street and Third Avenue North, Fargo	1891	75
German Grace Lutheran	Fargo (no church building)	1898	N/A

Immigrant churches in Fargo and Moorhead. From *Fargo and Moorhead City Directory, 1900.*

port its sanctuary, the congregation finally sold its property and moved to Fargo. It became the First Norwegian Evangelical Lutheran Church in 1892 and erected a building three years later. A Fargo home meeting in December 1877 organized the Pontoppidan Norwegian–Danish Evangelical Lutheran Church. After the Fargo fire destroyed its house of worship, the congregation immediately rebuilt. Sixteen charter members—a flour miller, a carpenter,

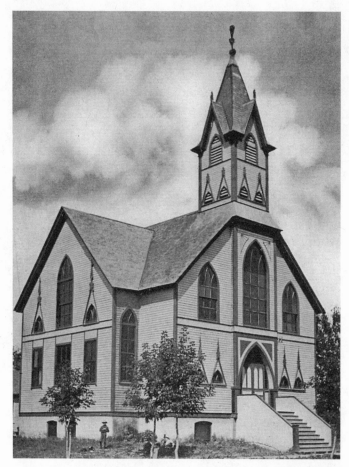

The Pontoppidan Norwegian–Danish Evangelical Lutheran Church, founded in 1877, erected this building immediately after the fire in Fargo in 1893. Courtesy Institute for Regional Studies, North Dakota State University, Fargo (2070.190.1).

a saloon owner, two farmers, and six storekeepers—founded the Moorhead Norwegian Trinity Lutheran Church in December 1882 without pastoral assistance. They erected a sanctuary in 1884 and, after a decade, built a larger one.[59]

Pontoppidan established what might have been the city's first temperance society in 1881. Other Lutheran bodies rallied to the cause. Pontoppidan pastor S. L. Romsdahl assumed leadership in founding Oak Grove Ladies Seminary in 1903 and St. Luke's Hospital in 1908. Both expressed traditions of the Norway state church, which for centuries had provided schools and institutions to care for the sick, aged, and poor. Therefore, middle-class Norwegian churchwomen in America initially embraced the nursing and teaching professions. They also played an important role in voluntary charity work.[60]

A Ladies Aid society sustained each Norwegian Lutheran congregation by raising money, supporting missions, caring for the unfortunate, and educating youth. Their stamina helped erect buildings and ensured survival. Women's societies originated from the Haugean mission movement in Norway. After their transplantation to the United States, Anglo-American Protestant women's groups influenced them. As congregations became more established, mission work assumed greater importance. By the early twentieth century, each synod had a women's organization, although women did not vote or hold office in most congregations until the 1940s. The Norwegian Lutheran Church, created from the merger of three synods in 1917, soon formed the Women's Missionary Federation. The North Dakota district met for the first time in 1919.[61]

Many nineteenth-century Norwegian immigrants insisted that churches and religious schools must use the "language of the heart" so long as families spoke it at home. Trinity and its sister congregations therefore worshipped entirely in Norwegian until after the turn of the century. A breech in this linguistic wall occurred in 1899 when Trinity hosted the Swedish and English Lutheran churches for a joint Reformation service. A combined Norwegian and Swedish choir furnished music. Pastors delivered addresses in Norwegian, Swedish, and English. The congregation sang Luther's "A Mighty Fortress" in all three languages simultaneously. Three Norwegian Lutheran synods wrestled with the language question at this time. To retain Americanized youth, the synods provided English hymnbooks, catechisms, and other religious materials. By 1917 the three synods conducted about 25 percent of their services and 50 percent of the Sunday school and confirmation classes in English. Trinity, as an urban congregation, shared its synod's concern for keeping the young. English Sunday school and confirmation instruction started in 1903 and 1909, respectively. After the three synods merged in 1917, Norwegian worship and teaching steadily declined. English became the official language at Trinity in 1919. It scheduled two English services and only one Norse Sunday school class. It ended Norwegian worship in 1939. Pontoppidan began English services in the 1920s, and discontinued the Norwegian one in 1942.[62]

Some Norwegians abandoned Lutheranism, and became Baptists, Methodists, and Congregationalists. Seven Norwegians and Swedes founded the First Scandinavian Baptist Church in 1883. The congregation numbered forty-five by 1888. Each Sunday, the Reverend J. A. H. Johnson conducted two worship services and Sunday school. According to the *Fargo Sunday Argus*, Pastor Johnson displayed "a great zeal and earnestness . . . in bringing young Scandinavian-born citizens of both sexes to join his congregation." Worship in the Norwegian language created dissension, however, and the Swedes withdrew to form a separate church in 1891. The First Norwegian Baptist Church erected a small building before completing a larger edifice in 1897 during the pastorate of the Reverend C. W. Finwall. He also created a Norwegian Baptist Young People's Union. After Norwegians and Swedes each adopted English in church, the two congregations merged in 1925.[63]

A Scandinavian Methodist church met for a time. Fifteen Norwegians organized the Fargo Mission church in 1891 that evolved into the Scandinavian Congregational Church two years later. Membership shrank as families left the city and the church struggled under a succession of pastors. It revived after becoming the Scandinavian Evangelical Free Church in 1910. It dropped Scandinavian from its name in 1933 when English replaced Norwegian as the official language.[64]

Like churches, newspapers affirmed ethnicity. The *Red River Star* published a column in Norwegian briefly for its "Scandinavian friends" in 1875. Norwegians warmly received the *Red River Posten,* which first appeared in April 1879 after relocating from Red Wing, Minnesota. Editor John Miller printed it on the *Argus* press and hoped to expand its circulation of a thousand readers. The *Fram* and the weekly *Fargo Posten* also appeared for a time. The *Red River Tidende* began publishing in Moorhead in January 1882 as the only Scandinavian paper in Clay County. It soon moved to Grand Forks. Populists—"broad-minded liberal thinking men who have the courage and honesty of their convictions," according to a like-minded publicist—founded the *Nye Normanden* at Moorhead in 1894. It reached a circulation of three thousand before relocating to Minneapolis the next year. The short-lived *Folkets Ven* replaced it locally.[65]

By the mid-1880s, "Little Norway" in Fargo occupied the area east of Broadway and within one to two blocks on each side of the Great Northern tracks. This concentrated Norwegian population attracted two churches, two hotels, a medical doctor, a brewer, a grocer, a druggist, two merchants, and two saloonkeepers. The anomaly of the Bohemian-born proprietor of the Scandinavian House suggests that Norwegians did not attain absolute physical segregation. Each summer, church schools instructed youngsters in Norwegian language, Lutheranism, and culture. A literary society—established with fifty members by 1882—aimed to provide a library, preserve knowledge of the language, and enlighten their fellows. It sponsored many speakers and cultural events during the following decades. Norwegians might attend concerts by local singing societies or a lecture by celebrated poet and composer Bjørstjerne Bjørnson. Norwegians also socialized at church picnics held at farmsteads or at Christmas parties hosted in homes.[66]

Norwegian ethnicity further expressed itself by establishing Concordia College, a prize for which both Fargo and Moorhead competed. Norwegians decided they needed a school for saving their youth from the Swedish Lutherans at Hope Academy and the Congregationalists at Fargo College or Moorhead Normal. The Red River Valley Lutheran Pastoral Conference organized the Northwestern Lutheran College Association. It negotiated the ten thousand-dollar purchase of six acres and the Bishop Whipple School building valued at thirty thousand dollars. Successful Fargo druggist Lars Christianson, who served forty-three years as the association secretary, gave Concordia College a business head and essential financial assistance during many emergencies. His practicality triumphed over Norwegian Lutheran piety in locating the college in Moorhead, a saloon town plagued by booze, brawls, and brothels. As Christianson recalled many years later: "When we heard of the opportunity to buy this place in Moorhead so cheap, we couldn't afford to turn down the offer."[67]

A college in name, but academy in fact, Concordia advertised itself as a Christian preparatory school for both sexes. It offered religious education, chapel exercises, and instruction to prepare students for business, teaching, or college. Practical training in parliamentary practice and the English language equipped Norwegians for American citizenship. Recent immigrants who came to learn English composed about one-half of the winter term enrollment of more than two hundred. From the start the school mirrored the dual identity of the Norwegian community that it served. Instruction in English prepared students to enter American civic and commercial life. Yet chapel services alternated between Norwegian and English. Many conversed in their native tongue outside of class.[68]

From the beginning, Norwegians affirmed their dual identity by annually commemorating the independence of both the United States and Norway. Their festivities confirmed they had "a home in America." Although they often celebrated July Fourth separately, middle-class Norwegian nationalists paralleled Yankees by championing individualism, enlightenment, and progress. On the other hand, as May 17 observances evolved from early picnics into grand processions, organizers solicited contributions from businesses and attempted to include all residents. The 1879 fete set the tone for the decade to follow. A procession of more than four hundred people headed by the Fargo Brass Band marched through the principal streets of both cities before gathering in Island Park for patriotic songs and speeches in Norwegian, Swedish, and English. The day closed with a ball at Chapin Hall. As the decade progressed, the event became more elaborate. It often began with booming cannons at the Cass County courthouse, displayed American and Scandinavian flags, and included an ever-larger parade.[69]

By the 1890s, processions disappeared from observances now planned by middle-class moralists. They appealed to the pious and temperate by substituting literary and musical programs for the alcohol and dancing of earlier celebrations. Concordia held a literary program in the morning and games in the afternoon. Four hundred people in Fargo heard patriotic

Norwegian Americans celebrated ethnic community by dedicating a Hans Nielsen Hauge monument in 1912 at Concordia College in Moorhead. Courtesy Concordia College Archives.

speeches and music delivered from a stage decorated with American and Norwegian flags.[70]

While Norwegians maintained loyalty to their motherland through worship, schools, and newspapers, they became American by participating in politics. To be sure, they pursued ethnic agendas while engaging in this American practice as they did in other areas. Nonetheless, politics brought them into face-to-face contact with Yankees and tied them more closely to present American social conditions. The supremacy of the Minnesota Republican Party before 1890 rested on a coalition of Scandinavians and native-born Americans. The *Red River Star* in 1873 admitted that without Norwegian support Republicans would be powerless. Although many had participated, few held Clay County office before 1885. Ethnic-based loyalties disintegrated as agrarian radicalism lured many Norwegians away from the Grand Old Party. In the election of 1890, only the towns of Moorhead, Barnesville, and Glyndon returned Republican pluralities.[71]

To prevent further defections to the Populist Party, the Republicans nominated Norwegian-born Knute Nelson for governor in 1892. His ethnic appeal enabled him to carry Clay County. Moorhead, with Scandinavians composing slightly more than 50 percent of the population, voted Republican for every office. Nelson's higher returns indicated ethnic loyalty. He received 6 percent more than other Republican state candidates and 20 percent more than President Benjamin Harrison. As economic distress grew, ethnic ties became less important. By 1894, poor conditions had fostered a Populist amalgamation of ethnic groups.[72]

Devotion to prohibition also drew Norwegians to politics and the Republicans. A Moorhead temperance meeting in 1894 attracted 350 Norwegian Grand Templars. A few years later, a Scandinavian WCTU speaker blamed liquor for the many idle men she saw on the streets of Moorhead, which had more saloons in proportion to its population than Chicago. She might have added that the blight resulted from her countrymen's work in making North Dakota dry. Often allied with the temperance effort led by pastors from the United and Hauge Synods as well as the Free Church, Norwegian immigrants by 1885 had formed thirty-three local abstinence societies with 1,550 members in the state. Under clergy leadership, these societies united to form the Scandinavian Temperance Party. Of the eight Norwegian-language newspapers published in the Red River Valley, only the *Fargo Posten*—edited by a man with Norwegian Synod loyalties—opposed prohibition. Persuaded by this extensive temperance campaign, Norwegian counties voted heavily for prohibition in 1889, thereby contributing to the dry victory.[73]

Like Norwegians, Swedes often qualified as honorary Yankees in the eyes of Old Americans. Their Nordic, Protestant, sober, and industrious traits made them desirable settlers. Hence, the Northern Pacific agent for Scandinavian immigration recruited many and helped them find jobs as railroad laborers, carpenters, and farmworkers along the line. Despite prohibitions by Lutheran authorities, almost one-third of Swedish men in North Dakota belonged to Masonic lodges. They saw membership as entrance into the Yankee establishment. Merchants, bankers, and physicians made up more than one-third of the 105 featured in North Dakota biographies, indicating that Swedes quickly moved beyond the boundaries of small Swedish communities into the American mainstream. Assimilation did not occur without controversy, however. In 1881, the Moorhead Swedish Lutheran minister chastised William Vedeen and his sister for attending the Knights of Pythias installation in Fargo. Vedeen responded in a letter to the *Moorhead Weekly Argonaut*. He asserted that the minister had violated the principles of American religious freedom. Moreover, secret societies that exercised the charity and benevolence taught in the Bible could not be harmful.[74]

At the same time they embraced an American identity, Swedes affirmed their traditional culture by founding churches. During the 1870s, Swedish

Lutheran circuit ministers conducted services in Moorhead homes or at the Erickson House, a hotel owned by a prominent countryman. Despite a missionary's belief that the small number of religious Swedes could not create a church, builder John L. Bjorkquist and a handful of others formed the Swedish Evangelical Lutheran Bethesda Congregation on May 4, 1880. They bought the old school, remodeled the upper story into a sanctuary, and made the first floor a parsonage. The Reverend J. O. Cavallin, the Swedish-born first minister as well as missionary for North Dakota, served ten fruitful years. He located many immigrants in the state. He increased membership to two hundred and enrolled a hundred Sunday school scholars. The Ladies Aid society paid synod and conference dues, supported missions, and maintained church property. Although devoted to ethnic community, the pastor and his congregation joined in activities with other Christians. Cavallin spoke in Swedish at the dedication of St. Mark's English Lutheran Church in Fargo. Bethesda hosted an annual meeting of the Clay County Bible Society. In 1907, the Reverend John Nyvall helped found the Northwestern Hospital in Moorhead.[75]

Ten members organized Elim Swedish Lutheran Church in Fargo on October 14, 1891. Served by Bethesda Pastor S. A. Lindholm, the fledgling body erected its first church in 1892 and soon created a Ladies Aid society, Sunday school, and Young People's Society. Although Elim did not call a resident minister until 1900, it became the mother of Fargo Lutheran churches because so many worshipped there until they built their own edifices. The congregation held on to Swedish services until 1938.[76]

Lutheran liturgy at times repelled pietistic Swedes. In 1883, some of these formed the Scandinavian Christian Mission Society of Moorhead, which eventually became an Evangelical Free Church. Fargo Swedes separated from their Norwegian brethren in 1891 and formed the First Swedish Baptist Church. It held union gospel meetings with the Norwegian Baptist and Scandinavian Congregational churches. The Ladies Aid helped pay for its building. Its ninety-four members in 1912 made it the state's second largest Swedish Baptist congregation.[77]

To educate Swedish children, Pastor J. O. Cavallin proposed an academy that he hoped would evolve into a college. A conference of Swedish Lutheran congregations formed the Lutheran Benevolent Society of the Red River Valley. It purchased an unfinished hotel located at Fifth Avenue and Eleventh Street North. Intending to make Moorhead an education center, boosters pledged five thousand dollars and building materials for Hope Academy, a coeducational school that welcomed pupils from all denominations. A large audience attended the dedication on November 1, 1888. The school opened with an enrollment of fifty-three. That doubled for the next term, filling the building to capacity. Pupils commemorated the centennial of George Washington's inauguration by listening to English and Swedish orations and by singing "America" and a Swedish anthem. On another occasion, performers dressed in Swedish national costumes presented a program in English and Swedish on alternative evenings. Although much appreciated by residents, these events did not raise sufficient funds to fulfill Pastor Cavallin's dreams. Enrollment shrank after Concordia College opened. The 1893 depression diminished financial support, forcing the school to close in 1896.[78]

Small numbers probably limited other expressions of Swedish ethnic community. According to a study of the 1880 Moorhead census by ethnic historian Joy Lintelman, the 111 Swedish-born residents included mostly working-age adults, with more transient male laborers than female domestic servants. In addition to a medical doctor, the two businessmen included wealthy John Erickson. He gave annual suppers and dances during the 1870s that "our Scandinavian friends" appreciated, according to the *Moorhead Advocate.* He served several terms as alderman and mayor before he went bankrupt in 1892. First- and second-generation Moorhead Swedes totaled 760 by 1900, with a more balanced sex ratio and children under fourteen constituting the largest age group. Lintelman concludes: "Those Swedes who had arrived as single adults in the 1880s and 1890s were now marrying and having children." The female population consisted of fewer domestics and more wives or children. More men had become skilled laborers—plasterers, carpenters, or bricklayers. Three saloon owners had joined the business class. The number of Fargo Swedes is not known, but the eight businessmen in 1884 included three liquor dealers, a farm machinery agent, a butcher, a tailor, and two hotel proprietors—one of whom owned the Germania House. *Folkvännen,* a Swedish monthly newspaper, appeared for a time at the start of the next decade.[79]

Oscar Euren later recalled how his Swedish family lived during these years. His experiences, Lintelman believes, probably typified a second-generation Swede. His father Emil—a plastering contractor—came to Moorhead with seven others in 1880. He built a house at 311 Tenth Street North in an area that was more than 25 percent Swedish by 1910. A Swedish immigrant and builder, John Gustav Bergquist, operated his first brickyard nearby. Oscar, born in 1881, completed common school before taking three winters of business courses at Concordia College. As a boy, he worked for Otto Peterson's grocery. He stocked shelves, filled and delivered orders, and cared for the delivery horses. He frequently worked late as farmers came to shop after supper. His family often visited his father's friends from Sweden. His mother frequently enjoyed coffee with neighbor women after they had pastured their family cows. Although the city had a reputation as a "Sodom of the Plains," the drunks did not trouble the boy. His experience confirms that the middle class had segregated vice successfully.[80]

In 1879, only forty-seven Germans lived in Fargo. Despite their small numbers, they founded lodges, kindergartens, newspapers, and churches.

They also helped form the city band and other musical groups. Such organizational zeal qualified them as desirable community builders and honorary Yankees. J. H. Warnken, a recently arrived machinery salesman, opened the Germania House, founded a German newspaper, and participated in organizing a German lodge in 1882. Warnken was a "jovial, wide-awake businessman and . . . a good landlord." Over the years, German women operated language schools and kindergartens in each city.[81]

The Sons of Hermann, a fraternal order similar to the Odd Fellows, preserved German language and culture. Members celebrated their installation with a parade, banquet, and speeches in their native tongue. Later that summer, they picnicked at the Randolph Probstfield farm. Piano, violin, and vocal music entertained members and their wives while they consumed lemonade, beer, cigars, ice cream, and other edibles. Despite an active first year, the Sons of Hermann disappeared when the Dakota Boom ended and the energetic Warnken departed. The *Dakota Banner,* which began with bright prospects, lived as briefly as most North Dakota German newspapers.[82]

German churches expressed ethnic community more permanently. The German Zion Evangelical Church in Fargo dated from 1877 when the Minnesota Conference sent a missionary to the valley. Two years later, the Reverend G. F. Hiclscher established the first regular pastorate and soon erected a sanctuary. Each Sabbath, the congregation held Sunday school and worshipped in German at morning and evening services.[83]

The German Grace Evangelical Lutheran Church of Fargo, organized in 1898, originated two decades earlier when circuit riders began visiting the area. Missionaries irregularly served the handful of German Lutherans for the next several years. Parishioners held services at St. Mark's English Lutheran, the Norwegian Good Templar Hall, and the Moorhead home of August Koenemann, the Great Northern roadmaster. Moved to Fargo in 1894, these meetings finally resulted in the founding of the Grace church. After they built their first sanctuary in 1905, the congregation numbered twenty-two voting members, ninety-one communicants, and two hundred souls. They established a day school in 1908. Lack of students closed it eight years later. Until 1911, they worshipped solely in German. English became the official language after the Great War.[84]

THE OTHERS

According to French Existentialist philosopher Simone de Beauvoir, "the other" is a fundamental category of human thought. Every group defines itself by setting up "the other" against itself as "the stranger," "the foreigner," "the different," or "the inferior."[85] Similarly, Protestant Yankees in Fargo and

Moorhead defined the other as those different from them. People might be excluded on the grounds of class, ethnicity, race, or religion. Prejudice and discrimination functioned on a continuum ranging from a high degree of acceptance to outright exclusion. In theory, booster ideology welcomed all peoples because they contributed to dual city economic growth. In practice, all groups suffered some prejudice and discrimination.

Anglo-Saxon Americans found middle-class Protestant, sober, industrious, and Nordic Norwegians, Swedes, and Germans less alien and most easily assimilated them over time. Anglo-Saxons most marginalized nonwhite races whose color, poverty, and sometimes alien culture made them undesirable. Although anti-Catholicism diminished after the 1850s, it did not disappear entirely. The popularity of the American Protective Association in the 1890s and the Ku Klux Klan in the 1920s reminded Roman Catholics of their second-class status. In the half century since their arrival, the Irish Catholic Celts had adequately prospered and sufficiently Americanized to make them somewhat tolerable economically and racially, if not religiously. Religiously strange and lower-class German Catholics benefited from being racially acceptable, whereas Anglo-Saxons stigmatized southeastern European Catholics as lesser Alpine and Mediterranean races as well as an unwanted class and faith. Anglo-Saxons similarly rejected Jews as lower-class, Semitic, and religiously foreign peoples. Middle-class German Jews, however, attained more acceptance than lower-class East European Jews. Prejudice did not prevent some of them from achieving prominence.[86]

Father Jean-Baptiste Genin—a Roman Catholic missionary from Canada—first visited Moorhead in 1872. He built a church the next year that served the Catholics of both cities. Father J. A. McGlone became the first resident priest in 1878, succeeded one year later by Father Lawrence Spitzelberger. Two Sisters of St. Benedict soon taught elementary subjects in English and German as well as needlework to forty girls. Father Augustine Brockmeyer's zeal enabled the construction of several buildings between 1886 and 1896: a sisters' residence, a six-room parochial school, and a rectory. John and Patrick Lamb—prominent businessmen and civic leaders—bestowed land for the original Catholic cemetery. They bequeathed twenty thousand dollars and a site for a new church and school during the 1920s.[87]

According to oral tradition, Father Charles A. Richard from Quebec conducted the first Fargo mass at the Opera House in 1877. After local men organized the parish three years later, he became the first resident priest. Purchase of the old Methodist church for only three hundred dollars shelved his grandiose plan for a five thousand-dollar Gothic edifice. This small building with additions served the city's largest congregation until completion of St. Mary's Cathedral in 1899. Like their Protestant sisters, Catholic women solicited funds and paid bills. Editors, who urged contributions from every-one, publicized their weeklong fairs. The women sold suppers, ice cream, fruit, fancy goods, lace, and embroidery. They sold votes and awarded prizes to the most popular hotel girl, policeman, or fire company. They held raffles for a pony with saddle and bridle as well as other goods. They sponsored dances, until Fargo's first bishop banished them in the 1890s. These events often raised more than two thousand dollars.[88]

Income from fairs, supplemented by one thousand dollars from the Catholic bishop of Dakota Territory, built the first parochial school in 1882. Such institutions developed as an alternative to godless public—or worse, Protestant—schools. Religious instruction made them central to Catholic evangelization. The availability of numerous women religious for teach-ing made them possible. The Sisters of Presentation thus taught at St. Joseph's Academy, which also cared for poor children. It became St. John's Orphanage in 1897 after the school, renamed the Sacred Heart Academy, relocated to North Broadway. By 1902, the academy had added a second-ary course. North Dakota bishop John Shanley called on Catholics to sacri-fice financially for the cause of Christian education. Sacred Heart remained the only Catholic school in the city until 1920, when the church erected St. Mary's grade school. The parish supported both institutions without tu-ition and fees, as the now long-dead Bishop Shanley had wanted.[89]

Seeking to boost the metropolis, *Argus* editor Alanson W. Edwards cam-paigned for relocating the Catholic see from Jamestown to Fargo. On the day in 1891 when Bishop Shanley occupied his Island Park home, Governor Andrew H. Burke and Mayor Wilbur F. Ball welcomed him to the city. The church meanwhile purchased the "diamond square" at Broadway and Sixth Avenue North and laid the cathedral cornerstone in November. Local con-tractor and former alderman James Kennedy as well as merchants O. J. deLendrecie and Ferdinand Luger served on the reception committee of prominent parishioners for that ceremony. By such events, New Americans of Irish, French, and German descent demonstrated their respectability to Old Americans. Although the foundation had been laid, the Fargo fire de-layed completion for many years. During this time, Bishop Shanley raised funds by conducting retreats, missions, and lecture courses throughout the East and Midwest. A fifty thousand-dollar loan from Antoine Robert of Montreal enabled St. Mary's Cathedral to be dedicated on May 30, 1899, be-fore an overflow crowd.[90]

After the bishop relocated, the Sisters of St. Joseph Carondelet opened St. John's Hospital in his former residence. The national Catholic crusade for charity encouraged hospitals and orphanages. Staffed by women reli-gious, such institutions served working-class parishioners in a traditional way. They helped individuals and saved souls.[91]

During the nineteenth century, American Catholic parishes shifted from congregational to clerical control. The supremacy of each bishop in his diocese and each priest in his parish mirrored the enhanced powers of the pope that the doctrine of papal infallibility symbolized. A more powerful ecclesiastical hierarchy exerted its control over a church increasingly fragmented by the ethnic diversity of its working-class members. Confessions heard in English, French, and German for many years in Fargo evidenced these divisions. Given the middle-class values and anti-Catholicism of numerous Old and New American Protestants, Catholics undoubtedly experienced prejudice in the twin cities, however rarely the booster press expressed it publicly. In a letter to the *Forum,* an angry resident articulated attitudes that many probably shared. The writer said that a new hospital should not be Catholic. Although the city had provided twelve thousand dollars to the Catholic see and residents annually donated generously at the fairs, Catholics had no right to expect aid from Protestants. They had not helped "anybody or any church but themselves." They had not done anything for Fargo. "All they want is the power in their own hands," the letter writer sourly concluded.[92]

Fortunately for Catholics, Bishop John Shanley had been a well-loved friend of all during his long pastorate at the cathedral in St. Paul. While there he had been a disciple of the liberal archbishop John Ireland, who had named him the first bishop of North Dakota in 1889. Shanley's understanding of American ideas, his openness to working with Protestants, and his winning personality attracted broad support and did much to overcome anti-Catholic prejudice in the state. An able scholar and linguist, he often addressed his diverse flock in their native languages. His keen sense of humor made him an effective speaker and newspaper contributor. He belonged to the Fargo Commercial Club. He campaigned against the ninety-day divorce law. He donated a

John Shanley, the first Roman Catholic bishop of North Dakota, did much to win acceptance of Catholics in the city during the 1890s and early 1900s. From *History of the Red River Valley, Past and Present.*

hundred dollars toward creating a city band because he believed that "great music is the art to raise the soul above earthly storms." He wanted Fargo to become "a city populous, a city beautiful, a city artistic, a city cultured and a city holy." At his death in 1909, the *Forum* praised his administrative skill. During his twenty-year tenure, priests increased from thirty-two to 115; churches expanded from three to 220; and $146,000 had been gathered for St. Mary's Cathedral, rectory, and bishop's residence.[93]

Bishop Shanley often worked with Protestant and civic leaders on charitable causes. In 1892, he asked them for names of deserving poor families so that he might furnish them turkeys and other food for Thanksgiving dinner. Three years later, he suggested a plan for having tramps work for their meals. He became the president of Associated Charities. He toiled with Mayor Wilbur Ball and the YMCA in raising funds and directing the effort. Even on issues of disagreement with Protestants, Shanley engaged them in discussion. In 1893, his letter to the *Argus* attacking the North Dakota prohibition law attracted a firestorm of criticism. At a crowded public meeting in the armory, the bishop explained that the Catholic church promoted temperance in all things, including alcohol. That goal might be attained by prohibition or other means. The church promoted temperance through total abstinence societies. For those who could not control their drinking, the church imposed an abstinence pledge. Shanley had worked with Ireland for abstinence in St. Paul and since coming to the state had administered the pledge to hundreds of Dakotans. He also endorsed the treatment of alcoholics by Fargo's Keeley Institute. Protestants could not deny that prohibition had not been enforced and that liquor consumption had increased. They praised the bishop for his public stand.[94]

Bishop Shanley presided over the expansion of Catholic fraternal orders in the city. The Vatican in 1894 had condemned secret societies like the Knights of Pythias and Odd Fellows, despite opposition by American liberal prelates. Responding to the impulses of a fraternal age, American Catholics formed their own associations. By 1900, the Catholic Order of Foresters met twice monthly at St. Mary's Cathedral Hall. The most successful Catholic fraternal association, the Knights of Columbus, organized locally in May 1903 with fifty charter members. It offered life insurance, promoted the brotherhood of man, and stimulated charitable acts at all times and all places. It advanced a distinctly Catholic, but American, nationalism that demanded civil equality for people of every religion. As the Knights of Columbus expanded nationally to more than three hundred thousand by 1914, it grew locally as well. The order numbered five hundred in September 1909 when it finished the three-story, forty thousand-dollar Temple on North Broadway.[95]

Annual community-wide observances of St. Patrick's Day offset Catholic otherness to some extent. According to scholar Orm Øverland, "The . . . celebration of ethnicity is a way of affirming . . . that a particular ethnic group has a home in America." The press favorably reported on the well-planned and self-disciplined festivities. Similarly organized as those for American and Norwegian independence days, the parade in 1874 marched from the Headquarters Hotel down Front Street into Moorhead. Festivities concluded that evening with a Grand Ball at Pinkham's Hall. The best American, Irish, and Scandinavian elements attended, according to the *Fargo Express*. Prominent citizens of both cities joined later celebrations as well. The elaborate 1889 celebration included a grand parade with two bands, one rifle company, the dual city fire companies, municipal officials, and ordinary citizens. Orators spoke to a packed Fargo Opera House that evening. The proceeds went to the defense fund of Charles Parnell, an Irish nationalist under investigation in England. As happened elsewhere in the United States, clergy assumed a larger role by the 1890s. Catholic church services followed by evening musical and literary programs replaced processions and liquor. Bishop Shanley often spoke at these events, which now raised money for the cathedral fund. Like his mentor Ireland, Shanley likely pointed to the need for greater Catholic temperance, industry, and respectability.[96]

Jewish residents date from 1880 when Alex Stern came and opened a clothing store. Like urban Jews elsewhere in the United States, Stern and other early arrivals were middle-class merchants, German and Reformed. They had capital and benefited from the opportunities afforded by an expanding city. Unlike Jews elsewhere, they did not develop a distinctive communal life. When an Orthodox rabbi arrived in 1891, he found only fifteen families. Orthodox services did not interest the Germans and the impoverished East European Jews could not support the rabbi, who soon left for Grand Forks. Several German Jews became prominent citizens. None of them had their homes or businesses in the lower Front Street neighborhood that later arriving and poorer Jews

By the 1920s, when this photograph was taken, Alex Stern had long been a prominent businessman and civic leader in Fargo. Courtesy Institute for Regional Studies, North Dakota State University, Fargo (P272.1).

populated. Isaac Herbst built a large department store and participated in community affairs. Max Stern evolved from clothier into successful banker and civic leader. Alex Stern belonged to the Masons, Shriners, and Elks; he served as an alderman in the 1890s, a state legislator later, and president of the Fargo city commission in 1917. When he died, Governor William Langer ordered flags of state offices lowered to half-mast. The success of these men suggests a lack of visible anti-Semitism in the city and state.[97]

Growing numbers of lower-class East European Jews arrived in the 1890s. They shared common bonds of poverty, Orthodox Judaism, and Yiddish. They lived in an area of shacks and frame buildings that extended from Broadway to the Red River and from Front Street to Third Avenue South. Most engaged in mercantile activities that included clothing stores, groceries, a kosher butcher shop, and peddling for the most recent newcomers. They supported one another with loans, discounts, and mutual self-help. Living in a blighted district often disrupted by disorderly transient white and black laborers, Jews protected their families by affirming their communal heritage. Although their distinctive European nationalities and traditions made it difficult for them to organize, they established an orthodox congregation and a Hebrew Cemetery Association in 1896. David Lesk served neighboring towns and approximately 125 families in Fargo as first permanent rabbi from 1905 to 1915. In 1907, they erected a synagogue with several classrooms and an auditorium seating 350 at Fifth Street and First Avenue South. A Hebrew school started that same year.[98]

African Americans shared with Jews the same impoverished Front Street area, but failed to achieve the same status as an ethnic community. Lack of an economic base and sufficient numbers, as well as the more severe disadvantages imposed by color, account for the difference. African Americans came to the Dakotas through the Missouri River trade, construction of the railroads, and homesteading. Most arrived in 1879 when General Thomas L. Rosser, Northern Pacific construction engineer, transported numerous blacks from the Mississippi Valley to their jobs in western Dakota. After tracklaying halted for the winter, the railroad allowed them to settle Dakota lands or return south. Most likely went home, but some remained in Bismarck, Fargo, and other places. William Montgomery became the most eminent among the small number of black homesteaders. He acquired a thousand acres in 1885 on the Fargo and Southern division of the Milwaukee Road. He built his own elevator and entered into partnerships with Fargo businessmen. After losses on grain futures in the 1890s, he sold his farm and joined these partners in Canadian land investments. The *Fargo Argus* respectfully reported his business ventures, visits to the city, and stays at the Headquarters Hotel.[99]

Few historical records and little information are available about African Americans in the dual city during the 1890s. The identities of these two young men in Moorhead are not known. Courtesy Clay County Historical Society.

The 1890 census showed sixty-seven blacks in Fargo and eight in Clay County. By 1910, there were fifteen in Clay and 120—sixty-seven men and fifty-three women—in Cass. African Americans worked as barbers, laborers, bootblacks, prostitutes, and a boardinghouse proprietor. Contractors only employed them if whites were unavailable. Professor Frank L. Gordon, a ten-year resident, succeeded as a barber in Fargo. The press described him as "a genial black man who talks Norske" and conducts a popular shop with three chairs. After he moved from Front to 205 Fifth Street North, he ran for first ward alderman in 1900. He and his backers appealed for white support, but he lost. Perhaps his defeat convinced him to leave the city. Political bosses earlier had attempted to deliver the colored vote in the 1884 election to the incumbent mayor, W. A. Yerxa. Although he won, blacks had preferred the former mayor, William A. Kindred. With these exceptions, blacks remained politically invisible.[100]

Newspaper accounts of African American events suggest a desire of respectable residents for community. They attempted to organize a Lodge of Colored Masons in 1889. That same year, Mrs. Eliza Anthony and her husband hosted the local Baptist minister and several other black notables for a dinner in their home. The Colored Knights of Pythias gave a concert in 1896 for which Mrs. Frank Gordon performed. Her barber husband advertised and sold tickets for the event. In 1899, John Fort and George Hayes arranged a "Colored Picnic" at Haggart's farm west of Fargo. More than fifty people departed from Fort's residence on Northern Pacific Avenue for the daylong festivities. A luncheon, cakewalks, dancing, and other amusements entertained them. Black church groups occasionally formed and met in white churches. In 1888, the Reverend Alex Moore conducted services for the colored at the First Baptist Church. Between 1916 and 1918, a group worshipped in the basement of the Fargo First Presbyterian Church as John the Hope (Colored) Presbyterian Church.[101]

According to historians William Sherman and Playford Thorson, respectable African Americans attempted to separate themselves residentially and in other ways from their disreputable brethren in Fargo and other North Dakota cities. Increased numbers of migratory blacks during the annual harvest influx threatened these distinctions. To protect themselves, permanent residents cooperated with the mayor and policemen, which helped preserve some order in their neighborhoods. Transient blacks certainly experienced greater suspicion, fear, and discrimination. Strong vagrancy laws kept them from settling in the city. Although cooperation may have minimized somewhat the hostility toward inhabitants, it never entirely disappeared.[102]

Antiblack prejudice and discrimination manifested themselves in a variety of ways. Most Fargo African Americans lived in the dilapidated housing of lower Front Street, which they shared with Jews, Asians, and white migrants. Most blacks worked

The popularity of minstrel shows at the Fargo Opera House indicated the attitude of many whites toward African Americans at this time. Courtesy Institute for Regional Studies, North Dakota State University, Fargo.

as laborers or in personal service occupations. One-half of the stories in Fargo and Moorhead newspapers about African Americans in the late nineteenth century reported their crimes—beatings, knifings, shootings, fornication, and larceny—and applauded their punishments. The use of "razors" or "coon" and "gorilla" stereotypes in news accounts described African Americans as less than human. On the other hand, they need not commit crimes for some whites to demand their exclusion. When the *Fargo Weekly Argus* reported that a black man had enjoyed the masquerade ball, two letters to the editor objected to such an expression of social equality. The negative stereotypes whites shared are evidenced by the popularity of minstrel shows at twin city theaters and the cakewalk sponsored by the Unitarian Ladies Tea Club. The women gave prizes to those who blacked up, dressed in the funniest costume, and walked in the most ridiculous manner. According to the *Forum,* the event "was heartily enjoyed by everyone of the large number who attended."[103]

On the other hand, the *Argus* publicized the lecture on freedmen churches and schools delivered by ex-slave J. C. Fremont at the First Congregational Church. Both the *Argus* and the *Forum* condemned the disfranchisement of Southern Negroes in the 1890s. The *Forum* concluded: "Some of them are welcome to come to North Dakota, which numbers many colored people among its law-abiding and prosperous citizens." That only the law-abiding and prosperous should come suggests limits in this statement of apparently color-blind boosterism. A subsequent article made these explicit. The solution to the race problem required several more generations. Negroes must heed Booker T. Washington's teachings: acquire an industrial education, emulate whites, and accumulate property.[104]

Native Americans also aroused fear and suspicion among whites. Their raids on Fort Lincoln livestock may have prompted rumors of Indian uprisings during the 1870s. The *Fargo Express* dismissed such talk as nonsensical because Indians could never agree on concerted action and could no longer subsist, except in small numbers. After the Battle of the Little Big Horn destroyed Custer's command, *Red River Star* editor W. B. Nickles rejected the peace policy advocated in Washington by Bishop Henry Whipple of Minnesota. Grown Indians could not be civilized because they "are full of murder and continually long for the scalp of whites." They could only be pacified through depletion or extermination. The memory of Custer's fate probably added to settler fears when Fort Abercrombie closed the following year. Rumors of uprisings circulated. Norwegian immigrant Christine Hagen recalled sitting on the roof of her farm home looking for Indians, while many neighbors sought protection in Fargo.[105]

The greater visibility of Native Americans in the early years of Fargo and

Moorhead aroused more anxious and prejudicial expressions than later. The *Red River Star* complained in 1874 about "the presence of packs of worthless Indians away from their reservation." The editor insisted that the military should keep "the aborigines where they belong." If it did not act, "the people of this section will be compelled to either relinquish their homes to the red men or drive the lazy, begging beings to their proper location." Later editors used less bigoted language. In April 1879, the *Clay County Advocate* reported fourteen Indians from the Red Lake Reservation on the "visiting path" to Sisseton. A sober and industrious Indian, who was a familiar face in the city, led the friendly band. A few years later, the newspaper noted an Indian woman on the streets of Moorhead one January day, "transacting her regular line of business, which is selling bead work." Whites did not always appreciate native enterprise. When they sold raspberries and blueberries to the Continental Hotel, one alarmed patron wrote to the *Argus*: "If your readers could see the dirty vermin covered Indians who pick these berries . . . I do not believe they would eat any more." Other Native Americans regularly came to Fargo for their treaty money. Many whites never overcame their fear of them, as an old settler later recalled.[106]

Sometimes editors commented sympathetically on the Native American plight. When settlers drove a band of Yankton Sioux from land on the James River, the *Fargo Times* stated that the land had been stolen by whites who should be made to "realize that even an Indian has some rights that a white man is bound to respect." A reader's letter heatedly disagreed. The Indians had no right to the land, which was on the market. An infantryman at Fort Sisseton responded that the band had been driven from ground promised to them by the U.S. government. At this time, the *Clay County Advocate* supported lumbering on the Red Lake Reservation because "cheaper lumber is of interest to us all!" A few years later, the *Moorhead Weekly News* favored opening either the Red Lake or the White Earth reservation for settlement. Editor George Lamphere argued that "sickly sentimentality" should not allow a few hundred Chippewa to obstruct the needs of thousands of white citizens for cheap land and lumber. Lamphere later said that Indians should receive allotments of pinelands, because it would not be fair to make them purchase timber from whites.[107]

Booster ideology often shaped editorial attitudes toward Native Americans, who must give way to settlement and surrender their resources to further white economic development. To survive, Indians must be civilized. Bishop John Shanley urged assimilation for the Catholic Indians of North Dakota. Justice would follow the salvation of Indian souls. They should avoid liquor, keep their land, and become respectable farmers.[108]

Few Asians lived permanently in the twin cities. Several came but seldom stayed. A Chinese laundryman arrived in Moorhead from Barnesville in 1886, worked for five months, then suddenly relocated to Wahpeton even though he had paid his rent in advance. Sam Lee established a laundry in 1879. Two decades later, his business at 24 First Street South still served transients and workingmen without wives. Newspaper accounts frequently ridiculed the Chinese, accentuating their odd dialect, clothing, and hairstyle. For example, the *Fargo Times* reported: "Ah Wing, a native of the Celestial Empire, has bought lots . . . for the purpose of erecting a laundry and tea store." His wealth from businesses in Rochester and Winona made Ah Wing less bizarre: "He wears United States clothes and keeps his cue done up in a bunch under his hat." A later *Times* account stated that mosquitoes had driven "the almond-eyed son of the celestial empire" back to Winona.[109] The editor's humor emphasized strangeness of the other and discounted Chinese humanity.

Railroad companies recruited and transported the many nationalities that peopled Fargo and Moorhead. Corporate managers believed these peoples could not prosper without religion and education. The Northern Pacific and SPM&M therefore issued passes to missionaries and educators. The Northern Pacific and its subsidiary LS&PS Company donated lots, or sold them at discounts, to individuals for establishing churches and to boards of education for founding public schools. The Northern Pacific also shipped materials for religious and educational buildings at reduced rates and at times transported them without charge. Aided by such corporate largesse, Yankees and European immigrants built churches and schools, which transmitted the religious, moral, and civic values that made prosperity possible.

Corporate and individual wealth seekers founded, settled, and developed the twin cities. The Northern Pacific profited from attracting settlers to the cities it had platted. All peoples migrated with similar expectations of gain and, not surprisingly, established churches and schools that reflected and perpetuated a culture of privatism. According to this culture, individual happiness depended on personal independence and the pursuit of wealth. The culture shaped Old American denominations, which advanced programs of private Protestantism that promoted individual salvation and corrected individual behavior. Immigrant churches and schools often accepted these American values. For example, pietistic Scandinavian Lutherans embraced liberal individualism and advanced prohibition as a solution to the evils of poverty and crime like their Yankee brethren. Bishop John Shanley similarly mirrored Protestants by calling for greater temperance, industry, and respectability among Catholics.

Public schools inculcated the common creed of individualism, self-help, and patriotism in children of every class, religion, and ethnicity. Although each child had an equal right to education at public expense, the community expected that each pupil—armed with the knowledge and values essential to individual success—must take care of himself or herself thereafter.[110] Private schools imparted the same creed to their students. The entire populace duly celebrated similar values each Fourth of July. Boosters welcomed Norwegians, Swedes, and Germans as honorary Yankees because their Protestant religion, work ethic, and whiteness made them desirable residents who would further the economic development of both cities and the valley. Even Catholics and Jews won some acceptance among the Yankees because they also contributed by their numbers and economic activity, which offset to some degree the strangeness of their religions, racial traits, and often lower-class status. Community celebrations of Norwegian independence and St. Patrick's Day eased the acceptance of Scandinavians and Catholics by diminishing their otherness. As Orm Øverland has observed, such expressions of ethnic nationalism aided the group's entry into the American nation.[111] Strong racial intolerance, however, prevented the acceptance of nonwhite African Americans, Native Americans, and Asians. Discrimination made them unwelcome in either city and limited their numbers.

Fargo and Moorhead shared a common origin as railroad towns, a culture of privatism, and a multiplicity of nationalities and religions. Yet the twin cities remained separate entities that rarely cooperated and often competed in most enterprises. Each community generally conducted its holiday celebrations, religious revivals, churches, and schools independently. Such separatism continued until the mid-twentieth century. As Concordia College president Joseph L. Knutson observed after yet another failure by that institution to extract funds from Fargo businessmen: "That Red River is mighty wide and mighty deep."[112] A sense of superiority stemming from Fargo's higher percentage of Old Americans in its larger population may have made it unwilling to help a Norwegian Lutheran institution in Moorhead. By 1900, the city had two and a half times more people, but just over half the percentage of foreign-born as its rival. Yet Moorhead's autonomy made it equally unwilling to aid most causes its North Dakota neighbor sponsored.

Domestic Virtues

MIDDLE-CLASS MORAL ORDER

The intellectual Woman's Club is a potent factor in . . . social advancement . . . for it is the channel outside of the home . . . in which the influence of women will be most distinctly felt.

—Mrs. S. J. Clapp, Fargo Woman's
Club president, January 4, 1895

The liquor traffic is responsible for at least 90 percent of crime committed. . . . The saloon is the hotbed of socialism and anarchy. Remove the saloon and you remove the cause of all these. . . . Prohibition is the only safety for the individual, for the home, for the nation.

—Elizabeth Preston, North Dakota
WCTU organizer, 1889

TRANSCONTINENTAL RAILROAD CONSTRUCTION ACCELERATED EXtensive change throughout the nation in the late nineteenth century. Industry expanded. Cities grew. Social and geographic mobility increased. Corporations and individuals intensified their pursuit of wealth, widening the gulf between rich and poor and elevating industrial violence between capital and labor. Poverty, alcohol consumption, prostitution, and crime all seemed on the rise, arousing middle-class fears throughout the country. How could individual virtue and social cohesion be attained in such a fluid and chaotic society? The Northern Pacific initially, and the SPM&M later, connected Moorhead and Fargo to this troubled national scene and brought some of its evils to the Red River Valley. The railroad also enhanced economic opportunities. Some men came with little, made fortunes and housed their families comfortably in fine mansions. Others achieved only modest wealth, but still aspired to genteel refinement, if on a less lavish scale. Some succeeded at first, yet suffered bankruptcy, losing all they had attained. Others failed perpetually, never accumulating anything.

In the urban-industrial world the railroad corporations called into existence, what enabled wealth-seeking individuals to cope with the problems they faced? As Alexis de Tocqueville had argued earlier in the century, associations let individuals carry on the civic work of a democratic society without increasing the power of government. U.S. citizens therefore voluntarily combined for thousands of varied tasks, which preserved public tranquillity and furthered civilization. Confronted by disorder, residents of Moorhead, Fargo, and other cities adopted this traditional strategy as historian Paul Boyer and others have documented. By participating in Bible, tract, Sunday school, and reform societies, Boyer argues, successful businessmen and upwardly mobile groups defined themselves as middle-class and developed communal norms. Their organizations embodied the bourgeois family ideals of self-disciplined rectitude and decorum as solutions to poverty, vice, and crime. Their search for order began in eastern municipalities and migrated westward with settlers who faced similar evils in new towns.[1]

Middle-class desire for moral order early expressed itself in the twin cities. The *Red River Star* celebrated its first birthday by discussing "Moorhead as it was, and should be." In July 1872, the city had contained "a large proportion that was characteristic of all frontier towns—a . . . floating element. Now . . . Moorhead contains a permanent, industrious class of people." Businessmen should form a League for the Public Good to carry out moral and material improvements. Meanwhile, the *Star* would support reform by condemning wrong and upholding right.[2] Middle-class men and women quickly heeded the editor's call. As discussed in chapter 4, they first established churches and schools. They also built homes for their families, created a material environment for perpetuating genteel culture, and founded an extensive network of voluntary groups. Through reform societies, women's clubs, the Young Men's Christian Association (YMCA), the Woman's Christian Temperance Union (WCTU), fraternal lodges, and women's auxiliaries they cared for the poor, initiated public libraries, upheld the Sabbath, and combated all vices that furthered disorder. Although Old Americans dominated these bodies, the immigrant middle class participated in some or worked toward similar ends through parallel organizations of their own. This chapter describes how homes, the cult of domesticity, gentility, Christianity, and associations established middle-class moral hegemony in the twin cities. What this meant for workers and the underclass is addressed in chapter 6.

The Middle Class: Home, Family, and Genteel Culture

The home, centered on the cult of domesticity and gentility, served as the keystone of middle-class moral order. When husbands and wives participated in associations and activities outside their domicile, they spread throughout society a bourgeois family ethos based on character, industry, sobriety, and thrift. According to historian Stuart M. Blumin, the middling sort organized their households as the separate female sphere. Women directed consumption of genteel dress and furnishings for new homes built by profits from the masculine sphere of business. Parents had fewer offspring and socialized them in the values of achievement and respectability. Children remained at home longer, received more formal education, and delayed marriage until sons had attained financial security. Thus the urban middle class shared a well-defined worldview and style of living. It developed a similar consciousness in Fargo and Moorhead even though the social hierarchy was less well developed than in larger cities.[3]

Solomon Gilman Comstock's family exemplifies the emerging middle class locally. Although Comstock attained a personal fortune, he never abandoned his middle-class identity or cultural values. Born to modest circumstances in 1842, S. G. (as he preferred to be called) descended from immigrants to seventeenth-century Massachusetts and Connecticut. His father, a Maine lumberman and Republican, served as selectman and state legislator. Educated at East Corinth and Maine Wesleyan academies, S. G. took the University of Michigan law course before he gained admission to the bar in 1869 at Omaha, Nebraska. Unhappy with the lack of opportunity for lawyers, he left to keep books for a railroad. Its bankruptcy soon left him unemployed. Comstock relocated to Minnesota. After an underemployed six-month stint with a Minneapolis lawyer, he decided to move to the Pacific coast by becoming a laborer for the Northern Pacific Railway as it built westward from Duluth. Stranded by winter at track's end in Moorhead, he began legal practice in partnership with Samuel G. Roberts. After election as the first Clay County attorney, he enjoyed a princely annual salary of $850.[4]

Two years later, Comstock married his partner's sister-in-law, Sarah Ann Ball. Born in 1844 to English immigrants who had made a poor living as farmers in Canada, Illinois, and finally Rockford, Minnesota, Sarah Ball had taught school for several years at the time of her marriage. She and her husband would have three children: Ada (1876), Jessie (1879), and George (1886). The Comstocks considered religion to be important, yet little is known about their formal church life. In the early years when Solomon contributed to the Presbyterian church, his apparently lax attendance brought a call from the Reverend Oscar Elmer. At the end of his life, a brief and simple funeral service took place at St. John the Divine Episcopal Church, although he was not a member. The Episcopalian minister conducted Sarah's service at a funeral home. Dr. O. J. Hagen's tribute called her "religiously distinctive, tolerant, solid, sane."[5]

Comstock served twelve years in the state legislature and became the friend and business associate of James J. Hill. He and his partner, A. A.

Solomon and Sarah Comstock and their children Ada, George, and Jessie, pictured here in about 1890, epitomized Victorian values. Courtesy Minnesota Historical Society.

White, secured the right-of-way for Hill and the SPM&M into Moorhead and northward to the Canadian border. Within a decade, his land transactions had created a two hundred thousand-dollar fortune that made him the only "really rich" man in the city, according to Henry Johnson's *The Other Side of Main Street*. As Comstock wrote Ada many years later: "My observation is that wealth usually comes from service." John D. Rockefeller and Woolworth stores served millions and produced great fortunes. On the other hand, "A washer woman who can serve only one family cannot hope for much return." Comstock placed himself and middle-class friends between these extremes: "The best people I know usually acquire something by industry, thrift and saving even though their talent does not lie along lines of great service or even production." For Comstock, his thrift and industry had secured a comfortable living and middle-class success.[6]

Sarah Ball Comstock managed the household according to the ideal of domesticity. She supervised the consumption of those goods required for meeting physical needs and denoting social status. Magazine advertising entered her home as it did all others of the middle class. It elevated her awareness about nationally distributed brand-name products. It encouraged her to see mass-produced goods as necessary markers of good taste and individuality. She selected furniture, carpets, china, and other objects of the latest fashion for decorating her home. She cared for her small children and trained a succession of "Scandinavian maids" to cook and clean. She encouraged several to finish high school and attend Moorhead Normal, evidence that her commitment to education and gentility extended beyond sending her own children to college. As a conscientious Victorian mother, she labored to transform her oldest daughter—and Solomon's favorite—from "tomboy" into a lady. Sarah may not have understood her intellectual first child, who shared her father's love for history, literature, and stargazing. Ada pursued a career in academe, eventually becoming president of Radcliffe College.[7]

As her household duties permitted, Sarah extended her maternal domestic role to caring for the community. She briefly held the presidency of the Ladies General Benevolent Society. She took part in the Moorhead Literary Society as well as a reading room that the temperance movement spawned. She belonged to the Clay County auxiliary of the Women's Columbian Exposition. She helped found the Moorhead Woman's Club and became its second president. Annual study plans devoted to the cultural history of Western civilization mentally stimulated homemakers. In addition, the club did some civic work for public health and a library. Sarah led the fund-raising, won a grant from Andrew Carnegie, and served as library board president.[8]

Comstock and other New Englanders transmitted Yankee traditions of schooling. He donated land for Bishop Whipple Academy and the Normal School. He assured the Swedish Hope Academy backers: "I am greatly interested in the Academy and am very glad to hear of its . . . success." He also encouraged education at home. Every room of his large house contained bookcases filled with the classics, literature, history, and biography. He chose the books that the family read aloud on winter evenings. Through their commitment to family, education, and community well-being, Sarah and Solomon Comstock socialized their children in the middle-class norms of moral and social order.[9]

As upwardly mobile members of the emerging middle class, Sarah and Solomon Comstock in 1883 constructed an eleven-room Victorian mansion with outbuildings at 506 Eighth Street South. Designed in the Queen Anne style by a Minneapolis architectural firm, it was built by local contractors according to family demands for the finest materials and workmanship. The first floor featured two stained-glass windows, oak door and window frames, an oak and butternut staircase, butternut mantelpieces on the three fireplaces, and hardwood floors in the principal rooms. The colorful interior evidenced

The Comstock mansion in Moorhead, built in 1883, materially expressed genteel refinement. Courtesy Minnesota Historical Society.

current Victorian fashions influenced by the Orient: a silk embroidered folding screen, a Chinese porcelain garden seat, and a Turkish parlor suite. An icehouse contained the privy and space for storing tools and food. A two-story barn sheltered three horses and carriages. The family fenced the grounds and landscaped with elms, fruit trees, and gardens. The large home stood out in a frontier community, but was not as ostentatious as others erected at the time. The Comstocks valued good taste over conspicuous display. The pine furniture for Sarah's room suggests her lack of extravagance. She ran an "orderly and scheduled" home, her daughter Ada remembered, but she was "kind and generous" to the servants. For many years, the mansion sat nearly isolated on a single city block without any view to the south but the Prairie Home Cemetery and miles of wheat lands.[10]

The Comstocks' privilege did not entirely insulate them from the ordinary life of a frontier community. Ada later recalled some of the rudimentary conditions of her childhood: "The streets were unpaved and in time of rain were deep in mud as black and slippery as axle grease. The sidewalks were of planks laid crosswise on risers, leaving a space beneath where rabbits or other little creatures could take refuge." The family's nearest neighbor lived across the street. To avoid paying the city levy, the cranky Mr. Sprague did not permit a wooden sidewalk on his property. Ada and her siblings often watched him shoo his chickens up the outside stairs into his house for the night. Ada considered it a bad arrangement to have the Scandinavian maids sleep on the second floor with the family. After completing her university education and taking a continental tour of Europe, Ada returned home in the summer of 1904. Her diary occasionally noted that it had been "a very dull day" as she spent her time visiting or receiving visitors. At other times, she walked across the footbridge to Fargo for dress fittings. For all the dangers of the downtown saloons at night, she evidently felt safe on residential streets during the day. Yet certain rules of female decorum governed her movement. Unlike men, she could not loiter on streets. Proper dress, eyes-forward behavior, and purposeful movement that defined her as a respectable woman afforded her protection in "navigating public space."[11]

Elegant residences and possessions displayed the genteel respectability that defined middle-class membership. Club meetings, social calls, teas, dinners, theater parties, and dances often took place in homes. These events required appropriate dress and knowledge of elaborate rules of etiquette. Although Comstock and other bourgeois participated in the public realm that boosted their cities from crude origins, their well-appointed homes and elaborate private lives set them apart from the populace. Newspapers hailed their mansions and society life as "evidences of civilization." At the time that the Comstocks' and other spacious Moorhead houses were built, the larger city of Fargo developed its own fashionable neighborhoods: Eighth Street South from Fourth to Seventeenth Avenue and Broadway from Fifth to Twelfth Avenue North, as well as the Island Park and Oak Grove districts. These areas of large homes, well-tended lawns, and many trees had pretensions toward exclusiveness. Such neighborhoods made an important social and cultural statement: the wealthy men and women who live here have the right and duty to define and enforce the communal moral order. The thirty thousand-dollar Tyler mansion in Oak Grove set the standard for elegance. The *Daily Republican* called it "a fit emblem of Dakota's wealth."[12]

St. Paul architect George Wirth designed "Castle Tyler" as a two-story structure built of locally manufactured cream-colored brick trimmed with red. It featured a western veranda built around a bay window, porches on nearly all sides, several balconies, and a seventy-five-foot circular tower on the southwest corner. The interior had several memorable qualities: cherry wood wainscoting in a large dining room, stained-glass upper portions of windows, and an imported tile border for the living room. Shortly after returning from Chicago where she and her spouse had selected carpets, draperies, and furnishings, Mrs. Evan S. Tyler died suddenly. The bereaved husband never occupied the residence of their dreams. He sold it quickly to G. S. Barnes, who lived there until 1906. Oak Grove Ladies Seminary then used Castle Tyler until 1933. Because the building was too expensive to maintain, the school abandoned it and razed it shortly thereafter.[13]

"Castle Tyler" in Fargo, photographed in 1884, displayed elegant standards of genteel respectability. Courtesy Institute for Regional Studies, North Dakota State University, Fargo (51.60.1).

Castle Tyler and the Comstock mansion displayed an elite, genteel culture that others emulated according to their more limited means. Many twin city residents similarly displayed standards of respectability through their possession of houses, furnishings, china, silverware, and clothing. The railroad enabled them to participate in the material culture of gentility even though they lived far from metropolitan centers. Aspiring local citizens also benefited from "the golden age of housing for the common people." By 1890 in the United States, owners occupied 36.9 percent of nonfarm dwellings. Balloon-frame construction (studs, joists, and rafters nailed together), stable or declining interest rates, machine-tooled components, and more modest single-family homes facilitated ownership. Abundant forests made available inexpensive lumber. Machine-made wooden doors, windows, frames, decorative trim, bricks, and pressed metal ceiling centerpieces lowered costs. Demand compelled architects and pattern books publishers to prepare standardized plans for inexpensive houses. To be sure, costs rose with central heating (1880s), plumbing necessitated by sewer connections (1890s), and standard wiring for electric lights (1906). Yet those who could afford them willingly paid for these comforts. The Victorian home—designed to shelter families from sordid commercialism—ironically depended on industrialism and merchandizing for its construction.[14]

Fargo and Moorhead mirrored these trends. Many with modest means acquired or built homes, thereby attaining an important marker of gentility. The *Fargo Forum* in 1899 reported that more than a hundred neat cottages existed in the city's north side. Anecdotal evidence suggests that members of the immigrant working class or the lower middle class erected or purchased these residences. They immigrated from Norway, Sweden, Switzerland, or Canada. They kept shops or worked for the railroad and waterworks. They rented initially. They supplemented wages and accumulated capital by varied means: cultivating gardens, renting rooms, feeding boarders, tending cattle, and selling dairy products. An exceptionally thrifty and ambitious few acquired additional property that they rented to others. Building and loan associations, which expanded rapidly after the Civil War, offered such families an opportunity to borrow. The Fargo Building Association, founded in 1880, had built more than sixty homes by 1883. It financed many more to the end of the century and beyond.[15]

The middle class applied the genteel standards for respectability to amusements outside as well as inside their homes. As the twin cities expanded, residents developed a full schedule of seasonal entertainments, ranging from summertime picnics, excursions, band concerts, circuses, baseball, lawn tennis, and other sports to wintertime balls, dinners, theatricals, and ice-skating. Baseball became popular by 1874. Episcopalian Benjamin Mackall served as secretary of the Red River Baseball Club, which played teams from neighboring towns. Women from the city provided refreshments at socials held after games. Editors publicized the more reputable circuses, recommending them as "clean, orderly, amusing [and] entertaining" for the entire family. Bicycling attained popularity with men and women during the 1890s. The Dual City Wheel Club and the Sycamore Cycle Club at times sponsored Sunday rides of twenty to forty miles. The sport declined after the Model T afforded a new diversion.[16]

Bourgeois mothers hosted birthday parties by invitation only in any season. These defined their child's peer group, inculcated refined manners, and taught boys that females planned formal parties. Members of the middle class also differentiated themselves through dance clubs. Fargo organizers often lived in stylish Eighth Street homes and scheduled their "society" events at the Headquarters, Continental, or other hotels until Lent suspended their frivolity. The Qui Vive met during the winter of 1882 for the "German" (waltz) and other dances. Members of "Fargo's best society" and some invited Moorhead guests attended. The following season, the Benedict Club with eighty members made its appearance. The newly formed

Bachelors Club dubbed them "married miserables." One dance provoked a Philadelphia lady to exclaim: "I wish some of those down-east people, who think Dakota is the jumping off place of civilization . . . could see this party! I think it would open their eyes to the fact that our society is as good and as good-looking as the best they have." At this time, the Moorhead Dance Club organized by Henry Bruns, A. A. White, Benjamin Mackall, and other gentlemen often staged balls by invitation to as many as one hundred couples at the Grand Pacific Hotel. Special trains or buses frequently carried guests from Fargo and back.[17]

Dance clubs continued into the next decade. For example, the Metropolitan, German, and Century clubs jointly sponsored the last dance of the 1898 season at the Odd Fellows Hall. Diary comments by Lily Haynes suggest the importance of such events for a mother with three young children: "I went out for first time in a long time . . . to [the] Masonic Reception and Ball . . . I enjoyed myself . . . [and] received many compliments; was dressed all in white and felt as young as any of them." Mrs. Haynes also reported attending, in the absence of her husband, a card party at the Headquarters Hotel, a New Year's dinner with Moorhead friends, and a dancing party at the Headquarters. She would have preferred going with her husband, but Frank Haynes's photography often kept him away. She hinted that he would not have attended even if he had been at home. Mrs. Haynes admired her husband's ambition and acumen. Yet her complaint demonstrates how the masculine pursuit of business at times interfered with the feminine social sphere.[18]

Respectable theatrical entertainment proved problematic and sometimes unavailable for the genteel. Liquor and "girlie shows" that catered to rowdy single men did not meet bourgeois cultural standards. For example, nightly disturbances at Schey's Opera House on lower Front Street led Sheriff John E. Haggart to arrest Schey and his troupe. He released the group on their promise to leave town, but charged Schey with maintaining a public nuisance. Benjamin Reynolds took control of the theater and renamed it the Music Hall. He promised minstrel and variety entertainment without vulgarity. A new company—guaranteeing to produce "a laugh from the most forlorn specimen of humanity"—soon drew sizable crowds nightly. Encouraged by a booming business, Reynolds and his partner Frank McCauley built the Coliseum Theater and Bar on Northern Pacific Avenue. Its program of singers, dancers, comedians, knife throwers, and countless new acts proved so popular that others established several vaudeville theaters. The *Fargo Sunday Argus* and its middle-class readers still craved more refined drama.[19]

After 1880, McHench and Chapin halls appealed to the middle class by hosting local entertainment, visiting lecturers, and traveling theater companies. During the 1881 season, McHench Hall presented eleven shows consisting of typical dual city theatrical fare: three minstrel, two variety, and five dramatic productions. A remodeled and enlarged Chapin Hall, which became known as the Fargo Opera House, soon supplanted its cramped theatrical competitor. Located on the northeast corner of Broadway and Northern Pacific Avenue, the opera house presented almost four hundred events—including sixty-six operas, seven Shakespeare productions, and thirty-six versions of *Uncle Tom's Cabin*—before the Fargo fire destroyed it in 1893. If management booked first-class attractions and advertised them well, residents filled the house. When management faltered, as it apparently did in the late 1880s, audiences declined. Renewed support in the next decade stimulated demands for a larger building.[20]

The great fire created an opportunity to build anew. C. P. Walker managed the new house, located at the southeast corner of Roberts Street and Second Avenue North, until it burned in 1912. Thirty-two stock companies, traveling on the Red River Circuit that included Grand Forks and Winnipeg, came to Fargo in those years. They generally performed seven shows during their one-week stay. Performers included comedienne Fanny Rice, comedian Eddie Foy, Sousa's Peerless Concert Band, several opera companies, and Marhara's Mammoth Minstrels. The *Forum* assured its readers that the minstrels gave "a strictly refined and moral performance," presenting "happy scenes of southern life" and "the colored race in all their natural comedy." Well-known local musician A. O. Rupert conducted the opera house orchestra that played overtures, the score for most performances, and several selections between acts. Rupert also directed a large concert orchestra as well as a dance band. The new facility opened in February 1894 with a performance of *Gloriana,* a three-act comedy, before a capacity audience dressed in formal evening clothes. Mary Darrow Wieble, daughter and wife of prominent local physicians, later fondly recalled this aspect of elite social life.[21]

WOMEN AND CIVIC HOUSEKEEPING

According to the cult of domesticity, naturally virtuous women tended morality. They kept house, maintained the home, and secured the social order by inculcating moral and civic virtue in their children. The logic of women's moral superiority propelled them over time beyond the female sphere into the male worlds of intellect, business, and politics. If women naturally nurtured children, could not their qualities directly benefit the community as well? Hence they engaged in church work and taught in the common schools. They promoted self-cultivation for everyone by establishing public libraries. They took charge of charity for the deserving poor. When they attacked the evils of liquor, gambling, and prostitution, however, they more directly confronted the male world. Although they were part of the battle against barbarism in the West, anti-vice crusades paralleled those of the East. Vice must be purged because it threatened home and family by destroying industry, thrift, and virtue. Women sought suffrage on similar grounds. The vote better protected wives and children by making mothers more effective civic housekeepers.[22]

Women led in promoting culture for the twin cities. Believing that cultured as well as virtuous people strengthened the social order, they went beyond self-improvement and increasingly devoted themselves to bettering others. Young women in 1873 organized a reading circle in Fargo. They gathered in the evening for reading selections, declamations, and singing. By the following year, women had constituted the Moorhead Literary Society. It met weekly in the homes of Sarah Ball Comstock and others. It gave occasional pubic entertainments that featured instrumental music and singing as well as a drama *(Loan of a Lover)* and a farce *(Thirty Minutes for Refreshments)*. The Moorhead Literary Society remained active into the next decade, but became for a time an association of men and women.[23]

The 1868 founding of Sorosis in New York and the New England Woman's Club in Boston may have inspired these early feminine efforts. Similar clubs soon appeared throughout the country, meeting the needs of married women with children. According to historian Karen Blair, female literary clubs, which eventually combined to form the General Federation of Women's Clubs, provided an alternative route toward women's self-development from that of the suffragists. Clubwomen utilized the attributes of the ideal lady to increase their autonomy, expand their education, and enlarge their influence outside the home.[24]

Twelve women created the Fargo Woman's Club in 1884 for the purpose of studying literary and household topics. At an 1886 meeting, members debated this question: "Which life is likely to produce the finest character in woman, business, society, literature or the domestic circle?" Their responses are not recorded, unfortunately. Two years later, at an annual reception held at the home of William H. White, seventy ladies and gentlemen enjoyed a program of music and literary readings. The club that year also staged an Oliver Goldsmith comedy. After the Dakota delegate to the Sorosis convention had been warmly applauded when presented in 1889, President Mary E. Bliss explained: "Perhaps it was a pleasant surprise to find that women of this new country were so well abreast of their sisters in plans for self-cultivation." When their self-culture benefited others through philanthropic work among the destitute, Mrs. S. J. Clapp said the Federation of Women's Clubs would redeem the race.[25]

After membership in the initial club numbered forty, those unable to join founded the Fortnightly Literary Club in 1896. Well-educated, upper-middle-class Congregationalists, Methodists, and Presbyterians constituted most of its twenty-five charter members. Their study programs ranged from the literature and history of France and Great Britain to discussions about good housekeeping and homemaking. Although the first club joined the General Federation in 1890, the first annual congress of the North Dakota Federation did not gather until 1897 in Fargo. In her annual report for 1900, which mirrored issues raised at the national meetings of the General Federation, President Martha Pollock called for closer cooperation of all clubs to beautify the city, promote public health, and foster harmonious relations between parents, teachers, and children. Pollock's suggestions came to pass as both clubs became more involved in civic affairs after 1902. They worked for a pure food law, juvenile court officers, police matrons, and organized charities. Some members furthered the WCTU and women's suffrage causes.[26]

After Moorhead ladies had collected material for the Congress of Women's Pavilion at the Chicago World's Fair, Sarah Comstock proposed continuing their association. Eighteen women assembled at the home of Mary Lord in 1893 and founded the Woman's Club of Moorhead, which two years later joined the Minnesota Federation of Women's Clubs. Focusing primarily on literature rather than civic work or women's rights, the first year's course of study concluded with an illustrated lecture on Egypt delivered by Professor John Paul Goode at Normal Hall to an audience that included Fargo club members, their husbands, and Normal School students. On other occasions, the club held receptions for their husbands and friends. A public library—a logical extension of their educational purpose—became a club project. In 1903 they approached Andrew Carnegie for assistance. He agreed, on the condition that the city provided a suitable site and that taxes be appropriated annually for maintenance. The club purchased a location at First Avenue and Sixth Street South and petitioned the city council for tax revenues. The council agreed to furnish at least $1,200 annually. The Carnegie Library opened on July 12, 1906. The Woman's Club continued its support. Sarah Comstock and Letitia Burnham served on the first library commission; members donated five hundred dollars in books and worked as volunteer library staff on Sundays until 1941.[27]

The Woman's Club succeeded where earlier attempts had failed. The Moorhead Lyceum and Library Association formed in 1875. Four years later, Fargo business and professional men attempted to raise funds by selling shares, but their project died. Renewed efforts in 1882 staged a benefit concert and created a new dues-paying society. After the library appeared many months later, people complained it was too small. The Public Library

Association sponsored socials, fairs, and a course of lectures to raise money and solicit books. It turned over 1,200 books to the YMCA in 1887 to be made available in its new building. Benefits continued to be held without much effect. The Fargo women's clubs took up the cause in 1897, winning support from Mayor J. A. Johnson, the council, the *Forum,* and many prominent citizens. Unfortunately, the library referendum occurred during a severe flood and failed. Opponents raised the specter of higher taxes, which carried the day with voters worried about extensive flood repairs.[28]

After the women's clubs asked for another vote on the question, a large majority authorized a public library in 1900 by an eight to one margin. Club president Martha Pollock justifiably called the outcome "a glorious achievement." Mayor Johnson further publicized the cause by soliciting autographed books from well-known U.S. officials. One year later, the council pledged annual funding and Andrew Carnegie donated twenty thousand dollars. The Fargo Public Library—located at Roberts Street and Second Avenue North on land granted by the municipality—opened in early 1903. Carnegie also funded libraries for NDAC in 1905 and Fargo College in 1910. These institutions stemmed from the national library movement that began in the mid-1880s, championed by Carnegie and other philanthropists. Swayed by their argument that reading books formed character and there-

At the end of the nineteenth century, the Women's Clubs of Fargo campaigned for this Carnegie Public Library in order to develop character through reading. Courtesy Institute for Regional Studies, North Dakota State University, Fargo (2070.277.1).

by reduced social evils, the Dakota Territorial Legislature enacted a Free Library Law in 1887, which permitted towns and counties to impose taxes for libraries. Women often led their formation in many communities.[29]

In addition to cultivating character through reading, middle-class women cared for the poor. They practiced stewardship by giving assistance to the deserving needy without undermining their character or virtues of industry, thrift, and sobriety. The new profession of social work or the new concept of poverty did not much affect their voluntary efforts. They retained the traditional view that flawed character or personal misfortune impoverished families. They did not perceive economic exploitation or environmental conditions as factors. They remained well-intentioned, neighborly (if somewhat morally superior) visitors who did not adopt the new professional standards for working with clients.[30]

The Moorhead Ladies Benevolent Society met regularly in homes after 1882 to make up clothing for widows or married women reduced to poverty through misfortune. Aided by physicians and clergy, they identified the destitute of every sect and nationality. When fund-raising socials fell short, they resorted to an annual charity ball in 1889. As demands for aid increased during the depressed 1890s, the ladies assisted Mrs. Nelson, an impoverished, terminally ill mother of five small children. After her death, the society acquired land, purchased lumber, and built a house for the family, aided by a fifty-dollar grant from the city council and seven days of labor donated by a contractor. When the local mill contributed twenty sacks of flour in 1894, the society distributed one sack to each family of deserving poor.[31]

As the women annually raised several hundred dollars and distributed gifts of money, clothing, food, and Christmas toys, they guarded against making recipients dependent. To validate need, they sent visiting committees to applicants' homes. They praised Mayor Art Lewis for compelling those on relief to saw wood for the city and thought their society should compel labor from all men whose families received aid. In all cases where the ladies could give work, they ceased charity. Given their desire to defend the middle-class work ethic, the expansion of city improvements in the mid-1890s fortunately increased opportunities for construction jobs. Middle-class dedication to identifying the deserving poor sometimes backfired, as Henry Johnson recounts in his autobiography. As chairman of the city poor committee, Johnson worked with Mary Lord in checking each applicant. When one died after being denied hospitalization, Johnson wondered if reducing expenditures was a virtue. His efforts did not receive any public praise. Instead, storekeepers complained that less relief translated into fewer sales for them.[32]

Fargo residents, and North Dakotans generally, prided themselves on their neighborly helpfulness that reduced the number of destitute and the need for organized charity. Dakota Territory nevertheless legislated poor relief based on the models of eastern states. The law required counties to bury paupers, assist indigent permanent residents, and temporarily aid nonresidents. Respectable opinion, however, stigmatized county relief as shameful, which reduced the number of applicants, as was doubtless intended. To provide temporary assistance during illnesses or other family emergencies, Fargo—like Moorhead—relied on the Ladies Aid societies of the several churches as well as a Ladies Benevolent Society because, according to the *Fargo Sunday Argus,* charity was women's work. They collected food and clothing for distribution, especially during the winter months when employment opportunities shrank. At times, city officials supported their efforts. For example, the council in January 1887 authorized paying the person who received and distributed charitable gifts.[33]

The great fire and the depression of 1893 changed circumstances and altered charitable organization, as well as the delivery of poor relief. The Cass County Hospital, established in 1879 to provide medical assistance to the poor, no longer met county needs. The commissioners constructed a new hospital and poor farm two miles north of the city. At the same time, proposals by the national charity organization movement affected local practice. To correct character deficiencies of the destitute, the movement recommended more direct influence by middle-class moral exemplars. To that end, charitable organizations more closely coordinated their efforts; they learned more about the lives of the urban poor and friendly visitors converted the indigent to their principles. Fargo women and men formed a new Citizen's Relief Society to look after needs of the many poor families during that first depression winter. The society divided the city into sixteen districts, appointed two members for each, and identified the needy. Two years after this temporary effort, the *Fargo Forum* called neighborly charity overwhelmed and proposed creating a central committee. A judicious investigator should identify the "deserving cases that need assistance" for the committee and the commissioners.[34]

The Fargo Associated Charities formed at the YMCA later that spring. This all-male organization elected Bishop John Shanley as president and Mayor Wilbur Ball as vice president. Six ward representatives joined them on an executive committee, which addressed the annual "tramp nuisance." Although the law authorized temporary relief for men like these, county officers ignored their requests for aid, forcing them to beg food and shelter. The association solicited funds and distributed fifteen-cent meal tickets to restaurants. Tramps earned a ticket with one hour's work in the city park or for householders. A few weeks later, alderman William Sweet reported on the plan's success: "From ten to twenty men daily avail themselves of the work offered—while the park . . . is rapidly advancing in permanent improvements." Associated Charities collected $320, drew $40 from the Fire Relief Fund, and distributed 2,500 meals during the season. Arrests for vagrancy decreased 75 percent; robberies declined and back-door begging diminished. Yet efforts to perpetuate the plan did not succeed. Perhaps hard times decreased giving or the city lacked sufficient public work or funds.[35]

In early 1896, Ladies Aid representatives formed the Fargo Union Relief Society. Any of these churchwomen might serve as an officer, board member, or friendly visitor. The society set annual one-dollar membership dues to become self-supporting and avoid the fund-raising burden. It immediately utilized rooms in the WCTU hall to collect food and clothing for distribution to deserving families. By June, it had assisted twelve families with money, clothing, and provisions. The society helped the poor find aid from other sources. Those with permanent needs became wards of the county. Still others, upon investigation, received no assistance. The Union Relief Society did not achieve self-sufficiency. It regularly requested clothing. It sought appropriations from the city council and the Cass County commissioners. It took donations from the Knights of Pythias and other fraternal bodies.[36]

Churches and other organizations still assisted particular individuals or institutions. For example, Mrs. Harry O'Neil of St. Mary's parish organized a charity ball in 1892 to pay Mrs. Dowd's home mortgage. O'Neil's effort exemplified the increased involvement of laywomen in the national Catholic charity crusade. In addition, the Gethsemane Church Ladies held a ball and card party to benefit the free kindergarten. Other dances assisted the McLean orphans and the orphanage. During Christmastime 1896, the Good Templars Lodge erected a large tree at the Odd Fellows Hall for those children who would not otherwise enjoy the holiday. The Fargo Packing Company provided free meat "to all deserving" for their festive meals.[37]

Turn-of-the-century charitable reform focused on protecting children. As a consequence, Fargo acquired more benevolent institutions than any other city in the state. These may have helped Cass County administer its poor relief more effectively than other counties. The North Dakota Children's Home, founded in 1891, provided residential care for all children or for their temporary placement in Christian homes. The Florence Crittenton Home opened in 1892. It assisted homeless families and helped them to live independently. It served unwed mothers and their children. If warranted, it separated children from their parents and permanently placed them in new homes. St. John's Orphanage, established in 1896, accepted destitute or orphan children and placed them for adoption. These institutions relied

St. John's Orphanage in Fargo protected children and inculcated Victorian values. Courtesy Institute for Regional Studies, North Dakota State University, Fargo (2006.57.2).

on middle-class charitable contributions. They also inculcated their charges with the bourgeois virtues of industry, thrift, and sobriety.[38]

A new "politicized domesticity" during the 1890s that protected children and promoted other forms of civic housekeeping also fueled a renewal of the women's suffrage movement. Although clubwomen came late to suffrage, they constructed the winning argument. The belief that naturally virtuous women voters would redeem society carried the suffrage amendment to victory. The Dakota Territorial Legislature in 1883 granted women the right to vote in school board elections. Nearly a decade later, the state elected its first female official, superintendent of public instruction Laura J. Eisenhuth. Despite these hopeful signs, the dominant Republican Party, the liquor interests, and many foreign-born stubbornly resisted full suffrage. Opponents employed duplicitous "tactics . . . throughout the long struggle," according to leading suffragist and longtime WCTU president Elizabeth Preston Anderson.[39]

Meanwhile, in Fargo, Fortnightly clubwoman Helen (Mrs. O. J.) deLendrecie combined domesticity with strong suffrage advocacy. Along with other female members of the Political Equality Club, she undertook the study of civil government in 1895. That same year she attended the first Woman Suffrage State Convention at Grand Forks. She responded to an address by Laura M.

Johns, a nationally known orator and organizer of the Political Equality Club. A few days later, deLendrecie reported to her Fargo sisters on the convention's work. The *Forum,* taking a benign view of these activities, commented: "Rational freedom is as wholesome for women as for men . . . as it has . . . strengthened the manliness of men, it cannot fail . . . to have like effect upon the womanliness of women." Agreeing that the women's vote will morally improve home, church, society, and government, the newspaper urged women to vote in large numbers for female candidates in an upcoming school election. Board member Alex Stern endorsed the lone woman aspirant after two others withdrew: "By all means let us have Mrs. deLendrecie's good sense and business ability on the board." Stern and deLendrecie finished first in the election. By autumn, women constituted almost 19 percent of the city's 2,575 registered voters. After traveling to Washington, D.C., for the 1898 national suffrage convention, deLendrecie pledged herself to lecture each Saturday on the suffrage cause.[40]

Helen deLendrecie campaigned for women's suffrage and served on the Fargo School Board. From *Fargo Souvenir* (1897).

RELIGIOUS FOUNDATIONS OF THE MORAL ORDER

Argus editor Alanson W. Edwards reflected the common American belief in God as the basis of both morality and citizenship when he called for a "crusade against infidelity and boastful blatant irreligion." Numerous sales of the *Infidel Bible* at a local bookstore had likely alarmed the editor. Perhaps the public talk of popular theater manager Ben Howard, whom the Reverend Oscar Elmer regarded as an "atheist of [the] materialist Evolution school," also disturbed Edwards. When Howard died in 1884, Elmer reported that a large number of lawyers and public men attended his funeral. Despite the anxiety of Edwards and Elmer, Protestantism remained potent intellectually and institutionally in the twin cities and elsewhere.[41] Its values, churches, and members collectively provided the foundation for the middle-class moral order. Its ethos permeated most social institutions and reform movements.

Protestantism pervaded the public schools. Most American educators viewed the United States as a Christian nation. They charged the schools with promoting social stability by training good citizens and inculcating basic American values. They believed that good citizenship rested on sound morality and that true morality required religious instruction. They therefore taught a civil religion that derived from Christianity and emphasized America as a special nation under the guidance and judgment of God. Textbooks, Christian teachers, and patriotic observances imparted these beliefs in classrooms. School readers and other texts contained explicit and implicit moral and religious lessons. Teachers modeled Christian moral and civic rectitude. Most attended church and participated in church activities. School commemorations of the American flag and national holidays taught patriotism. By these methods, public schools instilled a common set of moral and civic values.[42]

Protestant churches filled the social lives of numerous families every Sabbath with worship, Sunday school, and evening prayer. Several congregations sent delegations to the annual Sunday School Convention, which often met in Fargo. Members from many denominations attended the yearly meetings of the Cass and Clay County Bible societies. During the 1880s, the Fargo Methodist Lyceum offered a varied course of literature and music that attracted cultured people from both cities. In the next decade, the Moorhead Methodist pastor delivered a series of Sunday evening sermons on the topics: "Businessman as Public Benefactor," "What the Gospel Has Done for Laboring Men," "What the Gospel Has Done for Women," "Need of Prayer," and "Perseverance in Well Doing." Other churches offered similar programs that editors publicized and likely attracted a general audience of Christians.[43]

Many Protestants strictly observed the Sabbath. For example, "a Christian citizen" wrote to the *Moorhead Weekly News* in 1883 complaining about baseball games that transformed the "sanctity and quiet of the New England Sabbath" into "a European Sunday." *News* editor George Lamphere shared these sentiments. He called on citizens to prevent Sunday baseball because it "is very distasteful and shocking to people of religious and moral tendencies." He additionally criticized threshing crews and hunters of prairie chickens for breaking the Minnesota Sabbath Law. Residents frequently petitioned their city councils to enforce the Sunday closing of saloons. Moorhead ministers in 1886 formed a Law and Order League that cooperated with its Fargo counterpart in promoting stricter obedience of antiliquor and antiprostitution laws.[44]

Protestants fostered the YMCA in both cities. It had been transplanted from England in 1851 to Boston and New York. During the next half century, it attracted support from railroad executives, bankers, and merchants as it established 1,500 local associations and enrolled 250,000 members throughout the United States. Association facilities and services attempted to save thousands of unmarried young men from the temptations of urban vice by re-creating a Christian homelike environment as an alternative to the saloon, pool hall, and boardinghouse. It initially targeted the middle class, but a railroad department created in 1877 carried its message of "workplace domesticity" to the working class. According to historian Thomas Winter, the patriarchal household modeled this ideal. By developing an obedient Christian manhood among workers, middle-class YMCA officials hoped to resolve labor conflict. Laborers exchanged their loyal service for moral guidance from employers. Although the Y had failed in its initial purpose by the 1920s, historian Jessica Elfenbein suggests that "its willingness to maintain linkages with the public and private sectors" fundamentally altered United States civic culture by contributing to the rise of the welfare state.[45]

Establishing the Fargo YMCA required three attempts. An initial effort occurred at the Methodist and Presbyterian churches in August 1879. A second attempt by seventeen men three years later bore fruit, but the group disintegrated after only two years. Fargo ministers called a meeting in 1886 at the home of Samuel G. Roberts that finally succeeded. Meanwhile, the Moorhead YMCA formed at an 1881 Methodist church gathering. It began with twenty members and forty prospects. In addition to regular Sabbath meetings and a reading room, it sponsored well-attended concerts and lectures throughout the decade.[46]

At the turn of the century, the Moorhead association had a gymnasium equipped with new apparatus; its reading room offered the latest newspapers and periodicals; and its annual program featured four lectures, one recital, and one concert scheduled from November until May at Fraternity Hall. According to well-known local attorney, Congregationalist, and president George Perley, the association benefited the city by helping young men physically, mentally, morally, and spiritually. Through this fourfold program, Jessica Elfenbein observes, the YMCA became a comprehensive institution providing important caretaking and homemaking services. In addition, its educational programs fostered members' leadership skills and confidence, serving as schools for democracy. These achievements did not accrue without community support. Fortunately, many Moorhead Protestant church ladies rendered assistance. Female activist traditions equipped them for creating the required YMCA domestic setting. They formed an auxiliary, sponsored fund-raising suppers, decorated the hall, and hosted receptions at which up to four hundred might attend. Thomas Winter concludes, "The Women's Auxiliaries readily embraced the opportunity . . . [of] building manhood."[47]

By 1887, the Fargo YMCA had a building on Front and Seventh streets. Despite many members' fees, an annual city canvas, and endless benefits by the ladies auxiliary, the association struggled financially. The *Forum* endorsed its continuous appeals for funds, asserting that the Y did great good and deserved help from everyone. It bettered "public morals." It did not permit cards and billiards that might lead to gambling and prevent young men from rising in society. It sponsored an impressive program: weekly prayer meetings, Bible study, reading, lectures, gymnastics, tennis, and baths. Besides daily newspapers, religious and railroad publications, illustrated newspapers, and popular magazines, the reading room furnished a writing desk, envelopes, and paper, as well as an admonition—"Write a letter home!" Scheduling a social on Thanksgiving evening afforded an additional homelike experience. After assembling at the building, members took young men home for dinner before returning for apples, popcorn, and music. The 1896–97 annual report demonstrates how popular many activities were. Bible class and gospel attendance numbered 388 and 3,512, respectively; the reading room recorded 40,560 visits; 6,442 engaged in gymnastics; and 4,426 took baths. As YMCA officials frequently asked ministers for help, they did not schedule meetings that conflicted with church services.[48]

Historian Elliot Gorn has called the YMCA the most prominent institutional expression of muscular Christianity in the 1890s. By combining piety with sports, Christian men need not be soft, feminine, or sentimental. The well-equipped Fargo Y gym featured mats, a springboard and German horse, rings, parallel and horizontal bars, a punching bag, and sets of Indian clubs, dumbbells, barbells, and pulley weights. The remodeled handball court permitted playing the popular new game of basketball. Boys, businessmen, and ladies took gym classes. Large audiences attended an annual gymnastics exhibition and concert scheduled to raise money. Newly organized baseball, tennis, and bicycle clubs used a recently acquired athletic park. More than three hundred bicyclists paraded through city streets, whetting their appetites for refreshments sold by the ladies auxiliary to benefit the association.[49]

The Salvation Army—"the Church of the Poor" founded in England by ex-Methodist minister William Booth and his wife Catherine—came to North America in 1880. Among religious groups at this time, it best combined concern for poverty with biblical theology and morality. It attracted the poor by food, shelter, music, marching, and uniforms. It then rehabilitated them through regular work, sobriety, and responsibility. By 1900, the Salvation Army had 700 corps and 3,000 officers situated in U.S. cities. It first appeared in Moorhead on May 9, 1895, when 300 attended a meeting at "the barracks" on Fifth Street and Main Avenue. Captain Lindemann reported 100 converts by the end of June. A procession of eighty people invaded Fargo, marching to First Congregational. Many soon grumbled that bass drums and parades disturbed horses and the sick. Others objected that religious freedom and the right to parade should be upheld. Mayor Art Lewis offered a compromise that permitted parades without drums, kept one side of the street open, and denied street meetings. When Captain Lindemann and other officers departed after seven months' work, many gathered at the opera house to say good-bye. Captain Berriman and Lieutenant Lane soon arrived to carry on the "good work." Canadian division commandant H. H. Booth—fourth son of the founders—lectured in Fargo at this time. His jurisdiction included the Fargo corps.[50]

TEMPERANCE AND THE WCTU

Religiously inspired temperance crusaders attacked alcohol as an evil at the same time that they affirmed the bourgeois virtues of industry, thrift, and respectability. By the late nineteenth century, "the saloon had acquired the reputation of a mother of vices ranging from drunkenness and prostitution to crime and political corruption," according to western historian Richard White. Because the spread of prostitution in the United States matched that of the saloon, the campaigns against vice and liquor corresponded. Scholar Joseph R. Gusfield has argued, "Drinking and abstinence became symbols of social status." The middle class viewed sobriety and industry as necessary for economic success, self-respect, and social acceptance. For Catholic working-class immigrants, therefore, temperance afforded an avenue of assimilation into American middle-class culture. When too few chose abstinence, temperance became more coercive by the end of the century, culminating in state and national prohibition campaigns.[51]

The war on intemperance started early in the twin cities. It began with voluntary associations led by the native-born bourgeoisie and supported by Christians who may have been converted to the cause by revivals in their respective churches. Twenty-five men, including the Reverend Oscar Elmer, formed a Moorhead Good Templar Lodge in 1878. Another appeared in Fargo at the same time. The Templars battled with activities and meetings that replicated the fellowship of the saloons they intended to displace. They sponsored numerous speakers, who encouraged hundreds to wear blue abstinence ribbons. As a result, each city started a Reform Club. These proposed reading rooms—stocked with good books and periodicals—as wholesome alternatives to drinking dens. Men from several Fargo congregations founded a Christian Temperance Union in 1882. It publicized the demerits of high and low fee licensing systems. Its work soon affected municipal politics and divided congregations. For example, the Reverend Elmer electioneered for James Sharp against saloonkeeper John Mason in an 1881 contest for alderman. Afterwards he wrote in his diary: "Some of my people pretend to be troubled because of my politico-temperance zeal—Bah!" Meanwhile, more than two hundred Fargo voters pledged support for a temperance mayoral candidate.[52]

Catholics and Scandinavians also contributed to the struggle. The Catholic church sponsored total abstinence societies for those who could not control their drinking. Bishop John Shanley counseled the faithful to abandon the liquor trade because it might lead to sinful behavior. He administered the abstinence pledge to many others. Pietistic Scandinavian immigrants brought temperance convictions with them to the United States. They created their own societies and sponsored their own speakers, socials, rallies, and other events. In Fargo, they instituted a Norwegian Good Templar Lodge and Scandinavian WCTU. They founded a Moorhead Scandinavian Temperance Society at Trinity Norwegian Lutheran Church. Later, many Concordia professors and pupils eagerly joined. The college enforced the rules of a well-conducted Christian home. Students could not use tobacco, visit saloons, and purchase or drink intoxicating liquor. Principal I. F. Grose expelled those who did, which the *Moorhead Weekly News* called "reasonable." Professor Rasmus Bogstad gave temperance talks at Norwegian Lutheran churches. Concordia rejoiced when Clay County voted dry in 1915.[53]

Elizabeth Preston Anderson, pictured in 1882, became the president of the North Dakota WCTU (1893–1933) and battled for the adoption and enforcement of prohibition. Courtesy Institute for Regional Studies, North Dakota State University, Fargo (p4.3).

The WCTU strongly opposed the liquor interests. Founded in 1874 after a crusade by Midwestern women to close saloons, the WCTU had evangelical Christian roots. Led by middle-class, native-born Protestants who assumed the superiority of their own values, it supported varied humanitarian reforms for bettering society. Most specifically, by attacking alcohol abuse it protected the home and family from male violence and unreliability. Under the exceptional leadership of longtime president Frances Willard, the union projected a vision of what historian Sara Evans has called "the maternal commonwealth" that fused domesticity and politics. Willard waged campaigns for temperance education in the public schools, social purity, and protection of the American home. The union's reliance on moral suasion and a less threatening version of domesticity attracted sufficient Catholic and labor support to carry prohibition in several western states. Its threat to bolt to the Prohibition Party in 1888 forced adoption of an altered Republican platform that supported "'temperance and morality' and 'the purity of the American home.'" Historian of religion Sydney Ahlstrom suggests that the WCTU represented one way that social Christianity changed the consciousness of conservative evangelicals.[54]

After a short-lived previous attempt, women organized the Moorhead WCTU in 1883. Editor George Lamphere applauded its formation, saying only women could protect their sisters from the evils of liquor. The union soon petitioned the city council to enforce Sunday closing. It frequently sponsored lecturers who urged total abstinence and prohibition as the only solutions. It opened a reading room at the First National Bank building and placed a barrel of ice water on a business street in 1894.[55]

The Dakota WCTU—with Adelaide M. Kinnear of Fargo as corresponding secretary—appeared in 1882. Some bodies, including the indigenous Central Union, predated the territorial organization. At this time, women of every Protestant faith except Scandinavian Lutheranism formed the Woodford Union at the Fargo Methodist church. These unions soon created a Band of Hope embracing children who had signed a pledge forswearing intoxicating liquor, tobacco, and profane language. They later instituted a Young Women's WCTU. For all members, abstinence became the badge of respectability. All battled hard for the cause. They sponsored frequent socials to replenish their treasuries and finance their many activities. Like their Moorhead sisters, the women placed barrels of water on Front Street and Broadway, "thereby furnishing a drink that refreshes but does not intoxicate." They offered firemen coffee as a substitute for whiskey while battling fires. They held gospel temperance meetings. In 1887, they hosted Frances Willard—their founder, president, and champion of the woman's cause for "God, Home and Native Land." Speaking before a large audience,

Willard attacked the destruction caused by liquor and urged female suffrage in order to protect the home. The unions also petitioned the city council to deny liquor licenses to anyone already indicted or convicted.[56]

The WCTU—aided by the Scandinavian Total Abstinence Society, the Scandinavian WCTU, and Norwegian Good Templar lodges—secured prohibition in 1889 when the state narrowly ratified the constitution. Local members celebrated their "glorious . . . victory" with a "thanksgiving and praise meeting" at the Methodist church. Elizabeth Preston (later Anderson)—an organizer who succeeded Adelaide M. Kinnear as president in 1893 and served forty years—spoke frequently for adoption. She urged North Dakota voters "to rise in the nobility of your manhood and say by your ballots . . . that this enemy of purity in morals . . . politics . . . home . . . [and] childhood shall not enter here." She asserted: "The liquor traffic is responsible for at least 90 percent of the crime committed. . . . The saloon is the hotbed of socialism and anarchy." She concluded: "Prohibition is the only safety for the individual, for the home, for the nation." Having won a victory, Preston did not rest on her laurels. She devoted herself to organizing new associations throughout the state "to guard this law and its enforcement" by keeping "public sentiment awake." Her efforts battled the liquor interests and other opponents that annually attempted to repeal the law for many years.[57]

Saloons closed on July 1, 1890. Enforcement proved problematic. Many officials and state's attorneys did nothing. West river Germans ignored a measure imposed by Red River Valley Norwegians. The dominant Republican Party, controlled by Boss Alexander McKenzie and the old guard, blocked railroad regulation by threatening resubmission. Cass County Democrats supported a new vote and called for high license fees to prevent the evils of intemperance. Numerous city residents expressed doubts. Hostile workers viewed saloons as places of enjoyment and recreation. Municipal officials worried about reduced revenues from lost fines and liquor license fees. Businessmen fretted about diminished trade without saloons as an attraction. Even some temperance crusaders objected. For example, the *Moorhead Weekly News* articulated the views of several when it argued that law could not prohibit consumption. Only converting individuals to abstinence and strictly enforcing license laws would reduce drinking. Editor George Lamphere thus expressed Victorian bourgeois values: character must be changed to stop the trade.[58]

"The battle royal" of resubmission raged at every legislative session for many years. Elizabeth Preston attributed the victory of her cause to the "telegrams, letters and petitions" from the WCTU rank and file. Charles Pollock—known as "the father of North Dakota Prohibition"—later said that the WCTU deserved the most credit for the enactment and preservation of the law. Similarly, Frances Willard praised Preston: "It is a pleasure to see a young state president so capable and womanly." Preston demonstrated her worthiness in the message she sent for reading at Willard's funeral: "We pledge renewed consecration to the holy cause to which she gave the last full measure of devotion." Preston and the WCTU backed additional reforms: the 1893 women's suffrage bill, the 1899 repeal of the ninety-day divorce law, and subsequent antitobacco legislation.[59]

In narrowly defeating resubmission in 1895, the WCTU received support from legislator Alanson W. Edwards, an unlikely ally who earlier had opposed the measure. The *Forum* editor decided to honor the recently adopted prohibition pledge by the Republican Party. He now urged "rigid and strict enforcement" of the law. Immediately after narrowly winning this battle, Preston and her lawyer allies—Charles and Robert Pollock—organized the North Dakota Enforcement League at the prohibition state convention held at the Fargo First Congregational Church. During that week, A. C. Rankin— a former Pittsburgh factory worker converted to sobriety—delivered a series of lectures at the armory at which more than 1,200 took the abstinence pledge. The popular prohibitionist sentiment surprised delegates, who supposed that a majority of inhabitants favored open saloons. Indeed, the Baptist, Congregational, Methodist, and Presbyterian churches continued backing the WCTU antirepeal fight. They also welcomed Elizabeth Preston to the city in 1899 as she nurtured the local temperance unions.[60]

FRATERNAL LODGES AND WOMEN'S AUXILIARIES

By 1901, more than 5 million Americans belonged to an estimated six hundred fraternal orders that served many diverse groups—native-born, immigrants, Catholics, Protestants, blacks, whites, men, and women. Moorhead and Fargo echoed these national trends. The 1900 directory listed fifty-one fraternal bodies, which included fourteen Masonic, three Odd Fellow, four Knights of Pythias, two Ancient Order of United Workmen (AOUW), two Grand Army of the Republic (GAR), and many others. In addition, six women's auxiliaries had been organized. Scholars have variously interpreted this "Golden Age of Fraternity." Most explain how lodges fostered middle-class moral order. By promoting bourgeois values—sobriety, thrift, discipline, and self-reliance—they decreased religious and ethnic separation. By providing tangible benefits—business contacts, organizational skills, charity, and life or health insurance—they enhanced individual opportunity, defended the family, and fortified community.[61]

The popular and prestigious Masonic order imparted the model for most other fraternal bodies. This white, male, Protestant quasi-religious secret society conducted elaborate rituals and developed bourgeois virtues. The number of North Dakota Masons—drawn from the Yankee, Scandinavian, Protestant, and Republican elite—increased from 1,300 in 1889 to 13,000 in 1909. Membership afforded a means of getting ahead in business and a sign of success. The Masons established themselves as early as Christianity in the twin cities. As their descendants recalled more than a half century later, "They knew that the Masonic Lodge is a silent partner of the home, the church and the schoolhouse, toiling in behalf of law and order." Accordingly, early settlers organized the Fargo Shiloh Lodge No. 105 and Moorhead Lodge No. 126 of Ancient Free and Accepted Masons in 1872 and 1876, respectively.[62]

At the start of the new century, the Fargo Masonic bodies claimed 2,904 members. Many of these had undergone initiations to the several degree-granting lodges. These grew in number to facilitate the rituals for awarding thirty-three degrees. To house them all, the Scottish Rite Order built a new temple on the corner of Fifth Street and First Avenue North. It accommodated the lodges, the Scottish and York rite bodies, the El Zagal Shrine, the Order of the Eastern Star (OES), and the youth organizations. The Grand Lodge headquarters, library, and museum also located there. According to the dedication souvenir, the Masons led in an "age of clubs and lodges." Their preeminence "did not rest simply on ceremonies and mysteries." Instead, their morals and philosophy bound them to fostering "the brotherhood of man, and the fatherhood of God."[63]

Despite such disclaimers, Masonic "ceremonies and mysteries" defined their cultural role in forming Victorian manhood, according to historian Mark Carnes. Initiation rituals emphasized death, omitted reference to Christ, and evoked a powerful deity. Rites refuted the feminized liberal theology of nineteenth-century Protestantism at the same time that fraternal symbols—altars, God, and biblical oaths—suggested the unity of church and lodge. Rites enabled initiates to efface their ties to women and feminine values. Reborn initiates acquired a new masculine identity that prepared them to face the unpleasant realities of life. As Howard Chudacoff observes, initiation "symbolized a rebirth into the family of brethren as well as a rite of passage, rewarding man's worthiness for membership." The lodge thus provided a substitute for the feminized church and home with which Victorian men could not identify. Yet ritual for the highest Masonic degrees kept secret the feminine side of masculinity because members could not admit to themselves they were by nature both male and female.[64]

By the 1850s, the Masons allowed women to attend lodge banquets and lectures. This shift originated from the anti-Masonic charge that the order could not inculcate virtue without women's moral custodianship. Masons

MASONIC TEMPLE, FARGO, N. DAK.

The impressive Fargo Masonic Temple, built in 1900, testified to the importance of that fraternal order in the city. Courtesy Institute for Regional Studies, North Dakota State University, Fargo (51.130.1).

responded by establishing female honorary degrees. After the Civil War, the women insisted on creating their own auxiliary, the OES. Only the wives and daughters of Master Masons could become members. Their membership ceased if the order expelled husband or father, or the daughter married a non-Mason. The Worshipful Master of the men's lodge presided over OES meetings. Unlike the Masonic masculine religion, the ladies' degrees embraced liberal theology and true womanhood. Initiates emulated Ruth, a biblical model of female self-effacement. The OES had attracted five hundred thousand women by the 1890s. Without female support, the anti-Masonic campaign by evangelical Christians collapsed. Although limited by their ties to male lodges, auxiliaries furthered female public participation, according to scholar Mary Ann Clawson. "Sister Masons" early attended local lodge functions and served banquets. The Moorhead OES organized in March 1903. The Mecca Chapter in Fargo emerged a decade earlier. It met at the Masonic hall, which hosted the first annual session of the OES Grand Chapter in 1895. Mecca claimed 175 members by 1903.[65]

Masonry spawned many fraternal imitators, becoming the model for the structure, ritual, government, and function of other orders that reflected the growing ethnic and religious diversity of American society. Like

In the 1880s, a woman proudly wears the distinctive and mysterious dress of the Order of the Eastern Star, the women's auxiliary of the Masonic Order. Courtesy Institute for Regional Studies, North Dakota State University, Fargo (2006.94.20).

Masons, others emphasized ritual and fraternal brotherhood. Unlike Masons, they embraced insurance and provided fraternal aid based on the ethical principle of reciprocity. Before the 1930s, they provided most insurance. The Independent Order of Odd Fellows (IOOF) separated from its British parent in 1842. It became the most important and largest American fraternal trendsetter. Initially a working-class movement, it only later appealed to middling Anglo Protestants with good morals and incomes. It initiated guaranteed benefits. Even though every brother had the right to assistance, the order denied it to the habitually drunk, profane, and promiscuous. Moral selectivity and age-scaled initiation fees made IOOF insurance less expensive than that of its commercial competitors. IOOF lodges established themselves in Fargo by 1874 and in Moorhead by 1879. A visiting Grand Master articulated the order's basic principles: "An Odd Fellow's Lodge is a fountain from which should ever flow the healing tide of peace and love, of charity and kindness to all mankind, and a safe and sane asylum to all brethren." Two additional male bodies and the Ivy Rebekah Lodge composed of ninety-five women appeared in the 1890s. These met twice monthly and often conducted dancing parties during the winter.[66]

The AOUW, the first national life insurance fraternal order, attracted 450,000 members and numerous imitators by 1902. It centrally dispersed one thousand (later two thousand)-dollar death benefits that one dollar per capita assessments funded. As other orders regularized their insurance, they similarly grew. AOUW initiation paralleled that of the Masons, indicating how ritual appealed to workers and immigrants as well as the native-born Protestant middle class. A Moorhead AOUW lodge first met in May 1878. A more permanent body emerged in April 1890. The Degree of Honor—the women's auxiliary—organized in March 1900. The first Fargo lodge, instituted in 1882, had been replaced by another by 1889. When the lodge dedicated its new hall five years later, the Degree of Honor served the order's almost five hundred members. During its early existence, the lodge paid two thousand-dollar death benefits to two families. Cards of thanks for sickness assistance appeared in the newspaper. As one wrote, "It conveys to me that . . . brotherly love and charity which our noble order teaches."[67]

By the 1880s, the GAR had four hundred thousand members, making it the most important among several veterans' organizations. Like other fraternal orders, it emphasized ritual, brotherhood, and charitable assistance. The Fargo John F. Reynolds Post No. 44 organized with seventy enrolled in 1884. Membership eventually peaked at 287 before declining to only six survivors by 1929, dictating the end of the post shortly thereafter. The Woman's Relief Corps (WRC)—a women's auxiliary—served the first and all subsequent banquets, as well as refreshments at the many GAR dances. As was customary for all fraternal bodies, the women distributed surplus food from these events to needy families. Annual balls typically benefited poor veterans and their families. Both organizations met every two weeks. Often they arranged assistance in the form of food, clothing, rent, railroad tickets, or cash. The WRC hosted socials and formed sewing circles to provide for veterans' wives, sisters, or children; they transferred surplus funds to their male comrades.[68]

Additionally, the GAR and WRC jointly conducted annual Decoration Day observances, a collective rite of the dead that integrated the entire community. Several Northern and Southern towns claim to have originated the ceremony. Mrs. John Logan, impressed by the Confederate Memorial Day, spoke about the custom to her husband, a Republican congressman and newly elected GAR commander. He issued a general order in 1868 designating May 30 for decorating comrades' graves. Over the years, processions and ceremonies became more elaborate as a way of instilling patriotism. The Fargo public joined in paying tribute to the heroic dead. Flags were lowered to half-mast; city offices closed for the entire day and businesses for the afternoon. In the morning, schoolchildren placed flowers on veterans' graves. Following a dinner served at the GAR hall by the WRC, veterans, Militia Company B, firemen, policemen, and citizens paraded through the principal streets to Island Park for a commemoration, oratory, and music. During the 1890s, the Baptist, Congregational, Methodist, Presbyterian, and Unitarian churches conducted Union Memorial Sunday Services in the well-filled opera house.[69]

PROGRAMME

FOR THE

Grand Army of the Republic Memorial Services

John F. Reynolds Post No. 5, Fargo, N. Dak.

OPERA HOUSE, SUNDAY, MAY 27, 1894.

The Congregational, Baptist, Presbyterian and Methodist Churches will unite
in this service Sunday Morning at 10:30.

1. ANTHEM BY THE CHOIR.
2. INVOCATION — Rev. V. N. Yergin.
3. HYMN — Rev. A. H. Tebbets.
4. SCRIPTURE LESSONS — Rev. W. L. Van Horn.
5. PRAYER — Rev. E. W. Day.
6. HYMN — Rev. J. A. Strachan.
7. ANNOUNCEMENTS.
8. SELECTION BY CHOIR.
9. SERMON — Rev. Eugene May. Theme: "The Immortality of Heroism."
10. SELECTION BY CHOIR.
11. HYMN.
12. DOXOLOGY AND BENEDICTION.

Four Protestant churches in Fargo conducted a Union Memorial Day service in cooperation with Decoration Day observances sponsored by the Grand Army of the Republic and Woman's Relief Corps. Courtesy Institute for Regional Studies, North Dakota State University, Fargo.

Although the GAR planned Decoration Day ceremonies, the WRC played an important role. The women purchased flowers, prepared food, and served dinner "to all old soldiers and their families . . . that may be in the city." The women also encouraged patriotism on other occasions. They conducted socials on Lincoln's or Washington's birthday. At a union meeting of the two societies in 1895, the women presented a flag to the men. Comrade Samuel G. Roberts eloquently thanked them for their beautiful gift. Mrs. Gebhardt sang "The Star-Spangled Banner" and "Rally Around the Flag," with the audience joining in the choruses. The WRC then served the banquet. In addition, the women provided flags to all public schools and persuaded the board to mandate that flag salutes be conducted each morning.[70]

Profit-seeking railroad corporations founded, developed, and left a permanent mark on the cityscapes of Moorhead and Fargo. The Northern Pacific, SPM&M, and the Milwaukee Road afforded opportunities for economically ambitious dual city settlers. The corporations established the framework for private decision making. Individuals erected homes, businesses, churches, schools, and fraternal halls, many of which remain today. These structures could not have been built without the lumber, brick, stained glass, and machine-tooled components required by local contractors.[71] Railroads shipped all goods, which made it possible for residents to enjoy and display the most advanced material culture and genteel refinement of the East. In this sense, the railroads supplied the material environment for an emerging middle-class moral order.

A culture of privatism shaped Moorhead and Fargo as it did other American cities. Individuals pursued happiness by seeking wealth and the independence that it brought. They provided homes, security, and a prosperous future for their families. They built a community that maintained order among moneymakers and allowed opportunities to all.[72] Men such as Solomon G. Comstock and Evan Tyler made fortunes and built mansions that evidenced their success and their vision for the communal order. Such homes set a standard for gentility emulated by others as their pocketbooks permitted. The cult of domesticity ruled households in which virtuous women reared children, upheld the markers of social status, and provided a haven from the less than pristine commercial world. Home and domesticity became a keystone of dual city associational life. Women extended their influence beyond the home, at times spurred by revivals in their own churches. They founded libraries, aided the poor, and joined temperance crusades. These helped the threatened and needy help themselves. Books elevated character, increasing the odds for success. Assistance put the worthy poor back on their feet. The YMCA offered an attractive Christian, homelike atmosphere and kept young men from saloons. The WCTU took reform a step further. It aimed at saving home and family by abolishing liquor. Woman suffrage advocates politicized domesticity. They argued that female voters would morally improve municipality, state, and nation.

Middle-class men similarly joined voluntary associations in large numbers. Such organizations stemmed from self-interest and furthered community, as historian Richard White has observed. Fraternal orders afforded opportunities for self-definition to members of the emerging middle class. They provided the tangible benefits of business contacts, life or health insurance, and charity. They served the communal order by bringing like-minded individuals together and fulfilling their particular aims. They provided a means for attaining municipal goals against the powerful political and economic forces faced by all western cities.[73] Men who joined the Freemasons, Odd Fellows, and other lodges perpetuated middle-class virtues through their quasi-religious rituals. By establishing fraternal orders, reform societies, schools, churches, homes, and families, the emerging middle class socialized the young in the Victorian moral code. By all these means, it spread values of domesticity, respectability, industry, thrift, and sobriety throughout society and thereby established middle-class moral order in both cities.

Fargo and Moorhead had many similarities. Both cities depended on the railroad for prosperity and the good things of life. Both shared the culture of privatism. Both relied on voluntary organizations of individuals to curb the excesses of individualism. Both developed parallel institutions— homes, families, churches, schools, and associations. For the most part, institutions and associations functioned separately, each conducting its own affairs within its community. Thus the woman's club in each city founded a public library and temperance groups focused on cleaning up their town. There were exceptions. Members of the middle and upper classes occasionally crossed the Red River to attend dances, theatrical productions, and other events. Apart from such fraternization and occasional sponsorship of a few joint events, the communities and their voluntary associations carried on separate existences.

Most fundamental differences within the dual city stemmed from the fact that larger and wealthier Fargo dominated its state. Fargo therefore had characteristics Moorhead lacked. Although Moorhead claimed the Comstock mansion and a few other imposing homes, Fargo had three or four elite neighborhoods. The Fargo wealthy consequently had greater pretensions to exclusivity than their Moorhead counterparts, yet never completely eliminated modest dwellings in their midst. In addition, Fargo had an orphanage, a children's home, and a home for unwed mothers. Moorhead's small size and its relatively low status among Minnesota cities prevented it from developing comparable institutions.

Vagabonds, Workers, and Purveyors of Vice

A person who has never taken part in the celebration of a crew of prairie laborers can hardly imagine how wild such men can be. . . . Everyone immediately buys a round. . . . There are some . . . who . . . order five rounds at a time. . . . There is drinking and gambling, fighting and shouting for several days.

—Knut Hamsun (1887)

Let the saloons come. The more the better it will be for us. They pay more taxes than anyone else. How many temperance people . . . pay $500 a year in taxes?

—John Erickson in *Moorhead Weekly News*, March 1, 1888

Houses of prostitution are curses to any city, even when confined to quarters remote from respectable habitations; but to permit them to exist in the very midst of private dwellings . . . is an outrage on decency.

—*Fargo Daily Republican*, September 27, 1882

INDUSTRIAL AND WESTWARD EXPANSION CREATED MOORHEAD AND Fargo. Railroad corporations defined them as real estate to be purchased. Mobility and avarice fragmented community, leading historian Rowland Berthoff to ask, "Could so atomized a society ensure the stability and security . . . of its self-reliant members?" As we have seen in chapters 4 and 5, residents responded to instability by establishing institutions of middle-class moral order: churches, schools, fraternal lodges, women's clubs, and a plethora of other voluntary associations. The cult of domesticity held women responsible for communal moral health. Accordingly, historian Julie

Roy Jeffrey has argued, westward migrating women took upon themselves the mission of civilizing the frontier. Similar to urban middle-class experience elsewhere, a worrisome working-class culture and institutions often confronted dual city female civilizers and their male allies.[1]

Industrialization fostered commercial agriculture, depressions, and class warfare that affected even small cities like Moorhead and Fargo. Thousands of migrant laborers arrived each spring and summer to plant and harvest wheat on the Bonanza farms and their smaller successors. Urban workers formed labor unions that challenged the economic individualism of small businessmen. Whether they toiled on the farm or in the city, many workmen patronized the numerous saloons that the middle class associated with drunkenness, violence, prostitution, and other crimes. Fearing that these forces of barbarism would destroy the bourgeois home, family, and success ethic, respectable elements headed by clergy, the WCTU, and other temperance groups battled to enforce Sabbath observance and to eliminate liquor, the mother of all vice and crime. After the state banished alcohol, Fargo segregated prostitution in the "hollow." Moorhead limited vice to downtown saloons and brothels at Front Street east. Like those in the Kansas cattle towns of Robert R. Dykstra's classic study, reformers ranged from radicals who wanted to eradicate all vice to moderates who kept a minimum of law and order so long as "sin paid its way." For a long time, rectitude and its lack coexisted uneasily, as they did at the first Moorhead church service held in the Chapin House dining room. According to the Reverend Oscar H. Elmer, a drunken man was among the twenty-five who attended. He knelt in prayer and gave responses, but withdrew when Elmer began to preach.[2]

TRAMPS, HARVEST HANDS, AND URBAN WORKERS

"The tramp evil" first appeared in the United States following the depression of 1873. Observers coined the term to describe the host of homeless who traveled far over the new railroad network looking for work. These mostly young, white, native-born males frequently found temporary lodging in municipal police stations. The tramp army usually excluded poor females and African Americans. Likely harassment and violent life on the road dissuaded women. Many either joined the growing ranks of urban prostitutes or charitable houses cared for them. The South restricted black mobility and the numerous Irish transients rejected them. By the 1890s, observers variously estimated that "professional" wanderers totaled between fifty thousand and a hundred thousand. According to historian Kenneth Kusmer, they were "the natural result of a virtually unregulated capitalist economy." The relative newness of industrial unemployment kept most middle-class

Americans from perceiving it as the cause. They instead blamed illiterate, lazy foreigners. Hence, the thousands who annually arrived in the valley for planting and harvesting frequently received harsh treatment as tramps.[3]

As transients grew in number, they developed terms that scholars later adopted. Historian Frank Higbie states it well: "Hoboes wandered to find work, tramps worked only to facilitate their wandering, and bums neither wandered nor worked." He applies Robert Wiebe's term "indispensable outcasts" to the several million who toiled seasonally throughout the Midwest in the late nineteenth and early twentieth centuries. Although their labor made them economically indispensable, their social habits placed them outside the communal order. This mobile labor army included the Red River Valley harvest hands. After 1900, more than a hundred thousand worked the wheat harvest each summer, following it north from Texas to Canada. Variations from year to year support different interpretations about the composition of this multitude. Historian Thomas Isern divides them into approximate thirds among farmworkers—small farmers, their sons, or migratory hands; skilled urban workers; and unskilled laborers. Kenneth Kusmer

Each autumn a migratory labor army supplied the Red River Valley with workers for the harvest. This photograph was taken near Fargo about 1900. Courtesy Minnesota Historical Society.

argues that most were unskilled workers. Some drifted randomly from job to job. Others worked an invariant seasonal cycle, moving from lumber camps, mines, or construction to wheat fields. Many wintered in the migrant neighborhoods of Minneapolis and St. Paul or Chicago. They relaxed there in saloons and found female companionship in brothels. They lived in low-cost lodgings on their savings or earnings from occasional jobs until summer brought renewed opportunities for work. Their failure to labor for accumulation annoyed even sympathetic observers.[4]

Harvest hands faced multiple difficulties. It was hard to find work, transportation, good wages, and decent conditions among often hostile communities. Short-lived harvest jobs usually defied efforts at more effective recruiting by managers, states, and railroads. Harvesters usually responded to handbills distributed by farmers or erroneous newspaper accounts. Either might lead to an oversupply and lower wages for hands. Employers did not mind, but the men and the twin cities did. For example, misled by the eastern press, many desperate workers arrived one month early in the depression year of 1895. The large number of potential thieves and beggars worried municipal officials. Three years later, more transients arrived than ever before. By August, the police rounded up an average of two hundred each day. Authorities feared more crime because many would not find jobs. Apparently, news of the surplus and rumors of a small harvest affected subsequent supply. The following spring, valley farmers complained about a labor shortage, which they attributed to low wages paid in previous years, the return of national prosperity, and the large numbers serving in the Spanish-American War. Owing to adverse publicity about a likely light crop, the shortage of hands continued the next season.[5]

Railroad travel posed problems as well. Most men rejected harvesters' fares as too high. They rode illegally on freight trains, a dangerous and poor method for distributing workers. The rides they found did not always take them to the most plentiful jobs. Accidents killed thousands and criminals, who also rode the rails, robbed others. Workers' experiences with trainmen varied. They might be brutally beaten, assessed a fee, or given a free ride if they had a union card. The *Moorhead Weekly News* in 1886, for example, reported men arriving at the rate of a hundred per day, aided by Northern Pacific conductors who sold "free rides" for fifty cents or one dollar each. At other times, the railroad corporations gave more help. Pressured by towns to keep migrants moving, they added extra boxcars to handle the large numbers. Although some train crews continued waging war on tramps, others became more sympathetic. New technologies and rules made their work more dangerous while wages declined. Engineers, conductors, and brakemen became less inclined to aid the corporation and left the hoboes to company detectives.[6]

Once tramps arrived at a destination, those who could not afford cheap lodgings resided in "hobo jungles" until work could be found. The men placed these "marvels of cooperation" near water and railroad lines and away from the oversight of residents and authorities. A "code of hobo ethics" governed them, according to scholar Todd DePastino. Camaraderie based on the virtue of reciprocity enabled many to survive unemployment on the road and in the cities. To be sure, twin city residents did not observe life in the jungles located near the Red River at the Manitoba Railroad Bridge in Moorhead and the Northern Pacific Elevator in Fargo. Recent arrivals as well as hands biding their time between spring planting and fall harvest lived there. Suspicious policemen in plain clothes often watched them closely.[7]

Even when harvest hands found jobs, difficulties remained. What they earned varied according to national economic conditions. Although Minnesota and Dakota daily wages in 1901 were estimated at between two dollars and $2.50 including board, they had been much lower in the depressed 1890s. For example, Swedish immigrant H. E. Berggren's pay ranged from $1.25 to $1.75 during the 1894 harvest. Working conditions also varied markedly from farm to farm. At times, he slept in a cold, rat-infested elevator or storeroom and received poor food. After the harvest ended, he found it difficult to find any job on valley farms or in the twin cities. Thus he toiled for short times at a variety of tasks: plasterer, digging potatoes, sawing wood, planting trees, and building sewers. He avoided construction because contractors treated workers "like slaves and not free people." Employers immediately dismissed any rebel and replaced him with one of the many unemployed. Berggren finally found work with a farmer at eight dollars a month during the winter. Hard times had reduced his monthly wage by almost half. Berggren's plight makes clear that often little or no work could be had. With two exceptions, his experiences are probably representative of those without skills. He does not mention the paternalistic regulation of alcohol, profanity, and other behavior imposed by many farmers. As a Swedish immigrant, his relatives supported him during holidays, illnesses, and jobless periods. Not many native-born had willing families so close at hand.[8]

The annual influx of roughly clad strangers heralded the coming of spring and autumn in the twin cities. It aroused fear from the late 1870s to the end of the century and beyond. Break-ins and begging dramatically increased. Editors and officials mirrored the criticisms of "scientific charity" proponents who condemned the free handouts of traditional assistance. Instead, tramps should be forced to work for any aid they received. As the *Clay County Advocate* stated: "We have made up our minds no more of them will eat at our expense. We direct them invariably to the street commissioner, who can find at least temporary work for them, but only one so far has satisfied us that he

Strangers on Moorhead's Main Street bridge (ca. 1905) might provoke fear among residents. Courtesy Clay County Historical Society.

would do any work." The editor concluded that handouts only perpetuated "their vagabond life." He warned parents not to let children roam the streets after dark because they would "see and hear things they should not." Fargo city marshal Charley Foster arrested the thieves, drunks, and disorderly. He cleared others from the city. Work on the streets awaited those who refused to leave. Although the *Fargo Times* commended these efforts, the editor recognized that some strangers were harvest hands. These should be welcomed. They should be aided in finding housing and employment. Like its middle-class readers, the press wanted the benefit of seasonal workers without begging, theft, or disorder.[9]

Hostile community attitudes produced new vagrancy laws. Most northern states passed "tramp acts." Yet municipal governments never consistently enforced these statutes. Moorhead and Fargo tolerated transients if jobs beckoned. If not, or growing numbers caused complaints, twin cities police expelled them from both cities, arrested them for vagrancy, and sentenced them to street labor. When the Moorhead chief of police set them to work in 1885 instead of driving them to Fargo, the *Argus* responded with praise: "Moorhead will find this change a benefit as such gentlemen of leisure care very little for being driven out of town, but they do hate to have to do a full day's work." Often neither city had jobs for so many. Chief P. J. Sullivan and his patrolmen banished 160 on a single morning in 1895. Sullivan admitted that he could not distinguish the worker majority from tramps and criminals so he expelled them all. Fargo similarly harassed harvest hands and tramps, although at times editors expressed sympathy for their plight. In 1894 the *Forum* wrote: "That poverty is a crime is daily proved in Fargo." The police arrested all men sleeping in boxcars because "an ordinance passed in the interests of the railroad companies makes it a crime of vagrancy." Consequently, the police court sentenced them to serve "from ten to thirty days on the chain gang for being poor."[10]

After farmers finished harvest, the crews celebrated. Norwegian writer Knut Hamsun, who worked on the Dalrymple Bonanza Farm, later recalled his experience: "There is drinking and gambling, fighting and shouting for several days." Such behavior transformed the twin cities into Sodom and Gomorrah in the eyes of God-fearing folk. The liquor and prostitution businesses boomed while arrests rose for theft, assault, and disorderly behavior. The *Moorhead Weekly News* blamed victims for these crimes, saying their negligence caused most of their troubles. They drank too much, flashed their roll, and awakened the next morning with their money gone and without any memories of their previous night or companions. Thieves, gamblers, and prostitutes similarly followed the harvest. They reaped their rewards after the hands had finished farmers' fields.[11]

The first twin city settlers included urban workers. For example, an 1879 census listed 168 mechanics residing in Fargo, which had just slightly more than 1,400 people at the time. Many likely worked in the repair shops and the running trades based at the Northern Pacific division headquarters. The Brotherhood of Locomotive Engineers organized locally in 1874 because a large number lived in the city. Engineers were the most highly skilled and paid railroad workers. Their brotherhood promoted industry, sobriety, and civility, expecting that the corporation would reward their enhanced efficiency with higher pay. They embraced the YMCA as an additional means to inculcate these values and protect their craft. Firemen, brakemen, and conductors had organized brotherhoods throughout North Dakota by the 1890s. They aspired to the respectability of the engineers and emulated their association. Semiskilled firemen and brakemen entered the running trades with expectation of winning promotion to engineer or conductor within a few years. Engineers and conductors, skilled and amply compensated, formed an aristocracy of labor. Until the early 1890s, they strongly identified with the interests of management. Economically important to their community, they often set themselves apart from the mass of transient and unskilled workers, as western historian Richard White has observed.[12]

Twin city residents esteemed members of the railroad brotherhoods for their bourgeois qualities and aspirations. The *Fargo Express* praised them for providing death benefits to widows and for assisting families of disabled engineers. The *Fargo Argus* admired their personal qualities: "They are good citizens, first-rate operatives and have given Fargo . . . a good name by their upright conduct." To fund death and sickness benefits, each brotherhood sponsored an annual ball. As many as a hundred couples and forty or fifty visitors might attend these events that newspapers always reported on in detail.[13]

Despite the goodwill brotherhoods displayed toward railroad corporations, workers and managers collided in the late nineteenth century, as labor historian Shelton Stromquist has explained. Managers successfully transformed their labor supply from scarcity to surplus in all regions of the country. They centralized control in the heads of departments. They standardized work rules and wage rates. Already under way in the East by the depression of 1873, these changes affected the trans-Mississippi West thereafter. As a larger pool of workers became available, western trainmen lost the higher wages, improved conditions, and union recognition they had won in the previously tight labor market. Faced with worsening wages and conditions, the brotherhoods and unskilled workers naturally resisted. As a consequence, numerous struggles large and small racked railroads and the nation from the Great Railway Strike in 1877 to the Pullman boycott in 1894.[14]

These industrial conflicts alarmed middle-class opinion in the twin cities and throughout the country. For example, the *Moorhead Advocate* deplored the $100 million lost from property damage in the Great Railway Strike. Neither businessmen nor workers benefited from what the *Advocate* called "the great Communistic rebellion." It had been sparked by alien doctrines brought into the country by the worst elements of European society. The United States required both a stronger army and additional compulsory education in American values to control such mobs. These views agreed with those expressed elsewhere, demonstrating that America experienced its first red scare at this time. Haunted by the violent Paris Commune of 1871, editors and businessmen saw foreign-born tramps infected by communism as the cause of every strike. Middle-class perceptions thus shaped reality because most conflicts lacked tramps.[15]

As violent confrontations occurred frequently during the ensuing decades, local editors diverged on the issues of unions and strikes. The *Moorhead Weekly News* in the early 1880s defended the formation of a typographical union by printers and a walkout by telegraphers. Editor George Lamphere, who later became a Populist, appealed to the republican tradition. Individuals had rights to share the wealth their labor produced, organize for self-protection against wealthy exploiters, and strike for a living wage if employers would not negotiate and unions were not violent or did not destroy property. Higher wages benefited the entire society. Better pay furthered morality, education, patriotism, and happiness by promoting greater effort by workers. Lamphere did not blindly defend all strikes, however. When the Brotherhood of Boilermakers walked out against Great

Northern wage cuts in 1893, the *News* called it foolish. Workers should be grateful they still had jobs during a depression.[16]

The views of *Argus* editor George K. Shaw, a business-minded Republican, differed somewhat from those of labor sympathizer Lamphere. Shaw argued that unions should forgo strikes entirely and expend their dues on life, accident, and health insurance for all members. He believed that wealthy businessmen would cheerfully contribute funds if labor organized on such a fraternal basis. Condemning the destruction of property during a walkout by railroad men in Buffalo, New York, Shaw wrote: "The only safety for the state is for good citizens everywhere to frown upon mob violence." Real or alleged grievances did not justify illegal methods. Just and impartial laws were the only true solution for industrial conflict, according to Shaw. Many corporate managers held similar views. They therefore preferred dealing with the fraternally oriented railroad brotherhoods rather than militant industrial unions.[17]

The depression of 1893 and subsequent events made 1894 a critical year for the nation and the twin cities. The coming of Coxeyites, the successful strike waged by the American Railway Union (ARU) against the Great Northern, and the valiant struggle in the failed Pullman boycott stimulated a brief local flowering of worker activism and union organization. Several factors shortened its duration, however. In the watershed election of 1896, Republican William McKinley defeated Democrat William Jennings Bryan, whom the Populist "producer coalition" of farmers and workers had backed. As a consequence, business-oriented Republicans ruled the federal government for more than three decades. The Populists disappeared. Labor unions remained weak nationally in the face of overwhelming corporate power. They attracted even less support from the rural majority in agrarian North Dakota.

As unemployment grew with the deepening depression after 1893, Jacob S. Coxey proposed that industrial armies of the unemployed march on Washington, D.C. He hoped his "petition in boots" would secure federally funded public works projects for the jobless. In late March the Commonweal of Christ left Massillon, Ohio. They processed down Pennsylvania Avenue on May 1 with the hope that Coxey would address Congress. Instead, the authorities arrested and convicted him and others for trespass on the Capitol grounds. Thus ended ignominiously the first phase of Coxey's movement. The second stage lasted until mid-June as perhaps thirteen contingents numbering five thousand men from the Pacific and Mountain states made their way toward the federal capital. The more militant western armies not only stole rides but on at least fifty occasions seized entire trains. As scholar Todd DePastino suggests, "the movement . . . signaled that a new 'wageworkers' frontier had opened" in the "corporate capitalist development of the West." The armies thus provoked national hysteria.[18]

Some of these men passed through Fargo and Moorhead. On the last evening in April, five hundred unemployed marched down Front Street to Island Park, where they listened to speeches delivered by a man named Margrave, a Moorhead minister, and a Fargo citizen. Their audience may have included unemployed residents as well as Montana miners and teamsters. Afternoon and evening meetings continued for several days. By May 3, 228 men had been enrolled and planned to leave for Washington the next morning. These men were not tramps, according to both the *Fargo Forum* and *Moorhead Weekly News*. They were sober workers who became unemployed when western mines had closed. Such favorable press coverage is surprising given the public predisposition to perceive Coxeyites as ill-disciplined tramps. To overcome these prejudices, the movement consciously cultivated a favorable image. Speakers generally used temperate language. The men kept themselves clean. Camps followed military discipline.[19]

Members of rival Washington contingents from Seattle and Tacoma arrived later. Edward J. Jeffries, a journalist, lawyer, and state Populist Party leader, led the former. Democrat Jumbo T. Cantwell commanded the latter

A Coxeyite camp in 1894 at an unknown location for the "petition in boots" that demanded federal work relief. Courtesy Institute for Regional Studies, North Dakota State University, Fargo (2069.22.1).

group. Both left Spokane at the end of May with Cantwell's army following the Great Northern route while Jeffries's men traveled via the Northern Pacific. All agreed that harassment from federal deputies made North Dakota the most difficult state to cross. In early June forty men from Jumbo Cantwell's division of the Spokane Commonwealers arrived. Mayor Wilbur Ball greeted them kindly. Although the municipal government could not provide assistance, the mayor gave them permission to solicit supplies for two meals from businessmen. The *Forum* urged contributions, adopting the tactic employed by many communities of feeding the army in hopes it would quickly move on. The men managed to forage a good supper of fish soup, beef stew, and fresh bread furnished by Nordale Bakery and Hauser Brothers' Meat Market. They failed to find anything for their next day's dinner, however. Despite prevalent antitramp prejudices, the *Forum* expressed sympathy for these honest laborers who proved they were not tramps by taking a day to wash their clothes. For several days, other peaceful contingents arrived and departed. Some had provisions, but others begged.[20]

After Chief of Police Barnes offered one group construction work at $1.50 per day and they refused, he ordered them out of town. As the *Forum* reported: "Willing to help the needy, Fargo has no use for men who refuse work when tendered." Although a favorable public image required adherence to the work ethic, Coxeyites would not exchange their journey for a job. Indeed, on principle they refused the jobs of strikers or those local workers could perform. Speaking to an audience of five hundred assembled that evening in Island Park, General Edward J. Jeffries explained: "[My] men don't want work—they want to go to Washington and have fun with Grover." A more reputable leader than Cantwell, Jeffries moved with his men. He raised enough money to pay boat passage from Duluth, Minnesota, to Marquette, Michigan, so they would cross a state where previous armies had not traveled. A lifelong reformer, he was known as the "Knight of the Open Mouth and the Bleeding Heart." Cantwell left several hundred of his followers at Great Falls, Montana. Fortunately, his wife Carlotta ("Mrs. General") rebuilt their morale and moved them to Chicago before her health gave out. Meanwhile, Jumbo traveled alone by coach to the federal capital. One of his disgruntled followers later damned him for stealing the army's funds and fleeing to South America.[21]

By the end of June, most Coxeyites had passed eastward through the twin cities. Subsequent newspaper reports mirrored national trends by becoming less frequent and more negative. Without the contrary evidence of positive behavior, old prejudices appeared once more. A deputy marshal declared: "Half the men now going over the road are not Coxeyites but tramps and crooks who are taking advantage of the occasion to force people to furnish them food." At this time, Moorhead police chief P. J. Sullivan arrested ten armed men, who had stolen an engine near Dawson, North Dakota, and fired upon a U.S. marshal. Meanwhile, the armies arrived in Washington, D.C. There the movement disintegrated. Officials quartered the remnants on the Naval Observatory grounds for three days in August. District commissioners arranged railroad transportation to St. Paul, St. Louis, and Kansas City. They supplied bread, meat, and coffee for several days. After two hundred arrived in St. Paul, some rode the rails home to Washington, while many stopped in North Dakota for the wheat harvest. Coxey's Army challenged the idea that laziness caused joblessness and advanced the concept of federal responsibility for economic welfare. Nonetheless, the fear of government paternalism and faith in American opportunity never entirely lost its influence, as our own times attest.[22]

In April 1894, the newly formed ARU led by the dynamic Eugene V. Debs successfully struck the Great Northern in response to wage cuts, tying up the railroad from St. Paul to Spokane for eighteen days. Although President James J. Hill denied any pay reductions, a Moorhead car repairer claimed his wages had been reduced from $70 to $50 per month and those of section hands from $1.25 to 90 cents per day. *Forum* editor Alanson W. Edwards— reflecting his animus toward Hill for his bankruptcy and loss of the *Argus*— took the side of the workers, praising them for their orderliness and protection of railroad property. "They deserve high praise and no men ever entered on a strike against a monopoly that had fewer friends," Edwards wrote. "Purse proud and autocratic, the Great Northern is getting a portion of its long merited deserts." The *Moorhead Weekly News* also took the side of the workers, arguing the men deserved fair wages. Populist editor Lamphere called this the first time the Great Northern had reduced wages without a corresponding rate cut to farmers. As these editorial opinions imply, the public sided with the workers against what they perceived as Hill's monopoly. Most communities located north and west of St. Cloud, Minnesota, shared this rebellious attitude, while those to the south and east were more conciliatory. In part, the twin cities mirrored their hinterland, which had opposed railroad abuses in the Granger, Alliance, and Populist movements. As Olivier Zunz noted, middle-class entrepreneurs who feared corporate power backed working-class strikes. At times, this alliance stopped city officials from taking the police actions railroads demanded.[23]

After President Grover Cleveland ignored his angry demand for federal troops, a relieved Hill accepted an arbitration board recommendation in early May. He reestablished the wage schedule of August 1, 1893, and recognized the ARU. He startled Debs by congratulating him on his shrewd management of the strike. The *Forum* exclaimed: "The result is the greatest labor victory of the age." The men won because they respected the law and protected property, Edwards wrote. Fargo meanwhile rejoiced, as did several points throughout the Northwest. As a large crowd gathered at the depot to greet the trainmen, the *Forum* reported, "A rooster in the express car crowed several times and the crowd said it was a representative of the ARU." A public meeting held at the crowded opera house honored labor. Attorney Melvin A. Hildreth and others spoke. The crowd applauded "every reference to the ARU and its president, Eugene V. Debs," according to the newspaper account.[24]

Fired with the confidence gained from its victory over Hill, the ARU joined the national boycott called by Debs against the Pullman Car Company in Chicago. The company had failed to negotiate workers' grievances regarding wage cuts and had refused to reduce rents in George Pullman's model town. The ARU also struck the Northern Pacific for dismissing crews, who did not handle Pullman cars. The strikers sought public support for their cause with varied success. The Missouri River divided western rebellious and eastern conciliatory communities toward the corporation, according to Northern Pacific managers. Twin city community leaders manifested conciliation by adopting the stance of objective neutrality. As division headquarters, Fargo had always regarded itself as a Northern Pacific town. The many shop workers and train crewmen made the railroad payroll an essential part of the local economy. In addition, boosters had long sought company support for their metropolitan dreams. The municipal and business elite had developed a more cooperative relationship with the Northern Pacific than it had with the Great Northern. The elite displayed less hostility toward management in the Pullman boycott than they had toward the Great Northern three months earlier. Self-interest dictated neutrality. The press mirrored this attitude. The *Forum* and other local papers carried detailed, daily reports of the dispute from June 28 until July 13.[25]

Meanwhile, ARU members attended several crowded meetings held at the Old Masonic Hall. Unitarian minister William Ballou, attorney Taylor Crum, Methodist minister Carl Anderson, Coxeyite Carlotta Cantwell, and others delivered addresses. To win public support for the labor cause, resident leader Elmer H. Evans assured residents that the union rejected violence and would protect Northern Pacific property. Nightly ARU patrols enforced this promise. The men deserted the shops and yards. They flocked to join the union. On the boycott's first night, several hundred citizens assembled at the Northern Pacific depot to watch the arrival and departure of infrequent trains. The next day, no trains appeared. The *Forum* praised the strikers for preserving order and protecting property despite escalating anger against strikebreakers. The railroad managers, determined to break the boycott, dispatched Northern Pacific trains operated by scabs and pulling Pullman cars.[26]

In lieu of infrequent Northern Pacific trains, the Great Northern and the Milwaukee Road supplied the city. On the eleventh day, a crowd of four hundred attended a union rally, including "many members of the fairer sex whose presence cheered hearts of the boys." Speeches and music by the Banjo, Mandolin, and Guitar Club entertained the audience. The meeting formed a relief committee to aid strikers. Two days later, Northern Pacific train service started to improve. A large crowd watched No. 1 arrive four hours late, carrying a hundred "regulars" armed with rifles. A deputy marshal and a score of men carrying Winchesters accompanied the train westward. Given the overwhelming display of firepower, it is not surprising that "there was absolutely no trouble in Fargo," despite the strikebreaking engineer and firemen operating the train. Rumors the next day said that local engineers had met for several hours and would return to work when called. A businessman commented in the newspaper: "The boycott and strike cannot win in its present shape." The engineers agreed and reported for duty, although ARU firemen refused. With the engineers available, management operated more trains with strikebreakers as firemen.[27]

After Debs defied a federal injunction and President Cleveland sent federal troops, the ARU boycott dissolved. National opinion blamed workers for destroying Chicago property. The Fargo strike ended unhappily for labor by July 13. Engineers returned expecting to be put in their old jobs, but Northern Pacific managers treated them as new men and asked ARU members to resign from the union. Even though most unionists did not report, Northern Pacific freights moved more rapidly within one week. The company had hired many new men, giving it an almost full complement of workers. The Northern Pacific thereby demonstrated that its sufficiently large surplus labor pool could replace every man that struck. The local press maintained its neutrality and reported these replacements without comment. Editors, who had not condemned the ARU for its boycott, did not criticize the company for busting the union.[28]

The Pullman boycott dealt a severe blow to the ARU. At greatly reduced strength, the union lingered into the twentieth century. Debs received a six-month sentence for contempt of court. President Cleveland appointed a federal commission that urged capital to recognize and negotiate with unions. It also advised Congress to enact a system of compulsory arbitration for the railroads. By 1898, mediation had been enacted. Within this federal framework, Hill joined with other transcontinentals to regularize labor negotiations. After crushing the threatening industrial unionism of the ARU, management willingly worked with the responsible unionism of railroad brotherhoods. Trainmen accepted the bargain, winning greater benefits than most workmen until the Great Depression. The acceptance of this arrangement by the businessmen of St. Paul, Minnesota, paralleled the outcome in Fargo and Moorhead.[29]

Local businessmen agreed that the conflict created bitterness and materially injured their trade. They welcomed the industrial peace promised by compulsory arbitration. They ignored rural protests against railroads and identified their civic interests with those of the corporation. For example, Fargo benefited in the mid-1890s from lower rates granted by the Northern Pacific, Milwaukee Road, and the Great Northern. The city looked forward to becoming the distribution center for North Dakota. Twin city businessmen rejected strike leader Elmer Evans's condemnation of compulsory arbitration as un-American and his socialist demand for government ownership. They applauded editor George Lamphere's rejection of communism and anarchism as solutions. They embraced compulsory arbitration as sufficient recognition of workers' rights to life and comfort.[30]

Two visits by Eugene Debs in 1895 reveal some class division in local attitudes toward the cause of organized labor. Stopping in Fargo on his tour of western ARU locals, Debs delivered an address titled "Who Are the Conspirators?" at the opera house. The ARU Defense Fund received proceeds from the event. Local socialist Elmer Evans chaired the meeting. The Reverend William Ballou, who greatly admired Debs and also became a Socialist Party member, introduced the speaker. Debs spoke effectively for almost two hours to a mostly male audience diminished by the high admission

Unitarian pastor and Socialist Party member William Ballou of Fargo, pictured during the 1930s, sympathized with the workingman's plight. Courtesy Institute for Regional Studies, North Dakota State University, Fargo (SC 46.1.4).

fee. Workers who wanted to hear him and could not afford tickets on the main level crowded the galleries; businessmen who could pay were not interested. Debs blamed property destruction during the Pullman strike on the antiunion General Managers Association and the slum-dwelling scabs they hired. In a comment reported by the *Forum,* attorney Smith Stimmel called the speech a "very fair, candid and impartial presentation of the laboring man's cause." He added, "The ARU have every reason to be very proud of their able and gifted leader." On his return trip in early June, Debs spoke at the Unitarian church before meeting with the ARU local to discuss its ongoing struggle with the Great Northern. Rumors of an impending strike circulated for several days in early November. In the meantime, a Great Northern circular warned that any disloyalty by workers would lead to instant dismissal. The *Forum* displayed sympathy for labor (or Edwards's antagonism for Hill) by reporting that the Great Northern, backed by Chicago railroads, intended to bust the ARU.[31]

Labor activism and organization locally marked the 1890s. Hopeful signs nationally included new leadership for the Knights of Labor, the prospect of cooperation between the formerly antagonistic Knights and American Federation of Labor (AFL) as well as the growth of western ARU groups. Low wages, poor conditions, and activity elsewhere spurred dual city initiatives. Skilled artisans received a daily wage of $2.50. Unskilled workers

Carpenters at the Keeney Block in Fargo during the early 1880s represented part of the dual city's skilled laborers. Courtesy Institute for Regional Studies, North Dakota State University, Fargo (51.215.4).

earned the national standard of $1.50 for a ten-hour day. When contractor James Kennedy cut hours to nine and thereby reduced wages, twenty men struck. Kennedy immediately hired their replacements from among the jobless. In late 1892, resident unions responded to AFL president Samuel Gompers's call for aid. They scheduled a benefit for the Homestead workers who had lost a bitter strike against Carnegie Steel and had been indicted for killing armed Pinkerton guards. When the grand ball took place one month later, the sale of about three hundred tickets nearly filled the armory.[32]

Typographical Union 189, the first Fargo body, appeared in 1880. It most successfully modeled the AFL business-union approach. Because new technology did not eliminate skilled workers, the union controlled work, raised wages, shortened hours, and protected jobs. It supported the ARU Pullman boycott. It met monthly, elected officers for six-month terms, and sponsored an annual grand masquerade ball at the armory. In 1896 it hosted the Third Annual Convention of the Tenth District Union of the Allied Printing Trades. That same year, the printers proposed that the *Fargo and Moorhead City Directory* should be printed locally. Two years later, they successfully petitioned the council to have all city printing done only by union labor. Mayor J. A. Johnson, a sympathizer who supported the eight-hour-day movement, proposed that all public printing in the state should be done by union labor.[33]

The formation of the Fargo-Moorhead Trades and Labor Protective Union (TLPU) developed directly from the ARU and its success in winning the Great Northern strike. As a "union man" urged in the columns of the *Forum*: "Keep agitating the organization of a trades union in Fargo. It would be the best thing the *Forum* can do to aid the laboring man." TLPU permanent officers had been elected by early July. Members paid fifty cents to join and fifty cents each quarter. They soon totaled 178 with five hundred expected. The new organization immediately requested contractors to employ only Fargo workers and to pay artisans a living wage. It appealed to the self-interest of the municipal and business elite, arguing that higher wages enabled workers to pay taxes and buy more goods from merchants. Businessmen, aldermen, and contractors accepted the proposal. The *Forum* congratulated the union on its success.[34]

The TLPU additionally supported retail clerks, who had long sought shorter workdays. Employers initially accepted fewer hours during the winter months. Employees then suggested similar terms for the other seasons. In 1888 they secured 7:00 p.m. closing on all but two designated evenings each week. A petition signed by three hundred women, pledging to shop only on those evenings, aided them. Many merchants violated this agreement, however. By 1892, the newly formed Retail Clerks Association promoted closing at 6:00 p.m. for one year, beginning January 1, 1893. Clothiers, grocers, and hardware dealers accepted early closing for just six months while boot and shoe stores agreed for merely three. When some grocers ignored this agreement, the *Forum* urged a boycott by the many sympathetic union members. Eventually, the railroad brotherhoods and all other labor organizations in the city supported the clerks. Despite their support, the stores again resumed their regular long hours in April. Two years later, the Retail Clerks Association negotiated a ten-hour day and early closing at 7:00 p.m., Saturday excepted and all day Sunday until September 1, 1895. It received support from the seven hundred-member Federated Trades Council. The clerks renegotiated similar agreements annually for the remainder of the decade. Although some employers refused to abide by the terms, the *Forum* praised the efforts made to reach a harmonious understanding.[35]

Worker visibility and the limits of union power can be seen in the experience of first ward alderman Con Keefe, elected to three terms in the mid-1890s. Keefe, master of the Switchman's Mutual Aid Association, identified himself as a friend of workers. When he supported a council decision to purchase a Studebaker Sprinkler, however, fellow unionists attacked him. They backed a boycott called by the AFL-affiliated International Wagon-makers Union against the Studebaker Company for employing nonunion labor. As the dispute persisted through several meetings, the *Forum* commented facetiously: "Politics make strange bed-fellows and agitators sometimes go wrong." Union objections to this purchase proved as ineffective as earlier protests by the Knights of Labor against employing prisoners for street repair.[36]

Labor Day observances evidenced the power of twin city workers. The first celebration in 1882 occurred in New York City, organized by workers with ties to the Knights of Labor, trade unions, and socialism. A crowd estimated at twenty-five thousand attended the festivities. Even though the ideological harmony of that first day did not last, the Central Labor Union in 1884 made it an annual event on the first Monday in September. Oregon first legalized the fete three years later. Thirty-one states had recognized Labor Day when it became a federal holiday in 1894. Floats and parades of the pragmatic and nationalistic AFL displayed skilled labor's contribution to the republic. Unionists carried only American flags, delivered speeches only in English, targeted unorganized workers for membership, and invited capitalists to participate. As labor power grew, self-interested mayors, legislators, and other politicians accepted invitations to speak. Planners seeking a crowd soon added dancing and sports to the program of speeches.[37]

A joint committee from the Typographical and Cigar-Makers' unions planned the first Labor Day Ball at the Fargo Armory in 1891. The committee invited the railroad brotherhoods and other twin city labor organizations to participate. Republican governor Andrew Burke spoke, emphasizing that the foundation of society rested on labor and expressing the hope that Labor Day would become a legal holiday to recognize the dignity of manual work. A more elaborate observance followed the next year. Public buildings, banks, and many stores closed. A large number of citizens turned out for an afternoon parade from the Columbia Hotel to Island Park for a program of speeches. The *Forum* praised their conservative tone, which showed that "Fargo workingmen are a highly intelligent and responsible body of men." That evening Governor and Mrs. Burke led the grand march at the well-attended grand ball. Elaborate and well-supported observances continued until 1895, when street paving disallowed the parade. This did not prevent an enthusiastic celebration. A basket picnic in Island Park at noon preceded an afternoon of speeches and sports. Teams from twin city labor bodies played a baseball game. A grand ball concluded the day.[38]

Subsequent observances attracted fewer people. Workers planned no program in 1898, but public buildings, banks, and some stores closed in the afternoon and the YMCA arranged athletic exercises in the baseball park. North Dakota farmers killed a legislative bill to make Labor Day a legal state holiday because they did not want harvest crews disrupted. Republican governor Fred Fancher did not even issue a proclamation. The lack of celebration also testified to the weakening of unions in the twin cities. The ARU, TLPU, Typographical Union, and Cigar-Maker's Union all lost members. Workers also found that most Americans preferred recreation to hearing labor orations. Labor organizations elsewhere experienced a similar difficulty in gathering members for holiday parades and picnics.[39]

Republican William McKinley's decisive defeat of William Jennings Bryan's farm–labor coalition in the critical election of 1896 may have had a chilling effect on labor activity in the twin cities.

Democratic and Populist presidential candidate William Jennings Bryan campaigned unsuccessfully for Fargo and North Dakota votes in 1896. Courtesy Minnesota Historical Society.

Republicans portrayed themselves as the party of high wages secured by high tariffs. The McKinley campaign countered Bryan in Fargo by successfully appealing to workers. The *Forum* praised railroad laborers for creating a Sound Money Club, inferring that they supported McKinley. Republicans staged a torchlight procession of eight hundred men, many carrying "sound money" and other banners. They marched to the opera house where laborers occupied the front-row seats in a crowd of 1,500 for an address by A. C. Rankin, the "iron molder orator" from Pittsburgh. Speaking for three hours on the "money question" and the protective tariff, Rankin characterized Bryan as "the artful dodger." This large Republican rally stole some of Bryan's thunder when he appeared in the city two days later. Although an enthusiastic crowd of several thousand heard the great orator, Bryan lost the state.[40]

Unionism did not disappear with McKinley's victory or with the cessation of Labor Day observances. As North Dakota's largest city, Fargo attracted organizers. The building trades set up the Trades and Labor Assembly in 1906 and formed the Building Trades Council that virtually established a closed shop by 1912. This called forth the Fargo and Moorhead Master Builders' Council that successfully campaigned for the open shop, which spread statewide. Although the North Dakota Federation of Labor, established in 1911, claimed forty affiliated unions with 1,342 members in ten cities, it never overcame its rural environment. The sparse population could not support the locals created. Most Dakotans, engaged in family-owned production, disliked trade unions. Wages remained low, with minimal difference between union and nonunion workers. In addition, the AFL lacked resources for assisting state bodies. Its business unionism appealed only to skilled workers. It organized only a small percentage of the nation's workers and therefore remained weaker than powerful corporations.[41]

Businessmen did support unions when it suited their economic and cultural interests. As shippers they backed railroad workers in their struggle against the powerful Great Northern and James J. Hill. As merchants who benefited from expanded payrolls, they supported labor's demand that local contractors hire only residents for construction projects. As middle-class Victorians, they embraced those labor leaders who voiced the bourgeois success ethic of industry, thrift, sobriety, and genteel respectability. All sympathy for workers quickly evaporated, however, when laborers refused jobs that were offered, became drunk and disorderly, or embraced violence and destroyed property.

LIQUOR: THE MOTHER OF ALL VICE AND CRIME

Middle-class Victorians viewed liquor as the mother of all vice and regarded sobriety as necessary for success. Increased alcohol use alarmed many.

Imbibing hard liquor rose in the early nineteenth century with new distilling techniques and lower taxes on spirits. Beer drinking per capita grew ninefold from 1.5 gallons in 1850 to 13.6 gallons four decades later. Cork-lined metal crown caps, pasteurization, and the national railroad network enabled breweries to expand their production and distribution throughout the country. Saloons, 70 percent of which national breweries owned, numbered perhaps three hundred thousand by 1900. Fierce competition compelled many saloonkeepers to operate twenty-four hours a day, seven days a week. To prevent regulation, the liquor industry battled woman suffrage and corrupted politics by expending large sums on municipal and state politicians. Middle-class temperance crusaders abhorred the wicked Liquor Trust. It destroyed individual moral purity and industry, led to fiscal ruin, and harmed families. Associating saloons with working-class men, reformers tried to banish alcohol by imposing sobriety and other bourgeois values on workers.[42]

Saloons served "the non-domestic, mobile lifestyle of single men," according to scholar Howard Chudacoff. They functioned as workingmen's clubs, providing amiability, free lunches, newspapers, job news, and other services. Alcohol fueled male friendships with their distinctive talk marked by profanity, bawdy jokes, nicknames, teasing, boasting, treating, and toasting. Men also enjoyed chewing tobacco and cigars. In all these ways, Chudacoff concludes, the saloon "represented a victory of masculine working-class social standards over feminine middle-class morality." Saloons in the twin cities likely mirrored such masculine behavior. As alderman and temperance reformer Henry Johnson recalled, Moorhead saloons ranged from the poor to the palatial. They boomed during harvest when seasonal laborers filled the business streets, moving from bar to bar and to the brothels on Front Street east.[43]

Saloons appeared among other early businesses. Moorhead had one dozen and Fargo thirty-two by 1884. After North Dakota became dry many moved across the river, giving Moorhead forty-five in 1900. Native-, Irish-, or German-born workers typically became owners, hoping to advance economically by entering the trade. As genial and patriotic fellows, they normally drank with their customers but maintained order when necessary. Burdened by license fees, mortgage payments, liquor bills, and many competitors, owners often turned over quickly, producing discord within the supposedly unified Liquor Trust. Illegal practices of some barkeeps commonly tainted their honest brethren. The disreputable commonly broke the Sabbath and violated closing hours. They attracted customers with prostitution and gambling. The United States Brewers' Association attacked bar owners for causing crime. Retailers responded by blaming brewery saloons for criminal activities. Each was partially correct. Competition, meanwhile, escalated as hard liquor wholesalers added bars to their premises.[44]

Johnny Haas—the "Dutch Prince"—advertised himself as a "genial spirit" and "a successful caterer to the tastes of those who appreciate the good things of earth." He owned the Broadway Cigar Store (with billiard room) and Merchant Hotel in Fargo. He relocated his liquor trade, acquiring the Moorhead Midway Café in 1891. After he remodeled extensively, Haas offered working-class camaraderie in a palatial setting. The exterior featured imitation cut stone, fine plate glass, and an eighty-foot tower topped with a tall staff always flying the American flag. Patrons entered by a heavy mahogany door into an elegant interior finished in mahogany and decorated with brass grillwork, handsome chandeliers, frescoed steel ceilings, incandescent lamps, numerous mirrors, baseboards of Italian marble, and solid brass cuspidors. Several available rooms enabled social classes to drink separately or engage in illicit activities behind closed doors. The clientele ate in the public restaurant or one of three private dining rooms, drank in the barroom, and relaxed in the clubroom, smoking room, or musical garden equipped with a large pipe organ that played popular music.[45]

German immigrant and former Fargo brewer Thomas Erdel came close to matching the elegant standard set by Haas. Like Haas, he relocated near the North Bridge in order to better serve thirsty Dakotans. He built the elaborately lighted House of Lords and the German-decorated Rathskeller Over the Rhine. The latter initially catered to an elite clientele. Its family-friendly atmosphere reflected German traditions. It imitated "the original wine cellars in Germany." It offered "European beers" and "old-style German lunches" in an attractively decorated and well-appointed interior. Most saloons did not match the style suggested by these two examples. They varied widely in size, furnishings, quality, and service. North Bridge locations attracted the most elaborately decorated. South Bridge sites drew the most disreputable. Respectable places chose spots on Front Street farthest from the Red River. Only a few became substantial businesses. The numerous outlets for national breweries changed owners frequently. All sold nickel beer and provided free lunches subsidized by brewers. These featured salty foods to encourage drinking. Fred Ambs operated for many years on Front Street, selling quality liquor over the bar to standup and carry-out customers. With no tables or chairs, Ambs efficiently handled large crowds of strangers. Although some bartenders assured patrons they would be "treated honorably and courteously," others might beat rowdy drunks severely before tossing them out a back door without a stairway to interrupt their fall of several feet.[46]

The national liquor industry alarmed temperance advocates, who perceived drunkenness as a serious problem demanding immediate attention. Energized by religious revivalism, they expanded existing organizations and created new ones after the Civil War. The Independent Order of

In the 1890s, Fred Ambs handled large numbers of strangers in his Moorhead saloon, which had no tables or chairs. Courtesy Clay County Historical Society.

Good Templars, having grown to four hundred thousand members by 1869, helped form the National Temperance Society and the National Prohibition Party. The WCTU (1874) and the Anti-Saloon League (1896) soon joined the fight. According to historian Joseph Gusfield, these organizations successively embraced two types of reform. First, they fostered assimilation by sympathetically offering abstinence to the urban poor as a way to attain bourgeois status. Second, they embraced coercion and imposed bourgeois values on Catholic, immigrant workers who denied their legitimacy. As the moral suasion techniques of the first type failed to achieve the desired results, reformers adopted legal compulsion in state and national campaigns for the prohibition of liquor and other vices.[47]

Liquor posed a moral dilemma for the twin cities from the beginning. As pioneer and most prominent Moorhead resident Solomon Comstock explained, the "great problem was whether to be pure or prosperous." Ever since it had incorporated as a village in 1875 in order to gain sole control of license fees from thirteen saloons, Moorhead had relied on liquor revenues to finance urban improvements. Both the number and the amount grew with the years until by 1910 forty-eight saloons paid forty-eight thousand dollars in fees. Clay County residents adopted prohibition in 1915 and made Moorhead "pure," although the city had voted against the measure. The law banned legal liquor sales, but illegal consumption continued in several blind pigs. By that time Fargo had struggled unsuccessfully for a quarter century to stop unlawful sales. The moral lesson for both cities seemed to be that enacting prohibition did not thereby bring temperance.[48]

The Reverend Oscar Elmer early led the battle against booze. In May 1873, he secured signatures of the Clay County commissioners on a public notice, which required "all sellers to file bonds and take out licenses." After witnessing a drunken man pitched from a saloon into a muddy street, and hearing about a "drunken half breed dumped in timber to lie exposed in rain," Elmer visited several merchants, warning them "to post bonds as whiskey sellers." He called on the city fathers to demand Sunday closing. Although he aroused opposition, Elmer received some support. The second ordinance passed by the newly formed Moorhead Village Board of Trustees in 1875 regulated the sale of liquor. A dealer must pay the license fee, post a five hundred-dollar bond, and sell only in a designated building. He or she must not sell on Sunday, after 10:00 p.m. on other days, or before 6:00 p.m. on election day. Sellers must not allow gambling. Violators might pay a twenty-dollar fine and serve up to thirty days in jail. A later ordinance defined "drunk and disorderly behavior." The press publicized violations by reporting the daily presence of drunken men on Front Street and saloons open on Sunday. On the other hand, the *Clay County Advocate* proudly reported on July 1, 1880, that "the streets were those of a New England village" because the Sunday closing law had been obeyed.[49]

The newly formed Fargo council in 1875 passed a liquor ordinance, reduced the license fee from $100 to $50, and instructed the city attorney to enforce the law. Enforcement proved sporadic. An 1880 letter to the *Fargo Times* demanded: "Gambling Houses must be wiped out.

The Reverend Oscar H. Elmer founded Moorhead First Presbyterian Church and worked for the temperance cause. Courtesy Institute for Regional Studies, North Dakota State University, Fargo (328.9.3).

Sunday Saloon business must be stopped. . . . [And the] dozen or more houses of ill repute . . . [must be] wholly suppressed." Another letter rejected prohibition as neither efficient nor practical. Instead, the city liquor laws ought to be enforced. If saloonkeepers obeyed the law, they would be no more trouble to the moral order than any other businessmen. The *Times* observed that powerful liquor interests made it difficult to achieve either strict temperance or better law enforcement.[50]

As we saw in chapter 5, dual city temperance advocates had more effectively organized by the 1880s. Many men and women from the Baptist, Congregational, Methodist, and Presbyterian congregations signed temperance pledges. Numerous Norwegian and Swedish Lutherans did as well. Old Americans and Norwegians formed Good Templar Lodges and WCTU bodies in both cities. These forces of religious purity more strongly committed themselves to protecting the bourgeois family from the evils of drink through prohibition. They opposed those who thought regulation by licensing and strict enforcement would be sufficient. The Moorhead council nevertheless relied on licensing to regulate the trade throughout the decade. Temperance crusaders aroused the public conscience, promoted individual abstinence, demanded strict enforcement of Sunday closing laws, and called for higher license fees. Aldermen, backed by saloon owners, defeated all attempts to raise fees. Instead, they boosted municipal revenues by expanding the number of licenses issued. The *Moorhead Weekly News* supported efforts for stricter enforcement. The editor reported instances of compliance with and violations of Sunday closing. He also criticized the chief of police for failing to arrest everyone who broke the law against public drunkenness.[51]

The Fargo council meanwhile responded to similar temperance pressures by strengthening ordinances, raising fees, and urging enforcement. It increased the fee to $150 in 1884. The next year it banned the employment of girls in beer gardens and saloons. Violations continued as evidenced by petitions that demanded Sunday closing and a crackdown on gaming. Prohibitionists secured an 1887 local option election in which Cass County voted dry while Fargo voted wet. Arguing against a legal ban that threatened to bankrupt the city, Mayor Alanson W. Edwards and the board of trade insisted that higher liquor license fees best preserved moral order as well as municipal prosperity. At that time Fargo's forty-two saloons yielded twenty-one thousand dollars in revenue from the five hundred-dollar minimum fee mandated by territorial law. Additionally, well-capitalized breweries provided a livelihood for many families. Men such as Edwards believed that moral suasion promoted temperance better than prohibition. A high license more effectively curbed illegal sales and intoxication through closer supervision of fewer saloons. The forces of religious purity nevertheless prevailed. Thanks to speakers such as Elizabeth Preston (later Anderson), backed by the WCTU and Scandinavian temperance advocates, North Dakota became a dry state in 1889 when voters approved the constitution and its prohibition clause.[52]

Moorhead temperance crusaders knew that North Dakota prohibition would drive "the troublesome class" across the Red River. They feared lost business from temperate farmers shifting their trade to dry Fargo. To prevent their city from becoming "the Mecca of the departing Fargo liquor dealer," regulators insisted demand ought to drive license fees higher. Despite sentiments expressed by radical and moderate reformers for limiting the number of saloons, the city council—perhaps lured by the siren call of more municipal income—expanded the patrol limit, which enlarged an area for new saloons along the Red River. As a consequence, the number grew throughout the 1890s, reaching forty-five by 1900. As alderman Henry Johnson complained, "Fargo cynically regarded Moorhead as a segregated suburb for indulgences not tolerated in Fargo itself."[53]

During the 1890s, the Moorhead council divided on liquor. Arguing that license holders could not pay more, prosperity-minded aldermen resisted increases. Their purity-minded colleagues, backed by Mayor William Tillotson, proposed charging $1,000 before compromising on $750. Saloonkeeper and alderman Jacob Kiefer, pointing to depressed economic conditions, persuaded the council to adopt a $500 license in 1894. Even at this reduced amount, the city annually collected $17,000 in liquor revenues that helped pay for paving, lighting, and other improvements. Despite efforts to raise it, Kiefer and his backers preserved the rate until 1902.[54]

Liquor violations provoked constant complaints. Enforcement varied with officeholders. Reform mayor William R. Tillotson (1892–93) tried to uphold the Sunday and evening closing laws. Four-term mayor Art Lewis (1893–96 and 1897–98), closely allied with the liquor interests, generally did not. His failure led to his defeat in the 1896 election by reformer Samuel Frazier. Mayor Jacob Kiefer (1898–1900) selectively enforced the closing laws, which he believed could not be upheld during the busy harvest season. He and the chief of police strictly enforced them after the migrant workers departed and the owners more readily complied. As the *Moorhead Weekly News* pointed out, the saloons did not attract much business during the three months after Christmas. Compliance therefore saved them money on light and fuel. Temperance crusaders did not accept Kiefer's pragmatic compromise. They elected Norwegian-born Hans H. Aaker in 1900. As mayor, the Concordia College principal more strictly upheld the law, but with mixed success. Some violators lost licenses, but Clay County dismissed other cases based on weak witness testimony or refused to pay for prosecuting others that violated city ordinances.[55]

After North Dakota saloons closed on July 1, 1890, state enforcement proved difficult. The first governor and attorney general tried, but subsequent officials did little or nothing at all. Throughout the state and in Fargo, blind pigs sold liquor illegally and bootleggers even peddled directly to harvest hands in the field. Although Fargo residents blamed their drunks on Moorhead whiskey—easily obtained courtesy of the jag wagons that transported drinkers across the Red River—several well-known places in the city served liquor. Despite repeated demands from prohibitionists throughout the decade, municipal officials failed to close these establishments permanently. At times they lacked political will; more often they did not have adequate means. Although Fargo mayor Wilbur Ball personally opposed prohibition, he did not favor a wide-open city and pledged to enforce the existing law. Yet the small police force could not eliminate the liquor traffic, as Ball pointed out in 1891.[56]

Attorney Taylor Crum identified additional difficulties. Violators often believed the municipal authorities would protect them. Although Crum maintained that officials had not given such assurances, editors alleged repeatedly that someone "tipped" blind piggers about impending police raids. Crum also complained that low fines for violators did not pay prosecution expenses. Until heavy fines could be imposed and all police officers enforced the law, illegal sales would continue. To make the law effective, prohibitionists formed the North Dakota Enforcement League. As part of this effort, Cass County sheriff O. G. Barnes and state's attorney Robert M. Pollock staged many raids in the city and obtained several convictions. Spotters paid by the Moorhead Saloonkeepers Association—interested in eliminating its Dakota competition—assisted Barnes and Pollock. As the *Fargo Forum* wryly commented: "There are some queer bedfellows in this new deal." Tips to their intended victims frequently foiled these combined efforts, however.[57]

Political divisions further weakened enforcement. At each legislative session, antiprohibition forces—backed by the national liquor industry—fought for resubmitting prohibition to the people. Additionally, the powerful McKenzie Machine used the issue as a means of blocking railroad regulation. At this time Boss Alexander McKenzie, a Bismarck banker and businessman, tried to attract commerce and industry by controlling the Republican Party and state government in the interest of Minneapolis- and St. Paul-based corporations. After resubmission failed in the senate by only one vote in 1893, the *Fargo Republican* polled sidewalk sentiment. The varied responses reflected splits in the city as well as the state. Four said the legislature should have voted for resubmission. One of these favored prohibition if it could be enforced. If not, he wanted high license fees. Three others supported the legislative decision. Attorney Robert M. Pollack stated that it

A district judge dismissed charges of illegally selling liquor against Lars Christianson, pictured in his Fargo drugstore in about 1896. Courtesy Institute for Regional Studies, North Dakota State University, Fargo (51.27.2).

would now be easier to impose the law and called on the Republican Party to support enforcement. Attorney Charles A. Pollack said, "The death-knell of the saloon has been sounded in North Dakota. At the end of five years, public sentiment will be changed to support."[58]

Despite these optimistic assertions by prohibition leaders, liquor sales continued in Fargo, as the cases of Lars Christianson and Johnny Haas reveal. Christianson, a prominent druggist and Norwegian Lutheran churchman, helped found Concordia College. He served forty-three years as secretary of the Northwestern Lutheran College Association. The law licensed druggists to sell alcohol for "medicinal purposes." The amount that Christianson carried in stock and the amount that he sold each month, however, appeared suspicious to some observers. The *Forum* alleged that among the four hundred affidavits he presented for sales in one month some individuals obtained liquor each day and some bought it three times in a single day. Others purchased liquor without legally required affidavits. His inventory—reported at the beginning of each month as mandated by law—totaled 295 gallons divided among varied amounts of alcohol, whiskey, brandy, port wine, and sour wine. Christianson had earlier escaped conviction on the grounds that his clerks had sold liquor contrary to his orders. Despite what seemed incriminating to the *Forum,* the district court judge dismissed the Cass County case against him for insufficient evidence. The state subsequently renewed his druggist license. That Christianson and other druggists operating similarly escaped conviction suggests that North Dakota law allowed considerable latitude for the sale of liquor legally in a dry state.[59]

Newspapers regularly reported the antics of Johnny Haas—the most notorious and persistent of the Fargo blind piggers. The district court convicted him in July 1891 for illegally selling liquor. The *Forum* reported two years later that Haas planned to open two Fargo drugstores in addition to managing his Moorhead saloon. Haas did not become a "druggist," but likely established blind pigs in the back of two cigar stores located on Broadway and on Front Street. Additionally, he reportedly started gambling in each store's basement in order to fleece street-paving workers. Newspaper publicity may have attracted police attention; Haas allegedly relocated both "joints" to Moorhead. An article cleverly titled "Chips That Pass in the Night" stated that hard-drinking Hass had lost heavily in gambling. Adding to his woes, the police arrested Mrs. Haas for operating a blind pig at the Fargo Merchants Hotel. Despite the adverse publicity, arrests, trials, and occasional convictions, Hass continued his illegal operations. His ongoing activities suggest that he may have had political pull and that North Dakota law—weakened by many loopholes—failed to prohibit effectively.[60]

Middle-class Protestants and progressives nevertheless continued their assault on working-class saloons nationally and locally. Thirty-six states had adopted local option, four had set high license fees, and five had enacted prohibition by 1900. Congress in 1913 banned the interstate shipment of liquor into dry states, which totaled twenty-six before the end of the Progressive Era. These efforts elsewhere encouraged twin city reformers. Aided by the deciding vote of Mayor Tillotson, the Moorhead council narrowly passed a $1,500 license fee in 1902. Although the liquor interests managed to reduce the fee to $1,000 the following year, the commercial club and Loyal Liberty Protective League assisted in setting the license at $1,600 and limiting the total to thirty in 1913. That same year, the council passed an ordinance "prohibiting minors, . . . [Indians], . . . students, . . . prostitutes, spendthrifts, habitual drunkards or improvident persons from entering . . . any saloon within the city." After Clay County voted dry under the new statewide County Option Law in 1915, the council prohibited the "sale of intoxicating liquors." For almost the next two decades, Moorhead citizens struggled ineffectually, like their Dakota brethren, against the illegal sale of alcohol.[61]

In the minds of temperance advocates, liquor spawned the vice of gambling—whether by cards, dice, or roulette wheel. Although most forms had been outlawed by the 1890s, saloon patrons commonly wagered for small stakes. Professional gamblers subverted these friendly games by cheating drunken harvest hands. The middle class denounced such men as thieves for living without labor by taking wages from those who did. The only legitimate gain came slowly and honestly through work. They therefore condemned gambling among the rich as aristocratic pretense and among the poor as illusory. They even criticized selfish profit seeking by capitalists. Indeed, the older producer economy provided the basis for bourgeois censure of gaming dangers—irrational gain, expenditure without return, addictive passion, and corruption.[62]

During the 1893 harvest season, the *Moorhead Weekly News* complained about a gang of fifty "tinhorn gamblers." The editor demanded police action. Although Mayor Art Lewis claimed to have closed all saloons where gambling occurred, Clay County sheriff Hill, assisted by Chief Sullivan, arrested twenty-three of the fraternity upon orders of county attorney C. A. Nye. Nye ran six out of town and fined the others. Three years later, police detained four barkeepers for allowing games of chance on their premises. They seized tables, chips, wheels, and other paraphernalia. Authorities struggled to stop gaming because it occurred in so many bars and violators faced mild penalties. The notorious Johnny Haas had been arrested three times by June 1899 when the court convicted him and imposed the two hundred-dollar maximum fine. Some Fargo hotels and blind pigs offered gambling as well. It increased during harvest and persisted in the face of slight penalties. Apart from ordinances, the Fargo council did not address the problem between 1875 and 1911. Perhaps police harassment curtailed gaming sufficiently among seasonal transients to satisfy the city fathers. They likely tolerated it at other times.[63]

Twin city residents attributed most crimes to the lethal combination of the saloon and seasonal workers. Young, unmarried males lived without maternal restraint. They drank to excess. Once drunk, they robbed, assaulted, and murdered. The press reported numerous incidents of this kind. For example, drunkenness led to a double murder at Hanson's Saloon early one Sunday morning in 1873. The alleged murderer—railroad striker Patrick Sullivan—had arrived in town only a few days earlier. One of his victims had supported the railroad company in a quarrel earlier in the day. The *Red River Star* called the crime "Disgraceful!" and a "Blight [on the] character and moral standing of our community abroad!" Almost two decades later, the *Fargo Daily Argus* attributed a recent rash of robberies to professional thieves disguised as hoboes. The *Moorhead Weekly News* made the connection explicit in 1900. Most crime occurred during the wheat harvest. Drunkenness, larceny, and shootings declined in other months. The annual influx of laborers drew a large migration of gamblers and thieves seeking their own harvest from the wages of drunken farmworkers.[64]

Statistics confirm this anecdotal evidence. From his study of Moorhead police arrest records from May 1901 to April 1902, Clay County Historical Society archivist Mark Peihl has documented the seasonal nature of crime and established alcohol as the dominant cause. Of the 1,305 taken into custody, police apprehended nearly 82 percent in the three harvest months from August through October. After a sharp winter decline, the number detained climbed again as farmhands returned for spring planting. Alcohol-related arrests—which made up 71.7 percent of the total—rose to 83 percent at harvesttime. Drunks committed one-half the violent and two-thirds of the disorderly conduct crimes. Men comprised slightly more than 98 percent of those detained. Alcohol violations account for about one-half the jailed women, who were likely prostitutes. Only 20 percent of them received suspended sentences, while 67 percent of the men did. That a similar pattern prevailed in earlier decades is evident from the justice of the peace reports to the Moorhead council. Arrests totaled 958 in 1893; drunkenness comprised 72 percent (690) for July through October. Such statistics are less complete for Fargo. Drunkenness accounted for 65 percent of the arrests made by the police during August 1896 and October 1900, however.[65]

These statistics reveal a fundamental fact of Fargo and Moorhead life. From the onset of wheat monoculture in the 1870s, thousands annually inundated the twin cities, posing a moral dilemma for each municipality. On the one hand, migrants supplied essential labor for urban and agricultural prosperity. On the other, they endangered social and moral order, sparking a debate among middle-class reformers and city authorities about how best to protect families and the community. Citing liquor as the source for most crimes, religiously inspired teetotalers called for prohibition of alcohol. Failing abolition, they demanded high license fees and strict enforcement of liquor laws. Those worried about municipal prosperity, however, enacted license fees sufficiently high to produce revenue for the city without killing the liquor trade. They relied on moral suasion and effective regulation of saloons to curb the evils of drink. The debate continued along similar lines after North Dakotans closed their saloons in 1890. The forces of moral purity insisted on eradicating blind pigs, gambling, crime, and related evils. Their pragmatic opponents said pervasive lawbreaking proved the impracticality of purity, however desirable it might be.

MIDDLE-CLASS DEMONS OF DEMIMONDE AND DIVORCE

Bourgeois moralists demonized demimonde and divorce because each threatened Christian monogamy and the family on which civilized morality rested. During the nineteenth century, state and federal governments legislated Christian convention. States defined marriage as a lifelong contract that assigned economic and sexual duties to husbands and wives. Although the contract could be broken for specified reasons, Protestant and Catholic clergymen feared this prospect. By affording an opportunity for another sexual partner, divorce raised the specter of promiscuity. Congress, meanwhile, required monogamous marriage among Native Americans and Mormons. It defined birth control as obscene because separating sex from procreation weakened marital responsibilities. Congress excluded prostitutes from the immigrant flood. The Mann Act tried to eradicate the white slave trade. As scholar Nancy Cott concludes: "A refurbished alliance between national authority and Christian monogamous morality settled firmly into place." State and federal laws mirrored local opinion. Respectable dual city citizens barred prostitutes and brothels from their neighborhoods as "an outrage on decency" and feared "young girls are taken there and ruined."[66]

Except for "hog ranches" that served soldiers from nearby forts or drivers along freight routes, late-nineteenth-century prostitution was primarily urban. It grew wherever numerous unmarried men and out-of-town visitors gathered. From the largest cities to western cow towns and mining camps, officials segregated brothels either on the outskirts or in poor areas. In the trans-Mississippi West perhaps fifty thousand worked the seasonal sex trade that depended on the migration of cowboys, harvest hands, lumberjacks, or other laborers. Until mid-century, municipalities traditionally tolerated disorder and reluctantly curbed infamous businesses. Pressured by religiously inspired reformers determined to protect the bourgeois family, states and cities everywhere banned prostitution by the end of the century. Yet officials condoned lax law enforcement against brothels for the same reasons they tolerated illegal liquor sales.[67]

Despite the myth of prudish Victorians, recent historical scholarship shows that Victorian culture lacked a unified sexual standard. Historian Helen Lefkowitz Horowitz has discovered four contending sexual cultures in the nineteenth century. Evangelical Christian sexuality, backed by legislation and the courts, repressed the others and achieved moral hegemony by the 1870s. Middle-class Victorians agreed on the wickedness of prostitution, but disagreed about remedies and competed to impose their solutions on working-class men and women. Many regarded brothels as necessary evils, best controlled through regulation in which sin paid its way. Serving ineradicable appetites increased municipal income, expanded commerce, and preserved respectable morality through segregation. Purity crusaders rejected such pecuniary bargains with vice. They condemned the unholy alliance of prostitution with liquor interests and political corruption. They proposed aggressive policies for eliminating this sinful social menace. Anxious middle-class female reformers worked to preserve the purity of domesticity from the evils of liquor and prostitution. For them, soiled doves must be redeemed to elevate all women.[68]

According to author Francine du Plessix Gray, sex work is paradoxical because it can be seen as humiliating women as well as liberating them from male dominance. Scholars have long debated the meaning of this paradox and whether or not prostitutes were doomed to die in impoverished misery. Joel Best's study of the demimonde in St. Paul, Minnesota, describes women who were probably similar to their Moorhead and Fargo sisters. Most remained poor, but not doomed inevitably to miserable lives. They were women in motion. They commonly engaged in occasional prostitution, entering and leaving the trade as dictated by economic need. They frequently relocated to new cities or another brothel in the same city. Prostitutes were mostly twenty-something, single, and native-born, working in small houses with four or five others for a madam who had made a career of selling sex. Most were not abducted or tricked, but freely chose to escape unhappy family lives or to earn higher wages. They frequently coped with the stain of disrepute by conspicuous display in clothes and carriages. Many wanted to dress like ladies and even attract husbands. Madams sometimes protected their girls, many of whom left after a few years for marriage or other jobs. Contrary to Best's assertions, historian Anne Butler describes the self-destructive lives of those who remained in the trade. They experienced poverty, disease, and emotional as well as physical violence; they did not find solace in friendships, marriage, or motherhood; they became addicted to drugs or alcohol and many died from substance abuse or suicide.[69]

Sex work in brothels, dance halls and saloons, one-room shacks or rented shack-like rooms called cribs, and walking the streets formed the western prostitution hierarchy. Bordello inmates had the best status and creature comforts; crib workers and streetwalkers faced the greatest risks for the least income. Although these categories were fluid, lifelong prostitutes generally descended the hierarchy as they aged. For some western women, prostitution offered the best economic opportunity in an area with limited, low-paying employment possibilities. It drew employees from varied racial groups. A white majority, often of Irish descent, joined by African American, Native American, Mexican, and Chinese women in particular western locales, constituted the racial hierarchy of this stigmatized occupation. All were accustomed to hard work and few comforts, easing their adjustment to the sex trade. Whatever hopes they might have had for more money, most earned little from their daily working-class customers, who were poor themselves. Jail records reveal their destitution; only a small percentage had the cash to pay their fines. The rates they received for sexual services varied with situation and their haggling skills. They attempted to extract as much as possible through fees, alcohol sales at inflated prices, and even theft. During the 1880s in Helena, Montana, successful prostitutes earned from $179 to $339 a month. These high earnings declined in the next decade as conditions changed. At that time in Wichita, Kansas, the standard rate was five dollars for one customer for an entire evening. Payments to pimps, police, politicians, and more than 60 percent of their income to landlords left them with little profit. Few women accumulated savings or property. Prostitutes in the twin cities experienced similar economic conditions.[70]

Less is known about patrons than prostitutes. Harvest hands and traveling salesmen, who shared the promiscuous sporting culture of major American cities, accounted for most clients. As frequently happened elsewhere, the Fargo red-light district established itself near the principal hobo area. These men prized women who gratified sexual desire without marriage or courtship. Newspaper accounts at times condemned pimps or reported the arrests and fines of customers for consorting with prostitutes outside the designated sex area. Police also detained patrons if a brothel worker brought charges. A newspaper recounted the attempted suicide of prostitute Laura Spencer, who had been jilted by her lover, a baking powder salesman. Occasionally, middle-class residents became involved with the demimonde. For example, Mary E. Stephens sued for divorce in 1884 from Alfred—proprietor of Stephens and Sears Livery, Sale and Boarding Stable in Fargo. Although she had forgiven his earlier adultery with a servant, she charged that he frequently visited brothels and associated publicly with Dotty Smith, one of madam Rae Lawrence's girls. A decade later, the *Fargo Forum* reported that a married man had paid the monthly fine levied against madam Nettie Williams as well as a large sum of money that had furnished her bordello.[71]

Residents called the red-light district "Hell's Half Acre" in the early days of both cities. Belle Butler, Kate Bailey, and other madams operated on the eastern edge of Moorhead. Kittie Raymond managed the house she owned near the corner of present-day Center Avenue and Eleventh Street for twenty years. Three additional "houses of ill fame" appeared on her block in the 1890s. The Fargo district centered in an area north of First Avenue from Second to Third Street North. The 1884 *Sanborn Fire Insurance Map* euphe-

A Sanborn Fire Insurance Map from 1899 shows four "Houses of Ill Fame" on Front Street East in Moorhead. Courtesy Clay County Historical Society.

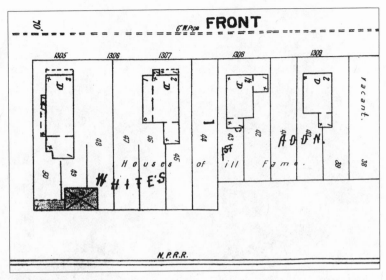

mistically identified the principal brothels as "female boardinghouses." "The flat"—later called "the hollow" or "under the hill"—had a large hobo jungle, impoverished lower Front Street, and Moorhead saloons conveniently located nearby. Inhabitants of the adjacent immigrant neighborhood known as "Little Norway" often launched anti-vice campaigns joined by many respectable businessmen from adjoining Upper Front Street, Northern Pacific Avenue, and Broadway.[72]

Early Fargo journalist Frank W. Pearson later recalled that prostitutes moved about the city during the 1880s. They plied three variety theaters and the forty or more saloons that enjoyed a booming trade. For example, the Coliseum combined vaudeville shows with a saloon and brothel. Waitresses served balcony booths that had tables, chairs, curtains in front, and doors to the rear. The demimonde frequently appeared on the streets fancily dressed and riding in carriages. Matilda Roberts, who owned a dressmaking and millinery shop, recollected "fancy girls" as her best customers, buying twenty-five-dollar hats. Indeed, hatmaking was the rumored trade of the finely dressed madam Clara Morton upon her arrival at the Continental Hotel. Morton shocked the guests when she established commerce of another kind.[73]

Outraged respectable folk and local editors complained frequently about the sex trade that flourished despite being forbidden by Dakota territorial law. The *Fargo Argus* published a letter from "Sufferer" who resided in the flat and demanded redress for "three notorious houses of ill fame" and as many as fifty "drunken loafers speaking profanely and firing pistols each night." He recommended licensing as a means of control. *Argus* editor Alanson W. Edwards urged publishing the names of madams and their clients; electing

In 1890, the Fargo City Council restricted prostitution to the area north of the Central Hotel (on left) at First Avenue and Third Street North. This photograph was taken in about 1909. Courtesy Institute for Regional Studies, North Dakota State University, Fargo (2006.3.3).

better men to municipal government; enacting new laws; and better polic-ing. Such complaints led to changes in municipal law. An 1885 ordinance prohibited employment of females in beer gardens and saloons. Two years later, another ordinance declared brothels "common public nuisances."[74]

In August 1890, first ward residents demanded abatement of the houses of ill fame in their neighborhood. The council referred their petition to the first ward alderman, who recommended that such houses be restricted to that portion of Third Street North of the Central Hotel known as "under the hill" or "the hollow." The council adopted his proposal. The madams contin-ued paying monthly fines, which paid for extra police patrols of the area. Two years later the *Forum* reported that either the madams had not all paid or the city treasury had not received all payments. The stench of possible graft mo-bilized sexual purity advocates; nine hundred residents signed a petition de-manding that the council banish all brothels from the city. The council did not act immediately, prompting the Norwegian Baptist preacher L. J. Anderson to write in a letter to the *Forum*: "Nights resound with voices of revelry, blas-phemy and curses . . . Let all Christian people arise and demand that the city administration do their duty." For Christians like Anderson, duty demanded prohibiting vice and expelling soiled doves from the city. For Victorian regulators on the council, however, sinful human nature rendered abolition un-attainable. They settled for driving all whores into the hollow and regulating them through improved policing financed by monthly fines.[75]

To make the system more effective and to placate critics, the council in 1896 enacted more comprehensive regulations. The new law declared broth-els illegal within the city limits or within one mile of Fargo; it subjected vio-lators to fines ranging from twenty-five to one hundred dollars. It imposed payments not exceeding one hundred dollars for now specified illegal acts: resorting to brothels, renting rooms or houses for lewd purposes, enticing persons to houses or rooms for sex, and brothel inmates appearing in public. It mandated that police report violations to the mayor and bring violators to court. Despite the more stringent laws, unofficially licensed prostitution in the designated area continued. Indeed, more careful record keeping and more systematic collection of fines attended the new ordinance. According to ledgers meticulously kept between April and December 1896, police ar-rested the principal madams each month. The women appeared before the justice of the peace, pled guilty, and paid $56.50 in fines and court costs. Before their release, four settled in full and two arranged installment pay-ments, as they were able.[76]

The arrangement unofficially licensed madams for another month of il-legal activity. The women cooperated because the understanding protect-ed them from predatory customers, police, and city officials. Despite the plan's promise of reducing disorder and increasing control, purity crusaders criticized municipal authorities for tolerating immorality and violating law. Offended purists continued to demand abolition. In addition, keeping pros-titutes in the designated district required constant vigilance. Police regu-larly arrested and jailed them for streetwalking or for keeping or resorting to rooms for immoral purposes in other parts of the city. When destitute women could not pay their twenty-five-dollar fines judges expelled them from the city. This served the policy of segregating sex in a single area.[77]

Prostitution in Moorhead paralleled that of Fargo. It boomed during late summer and autumn after the harvest hands arrived. Purity advocates con-demned the trade in letters to the press: "Is there no law to suppress the dens of infamy that exist in this place . . . which are leading our young men to destruction? . . . Houses of ill fame . . . [are] contaminating the whole vil-lage . . . by night, and even at mid-day." The council adopted new ordinances for suppressing vice and immorality. The state made it a felony in 1886 to keep a house of ill fame.[78]

Like their sister city, moreover, Moorhead officials selectively enforced laws and unofficially licensed vice. Surviving records of the municipal court presided over by Judge Daniel Titus demonstrate that Kittie Raymond and other madams regularly paid monthly fines from October 1, 1888, through February 1, 1896. These fees increased dramatically from twelve dollars to fifty dollars in July 1892, probably at the behest of reform-minded Mayor William Tillotson, who wanted to curtail the sex trade. Aldermen, seeking to enhance city revenues, supported the measure. Newspaper accounts show that this licensing system originated in the 1870s and persisted until the end of the century. Officials used jail terms, expulsion from the city, and denial of liquor licenses to eliminate streetwalkers, close "unlicensed immoral houses," and exclude prostitutes from saloons. These actions segregated vice on Front Street east.[79]

Although the city attempted to impose order through fines, jail, and expulsion, disorder did not disappear completely, as several incidents involving madam Kate Bailey demonstrate. Bailey's house gained even greater notoriety when Edgar Vandecar murdered his mistress there in August 1878. As he fired the shots, the girls scurried for other rooms and the male visitors exited for the nearest ditch. Three weeks later someone set her house afire by boring holes and pouring oil between the walls. The following March, "Fargo bloods" busted her door. The sheriff arrested both vandals and whores. The next day at court, however, the women told such contrary stories that the judge released the men. Later indicted for keeping a house of ill fame, Bailey pled guilty in district court and received a suspended sentence until the next term. She accepted the judge's implicit invitation to leave town.[80]

As Vandecar's murder of teenager Frances Clark suggests, prostitutes in the two cities lived at risk. Newspapers abandoned what social purity reformers had attacked as "a conspiracy of silence." Editors now reported such incidents in considerable detail and with a scandalized tone. Purity advocates wanted the sordid sex trade publicized in order to mobilize support for its abolition. Local editors often backed these campaigns with stories describing the lives and deaths of soiled doves. Both the *Clay County Advocate* and the *Moorhead Weekly News,* for example, portrayed Clark as the tragic victim of an abusive, drunken, gambling villain. A domestic from Brainerd, she had been lured into prostitution. She had supported him with her earnings. When she left him in order to marry a respectable man, she took refuge with Kate Bailey and swore out a peace warrant against him. Evading Deputy Sheriff J. B. Blanchard by fleeing to Fargo, Vandecar later returned to Bailey's house and shot Clark with a concealed pistol.[81]

"Wanted to Die"—an 1895 story published by the *Fargo Forum*—similarly evoked the sympathy of readers for the plight of another fallen woman. The reporter described Viola Lyons as a tall, slender blonde who would be attractive except for the mark of dissipation on her face. After her husband abandoned her and joined the Salvation Army, circumstances forced her into Cad Devine's brothel. She quarreled with the madam, who dismissed her. While drinking whiskey with a soldier in a Moorhead saloon, she grew despondent and took laudanum. After being revived by a physician, she was expelled from the city, only to be arrested in Fargo. While in jail, she attempted to cut her wrists with a penknife. When the knife was taken from her, "she threw herself on the hard bench of the cell with a wail of despair and began to cry as though her heart would break."[82]

These sympathetic newspaper accounts of Clark and Lyons portrayed them as victims of faithless men and economic circumstances. Editors implied that such women could be redeemed. For female reformers to set redemption as a goal, they had overcome their middle-class prejudices against prostitutes as "polluted" and "irrevocably fallen." They attempted to provide the girls with new homes, religious instruction, and employment. Two *Forum* accounts from the 1890s illustrate these tendencies. The newspaper condemned its rival, the *Argus*, for reporting a motherless young girl who had been convicted for prostitution. By breaking a pledge not to publish, the *Argus* prevented the girl's reformation through a commendable effort by respectable ladies. The *Forum* may have been more upset about its rival's scoop than by publicity about the victim. The newspaper seems to have believed that exposure would further the reformation of Signa Setterstrom, a Moorhead prostitute arrested for stealing a sealskin coat. The daughter of a respectable South Dakota family, Setterstrom had fled her stepfather and had been ruined by a married man. She moved to Fargo, but the bad company of a traveling man and a prostitute derailed her attempt to lead a proper life as a stenographer: "A few wine suppers [with them] led to her complete downfall." Nonetheless, the account called her unfortunate and concluded: "[She] is anxious to abandon the life she recently started and will make a home with a family in Fargo." Redemption frequently failed, however, because it did not move beyond spiritual appeals to the practical assistance required for reentering society by stigmatized ex-prostitutes.[83]

Purity campaigns in Fargo and Moorhead at the turn of the century echoed national and international trends by seeking to impose sexual repression on working-class culture. Like progressives elsewhere, Fargo authorities employed vagrancy laws to eliminate streetwalking. For example, police arrested Mrs. Jennie Stoltz, who plied her trade among the men and boys of Island Park. The judge fined her, but suspended the sentence on condition that she and her shiftless husband leave town in three days. Henceforth, officials warned, others would be similarly prosecuted for vagrancy. Meanwhile, Andrew and Anne Brandon Johnson—the Swedish- and Norwegian-born proprietors of the workingman's Central Hotel—joined with other respectable citizens and organized the First Ward Improvement

League. They found willing allies in the State Enforcement League, Judge Charles A. Pollock, and Cass County peace officers. Monthly fines paid to the city did not include county officials. The First Ward and State leagues closed houses in the hollow at least three times in the next decade.[84]

In a December 1898 raid, the sheriff arrested four madams. He charged Nettie Williams with selling beer and the others with contempt of court for violating a previous injunction against beer sales. Madam Clara Morton— who "had the reputation of being pretty smooth"—claimed illness and avoided detention. She soon skipped to Moorhead and then to Kansas City. "The officers are satisfied," the *Forum* concluded, "Fargo is not likely to shelter her soon." The others posted bond, were released, and resumed business. The Improvement League then demanded that Mayor J. A. Johnson close the brothels, which depreciated their property and threatened the morals of their wives and children. Complying with the committee's request, the mayor ordered the madams to vacate. As property owners, they refused to be driven from their homes. All demanded the protection for which their fines had paid. Four years later, the council closed all ten houses, but the madams fled to Moorhead and again returned. Another anti-vice campaign followed in 1908.[85]

Some Moorhead city officials similarly took tougher stands on prostitution as the movement for moral reform grew after the mid-1890s. Purity crusaders wanted to abandon the customary practice of having the madams pay monthly fifty-dollar fines. Declaring them a menace to the community, city justice Michael Syron promised to stop the "streetwalking business" by imposing the full penalty of the law. When reform-minded Mayor Samuel Frazier ordered Chief Nels Holbeck to bring the women before Judge James H. Sharp, the justice rejected their offer of payment because no case had been made against them. Upon their release, the women fled to Fargo, fearing legal action. Meanwhile, Justice of the Peace Peter Odegaard continued to accept "fines" from the madams, increasing city revenues by letting sin pay its way.[86]

As prostitution emerged as a national issue during the Progressive Era, the drive to end red-light districts succeeded in the twin cities and the two hundred largest American cities by 1920. A broad coalition of groups—the WCTU, women's clubs, purity crusaders, social hygiene advocates, and medical professionals—had long opposed the effort to control prostitution through regulation. They agreed that it had increased crime, fostered disrespect for law, and did not stop venereal disease. They feared that commercial sex threatened the purity of women and the bourgeois family through the unchecked spread of white slavery and venereal disease. After the United States entered the Great War, the Commission on Training Camp Activities suppressed prostitution in adjacent cities and towns, curtailed saloons, treated soldiers infected with venereal disease, and promoted wholesome recreation. Although the red-light district disappeared from Moorhead in 1906 and Fargo in 1916, prostitution did not end. It shifted to bars or hotels and to streetwalkers or call girls.[87]

With the exception of Malvina Massey Rae, it is not known what became of the madams and their girls after the bordellos closed. For a period of at least two decades, the African American Massey operated three different houses before occupying the Crystal Palace at 201 Third Street North. She provided black women for mostly white patrons. She survived a fire-related loss of her first house, valued at $1,800, only partially covered by insurance. She avoided extortion from Walter and Chester Bill, two agents of the State Enforcement League. When they demanded one hundred dollars to keep her place open while they shut down the others, she shrewdly refused payment until they had closed her rivals. Having paid monthly protection money to the city, Massey survived assaults by customers on her girls and avoided municipal police raids. After county authorities closed her brothel at the turn of the century, she cleaned houses in Fargo and worked as a chambermaid at the Moorhead Lafayette Hotel. Upon her death in 1911 at age fifty-two, fifty-nine, sixty-five, or perhaps seventy-three, she bequeathed the Crystal Palace, household goods, and all other personal property to her son, Henry Massey. Henry Rae, her husband, received one dollar and the empty lot adjoining her house. She claimed that Rae would have been worth several hundred thousand dollars if he had not carelessly spent the hundreds of dollars she had given him. In addition to furs valued at $250 and a savings account of slightly more than $200, her personal property totaled just over $1,600 and her house was assessed at $1,450. The Dakota Trust Company

This building at 201 Third Street North in Fargo, photographed in the 1920s, housed the Crystal Palace, which was operated by African American madam Malvina Massey until her death in 1911. Courtesy Institute for Regional Studies, North Dakota State University, Fargo (FHC 106-2).

distributed nearly $1,000 to creditors, enabling Massey's son to occupy the house without selling her personal property.[88]

Such were the wages of sin for one woman in Fargo. Did sex work liberate Massey or subject her to male domination? In a manner that her middle-class opponents ought to have appreciated, she accumulated property and preserved it for the sake of her son. By all accounts a shrewd businesswoman, she likely enjoyed more independence and prospered more in the illicit sex trade than she would have in the other lines of work open to her. On the other hand, when the Enforcement League and county officers temporarily shut her business down, they reduced her to working as a hotel chamber-maid and as a domestic servant. Additionally, she obviously felt betrayed by her feckless husband, who had squandered her earnings. Clearly, men—her husband, municipal and country officials, ministers and other moral reformers—limited her economic independence and security. The same men and their wives—who perpetuated the virtues of domesticity throughout society—dominated the middle-class moral ethos of Fargo and Moorhead. That ethos forever excluded women like Massey, however wealthy and inde-pendent they became, from genteel respectability and social acceptance.

Moral crusaders such as Roman Catholic bishop John Shanley and WCTU president Elizabeth Preston Anderson had battled prostitution and alcohol because they undermined the Christian family and civilized morali-ty. The two reformers opposed easy divorce in North Dakota for similar rea-sons. It violated God's law. It fostered adultery and promiscuity, which par-alleled prostitution. Hence, it gave the state an immoral reputation. State officials who defended the law for economic reasons especially disgusted both Shanley and Anderson, who rejected divorce on moral grounds.

As the *Moorhead Weekly News* pointedly stated in 1894: "There is one manu-facturing establishment in Fargo which flourishes in spite of hard times, and that is the mill where they grind out divorces." Actually, the city had acquired its reputation for this vice just recently. Before 1877 in Dakota Territory, an applicant for divorce could initiate action the day she or he arrived. That year, territorial legislators established a ninety-day residency requirement in order to make separation more difficult without discouraging settlement. Despite this intention, *Argus* editor Alanson W. Edwards—already alarmed in 1881 by the number of temporary residents who came solely in order to terminate their marriages quickly—warned that Fargo should avoid becom-ing a divorce mill. That did not occur for some time, however. Only after 1893 did North Dakota grant thousands of divorces, as South Dakota fol-lowed many eastern states and enacted more restrictive legislation. Those in Fargo increased from only twenty-seven in that year to 148 three years later. During that decade, Fargo's divorce rate averaged more than twice that of western states. At 65 percent of the total, the number of migratory divorce seekers much exceeded all other regions of the country. The grounds remained the same as elsewhere—adultery, cruelty, and drunkenness. An extremely lenient third district judge at Fargo, W. A. McConnell, facilitated these trends. The judge also insisted that applicants lead an exemplary life, according to attorney Melvin Hildreth, who called him "a stickler for high morality and good conduct" as well as a "lasting disgrace to the bench." After McConnell left in 1897, the more meticulous Charles A. Pollock replaced him. In the next year he granted only fifty-three divorces. That led many to file with more indulgent judges elsewhere in the state, although they still fulfilled the residency requirement by living in Fargo.[89]

Attracted by "real hotels" and an "endurable" theater, a wealthy divorce clientele flocked to the city from the eastern United States, Canada, England, and even the European Continent. Several of these rented apartments or houses on Eighth Street between First Avenue and Third Avenue South. Many worshipped at the nearby First Baptist Church, attracted by the eloquence of the Reverend Homer M. Cook and an excellent choir led by Mrs. Cook, an accomplished singer. It is not recorded what they thought of Cook's sermon on adultery as the only biblical grounds for divorce. Forty-three lawyers and many hotel owners reportedly made a good living from the lucrative divorce trade. Hildreth perhaps gave a more realistic assessment in a letter to his brother in the midst of the depressed 1890s: "The only business that now brings in any money, and that not much is the divorce business."[90]

As had prohibition and prostitution, this issue pitted proponents of purity against those favoring prosperity. According to the *Moorhead Weekly News,* the *Argus* "gloats over the gains to hotels, liveries, lawyers and other lines of business, which the divorce mill . . . brings Fargo." Those who benefited economically opposed modifying the law. Those who demanded moral purity, such as Bishop Shanley and Elizabeth Preston Anderson, campaigned to rewrite the law and condemned legislators who put money before God. Despite the multithousand-dollar industry, the divorce reform bill finally passed during the 1899 legislative session. The new law changed the residency requirement from three months to one year. Only U.S. residents, or those who had declared their intent to become citizens, could initiate divorce proceedings. As Reno replaced Fargo as the U.S. divorce capital, many lawyers and hotelkeepers relocated.[91]

The Northern Pacific railroad brought prosperity to the twin cities by defining them as real estate to be purchased, establishing the Bonanza wheat farms, and connecting the northern plains to metropolitan markets. Yet railroad corporations contributed to other activities that tested the reigning culture of privatism. Individuals who chose seasonal work, unions, strikes, saloons, brothels, gambling dens, and easy divorce contested fundamental assumptions of the middle-class moral and social order. These personal decisions displeased local family-oriented producers. Preservation of family, home, and business required curbing destructive individual actions.

Anxieties of middle-class residents increased as the railroads brought Coxeyites, organized labor, and strikes to the region. Violent work stoppages threatened private property with destruction. Collective action by unions challenged the economic individualism of small businessmen. Yet pervasive bourgeois hostility admitted exceptions. The work ethic and aspirations for respectability expressed by railroad brotherhoods earned middle-class esteem. Many businessmen sympathized with local members of the ARU in its strike against James J. Hill and the hated Great Northern. Businessmen adopted a neutral stance when workers struck the Northern Pacific because the corporation employed so many men in the city. Merchants, anticipating that more wage earners translated into more sales, backed laborers in their campaign for jobs from local contractors.

Each autumn, a "crime wave" engulfed the twin cities as hundreds of migratory workers arrived illegally by rail to harvest wheat, and thieves followed to reap their wages. Temperance crusaders blamed the increasing turmoil caused by this annual influx on liquor, which had been made more plentiful by national distributors using the railroad. Drunkenness led to disorderly conduct, theft, physical abuse, assault, and murder. The saloons and the closely linked houses of prostitution defied law and morality by paying bribes. Profits from vice, municipal income from licensing fees (official and unofficial), and the seasonal nature of crime made moral disorder bearable for many. City officials chose prosperity over purity and looked the other way so long as sin paid its way. A similar attitude made Fargo into a highly lucrative divorce mill that offended pious citizens. Businesses that traded in vice called the individualistic assumptions of privatism into question. How much restraint should be imposed on sinful individuals? Purists refused to compromise with sin. They demanded prohibition of saloons, brothels, and gambling dens. Others said that licensing and moral suasion afforded more effective control. Until all sinners voluntarily gave up vice, it could not be eliminated. The debate between purity and prosperity finally ended in a partial purist victory. By 1920 both cities had closed their saloons and brothels, but had not ended prostitution or drinking.

Fargo and Moorhead shared the culture of privatism and a commitment to middle-class moral order. Both debated whether to be pure or prosperous. External governments forced both wet cities to become dry. North Dakota entered the Union as a dry state in 1889, but not until 1915 did Minnesota adopt "county option." This difference meant that Fargo had battled the illegal consumption of alcohol long before Moorhead began a similar struggle.

Building a Better Community

*Moorhead has set Fargo an example which it will be well to heed,
and the voters here in selecting their municipal government should
cast their ballots for reputable businessmen rather than for those
whose financial interests are slight or who are in any way identified
with the bars of Moorhead.*

—*Fargo Forum and Daily Republican,*
March 18, 1896

*During the past few years streets have been improved, long stretches
of thoroughfares have been repaved on a concrete foundation; miles
of concrete sidewalks laid, water systems extended and health and
sanitary conditions have been improved as far as possible. A paid fire
department is maintained, and the peace and safety of the community are looked after by a small but efficient police force at the head
of which is the mayor of the city.*

—*Fargo Forum and Daily Republican,*
July 19, 1907

NEWCOMERS TO THE TWIN CITIES IN 1880 ENCOUNTERED A BLEAK
reality. Slightly more than four thousand people resided in a few hundred wooden structures built on a prairie bog. Neither town had sewers,
water, or gas mains, telephones or electric lights, recalled former journalist Frank Pearson a half century later. Boosters nevertheless shared a metropolitan dream. They optimistically projected twenty-five thousand or
more residents for each municipality within the decade. They avoided the
appearance of country towns by putting on "city airs." They conformed to
the "booster model" of municipal government defined by Robin L. Einhorn.
Businessmen governed the dual city, creating services that drew people and
ensured their own commercial success.[1]

During the 1890s, residents demanded more from urban government. Aided by engineers, civil servants, other experts, and middle-class reformers, civic and business leaders developed more professional budgets and services. New conceptions of threats to public safety and obligations to protect the community drove the growth of what Eric Monkkonen has called "the service city." More elaborate codes for health, building, fire, and crime, as well as expanded health, fire, and police departments, entailed new expenditures, greater revenues, and more responsible budgeting. A politics of service emerged in which civic leaders fulfilled public demands for amenities economically while balancing budgets, limiting bonded indebtedness, and holding down property taxes. To facilitate these changes, Fargo, Moorhead, and other western cities borrowed from the planning and technical advances of eastern municipalities.[2]

The local civic and mercantile elite realized that publicly financed prosperity could only be attained through communal unity. They therefore embraced ethnic participation in municipal affairs and promoted group harmony by annually celebrating the holidays of St. Patrick, Norwegian independence, and July Fourth. Old and New middle-class American businessmen advanced their self-interest through fostering good government and services. They divided, however, on the question of whether regulation or prohibition of liquor and prostitution best protected the community. Local workers, meanwhile, benefited from the jobs created by urban improvements. Both Old and New American working- and middle-class families enjoyed the enhanced convenience and comfort that new services afforded. Yet single male seasonal workers neither gained economically nor received an improved quality of life from the new service city.[3]

BOOSTER GOVERNMENT, POLITICS, AND FINANCE

U.S. cities were not naturally born, Eric Monkkonen has remarked, but formed by enabling legislation. Although the Dakota territorial and Minnesota state legislatures created Fargo and Moorhead, the dual city actively shaped its own development. For example, each city campaigned successfully for the county seat designation. Local boosters valued this prize that attracted many officials, lawyers, and much legal business to their town. Indeed, Moorhead lobbied hard to defeat neighboring Glyndon's three attempts to capture the courthouse. Glyndon finally surrendered after an 1879 bill authorizing the move died in the legislature.[4]

As settlers grew in number, they formed municipalities. Moorhead evolved from a town (1873) to a village (1875) and finally a city (1881). At each stage residents took appropriate steps and secured the necessary state legislation. The first village meeting elected entrepreneur Henry A. Bruns chair of the board of trustees and appointed a clerk, street overseer, and marshal. After citizens drafted the new city charter, the act of incorporation established a mayor and alderman plan of government and divided the city into three wards. Each ward elected two aldermen for staggered two-year terms. Several boosters and businessmen took the oath of office in March: Mayor Bruns and aldermen John Erickson, Andrew Holes, and John Lamb.[5]

Fargo also adopted the mayor and ward alderman plan. Official government did not begin until an April 12, 1875, council meeting held just days after the first election. The city had been incorporated on January 5 by the Dakota Territorial Legislature, which enacted a bill introduced by Fargo delegate Andrew McHench and demanded by a meeting of citizens a few weeks earlier. Pennsylvania-born Captain George Egbert, the first mayor, owned a saloon and billiard parlor with an upstairs meeting room. He helped found the first Masonic lodge and dealt in real estate. After merchant Evan S. Tyler succeeded him, Egbert won three successive one-year terms. Known as a man of rugged integrity, he "kept the city's money in one pocket and his own in another and never did the funds get mixed."[6]

Events soon rendered inadequate Mayor Egbert's "pants pocket" management of city finance. The rapid growth that challenged other American municipalities during the nineteenth century tested Fargo and Moorhead as well. An urban America demanded new services and protections unknown to a rural republic. Yet inexperience, ignorance, and greed often hindered their development. Property owners and businessmen dominated booster politics and dictated municipal expenditures. They urged cooperation among varied groups demanding services. Yet they competed for economic spoils and political advantage. The intensity of twin city municipal campaigns varied according to the issues advanced by contending or cooperating Republican or Democratic factions composed of businessmen, workers, and reformers. Occasional hotly contested elections between

Businessman "Captain" George Egbert served as Fargo's first mayor in 1875. Courtesy Institute for Regional Studies, North Dakota State University, Fargo (MSS 1970.54).

contenders arguing significant economic or moral issues attracted considerable voter interest. More frequently, unopposed mayoral candidates failed to engage an indifferent electorate.[7]

Twin city politics mirrored some new post–Civil War developments. Activists remained involved with community organizations. Participation declined, as evidenced by vague terms such as "comfortably filled" or "well attended" in the Fargo press accounts of the Republican city convention. Democrats apparently lacked sufficient numbers to fill a room; after the early years the party infrequently held city conventions and Democratic candidates ran as Independents in Fargo elections. In both cities popular rallies sometimes preceded elections or celebrated victories. For example, an 1884 caucus presented a petition with five hundred signatures requesting that Mayor Woodford Yerxa run again. After his reelection, supporters formed a torchlight parade led by a band and a carriage carrying the winner. They halted at the city park for speeches. Yerxa thanked the crowd and proposed three cheers for his opponent, who then spoke. William Kindred said he had been defeated by Yerxa's popularity and not by "the ring" headed by Republican stalwarts John E. Haggart and Alanson W. Edwards. He asked everyone to work for the prosperity of Fargo. Moorhead citizens similarly celebrated elections. The band paraded and supporters gathered for speeches, which they washed down with lots of beer at the Grand Pacific Hotel—owned by first mayor Henry Bruns—or at the Jay Cooke House with proprietor, council member, and second mayor John Erickson.[8]

Like other small U.S. cities then and since, Fargo and Moorhead governments did not support full-time paid politicians. Municipal contests usually lacked heat. Public-spirited devotion to progress and economy outranked party affiliation in electing officials. Considerable real-estate holdings by aldermen ensured that tax rates would be watched. After Fargo mayor George Egbert declined to seek a fifth term, a citizens' delegation recruited Democrat, booster, and saloonkeeper Jasper B. Chapin. His candidacy provoked opposition among the city's better citizens who nominated First National Bank president Ezra B. Eddy. Character, not party, defined the campaign. Dubbed "Bible-bangers" by their political enemies, Eddy's partisans charged that the people's ticket headed by Chapin had originated with "hoodlums and rum mills" and had "crystallized the influences of atheism and alcohol." Perhaps these attacks gave Eddy second thoughts because he abruptly withdrew. Chapin triumphed easily. The following year, Eddy again ran against Chapin. Although voter turnout increased 60 percent, the incumbent nevertheless won by a two-to-one margin. Even *Argus* editor Alanson W. Edwards, a staunch Republican who rarely spoke kind words for any Democrat, perceived Chapin to be honest, vigorous, enterprising, and public-spirited.[9]

DATE	MAYOR	VOTE	OPPONENT	VOTE
1875	George Egbert	86	Patrick Devitt	51
1876	Evan S. Tyler			
1877	George Egbert		Terrence Martin	
1878	George Egbert	103	Evan S. Tyler	50
1879	George Egbert	339		
1880	Jasper B. Chapin	154	J. B. Burgar	38
1881	Jasper B. Chapin	547	E. B. Eddy	249
1882	William A. Kindred	814		
1883	Woodford A. Yerxa	1,080	George Egbert	616
1884	Woodford A. Yerxa		W. A. Kindred	
1885	John A. Johnson			
1886	Charles A. Scott	776	J. W. Von Neida	687
1887	Alanson W. Edwards	771	J. W. Von Neida	607
1888	Seth Newman	621	Henry Capehart	596
1890	Wilbur F. Ball	625	C. H. Mitchell	11
1892	Emerson H. Smith	717	Fred B. Morrill	463
1894	Wilbur F. Ball	683		
1896	John A. Johnson	876	Wilbur F. Ball	714
1898	John A. Johnson	919	O. G. Barnes	592
1900	John A. Johnson	1,128	J. A. Chesley	764

Fargo mayoral elections, 1875–1900. Compiled by John E. Bye, North Dakota Institute for Regional Studies.

Chapin's mayoralty dramatized dilemmas of booster government. Services fueled expansion but forced higher taxes, threatening growth. Although the mayor preached economy, spending increased. His administration erected a city hall that contained the jail, council room, and clerk's office; and it created water mains, hydrants, electric lights, and other rudimentary services. Committees from each municipality began discussions about constructing a permanent Red River bridge.[10]

Resolving difficulties of service-driven growth created controversy. Some citizens condemned "extravagance" and called for reform. To clarify whether the city poll tax or private subscriptions had paid for improvements, Gordon J. Keeney demanded an accounting of how officials spent public money. In addition to accountability, the public debated whether or not to fund expanded services with bonded indebtedness, as adopted by other American cities. When the council called a citywide referendum on the question, the *Fargo Evening Republican* stated that necessary improvements ought to be financed without the "curse of heavy public bonded indebtedness" that could only be repaid through increased property taxes. Others worried that "the floating population" who did not pay taxes might vote irresponsibly for both bonds and improvements, thinking that construction afforded them jobs. City attorney Samuel G. Roberts and Mayor Chapin strongly opposed the bond issue and citizens decisively rejected it. Although nonpropertied voters condemned the result and attacked the "bloated land owners who would rather see us as serfs," they had not voted in sufficient numbers to carry the measure. The Democratic *Fargo Times* applauded the outcome and called on the council to reduce expenses and collect taxes more efficiently.[11]

The council responded in several ways. It initiated more precise accounting procedures. It prepared an assessment tax list based on the city valuation of the county assessor. By the end of 1881, it had increased city taxes to fourteen mills on the dollar. In June 1882, it proposed nine thousand dollars in sewer bonds that voters approved. The electorate usually passed the larger bond issues presented thereafter. Clearly, voters had changed their minds. Better record keeping and management after the inefficient Chapin administration partly explains this shift. Perhaps better-administered city finances made taxpayers somewhat more willing to bear the burden of bonded indebtedness for the services they wanted.[12]

When Chapin announced in mid-February 1882 that he would not seek reelection, it surely pleased *Fargo Evening Republican* editor J. B. Hall. Fearing that rising debt and higher taxes would drive out capital, Hall criticized Chapin's administration for "a loose, careless, irresponsible management of city affairs." After the mayor finally published the treasurer's report, the *Republican* called it "woefully inadequate." It showed that public debt had doubled to more than fifty-four thousand dollars in a single year, but did not account for how these funds had been expended. Chapin responded: "The *Republican* knows that if I had been robbing the city I would be smart enough to get away with it." He insisted that the expenditures had funded those services needed for promoting prosperity. Hall dismissed Chapin's defense. He applauded the election of a reform-minded council and an able, honest businessman, William Kindred, as mayor: given a "judicious and faithful chief magistrate . . . and . . . city council . . . the people and . . . law will be obeyed."[13]

The Fargo council had already taken steps for better accounting. In 1879 it ordered the treasurer to present monthly itemized reports of disbursements and receipts. It instructed the city clerk to prepare vouchers, which truthfully stated billed amounts, goods, and services. Without this sworn statement, the council refused payment. Although these changes had not curbed Chapin's irregularities, the Kindred administration embraced fiscal reform. Both the mayor and the council president now signed all warrants. The council published more exact financial statements on the first of April and October. It formed a board of equalization to adjust tax assessments. With the city financial house in better order, voters approved two bond issues totaling almost one hundred thousand dollars to fund floating indebtedness and a sewer system. Citizens had decided that improvement advantages outweighed tax disadvantages.[14]

Mayor William Kindred's election marked an emerging consensus on orderly budgets and government by honest businessmen. After Chapin's backers nominated George Egbert in 1883, *Argus* editor Alanson W. Edwards insisted his victory would hurt the city. He endorsed the business ticket headed by Woodford Yerxa, who outpolled his opponent in one of the largest municipal votes until 1900. His victory signaled a succession of business mayors for the remainder of the century. The dominant Republican Party, which comprised the majority of voters and commanded the capital for development, claimed responsibility for municipal administration. The nominating process shifted from a mass meeting to the wards. Each ward nominated its own alderman and elected delegates to a city convention that named candidates for municipal offices. A new charter in 1887 promised more efficient government by having the mayor preside over council meetings.[15]

Moorhead similarly wrestled with paying for services that booster government required. As a village from 1875 to 1879, expenses had ranged from about $1,600 to just over $1,800. A decade later, dreams of urban expansion

MAYOR	DATES	MAYOR	DATES
Henry A. Bruns	1881–84	Samuel Frazier	1896–97
John Erickson	1884–86	A. G. Lewis	1897–98
Patrick H. Lamb	1886–89	Jacob Kiefer	1898–1900
Erick Hansen	1889–92	Hans H. Aaker	1900–1901
William R. Tillotson	1892–93	William R. Tillotson	1901–3
A. G. Lewis	1893–96	Carroll A. Nye	1903–7

Moorhead mayors, 1881–1907. From John Turner and C. R. Semling, *History of Clay and Norman Counties* (Indianapolis: B. F. Brown, 1918), 1:269.

had increased expenditures nearly tenfold. Responding to a call from the *Moorhead Weekly Argonaut* for electing officials who would continue healthy urban growth, residents selected two booster businessmen as mayor: Henry A. Bruns (1881–84) and John Erickson (1884–86). Their administrations built miles of sidewalk and sewers, two iron bridges, a waterworks, and a city hall, which housed the mayor, council, police, and firemen until it burned in 1918.[16]

During the first election, the press advised selecting a financially astute mayor to check an extravagant council desiring improvements possessed by larger places. In a process similar to that of Fargo, ward caucuses nominated two candidates for alderman and elected delegates to the city convention. Surprisingly, convention delegates nominated Franklin J. Burnham for mayor, likely expecting the Vermont-born, propertied attorney and staunch Presbyterian to curb the liquor trade. If so, voters dashed their hopes and selected Henry Bruns by a two-to-one margin.[17]

Mayor Bruns's extensive personal interests related closely to those of the city. As an efficient and capable official, he helped create the first city waterworks and the first system of electric arc streetlights. As a businessman, he pumped the water from his flour mill and incorporated the Moorhead Electric Light and Power Company after the initial firm failed. He moved the generator to the Foundry, Car and Agricultural Works in which he had invested heavily. He led the campaign for bridging the Red River, hoping to capture the Dakota hinterland for Moorhead merchants. Two permanent iron bridges, completed in 1884, more effectively linked Fargo and Moorhead. Two ferries initially had crossed the river before a wagon bridge had been built in 1873. The bridge, located just north of the railroad span, rode unsafely low in the water and required annual reconstruction. Without a permanent crossing, Moorhead residents annually lost an estimated six hundred thousand dollars in Dakota trade.[18]

Petitioning the Minnesota legislature for bridge appropriations from 1874 on became an annual exercise in futility. Meanwhile, the council expended several hundred dollars each year repairing bridge damage from ice flows, flooding, and steamboats. An 1879 state law, authorizing Moorhead bond issues for roads and bridges, triggered new efforts for a permanent structure. Confident of a tenfold population increase in the dual city, Bruns suggested two bridges in early 1881. He appointed site selection committees, but his proposal failed to attract immediate support from either citizens or officials.[19]

The Fargo council did not start discussing a permanent bridge until October 1881. Committees from each city began meeting together the next month. Early in the new year, the Minnesota legislature appropriated $2,500 and authorized a $20,000 bond issue by Moorhead. Yet competing interests complicated negotiations and delayed progress. Fargo north- and south-side residents disagreed about the site of a single crossing. Several Fargo capitalists feared "it will not pay" because a bridge benefited their smaller rival more than their own city. Bruns's original proposal resolved these difficulties. By July, Fargo residents solicited subscriptions for two structures. The Moorhead council in August funded two iron bridges—one connecting Moorhead Main and Fargo Front Streets and the other joining James Street (present First Avenue North) with Northern Pacific Avenue. The *Moorhead Weekly News* urged devotion to the combined interests of the dual city and elimination of the river barrier. Through cooperation merchants might command the Northwest wholesale trade.[20]

Progress accelerated during 1883. The Fargo council debated the relative merits of funding by subscriptions, city appropriations, or bonded indebtedness. Fargo voters approved a $20,000 bond issue after subscribers did not pay their pledges. Cass County commissioners appropriated $5,000 for constructing the Front Street Bridge, while the Moorhead council approved a $20,000 bond issue for building two. Mayor Bruns solved the difficulty of obtaining right-of-way for the approaches on the Moorhead side by offering to deed the Main Street land if that on James Street could be similarly obtained. Bruns also convinced the Clay County commissioners to appropriate an additional $2,500, arguing that completion of the Fargo and Southern railroad company would boom the city and quickly repay their investment. Fargo secured its access to the southern span by removing shanties from land deeded by John Erickson, Moorhead's new mayor. The Fargo-Moorhead Bridge Committee awarded contracts in April. Work began once spring flooding receded and proceeded rapidly.[21]

The South Bridge, built by the dual city in 1883, remained in use until its demolition in 1936. Courtesy Institute for Regional Studies, North Dakota State University, Fargo (2070.149.3).

Editors enthusiastically announced completion. The *Moorhead Weekly News* waxed poetic, reporting how "magnificent iron bridges span the stream, and the dual cities are become one." The *Fargo Sunday Argus* agreed, calling them an incalculable benefit and "permanent evidence of the dual city's great commercial prosperity." The South and North Bridges opened to vehicular traffic on February 14 and May 16, respectively. Operation and maintenance created new conflicts. Both councils soon responded to complaints and outlawed fast driving. After the improperly opened North Bridge damaged both the *Grandin* and the *Pluck*, the Fargo council did not pay damages, suggesting instead that the steamers lower their smokestacks. Following damage caused by improper lubrication of the North Bridge, the Fargo council assigned span operations to the city's police chief. Difficulties notwithstanding, the twin cities used the structures until the 1930s, when a three-bridge plan replaced them.[22]

Despite his contribution to the successful bridging of the Red River, Mayor Bruns resigned suddenly on the first day of 1884. He created "a sensation," according to the *Fargo Daily Argus*. Why did he retire? Did he consider his work in booster government complete? Did he detect financial clouds on either the public or his personal horizon? Imminent collapse of the Moorhead boom threatened his financial empire. Only three days after the council accepted his resignation, it heard about treasurer Peter Czizek's defaulted accounts. During the real-estate boom of the previous year, Czizek had appropriated between ten thousand and twelve thousand dollars of city funds. Because of the embezzler's fragile health, the city's case did not come to trial until June 30, 1885. The jury acquitted Czizek, despite the judge's instructions to find him guilty. Yet the state convicted him two years later.[23]

The case shows how easily the line between public and private became blurred in booster government. Because municipalities expended monies on improvements that benefited private parties, an official perhaps more easily appropriated money for his own use. In addition, private citizens expected to benefit from their public service at this time. Finally, the well-intentioned Czizek promised to make things right. The public therefore sympathized with him throughout his long ordeal and welcomed him back into the community once the prison released him.

Moorhead civic leaders badly managed the municipal budget during the 1880s. Booster demands for Red River bridges and other services drove expenditures far beyond revenues. After the total bonded debt reached $120,000 by 1888, Fargo citizens mocked their rival's fiscal irresponsibility. Yet Fargo similarly teetered on the edge of bankruptcy as it reached taxation and borrowing limits. That prospect appeared imminent, as "cold water moralists" demanded the abolition of alcohol and brothels. The prohibition-

ists won and the city lost fourteen thousand dollars in annual liquor revenues.[24] Moorhead's comparable plight committed it to letting sin pay its
way. Hence, attempts to resolve budget woes while providing the services
voters demanded drove twin city politics during the 1890s.

BUDGETING MORE RESPONSIBLY

After the Civil War, municipal spending became more diverse. Debt expanded from just over $328 million in 1870 to more than $761 million in 1890.
Initially, states imposed de facto limits, stipulating that expenditures could
not exceed revenues. Later, most restricted indebtedness to 5 percent of
the assessed value of real property. Although local debt grew absolutely, it
dropped slightly in per capita terms. Newer, Northern states and small cities
had larger deficits because they had to build their entire infrastructure from
nothing. Lacking sufficient current revenues to pay for needed improvements and an established community to perform necessary tasks, new municipalities like Moorhead and Fargo followed booster principles of finance.
They built for an anticipated growing population, provided services to increase their numbers, and issued bonds to defer their costs over time.[25]

Class, ethnic, and party differences affected the positions that individuals might take on the public deficit question. Those with little or no property willingly supported bond issues and debt repudiation, thinking they had
everything to gain and nothing to lose by promoting growth. For similar
reasons, Democrats and the Irish more readily favored repudiation. Small
capitalists accepted debt that would make the city grow, but they supported
repayment when feasible, or readjustment when not, in order to maintain
good credit. The wealthy, most likely to be bondholders, used debt to finance expansion and always demanded repayment.[26]

In the struggles over twin city budgets, Republicans—Yankees, other
Old Americans, Scandinavians, and Germans—backed debt retirement to
maintain sound credit and responsibly financed services. Although citizens
grumbled about taxes, pragmatists contended that improvements expanded businesses, created more comfortable homes, and thereby increased tax
revenues. By 1900, twin city civic leaders more responsibly used debt and
taxation, spreading capital costs over time and space, to provide services
and to promote the local economy. Their success mirrored national trends.
American municipalities achieved greater fiscal honesty, refinanced indebtedness at lower rates of interest, and eased their debt burdens. As urban
historian Jon C. Teaford concludes: "The cost of municipal services during
the last two decades of the century hardly imposed an onerous burden."[27]

Fargo's debt in the early 1890s prevented additional streetlights or water mains. The fire of 1893, the flood of 1897, and the Citizens National Bank failure that same year further strained an already weak fiscal condition. A few months after the council had been informed that the city could incur no further indebtedness, an audit of the former treasurer's accounts revealed an $8,000 shortfall. No wonder the *Moorhead Weekly News* concluded that Fargo managed its affairs more poorly than Moorhead. Fargo's debt in 1900 totaled just over $487,000, divided almost equally between outstanding warrants and bonds. Moorhead's amounted to about $172,000, of which unpaid warrants constituted only $34,000. Yet its $46.24 per capita debt almost equaled that of its rival.[28]

Moorhead battled indebtedness and taxation throughout the decade. Although a board of equalization annually adjusted property valuations, the *Moorhead Weekly News* complained about paying assessments of 4 or 5 percent in depressed times. A report deplored disorderly finances. Customers used water without payment and collections had not been made. The council requested new bookkeeping procedures for the city collector, treasurer, and recorder. Alderman and finance committee chair George Perley presented several recommendations. First, the city attorney should collect all unpaid bills. Second, saloonkeepers in default on licenses should pay or be closed. Third, the city's higher costs in caring for the poor than that paid by other cities of comparable size should be reduced. Fourth, the new Electric Light Plant and Water Works should be operated efficiently. Fifth, the city should be put on a cash basis, which required changing warrants totaling eighty thousand dollars into bonds. An indebtedness larger proportionally than any other U.S. city demanded immediate action. Spurred by Perley's report, a forty thousand-dollar bond issue in late 1896 retired one-half the unpaid warrants.[29]

Moorhead alderman George Perley battled for more responsible fiscal management. From *History of the Red River Valley, Past and Present.*

Two years later, the municipality paid all bills in cash instead of warrants. Fiscal reformer Perley publicly called for electing an honest, business-minded mayor. Normal School president Livingston Lord demanded strict economy until the debt had been reduced from almost 22 percent to the legally required 5 percent of the assessed valuation. Yet *News* editor George Lamphere said the large debt should not cause alarm. Solvency could be reached through annual payments of fixed amounts from liquor revenues. The council did adopt more judicious fiscal management. By 1900, new electric and water meters yielded an $8,500 surplus put toward debt reduction. One-half of the money received from liquor licenses now funded a deficit that would be retired in ten years. With a debt of just forty-one thousand dollars by 1918, reformers had attained their goal. Yet new needs dictated new spending.[30] As even reformers should have realized, debt could be managed but never eliminated. It paid over time for the services most citizens wanted.

Desire for services in Fargo did not abate with revenue shortfalls. By the mid-1890s, new demands included a city hall addition to house the municipal court and jail; a water filtration system; paved streets, concrete sidewalks, and brick sewers. Mayor and aldermen wrestled with giving the public what it wanted without oppressive taxation or municipal bankruptcy. They now stressed collecting unpaid taxes. New state legislation ended tax exemptions for the Northern Pacific, Great Northern, and Milwaukee railroads. After the Cass County commissioners established a valuation he considered too low, Mayor J. A. Johnson twice appealed their decision. When they refused to reconsider, he appeared successfully before the state board of equalization. Boosting the Northern Pacific assessment by 25 percent, Johnson added almost eighty-five thousand dollars in assessed value to the municipal tax rolls as well as collecting back taxes since 1890. He also tried to recover twenty thousand dollars in road and bridge levies paid by the city that Cass County had not remitted. The council meanwhile sued individuals for unpaid property taxes.[31]

As a corporation formed by the North Dakota legislature, Fargo could not issue bonds exceeding 5 percent of its assessed valuation. The state also mandated an annual interest payment, a sinking fund for repaying principal, and elections for approving bond issues. Because Fargo had reached its debt limit, but needed sewers and other improvements, legislators now provided an exception. A new law permitted municipal sewer bonds not exceeding 4 percent of the assessed valuation. Levies on property holders who benefited directly repaid this debt at not more than 7 percent per annum over a twenty-year period.[32]

Fargo thus followed what Robin Einhorn identified as "segmented municipal financing." For example, businessmen paid eighty-five dollars per lot in 1895 for paving several blocks of Broadway, Front Street, and Northern Pacific Avenue. Their payments redeemed warrants issued to the contractor. This success generated many new demands. To fulfill pavement requests and build brick sewers, the council in 1898 established nine improvement districts that had been requested by a majority of lot holders. The North Dakota supreme court ruled these levies constitutional, forcing disgruntled opponents into compliance. The Cass County auditor annually collected one-twentieth for two decades, fully paying the costs.[33]

GOOD GOVERNMENT AND THE POLITICS OF SERVICES

Honesty and efficiency defined good government in both cities at this time. Twin city mayors and aldermen strove to provide at reasonable cost all the new services that citizens demanded. Although civic leaders found improvements alluring, they often disagreed about how to proceed. For example, purity crusaders waged anti-vice campaigns, ensuring the virtue of citizens and thereby protecting their prosperity. Regulators fostered security by segregating brothels and licensing liquor, paying for expanded services with these wages of sin. This contest between the forces of purity and regulation shaped Moorhead and Fargo politics throughout the 1890s. Pressed to pay for the favored improvements, Moorhead mayors relied on income from the liquor and sex trade. Fargo officials paid for expanded services without liquor proceeds. Yet dual city citizens condemned those leaders who did not strictly enforce the laws against alcohol and prostitution. Those striving for good government therefore found it difficult at times to be both honest and efficient.

The staffing and funding of twin city police departments exemplified several issues involved in the politics of service and good municipal government. Salaried, uniformed police spread during a period of four decades by diffusion from the London Metropolitan Police (1829) to large U.S. cities on the eastern seaboard and thence to smaller municipalities. Police departments marked the initial emergence of urban service bureaucracies. They served by controlling the dangerous class either by boarding them in station houses or by arresting them for vagrancy and crime. Their inability to distinguish among the poor, tramps, and criminals who were the underclass complicated their task. Political ties rather than professional knowledge determined appointments, making the police highly politicized. A skeptical public thus assumed that police corruption accounted for the persistence of illegal saloons and brothels.[34]

Like other American cities that established paid, uniformed policemen who reported to mayors, Fargo and Moorhead recognized an obligation to protect persons and property from crime. This seasonal problem worsened

Chief Ben Wade and uniformed Fargo policemen (ca. 1906) marked the emergence of an urban service bureaucracy. Courtesy Institute for Regional Studies, North Dakota State University, Fargo (2006.70.8).

with the annual arrival of migratory harvest labor. Although the *Fargo Daily Argus* normally favored reduced spending, it equally desired public safety. Citing threats to security, the *Argus* editor demanded night patrols, nighttime police station staff, and electric lights on the Red River bridges. Desires for protection, however, did not displace wishes for economy. During the seven months from January through July, each city reduced its force to three patrolmen. For the harvest and threshing months, Moorhead increased its force to five or as many as the chief deemed necessary. Fargo expanded to seven or sometimes ten patrolmen. Each city manned daily and nightly beats on the principal business streets. An additional officer patrolled the red-light districts at night. Another at the station responded to emergencies. Electric lights on the bridges, a favorite criminal haunt, deterred those who rolled the numerous drunks passing to and from Moorhead saloons and Fargo brothels.[35]

The Moorhead lockup battle demonstrated how contentious service politics could become. As the council planned a modern brick structure adjacent to the city hall in 1892, the state board of corrections imposed standards that increased costs by almost 28 percent. After aldermen surmounted this hurdle, public opposition to the city park location confronted them. Proponents argued the city had no other ground for a police headquarters and jail. They said convenience required placing it near the courtroom and the scene of most arrests. Opponents asserted that the site damaged their adjacent businesses. They objected to exposing citizens to sordid tramps, thieves, and drunks. They deplored losing the only municipal green spot where the public might gather. They insisted the LS&PS Company had deeded the land specifically for a park. Although an injunction halted construction temporarily, municipal officials finally built their jail. After dissenters took their case to the state supreme court, it ordered the building removed at the end of the decade.[36]

Emergencies like the disastrous Fargo fire in 1893 and the record-breaking flood in 1897 posed special challenges for the politics of service. Both demanded unplanned and large expenditures from municipal governments. Both raised questions about the quality of some services. "Fire! Horror upon Horrors!" headlined the *Moorhead Weekly News,* the day after the conflagration. Aided by a strong southern wind, a small blaze that began in the rear of a Front Street dry goods store spread rapidly north and east. In just six hours it destroyed everything in its path on the east

The tent of African American barber Frank Gordon sits in the foreground of the business district that was devastated by the Fargo fire in 1893. Courtesy Institute for Regional Studies, North Dakota State University, Fargo (51.30.21).

side of Broadway between the Northern Pacific and Great Northern tracks. Fueled by many wooden buildings, the wind-driven flames exceeded the capacity of the Fargo and Moorhead volunteer fire departments. Hundreds of homeless spent that night on the streets, made miserable by heavy rains. Moorhead residents opened their homes to victims and solicited clothing and money. Notorious saloonkeeper Johnny Haas reportedly contributed five hundred dollars to the relief committee. The three railroad companies reduced rates by 50 percent on building materials. James J. Hill housed homeless at Moorhead's Grand Pacific Hotel, which he had just acquired by foreclosure from the bankrupt Henry Bruns. The council made a tent city for temporary shelter and food distribution. It set maximum hauling fees for removing rubble and trebled the police force to prevent looting.[37]

"The fire was exceedingly disastrous," wrote Solomon Comstock to Hill, "but people are plucky and will build up the town again." Attorney Melvin Hildreth similarly reported: "The people with wonderful energy have commenced work. . . . We hope that . . . we will erect a better Fargo than ever." *Forum* editor Alanson W. Edwards led the campaign from his newspaper columns. He urged: "Don't Give Up! Rebuild at Once!" He praised businessman Alex Stern's hustle for having 125 men clearing his lots two days after the blaze. Stern promised to rebuild his Palace Clothing Store, the opera house, and the Knights of Pythias building. At Thanksgiving the *Forum* rejoiced: "Broadway, lately a mass of smoking ruins is the most beautiful street west of Minneapolis." That reconstruction proceeded in spite of a depression and small harvest demonstrated that Fargo "is the leading city of North Dakota."[38]

Although a short-term calamity, the fire had beneficial long-term effects. As insurance payments totaling $1.3 million pumped cash into the depression-starved local economy, many businesses quickly rebuilt. Already in August, the *Forum* reported: "The brick blocks keep flying skyward at a most gratifying rate." Five years later, 246 new buildings had been erected in the destroyed area. With its business trebled in volume and its population doubled, the city had made a strong recovery by 1900. An amended fire prevention ordinance regulated construction, required inspection, and ensured that the city would be rebuilt in brick and stone. Public infrastructure also benefited: larger water mains, concrete sidewalks, firewalls every fifty feet, and a modern post office. The disaster demonstrated the need for improved fire protection. The council placed the three companies in one building and purchased the Mutual Telephone Company fire alarm system. It recognized the need to make firemen more professional and to improve equipment. Yet cost kept it a volunteer force.[39]

Just as a new city rose from the ashes, the Fargo Fire Festival emerged to mark that metropolitan resurrection. Although some denigrated the folly of celebrating catastrophe, others insisted that it appropriately commemorated the best thing that had happened to the city. On the first anniversary, the *Forum* observed: "Fargo promises to become greater and grander than ever." As reconstruction materially realized these expectations, the festival evolved from a small parade into an elaborate three-day carnival, attracting thousands of visitors from the region. Mayor Johnson arranged special round-trip railroad fares from Minneapolis, St. Paul, and other locales within two hundred miles. Several parades, sporting events, and musical shows entertained the large crowds. Fargo business had not only risen from the ashes, it had capitalized on its success by sponsoring the festival, a commercial bonanza that endured until the 1920s and displaced the traditional July Fourth as a community fete. The festival committee embraced middle- and working-class members: the mayor, the senior alderman of each ward, prominent businessmen, as well as the presiding officers of each fraternal lodge, railroad brotherhood, and GAR.[40]

The 1897 flood crested at forty feet, making it the worst in a century. Municipal and railroad officials placed steam tractors and locomotives on the Red River bridges, saving them from being swept northward. Recently

Residents weighted the North Bridge with steam tractors to prevent it from floating away during the flood in 1897. An inundated Moorhead is in the background. Courtesy Institute for Regional Studies, North Dakota State University, Fargo (51.326.23).

laid wood paving blocks on lower Northern Pacific Avenue and Front Street threatened to float away. Waters inundated Island Park, the Fargo Water Works, and the emergency pumps located on higher ground, leaving the city without fire protection. Overland flooding from the Buffalo River covered the prairies to a depth of two feet between Moorhead and Glyndon, compelling thirty-eight Moorhead families to abandon their Woodland Park homes. When a small Northern Pacific culvert dammed waters from the Sheyenne River, the Big Coolie overflowed, flooding the entire Fargo west side between Eighth and Sixteenth streets.[41]

Hundreds of dual city residents lost everything. The flood damaged the stocks and buildings of many merchants. The initial estimated costs exceeded sixty thousand dollars for repairing twin city sidewalks and pavements. After rope booms saved the wooden blocks from more than a mile of damaged pavement, the Fargo council planned to relay them. As soon as water receded, work began and proceeded rapidly under the supervision of alderman James Kennedy and contractor Harry O'Neil. The council also appropriated four hundred dollars and employed workmen to replace buildings onto their foundations. It hired additional policemen. It brought a suit for $6,400 in damages against the Northern Pacific Railroad for its defective culvert.[42]

Unlike the 1893 fire, no insurance windfall assisted individuals in rebuilding. Relief remained largely private and local by the will of the middle-class majority. Bishop John Shanley, the Reverend J. G. Dudley, and Methodist layman S. S. Lyon appeared on behalf of victims before the Fargo council, which appropriated one thousand dollars and named two aldermen to work with Cass County commissioners in distributing the money. Mayor Johnson appointed a relief committee that appealed for clothing donations. A ladies' committee distributed provisions to the hungry and the Armory sheltered the homeless. After the U.S. Congress appropriated two hundred thousand dollars to aid victims of Mississippi and Red river flooding, twin city residents debated whether or not to accept federal relief. City officials concluded that these insufficient funds could not even be used for repairing damaged buildings. The council therefore rejected outside assistance and cared for its own needy.[43]

The *Fargo Forum* condemned the "queer idea" of federal aid. A letter from "Flood Sufferer" approved the *Forum*'s stand and praised extensive local relief that municipal governments and traditional charitable giving funded. Another letter condemned the rejection of federal assistance. Municipal officials had not asked the destitute, who could not live on "favorable press clippings about plucky Fargo" or on "laudatory letters from Congressmen." It did not take pluck to reject funds needed by someone else, the writer objected. Evidence from Moorhead confirms that the debate divided along

class lines. Seventy-five families totaling 325 people, mostly common laborers, had been flooded out. Workers who had suffered the most desired the
assistance rejected by the middle class. Although the Moorhead council received 7,500 federal rations to feed the needy for thirteen days, they did
not get monies for repairing fifty homes floated off their foundations and
twenty-five additional water-soaked buildings.[44]

Advocates of good municipal government called for electing honest,
competent, and efficient businessmen. Any work such men had done for
the city additionally qualified them to hold office. For example, Fargo aldermen Harry O'Neil and James Kennedy received many of the municipal
contracts for paving, sewers, and other improvements that amounted to
well over $150,000. The *Forum* praised the two men for employing resi-
dents and helping the city. After all, "the money has been spent in Fargo."
Mayor Johnson explained another advantage of using native contractors.
O'Neil had repaired the previous season's paving and curbing without pay
and without request by the city. The *Moorhead Weekly News* in 1893 similarly defended alderman Lars Anderson. An honest, industrious, and sober
wagon manufacturer, Anderson employed ten to forty men throughout
each year. To the *News,* it did not matter that Anderson had done work for
the city. Such men made the best civic leaders precisely because their private interests served the public good that, in turn, benefited them.[45]

A business background did not always deliver the honesty expected,

as shown by a Moorhead Democratic
mayor. Arthur G. Lewis served four
terms during the mid-1890s. Before
he died of cirrhosis of the liver at age
forty-two in 1900, the Ontario-born
Lewis had been one of the most popular
men in Clay County. After arriving in
1879, he worked for Bruns and Finkle,
the SPM&M railroad, and the Jay Cooke
House before becoming a successful fire
insurance agent. He embodied generous

Popular Moorhead mayor Art Lewis, a
"sporting man," protected the saloons and
promoted urban services during the 1890s.
Courtesy Clay County Historical Society.

charity as a member of the Odd Fellows, AOUW, Knights of Pythias, and the Episcopalian church. As city recorder (1887–90) and mayor, he assisted those in need and promoted paving, water, electric lights, and other improvements. Although the Democratic Party generally opposed the strict regulation of the liquor trade that Republicans often favored, mayoral candidate Lewis promised he would strictly enforce the gambling and Sunday closing laws. Even a member of Populist R. M. Probstfield's family thought Lewis would be a great credit if elected. As mayor, however, his lax law enforcement and excessive spending alienated respectable citizens concerned about morality and economy.[46]

When Lewis narrowly won a third term the *Moorhead Weekly News* lamented his victory. The *Forum* chronicled the mayor's moral failings. The newspaper alleged that Johnny Haas and other tinhorns dictated to all officials except Chief of Police P. J. Sullivan. After Sullivan closed saloons, the mayor reopened them if bribed. Just before the election Lewis fired Sullivan and did not replace him. According to an indignant *Forum*: "The two bridge streets . . . are honey-combed with gambling dens and lewd resorts. . . . Never . . . has crime been allowed to conduct its traffic so wide open."[47]

Outraged, respectable citizens mobilized to defeat Lewis. Their efforts paralleled campaigns by other native-born middle-class reformers against corrupt bosses in other American cities. No city convention met and several candidates ran independently without party backing. Newcomer Samuel Frazier, manager of the local flour mill, committed himself to strict law enforcement and received backing from a coalition of labor union members, respectable saloonkeepers, and middle-class reformers. Dubious of Frazier's ability to win, *News* editor George Lamphere endorsed John P. Hansen, a better-known businessman who had more time for the office. Lewis played the dismissal of Chief Sullivan for support among saloon owners and hoped to benefit from the divided reform camp. His opponents complained about paying high taxes for improvements they did not want and maintained that Lewis never would enforce the laws against saloons and gambling. Frazier won the three-way race by the narrow margin of two votes. Reformers controlled the council. Lewis challenged the outcome in court, but failed to prevent Frazier from taking office. The mayor and council appointed a new police chief and five new patrolmen, who more strictly enforced the antigambling and saloon-closing ordinances. A judge rejected Lewis's case contesting the election.[48]

Art Lewis gained a fourth term in 1897. The financial clout of the revenue-producing saloons and extensive patronage powers of the mayor explained his success, according to Normal School historian Henry Johnson. The saloons paid twenty-two thousand dollars annually in license fees. Lewis had been the most important municipal official in tax assessment, employment, and purchasing. Additionally, he had created the income-producing Municipal Electric Light and Water Plant. Although backers overlooked his paying municipal bills by illegal warrants and exceeding bonded indebtedness limits, opponents did not. A better-organized opposition thus denied Lewis his fifth term in the next two elections. Opponents gathered at a mass meeting chaired by Solomon Comstock. Addresses by alderman George Perley and Moorhead Normal president Livingston Lord demanded property tax relief and municipal debt reduction. Perley surprisingly nominated a bar owner and wholesale liquor dealer to carry out these proposals. Jacob Kiefer ran a "respectable" place. He deplored illegal saloon practices and municipal corruption. He campaigned for honest city government.[49]

Drawing support from both respectable and liquor interests, Kiefer bested Lewis with a plurality of fifty-nine votes in a three-way contest. He defeated Lewis again the next year. Kiefer promised a businesslike government, but his silence on moral issues worried reformers. They feared that violations of liquor and gambling laws would not cease because saloon interests had supported Kiefer. The mayor pursued a practical course between enforceable and unenforceable laws. He did not permit orgies by either saloons or bordellos. He tolerated orderly after-hours and Sunday business at saloons during the harvest season. He allowed the red-light district to operate under similar restrictions. He vetoed stricter council measures. Although his pragmatic compromise offended many respectable people, Lord and Comstock praised his honesty and efficiency. The *Moorhead Weekly News,* meanwhile, attacked alderman Henry Johnson's overzealous campaign for economy. Johnson proposed reducing the number of streetlights and policemen, as well as not purchasing a fire wagon team. Kiefer did not appreciate Johnson's attacks. Undeterred by criticism, the professor again called for retrenchment at the start of Kiefer's second term on March 30, 1899.[50]

As the 1900 election loomed with another Lewis candidacy, the businessmen's association backed Kiefer on economic grounds. Purity crusaders, unhappy with laxly enforced saloon, gambling, and prostitution laws, drafted a third candidate, Concordia College principal Hans H. Aaker. Despite fears that his candidacy would elect Lewis, Aaker prevailed. Large majorities from the south-side second and fourth wards gave him a plurality of 129 votes. Quarrels with aldermen over executing his moral mandate marred his administration. Potentially divisive issues included the police chief appointment, liquor license fees, and a 9:00 p.m. curfew for children under sixteen. The curfew, signaled by blowing the fire whistle each evening, easily passed the council, which readily set the license fee at five hundred dollars. Mayor and council battled passionately, however, over Aaker appointing and then

removing Chief of Police George F. Fuller for failing to enforce Sunday closing. The feud finally ended when Fuller resigned and the council later accepted Adolph Simonson. The stormy council meetings had attracted many
spectators and prevented Aaker from being a candidate for reelection. Yet
it mortified most residents when "hoodlums" assaulted the mayor "on his
wedding night." Reformers William R. Tillotson and Carroll A. Nye succeeded Aaker; they set high license fees and closed the red-light district.[51]

The new city charter in 1900 also divided Moorhead along lines of class
and morality. Under an 1899 Minnesota law, the council ordered circulation of a petition for drafting a new charter. Once the signatures of at least
10 percent of the voters had been obtained, the council submitted twenty-
five names to the district judge, who appointed a charter commission. After
the commission reported at the end of March, the council ordered a special
election in mid-May. The charter greatly reduced mayoral powers, revers-
ing a governmental trend toward strengthening executives that Moorhead
had shared with other cities. Liquor interests bitterly opposed this change
because strong mayors had protected their interests from purity reformers
on the council. In addition, the charter barred officeholders from making
municipal contracts. The *Moorhead Weekly News* questioned the illegality of
contracts while municipal funds must be deposited in a bank even though
the banker might be an alderman. Despite these criticisms, citizens approved the charter. The wealthy and reformist fourth ward provided the
victory margin.[52]

Fargo municipal politics paralleled that of Moorhead. The civic-minded
called for electing honest businessmen as strong mayors and aldermen,
who delivered good government and services efficiently. Yet Fargo differed
in being dry and even more Republican. From its territorial days, North
Dakota had been a one-party region. During the 1890s, the Republican majority expanded as the Democratic/Independent vote for governor declined
from 52 to 40 percent and its legislators decreased from forty-one to twelve.
Fargo reflected these trends by selecting a conservative and two progressive
Republicans as mayor. Conservative attorney Wilbur F. Ball won terms in
1890 and 1894, running unopposed. He belonged to the "Old Gang"—also
known as Boss Alexander McKenzie's Machine—that usually controlled the
state's Republican convention.[53]

Former superintendent of schools and Republican Emerson H. Smith
campaigned as a reform candidate in 1892 and bested his party's nominee.
Another reformer, implement dealer J. A. Johnson, defeated Ball in 1896.
Johnson overcame Republican Party opponents two more times before narrowly losing a three-way race in 1902. These mayors worked with a more efficiently organized council. It selected a president and vice president as well as

members to standing committees that mirrored the municipal services now provided: finance, fire and water, streets and bridges, sewers, lights, police, building, parks, and board of health, among others. Additionally, the mayor's appointments for chief of police, fire chief, superintendent of waterworks, engineer, and auditor required council approval. Aldermen usually ratified nominees, ensuring that the "mayor's men" held executive office.[54]

The Pennsylvania-born "Colonel" Ball served in the Second Ohio Cavalry during the Civil War. He migrated in 1868 to Alexandria, Minnesota, and relocated to Fargo a decade later. One of the best attorneys in North Dakota, he had been mentioned for the U.S. Senate but did not seek the office. He had no desire to become mayor either. After stepping down in his first term, he consented to run again in 1894 after his unanimous nomination by the Republican city convention. Without an opponent, his campaign drew little interest, although contested races for aldermen took place in four wards and a large number campaigned for municipal appointments. Ball said he would consult "the best interests of the business men as to who should be city assessor and chief of police." Speaking to the newly elected council, Ball pledged himself to "economy and good order." Although he personally opposed prohibition, he rejected a "wide-open policy" on blind pigs, gambling dens, and houses of ill fame. When the council confirmed his nominees, the *Forum* declared: "Ball is a man who understands his business."[55]

Dissatisfied with the failure to prevent blind pigs, gambling dens, and brothels, reformers mobilized in 1892. Emerson Smith received support from five hundred citizens and two Fargo dailies—the *Argus* and the *Republican*. His supporters asserted: "If a city wishes to be successful it must follow . . . business methods." The Republican Party nominated attorney Fred Morrill, a former council member. After the party labeled Smith a middle-class candidate and portrayed Morrill as the worker's friend, Smith countered, claiming: "My supporters are . . . businessmen, property owners and honest laborers." Voters agreed, awarding him 60 percent of the almost 1,200 ballots cast. The *Argus* rejoiced: "The old gang is downed. The honest citizens are on top." As mayor, Smith strove for economy and strict law enforcement, aided by Democrat Melvin Hildreth, whom he appointed as city attorney. Norwegian-born druggist Lars Christianson urged Smith's reelection, calling him "the best mayor Fargo has ever had."[56]

Reform proved temporary. When Smith did not again seek office, Ball won an uncontested second term. His lax law enforcement, however, brought forth another reform candidate. At that time the Republican Party coalesced behind prohibition. The *Forum* urged "electing a Republican mayor with a platform in accord with the party—enforcement of the laws." The newspaper also advised Christians to join the fight for good government. Methodist

S. S. Lyon concurred: "Running blind pigs is unlawful." Even Mayor Ball announced that he supported "enforcement . . . in obedience to the changed sentiment of the community." Ball's statement secured the Republican nomination but did not prevent the independent candidacy of fellow Republican J. A. Johnson, whom reformers nominated by petition. A large turnout of almost 1,800 voters elected Johnson by a plurality of 162 votes. Labor organizations celebrated the victory with a fervent meeting, parade, and serenade at the new mayor's residence.[57]

During the next decade, citizens reelected Johnson three times before he died in office. The Swedish-born mayor, who immigrated to Minnesota as a child, had led a varied life. After serving in both the Confederate and Union armies during the Civil War, he farmed, engaged in lumbering, and studied law; citizens elected him town clerk of Marine Mills, Minnesota, as well as three-term sheriff of Washington County. He moved to Fargo in 1879 as an agent for the Seymour, Sabin & Company machinery house. His second mayoral term began harmoniously with the council supporting his appointments and economizing efforts. It also formed a retrenchment committee, which presented recommendations the following year. Johnson made the police station more accessible by keeping it open twenty-four hours each day and installing a telephone. He made himself more available by holding daily office hours at the council chambers. He enforced all city ordinances,

Fargo mayor J. A. Johnson brought great energy to the office, inspiring this cartoon. From *Hon. J. A. Johnson: A Partial Copy of His Letters, Travels and Addresses.*

UNDOUBTEDLY A COMING MAN.

The new Northern Pacific depot, built in 1898, made Fargo appear more metropolitan to arriving salesmen and other visitors. Courtesy Institute for Regional Studies, North Dakota State University, Fargo (2006.55.18).

including entertainer licenses, sprinkling permits, sidewalk cleaning, and Sunday closing of barbershops, as well as laws against boxing, blind pigs, and gambling. The *Forum* praised Johnson's unorthodox prohibition methods in battling the jag wagons that ferried thirsty and inebriated Dakotans to and from Moorhead saloons. He ordered the police to arrest jag wagon drivers for stopping in Fargo. In addition, he secured an ordinance that licensed drivers and prohibited their soliciting for the liquor trade.[58]

Mayor Johnson impressively promoted Fargo. He arranged a street fair in early October and secured excursion rates from the railroads. He attended a meeting of North Dakota mayors, which supported legislation for decade-long payment of street paving. After the legislature enacted the law, he recommended paving improvement districts to the council. He attended the National League of Municipalities meeting in Columbus, Ohio, where he reported on North Dakota leadership in securing uniform municipal legislation. Johnson's participation in this organization brought him into discussions about more effective government administration informed by corporations, science, statistics, and cost accounting. Upon his return, Johnson called an organizational meeting of the North Dakota Municipal League. After several years of agitating for a new Northern Pacific depot, Johnson called for a Union Station that would accommodate the Great Northern and Milwaukee railroads as well. Although this effort failed, Johnson negotiated paving, underpass, and station deals with the Northern Pacific. He secured a new, commodious, steam-heated brick structure valued at thirty-five thousand dollars. The *Forum* called it "the pride of Fargo," giving salesmen and other travelers "a higher estimation of the city."[59]

In spite of his sterling record and being recommended by Senator Henry C. Hansborough for appointment as U.S. consul to Sweden, the Republican Party did not nominate him in 1898. By just a two-vote margin, the convention named O. G. Barnes. Although Johnson said he would not run, he accepted a popular draft. His efforts at curbing corporate power, Johnson alleged, had provoked party opposition. He had compelled railroads to pay municipal taxes and erect gates at crossings. Barnes worked as general counsel for Fargo Gas and Electric, chartered by the municipality for another seven years despite its relatively high rates.[60]

Throughout the campaign, Republican city committee secretary Arthur B. Lee subjected Johnson to withering criticism. He dishonestly broke his word to the party by running as an Independent. He had not paid personal and real-estate taxes since 1893. He had not originated the retroactive railroad tax or secured votes for it. Indeed, his lobbying expenses had exceeded the city revenues actually collected. Debt and taxes had risen because he had signed unconstitutional warrants totaling fifty thousand dollars. His incompetent police management produced the most burglaries in local history. Although the *Forum* conceded that Johnson had expended more time and attention than any previous mayor, Republicans should vote for Barnes, a first-class businessman and the party nominee. Mayor Johnson's friends countered opposition claims. They admitted that indebtedness had increased, but the council shared this responsibility. Additionally, about twenty-five thousand dollars had been expended unavoidably for interest and flood expenses. Special assessments totaling forty-five thousand dollars had prevented larger debts. The mayor's popularity enabled him to prevail, winning 61 percent of the 1,511 votes cast.[61]

Mayor Johnson's message to the council in 1898 called for working harmoniously to better the city. He requested lowering the tax levy. He proposed testing the lights provided by Fargo Light and Power. If the company did not supply the contracted amount of electricity, he wanted a discount. He backed the engineer's recommendation for detailed sewer maps and records. The *Forum* praised his businesslike address and his detailed attention to municipal affairs. The council unanimously confirmed his appointees. Mayor Johnson still energetically promoted the city. He invited the Danish-Norwegian Press Association, the Interstate Grain Growers Convention, and the National Flax, Hemp and Ramie Association Convention. All accepted. The National Flax meeting publicized Fargo's new Flax Fiber and Linseed Oil Mill that processed a crop, ranking second in national production and second to wheat in the state. An appreciative council appropriated three hundred dollars for this work and considered a $1,200 salary, but the strained budget made it impossible despite endorsement by the *Forum*.[62]

Mayor Johnson captured his fourth term in 1900, winning almost 60 percent of 1,892 votes cast in a contest with Republican businessman J. A. Chesley. Running on a record of unparalleled public and private growth during the previous four years, he carried each of the six wards. The tax levy decreased 25 percent despite constructing several miles of pavement, curbs, water mains, and brick sewers. These improvements provided employment for many workers. City warrants now sold at par and not at a discount. Only citizens might demand special assessments. Because business had never been better, supporters rejected the opposition's claim to be the businessmen's campaign. When the *Argus* implied that saloons and gamblers had bribed Johnson, he threatened a libel suit. He rejected opposition by the *Fargo Morning Call* as neither manly nor honorable, because he lacked the three hundred dollars to purchase its support. His record finally won an endorsement from the *Forum*: "Fargo has never . . . had a mayor who devoted so much of his time and energy to the furtherance of the city's interests." It is not surprising that he won handily or that a thousand people called at his home to celebrate.[63]

FROM RUDIMENTARY TO PROFESSIONAL URBAN SERVICES

The Moorhead and Fargo police epitomized the development of professional services from rudimentary ones. The dual city constabulary evolved from a city marshal into a uniformed chief and patrolmen by the early 1880s. The elementary state of services is evidenced by the wide-ranging duties assigned to them. They tended the bridge, collected poll taxes, enforced health ordinances, corralled stray animals, inspected stovepipes, prosecuted illegal sewer connections, and planted trees on Arbor Day. They could not easily perform so many tasks. A patrolman's letter "To the Disgruntled" in the *Fargo Daily Republican* articulated his frustration. Criticized by citizens for not being on his assigned beat, he pointed out that conflicting orders from the chief, aldermen, and health officers often called patrolmen elsewhere. As noted by Eric Monkkonen, municipal officials naturally assigned varied tasks to the uniformed and centrally organized police department. Easily identified policemen worked around the clock, making them available for many jobs. The police thus imparted a practical model of service government. They made criminal prosecution a publicly funded service and an exemplar for streets, public health, and other agencies. Their many duties naturally evolved into specialized departments in the twin cities and elsewhere as urban populations grew and needs became more complex.[64]

Wet spring weather turned the clay-based soil of the dual city into a mud capable of miring people, horses, and wagons. This ensured that the first public tasks included wooden sidewalks, crossings, graded streets, and ditches. Councils determined sidewalk location—often in response to petitions by businessmen or lot owners—and specified the dimensions and types of materials used. Standard widths were generally about six feet on most streets, except for the ten feet ordered for Broadway, Northern Pacific Avenue, and other busy Fargo streets. As both cities grew, the councils struggled to keep pace. They assessed property holders to fund expansion and cajoled those who ignored ordinances. They received many complaints about uncut weeds, unfinished sections, and poorly built walks.[65]

The 1893 fire enabled the Fargo council to move forward on "the speedy reconstruction of sidewalks" inside the fire district with noncombustible materials. Although the Fargo Tile Works received the first contract in November, most sidewalks remained wood. Two years later, alderman William Sweet proposed building cement walks throughout the town. He said the fire ordinance should be enforced citywide, that eastern cities had already adopted concrete, and poorly repaired walks left the municipality liable for injury lawsuits. Angry homeowners balked at the expense and the council rejected Sweet's proposal. The *Forum* condemned this action as "pennywise and pound foolish." Eventually aldermen in both cities agreed and exchanged plank for cement at the start of the twentieth century.[66]

Councils in the twin cities early imposed poll taxes for the grading and ditching of principal streets. Moorhead required two days' work or three dollars from each property owner. When collections proved difficult, the chief of police assumed the task. Fargo levied one day's labor or its cash equivalent on every able-bodied male between twenty-one and sixty years. As in Moorhead, tramps labored in lieu of paying fines for vagrancy. Dirt streets provoked constant complaint. Rain and heavy traffic immediately undid the grading and often rendered some streets impassable. Hence the first residents soon dreamed of pavement.[67]

Paving with small granite blocks began in eastern cities at about the time of the Civil War. By the mid-1870s, Midwestern towns surfaced with brick or wood. Shortly thereafter dual city authorities investigated the issue. After the Fargo city engineer presented two methods for consideration— the "Phillips round cedar block" or the "Stowe ordinary pine block"—the council inconclusively discussed paving Broadway. A two-year public debate followed about the relative merits of wooden blocks, plank, and gravel.

Although land agent C. A. Morton called plank "a swindle that would not last," most businessmen favored that method. When it received only one high bid for surfacing Broadway and Front Street with planks, the council—already overextended with sewers and bridges—dumped the project. Citizens endured ruts and mud for the duration of the decade. Not until May 1895 did the council approve cedar block paving for portions of Front, Broadway, and Northern Pacific. Lot owners who benefited paid the contracts, totaling just over fifty-three thousand dollars. The *Forum* and council celebrated the project, saying, "it will tend to benefit and advertise the city." Paved streets did not end complaints about dirt. After a mechanical sweeper had been purchased, some called it "a menace to health" because it filled "the air . . . with dense clouds of vile dust."[68]

During the next season, completed sections of six streets allowed the *Forum* to claim nearly five miles of pavement for "the biggest little city in the West." A court injunction halted levy collections for a time, but the North Dakota supreme court ruled them constitutional in June 1898. Later that summer contractors finished downtown paving according to the city engineer's specifications. Unfortunately, the first-laid blocks already showed signs of decay. This eventually compelled resurfacing Broadway and other streets with three-and-one-half-inch creosoted blocks laid on a six-inch concrete foundation. The Fargo experience paralleled that of other American cities. Officials paved many miles, but achieved mixed success with a variety of imperfect paving surfaces. Still, cedar block paving on Broadway and other streets endured until the 1930s when New Deal Public Works Administration grants funded their replacement.[69]

Moorhead mayor Art Lewis also pushed paved streets. At a special meeting in April 1894, a Minneapolis firm recommended cedar blocks as the only suitable material for Red River Valley soil. Armed with a petition from Front Street merchants, the council advertised for bids and awarded a contract despite some opposition. It requested that all materials be shipped on the Northern Pacific, which granted a 50 percent rebate. The *Moorhead Daily News* reported that paving will "give Front Street a metropolitan appearance, if it don't break her." Lot owners paid $7,000 of the $12,000 cost. Businessmen or residents on some other streets presented additional petitions. When large assessments on James Street and Ridge Avenue lots threatened to cripple owners, the council decided not to proceed. It resumed paving in the early twentieth century. By 1918 Moorhead had between three and four miles surfaced either with creosote wooden blocks or reinforced concrete. Not until 1937 did concrete replace the wooden blocks on Front Street (present-day Center Avenue).[70]

Like other municipalities, the dual city planted trees along streets for

Moorhead paved its principal business street with cedar blocks in 1894. Courtesy Clay County Historical Society.

utility and beauty. The *Fargo Express* in 1874 suggested a "tree brigade" to protect properties and people from the prevailing northwest winds. A few years later, the Red River Forestry Association headed by Andrew McHench informed the public about planting. Booster Alanson W. Edwards, who called for beautifying the city with elms, estimated that citizens planted five thousand during May 1883. With the designation of Arbor Day four years later, officials urged residents to "spend the day planting . . . and adorning public and private grounds." Newcomers hardly noticed these trees. When Judge Charles Pollock remarked, "They are really beginning to show a little shade," Jennie Burns Angell considered him "one of Fargo's brightest optimists." What citizens had undertaken in the early years became the responsibility of city councils. For example, Moorhead aldermen ordered trees planted along streets surrounding the new Normal School and provided another thousand for other streets a few years later.[71]

Like town dwellers elsewhere, Fargo and Moorhead residents confronted the problems of waste and its removal. During the 1840s, American cities had based sanitation on the theory of miasmas, which held that filth and foul smells caused epidemics. Officials focused on securing a sanitary water supply and, to a lesser extent, began laying sewers. They did not perceive garbage removal as a municipal problem. Cesspools, privy vaults, and scavengers sufficiently disposed of human and household waste for communities that did not grow rapidly. Knowledge of the germ theory of disease and mushrooming urban populations in the late nineteenth century, however, impelled the creation of modern water and sewer systems. More responsive city governments with larger fiscal resources better protected public health. Sanitary engineers and other scientific professionals, aided by bacteriological laboratories, joined with progressive reformers to create a more healthful and aesthetic urban environment.[72]

Waste from horses, cows, and other livestock, whether stabled or wandering about freely, posed serious sanitation problems for the twin cities. In addition, residents used streets and yards as dumping grounds. The *Red River Star* railed against the "disgraceful state of our streets" and the failure of officials to keep the town clean. Booster-minded Fargo editors waged similar campaigns, fearing that an unattractive city and epidemics repelled newcomers. As the *Daily Republican* warned: "Filthy streets and alleys are the gateways to disease, pestilence and death." Civic leaders, who accepted the miasmatic theory that "noxious, poisonous vapors" carried

Horse dung litters Front Street in the mid-1890s, indicating one problem of waste removal confronting Moorhead. Courtesy Clay County Historical Society.

"the seeds of disease," ordered property owners to remove from the city "all manure heaps, slops, decaying matter and other collections of filth." Many ignored these injunctions. The municipalities responded by enacting additional health ordinances. For example, the council licensed the Fargo Rendering Company to remove dead animals, garbage, and putrid matter. It created the Fargo City Scavenger in 1883 to clean streets, backyards, slaughterhouses, stockyards, warehouses, and stables. At night he emptied privy vaults into a tank, removing the contents for burial outside the city. Problems nevertheless remained. At the end of the decade, the *Moorhead Weekly News* reported that shanties, stables, and barnyards lined the Red River west bank. This manure and garbage contaminated the river water that people drank.[73]

The twin cities took steps to improve sanitation by creating boards of health, building sewers, and seeking clean water. The American Public Health Association, formed in 1873, encouraged over time more public campaigns against disease. By 1902, boards in Minnesota and other states supervised municipal water and sewer systems. Moorhead town supervisors served as its first health officers, but Fargo did not create a board until later. As mandated by Minnesota law, Moorhead formed an elected body in 1885 that medical doctor John Kurtz chaired. Even without money for adequate enforcement, dual city officials called on residents to clean their property thoroughly each spring. For example, the Fargo board recommended disinfectant for cesspools, drains, ditches, and sewers. It specified that garbage should be buried in back corners of yards and wastewater emptied in different areas. It battled epidemic diseases by quarantining smallpox, diphtheria, and scarlet fever cases. It secured hospitals for the infected. It ordered smallpox vaccinations in 1881 for those who desired them. It even funded shots for the indigent.[74]

City dwellers did not perceive garbage as a municipal problem before the 1880s, when the sheer accumulation of horse droppings, ashes, rubbish, and other wastes overwhelmed them. Not until 1895 did New York City develop the first comprehensive municipal refuse management system. Smaller cities with less waste volume retained private collection longer than larger ones. By the twentieth century, women's organizations and other civic groups publicized sanitary reform by accentuating morality, beauty, and health. Upon a board of health recommendation, Fargo secured a dump ground in 1886. It required scavengers to cover their unloaded refuse with dirt each morning. Moorhead for many years simply deposited its garbage on unoccupied ground outside the municipality. Not until 1896 did Mayor Samuel Frazier call for a designated area. The city purchased land from the county five years later. It instituted user fees for citywide garbage collection and removal in 1913.[75]

Epidemic diseases like diphtheria or typhoid fever were an ever-present worry. After an upstream North Dakota city installed sewers, dual city citizens—alarmed at the prospect of drinking polluted river water—called for a municipal filtration plant. Parents demanded that public schools serve their children artesian well water. The Fargo board of health minimized the danger, but warned residents to boil all water and milk before using. When a pupil died of diphtheria in 1897, Fargo officials closed the school, fumigated the building, quarantined the family, and disinfected their home. Confronted with several diphtheria cases in 1898 and 1900, the Moorhead health officer responded similarly. He quarantined infected families, delayed opening public schools, and instructed parents to place children with sore throats under a doctor's care. As in earlier epidemics, the boards located houses for the infected and provided for those too poor to pay doctors. Immunization now controlled smallpox, an earlier scourge.[76]

Community complaints and knowledge of the germ theory of disease eventually made public health more professional. For example, the Moorhead council licensed milk dealers, inspected dairies, and prohibited selling impure milk and dairy products by 1908. It licensed vendors of artesian drinking water and the board of health banned using Red River ice for anything but refrigeration. The Fargo council similarly passed milk and meat ordinances, and appointed a municipal milk and meat inspector at this time.[77]

Medical advances in bacteriology and improved public health standards reduced death rates in New York and Chicago during the 1890s. Yet American officials lagged behind Europeans in addressing polluted water and food supplies. Hence infant mortality remained high for Fargo, Moorhead, and other American cities in the late nineteenth century. According to Clay County Historical Society archivist Mark Peihl, children less than twelve years of age constituted half the 1,118 deaths recorded in Moorhead between 1872 and 1899. The city's infant morality rate of 175 per 1,000 exceeded that of third-world countries today. The 1890 U.S. rate of almost 206 dropped to just over 165 by 1900. The largest Minnesota cities in that year had even lower numbers: 97 (St. Paul), 102 (Minneapolis), and 111 (Duluth). Most Moorhead children died of infectious diseases such as tuberculosis, typhoid fever, and diphtheria transmitted by tainted food, milk, and water. For example, typhoid killed fifteen in 1882; eleven died from diphtheria in 1882 and 1892.[78]

Better sewer and water systems provided superior sanitation and fewer deaths. American cities excelled in adopting technology and built the most extensive sewer systems in the world. Yet lines did not extend to every neighborhood, and faith in dilution of sewage in streams did not protect drinking water supplies. Commitment to seeking private wealth held back such public health measures, as historian Sam Bass Warner has observed.

The twin and other American cities laid storm sewers first. The Moorhead council in August 1878 put down a line along Front Street from Fifth Street to the Red River. Lot owners paid the costs. The city had installed ten miles of combined storm and sanitary line by 1906, when it constructed a great trunk sewer. It thought this system adequate for the next half century. Fargo also laid storm sewers before it began work on a sanitary system in early 1881. Voters approved a fifty thousand-dollar bond issue in September, but precarious municipal finances delayed sale by a New York bank until the following March. City engineer Randall Hunt planned the system, which the *Daily Republican* called "as fine . . . as any city in the country." Vented and equipped with flush tanks, it quickly removed waste and all subsoil or surface water to the river.[79]

The Fargo engineer designed a more modern system with thirty-six-inch brick trunks fed laterally by twelve-inch pipes a few years later. The city paid costs with interest-bearing bonds or by special levies on lot holders who benefited. Those specially assessed often complained, but once Fargo had reached the legally imposed limits on bonded indebtedness no further expansion took place, except by petition from the majority in a neighborhood who desired sewers.[80]

The twin cities drew water from the Red River or relied on individual wells. By 1878, a centrifugal pump located at the Moorhead flour mill forced river water into the Front Street main that extended east to Ninth Street. One year later, Harry O'Neil pumped from the west riverbank into tank wagons that met family cooking and drinking needs for a monthly fee. Meanwhile, a representative of the New York–based Holly Manufacturing firm established a joint-stock company that built a waterworks. Residents raised thirty-five thousand dollars in addition to capital invested by the Holly family and other easterners. The city retained an option to purchase after ten years at a valuation fixed by appraisers. The plant supplied water at the end of 1880. Daily use constituted only 20 percent of the 1 million-gallon capacity sufficient for supplying twenty thousand people. Six miles of pipe had been laid by the next autumn, connecting about two thousand users residing in 150 homes and hotels. Drinking fountains, an ornamental Island Park fountain, and forty-five fire hydrants had been placed. Such growth seemingly justified civic pride in the venture. Boosters used the plant as a tool for promoting economic growth.[81]

Water supplied inexpensively and expediently by private contract, however, did not solve all problems. The council discovered defective hydrants. Customers grumbled about bad taste and odor. The company moaned about losing money since its start, despite a 20 percent rate increase. It blamed wastefulness, which it proposed to eliminate by adopting water meters without raising fees. Alarmed by usurpation of its authority, the council launched an investigation and examined the cost of fire protection in other cities. Unable to satisfy these many demands and remain profitable, the company offered to sell. The city bought in 1890 after an appraisal and an eighty thousand-dollar bond issue.[82]

Moorhead voters in September 1880 approved installation of the Holly water system by the Fargo Water and Steam Company. High costs evidently changed these plans. One year later, the council approved a fifteen thousand-dollar bond issue for a city waterworks and accepted the offer of Mayor Henry Bruns to continue pumping from his flour mill. The works soon extended its mains southward to Bishop Whipple School and built a large reservoir underneath the mill for settling and filtering water. The chief of police collected rates quarterly, the city recorder kept accounts, and the treasurer issued receipts. Persistent public unhappiness about inadequate purity and pressure, however, prompted an ill-fated drilling of an artesian well. This unfortunate episode epitomized the defects of booster government: undue optimism combined with insufficient knowledge produced excessive expenditures for intangible results. The unfortunate drillers had ground through nine hundred feet of rock in ten months when they finally gave up in November 1888. The city paid 50 percent of the firm's bills and received free use of its equipment until May 1, 1889. When no results had been achieved at that time, businessman Samuel Partridge sent drilling samples to the Minnesota State Geologist. He reported that the sand rock had been fabricated, probably by the drillers, and no water would be found. The council did not accept the bitter truth. It continued work for several months and expended twelve thousand dollars before finally giving up.[83]

Costly waterworks and sewer systems generated intense debates about the relative merits of private versus municipal ownership. All U.S. cities had municipal sewers by 1899, but private waterworks still constituted 46 percent of those serving cities. The twin cities eventually embraced municipal ownership, as did 73 percent of Midwestern cities. After the Fargo Municipal Water Works formed, it appointed a superintendent who extended the system. Anxious citizens, fearful of disease, questioned water quality. A public debate ensued. Banker S. S. Lyon called for analysis, saying: "If the river water is dangerous to life or health, then the supply must be purified. It is not a question of cost." After test results became known, contractor James Kennedy agreed about "the urgent necessity of a filtering plant" but rejected "raising the assessed valuation . . . to secure the money." Although municipal debt delayed a filtration system until 1906, the works proved profitable and modernized in other ways. It supplied twelve miles of pipe and more than a hundred fire hydrants by 1897. It later purchased two

This photograph from the 1910s shows the Fargo Municipal Water Works, created by the city in 1890 after a private company provided unsatisfactory service. Courtesy Institute for Regional Studies, North Dakota State University, Fargo (2070.252.16).

high-capacity pumps and laid fourteen-inch mains on Broadway and First Avenue, enhancing fire protection.[84]

An 1892 report to the council detailed Moorhead water difficulties. First, the Fargo sewer that emptied into the river near the pumping station tainted the supply. Second, the private station cost more than a municipal plant. Third, fire endangered pumps located in the wood-frame mill. Fourth, the system did not support itself. An 1895 public meeting approved constructing a municipal water plant valued at almost forty-eight thousand dollars. When completed it had two pumps with a daily capacity of 1 million gallons. It greatly improved quality. By establishing meters, quarterly fees, business rates, and disconnection procedures, the municipal plant collected rates more efficiently. Yet new worries about quality and supply developed in 1900 when the Red River reached its lowest level in many years. Moorhead finally developed an efficient and safe system by 1915. Three wells met ordinary needs; the river might be drawn upon during emergencies. A three hundred thousand-gallon storage tank, standing 126 feet above ground, provided sufficient gravity pressure for home use and fire protection.[85]

Modern water plants not only protected public health, they increased firefighting capacity. Flames frequently endangered the dual city from the beginning. For example, Moorhead residents battled for more than two hours in October 1872, narrowly escaping a prairie conflagration that nearly swept into town from the south. Then, one windy January day three roof fires threatened the entire community. Fargo faced similar perils when several buildings or an entire block burned. Moorhead created a fire committee that inspected chimneys and stovepipes. A volunteer company then provided more protection, as it did in all American cities before 1850 and still does in all small towns today. Thirty-seven men soon organized and established a subscription list for purchasing a hand-drawn reel, hose, and hook and ladder wagon. At the height of the boom in 1882, thirty men founded the more permanent Eagle Hose Company. It provided both better security and social life as the men appeared in their blue and red–trimmed uniforms at annual balls. The Key City Hook and Ladder Company organized later that year. The companies put a telephone in the station, built a bell tower, and set up dual city fire signals.[86]

After Fargo incorporated in April 1875, the council appointed fire wardens. The Pioneer Fire Committee organized, canvassed for subscriptions, and purchased a hook and ladder wagon in 1877. Rapid growth induced by the Dakota Boom and a bad fire in January 1880 prompted creation of several volunteer companies in the next few years: Hook and Ladder No. 1 Hard, Continental Hose Company, Hose Company No. 2, Yerxa Hose Company No. 3, and Rescue Hook and Ladder No. 1. In addition, the fire patrol formed to protect property from water damage and thieves. Volunteers represented many occupations and nationalities. After all, middle-class property holders—whether Old or New American—had tangible interests to protect and every member enjoyed enhanced status in the community. The council took additional steps to improve fire protection: fire escapes for two-story buildings (1882), an alarm system (1884), a bell tower (1885), fire horses (1888), and a horse-drawn hose wagon (1889).[87]

Community-based fire protection pressed property owners into deciding between the costs of safety and potential losses. An 1884 motion to repeal the fire ordinance illuminates this process. Alderman Gordon Keeney seemingly spoke for those constituents who wanted to build but could not afford brick. Prolonged discussion revealed that insurance companies would raise rates dramatically without the ordinance. Perhaps that is the point that Keeney wanted to make. He withdrew his motion and the law remained to be strengthened as dictated by subsequent fire losses and insurance agents. The community depended on the volunteers for protection and the companies needed community support. "Fire laddies" held annual balls and often paraded in uniform to solicit funds. Booster-minded editors usually reported the number of tickets sold and the number attending. They generously praised the men: "Here were represented . . . an assemblage of noble-hearted men who ever stand ready to save property of the dual city." Editors expected property holders to purchase tickets whether they attended or not. They urged the council to "encourage the boys" and assist them more generously. Such tribute represented payment from the

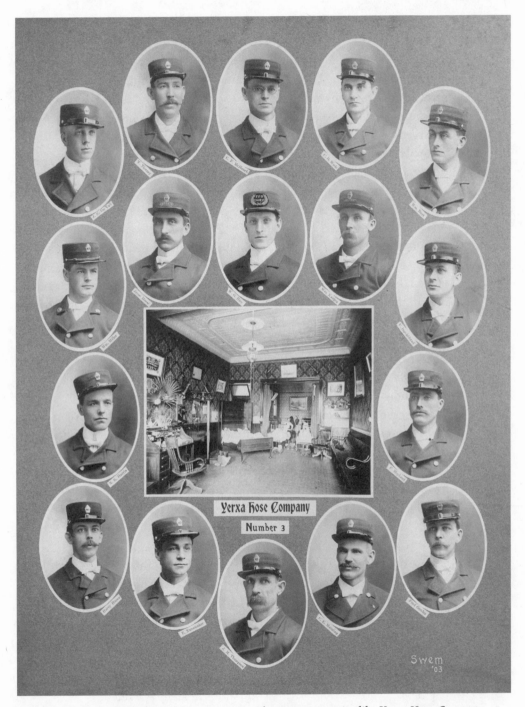

Until creation of a professional force in 1903, volunteer companies like Yerxa Hose Company Number 3 protected Fargo from fire. Courtesy Institute for Regional Studies, North Dakota State University, Fargo (2070.501.1).

community. Volunteers received tangible rewards with firehouses, equipment, and uniforms.[88]

The 1893 fire demonstrated the need for better protection. The Fargo and Moorhead councils continued earlier efforts to improve equipment and professionalize their volunteers by banning liquor and cards from fire halls. The municipal water plants purchased more efficient pumps and extended enlarged water mains to ensure adequate pressure for battling blazes. The councils prohibited wooden buildings and combustible materials within newly established fire limits. They cooperated with state inspectors in maintaining fire escapes on hotels and schools.[89]

Municipal budgets and volunteer companies limited professionalism, however. Budget crises of the 1890s prevented councils from paying firemen. Although Fargo created a professional department in 1903, Moorhead still relied on twenty-four volunteers in 1918. Paid chiefs secured their appointments through a political process. For example, each of the Fargo companies in turn nominated one of their members, whom the mayor appointed for one year if confirmed by the council. In addition, volunteers socialized as much as they fought fires. A company offered them a masculine culture freed from middle-class constraints and domesticity. It gave them "an opportunity to race, parade, wear a uniform, and match strength with other like-minded men, regardless of occupation," as historian Amy Greenberg has observed. For example, they joined their brethren from North Dakota and Minnesota towns at annual three-day tournaments at which companies tested their skills in competitive events. Horse races, concerts, balls, banquets, and speeches entertained the men. Twin city companies at times hosted each other in socials at which they sang songs, delivered speeches, and consumed refreshments. Companies celebrated anniversaries. Several hundred attended the annual Continental Masquerade Ball, a major social event to which the mayor and aldermen received special invitations.[90]

The twin cites early sought the amenity of well-lighted streets. Baltimore pioneered illumination in 1816, using gas made from coal. Standard Oil began piping and selling natural gas by the 1870s. Electricity soon offered an alternative. Urban America embraced this technology earlier than Europe. Private firms prevailed at the end of the century. Municipalities owned less than 2 percent of 945 gasworks and just over 15 percent of 3,032 electric light plants.[91] Fargo and Moorhead chose electric lights, but struggled in paying for systems that private companies initially provided.

Police tended kerosene streetlamps that gave Moorhead and Fargo "a city appearance" during the late 1870s. Yet electricity had greater appeal for metropolitan dreamers. In 1881 the council franchised the Fargo Electric Light and Power Company, which proposed one or more 150-feet-high

The base of an electric light tower stands in the foreground of this 1889 Fire Tournament Parade on Broadway in Fargo. Courtesy Institute for Regional Studies, North Dakota State University, Fargo (2070.150.8).

towers, topped by lights totaling twenty thousand candlepower. The firm put its power station near the Manitoba depot and its tower on the corner of Front and Broadway. Despite mechanical problems, Fargo's first experiment in electric lighting succeeded on April 12, 1882. As the *Republican* reported: "None expected to see the streets and alleys, and buildings all flooded . . . with so subdued . . . radiance." Subsequent breakdowns caused complaints, but whenever the system worked boosters praised "the ambitious young metropolis of the Red River Valley." After a storm destroyed the structure in August 1885, aldermen approved replacing it with three towers: one located near the Cass County courthouse, another near the SPM&M depot, and a third rebuilt at its former Broadway and Front Street site.[92]

Meanwhile, the newly organized Fargo Gas and Electric Company consolidated existing firms, obtaining their franchises for the towers, home lighting, and eighteen streetlights. As prohibition ended annual liquor revenues, the city struggled to pay its bills, while some citizens protested the high costs for all-night lighting. Then an 1890 tornado damaged the towers, which the council razed and sold for scrap. Despite the additional expenses and the complaints, aldermen approved a five-year contract with the company for a system of suspended arc lights. In 1895 the council renewed the pact for ten years, provided that the firm furnished twenty-five

incandescent lights at the city hall and the water plant. The new arrangement supplied lighting to the northern and southern outskirts. A citizen
called it "an excellent contract" because "the additional streetlights are very
much needed." When the Hughes Electric Company offered the city substantial savings in 1898, the council sought to cancel its agreement. Fargo
Gas and Electric secured an injunction, but the state supreme court voided
the deal in 1901. After the two firms merged one year later, Union Light,
Heat and Power assumed the former franchises upon council approval.[93]

At the height of its boom-inspired metropolitan dreams, Moorhead became perhaps the first Minnesota municipality outside Minneapolis to
have arc streetlights. In late 1882, it placed eleven lamps at the principal
Front, Main, and James Street crossings. The recently established Red River
Manufacturing Company generated the electricity. The *Moorhead Weekly
News* praised the brilliant lights enjoyed by all. Its pleasure did not last. At the
end of boom times in March 1884, the council canceled street lighting until
further notice. In the ensuing debate many agreed that lights needlessly burdened taxpayers. Others maintained that illumination favorably impressed
strangers, advertised the city, and benefited residents. The *Weekly News* suggested retaining only the Front Street lights, except on moonlit nights. The
budget-minded won and Moorhead remained unlighted until the end of 1885.
It then reached an agreement with the local wagon maker for seven lamps,
lit for three months at the nightly rate of fifty cents per light. Its straitened
finances kept the city mostly in the dark until the next decade.[94]

After the Moorhead council accepted a bid by Fargo Gas and Light for five
streetlights in 1891, the need for economy caused talk of removal. Residents
objected that the "dark would be a cover for hoboes, thieves and drunks." Safety
concerns carried the day. Downtown streets remained lighted. Following years
of turmoil with private companies, citizens welcomed municipal power in
1895. They celebrated with a marching band, fireworks, and firing the town
cannon. They also lit twenty-five arc and five hundred incandescent lights.
Alderman Jacob Kiefer urged appointing a superintendent of the Electric
Light and Water Works who would run the plants on business principles without political interference. As had been the case for several years, concern for
economy restricted use with a moonlight system of public lighting.[95]

Alderman Henry Johnson, who chaired the Electric Light and Water
Works Committee, strongly criticized the earlier mismanagement of the
plant by Mayor Art Lewis. Johnson's committee curtailed expenses by cutting salaries and increased revenues by collecting delinquent bills. Johnson's
report to the council of these achievements received applause and his ap-
plication of business principles achieved results. Adopting meters equita-
bly solved the old problem of assessing and collecting rates. The plant had

surplus earnings of ten thousand dollars by 1899. Yet purchase of a new engine, condenser, and dynamo dictated continued economy.[96]

An 1898 letter written by one of R. M. Probstfield's daughters describes the effect of electric light on the twin cities. As she returned from an NDAC concert, the large number of people, bicycles, carriages, and hacks on the streets at 11:00 p.m. surprised her. She also marveled how John Haas's place "was simply superb lit up with thousands of colored lights." However pretty, the brightly lighted tavern and restaurant caused controversy. Alderman Lew Huntoon charged that bar owners paid only midnight rates but used electricity all night. Haas's contract with the city called for lighting 250 sixteen-candle lamps at the rate of one hundred dollars per month. Apparently, he did not pay even these reduced rates and the council did not renew his contract. Such abuses enabled adoption of meters that same year.[97]

The first Fargo street railway appeared in 1882, called into existence by metropolitan dreams stimulated by the Dakota Boom. Horse-drawn cars followed tracks that ran south on Broadway from the Manitoba railroad to Front Street and then west and south to the prairie. The company ceased operation after its car barn burned. The council tabled a petition for track removal, probably hoping for more franchise applications. The rails disappeared into street gumbo in the meantime. A Moorhead company, which had hoped for Fargo connections, also expired with the boom's collapse and the shrinking urban population. Aldermen chartered five more companies before service finally returned in 1904.[98]

The Fargo and Moorhead Street Railway Company headed by future North Dakota governor L. B. Hanna assumed control of the franchise held by a Pennsylvania firm. At this time throughout the United States, many municipalities chartered streetcar firms. After a decade-long national boom, thirty thousand miles of urban railway had been 98 percent electrified by the end of 1903. The system provided rapid transit for millions daily, whatever profits it made for traction entrepreneurs and corrupt politicos. As urban historian Kenneth Jackson has noted, "The electric streetcar was a source of pride; the very symbol of a city." The completed Fargo line looped southward to Ninth Avenue South and northward to the NDAC with a branch to Oak Grove Park before it crossed the North Bridge into Moorhead. Electricity from a Union Light, Heat and Power Company generator powered the cars. A Pennsylvania firm purchased the generator in 1910, acquired the railway in 1911, and changed its name to Northern States Power in 1916. The popular dark green—later yellow—streetcars remained a familiar sight until 1937 when the firm suspended service at the expiration of its franchise. Buses replaced the trolley cars. The streetcar bridge became scrap metal during World War II.[99]

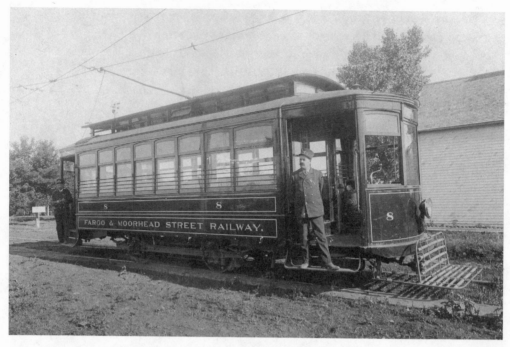

The arrival of the electric streetcar in 1904 manifested the metropolitan dreams of Fargo and Moorhead. Courtesy Institute for Regional Studies, North Dakota State University, Fargo (Folio 76.1.2).

Moorhead joined the system in November 1904 after the council had haggled for several months over the route, a streetcar-only bridge, and a ten thousand-dollar bond for removing track if the company failed. The line ran from the North Bridge to Fourth Street, down Front Street to Sixth and three other streets to the Normal School. Service later expanded northward to the Clay County courthouse on Eighth Avenue North and eastward to Dilworth for the benefit of Northern Pacific employees. The company afforded satisfactory service for three decades. It sparked a real-estate boom north of Concordia College and west of the Normal School.[100]

The progress achieved by streetcars and other services at the end of the century had been glimpsed by the *Fargo Sunday Argus* in 1883 when it announced: "The streets are already a network of the iron and steel pipes and wires which tell of the accessories of civilization." When booster editor Alanson W. Edwards wrote these words, he had in mind the water mains, gas lines, electric light tower, and telephone wires on every street. Among the many telephone and telegraph companies franchised by the dual city at this time and subsequently, the one awarded to the Tri-State Telephone and Telegraph for long-distance service in the early twentieth century more completely integrated the twin cities into national urban, political, and communication networks. As material culture historian Thomas J. Schlereth has suggested, new utilities significantly altered everyday life. They changed the physical landscape, made "system" an image for modernity, and ended household independence, making it dependent on several outside forces that unified domestic surroundings. Such technological feats were necessary but not sufficient for decent urban life, as civic leaders recognized. Although municipal governments created parks, libraries, schools, and welfare institutions, they did better at providing material comforts and cultural amenities for middle-class residents than they did in providing them for the poor. This discrepancy stemmed from the dominance of private institutions in the municipal order and production.[101]

As transcontinentals propelled the United States westward throughout the nineteenth century, the railroads created Fargo, Moorhead, and many other cities. Early settlers attempted to transplant the island communities of their youth, but nationalizing technologies compromised these efforts. Two transcontinentals, the telegraph, and the telephone integrated the dual city from its inception into national networks of commerce, culture, and politics. The Northern Pacific, Great Northern, and Milwaukee Road directly benefited city government and services. After the Fargo fire, the railways aided reconstruction by 50 percent rate reductions on building materials. They offered similar discounts on other major municipal projects. They assisted the annual Fargo Fire Festival by granting Mayor J. A. Johnson's request for special round-trip fares for the thousands who attended. Other twin city mayors made similar arrangements for other fetes, conventions, and fraternal gatherings. The new Northern Pacific depot made arriving in Fargo a more metropolitan experience. Rail networks enabled cities like Fargo and Moorhead to join state and national municipal leagues. Hosting and attending league meetings better informed civic leaders about possibilities for improving their communities through more professional public administration.

The culture of privatism, which prized personal independence and profit, complicated urban improvements. Private property owners confronted a dilemma: Was it better to be cost-effective or safe? Initially, the desire for lower costs prevailed. Residents used yards, riverbanks, and streets as dump grounds for manure and rubbish. They piped raw sewage into the Red River that supplied them with drinking water. They built with wood rather than brick. Public health concerns, spawned by knowledge of germs and fear of epidemics, eventually altered behavior. Citizens decided that safety justified removing waste and taxing themselves to pay for modern water and sewer systems. Yet worries about municipal debt slowed progress. Fargo delayed a filtration plant until 1906 and sewage disposal waited until 1934 and federal funds from the New Deal. Moorhead finally developed a safe and efficient water system in 1915. Devastating fire losses similarly altered behavior. New codes mandated brick inside fire zones. Fargo transformed its volunteer fire companies into a professional force by 1903.

The twin cities retained the close ties between business and politics that marked their founding by entrepreneurial boosters. These men developed rudimentary services to attract residents and expand trade. They assumed that what benefited commerce helped the city. They believed that men pursuing private interests best served the public. They therefore elected businessmen to office. They awarded municipal contracts to local builders, even if they served on the council, because such men hired inhabitants, kept tax money in the city, and fueled trade. Mercantile-minded municipal officials attempted to make thriving cities with elegant buildings and modern conveniences. As services expanded in the 1890s, the burdens of bonded indebtedness and tax assessments increased. To keep taxes low, citizens demanded fiscally responsible governments with comprehensive, comprehensible, and balanced budgets. Rate collection, budgeting, and administration became more professional as a consequence.

Fargo and Moorhead each had its distinctive qualities. Larger Fargo attained benefits beyond the reach of its smaller neighbor. It had a professional fire department as well as more miles of paved streets and improved sewer lines. Moorhead's higher percentage of foreign-born citizens translated into more ethnic mayors and aldermen than were elected by its rival. Yet the twin cities had much in common. They shared metropolitan aspirations. Both struggled to create honest municipal government and efficient services. Both battled the culture of privatism and its aversion to taxes to pay for improvements. Both achieved a modern infrastructure of paved streets, electric lights, streetcars, water mains, and sewer lines that increased convenience and comfort for both Old and New American working- and middle-class families. The infrastructure promoted economic growth for middle-class businessmen, while it enhanced job opportunities for resident married workers. The infrastructure signaled an institutional maturity that sustained the dual city throughout the new century.

Conclusion

THE TWIN CITIES OF THE NORTHERN PLAINS ACHIEVED AN INSTI-
tutional maturity by 1900 that provides an appropriate ending for
this study. Transcontinental railroad, telegraph, and telephone networks
integrated Fargo and Moorhead into the national economy, culture, and
political system. An ideology of progressivism, drawn from the evangelical Christian tradition as well as the modern ideals of rationality and science, influenced the dual city commercial and civic elite. Borrowing ideas
from progressives elsewhere, officials fostered honest, efficient, and orderly
municipal government. They built a middle-class moral order and an infrastructure of modern services that enhanced the safety, convenience, and
comfort of most long-term residents. Yet people of color, the poor, and the
transient single males who composed the essential seasonal labor force for
the region's wheat monoculture found no permanent place in this more
rational moral and social order. Religious prejudice and efforts to impose
Protestant cultural values through Sunday closing, prohibition of alcohol,
and compulsory education at times alienated Catholics, Jews, and workers.
Hostility toward labor unions and strikes estranged the working class.

Northern plains geography and climate shaped and limited dual city
growth from the start. The region's subhumid prairies yielded bumper
wheat crops but did not support large populations. Dependence on wheat
also meant uneven profits and lower than average per capita incomes.
Remote location from large markets elevated transport costs, prevented
manufacturing, and fostered colonial dependency on the railroads, grain
elevators, flour mills, and banks of St. Paul and Minneapolis. Main street
merchants of the twin cities, who may have profited from their ties to these
Twin City corporate interests, endured attacks by Populists and later agrarian radicals from their less-favored western hinterlands as a consequence. In
addition, the dual city never attained the population and economic power of
Omaha and Kansas City, the southern gateways that had excellent connections to Chicago and other metropolitan areas. They attracted more eastern

capital and served regions in Nebraska and Kansas with more than three to four times as many people as North Dakota.[1]

The Northern Pacific and other railroad corporations nevertheless put Moorhead and Fargo on the map; connected them to an expanding national economy; promoted settlement, farms, businesses and towns; and brought the essentials of civilization to the northern plains. Fortunately for both corporate and private businesses, each recognized that the growth of one required the growth of the other. The new managerial middle class at times collaborated with the old producer middle class in building the churches, schools, businesses, and homes that made the twin cities viable communities. Yet these efforts at community building involved complicated negotiations between the inhabitants of competing cities on the one hand, and often-conflicting railroad corporations on the other. However companies resolved their disagreements, managers necessarily worked with residents and relied on their capital for developing the dual city and the Red River Valley. The early history of the twin cities therefore demonstrates that the incorporation of America resulted from the complex and dynamic interaction of managers with each other and with local businessmen as each group sought prosperity through growth.

Yet growth proved elusive for resident entrepreneurs. Each city and its

A steam locomotive and train at Fargo's Great Northern depot in 1909 signified the railroad's ongoing importance. Courtesy Institute for Regional Studies, North Dakota State University, Fargo (2006.54.15).

boosters followed similar strategies. Because promoters believed that great cities could not depend on agriculture alone, they attempted to achieve self-sufficiency through building manufactories, mercantile establishments, and expanded transportation networks. These efforts either failed outright or yielded poor results. The steamboat trade stimulated early growth but proved a fragile basis for long-term Canadian commerce. The arrival of the SPM&M railroad created a boom that eventually disappointed expectations. Competition from national corporations that mass-produced and distributed goods more cheaply finally destroyed each city's industries—flour mills, breweries, brick manufacturers, and iron foundries. Their collapse bankrupted many, including foremost entrepreneur Henry Bruns, who had gambled on making Moorhead the key city of the region. Whereas his personal dealing with railroad magnate James J. Hill undid Bruns, Solomon Comstock showed how one might win and hold a fortune while working with a corporate giant. Despite Bruns's and Comstock's extensive efforts on behalf of their municipality, Fargo assumed regional dominance by capturing farm implement and other wholesale houses attracted by the favorable rates offered by three competing railroads.

While Fargo proudly proclaimed itself "Gateway City" to the "breadbasket of the world," Moorhead glumly resigned itself to its fate as a secondary market center. Although Moorhead's success contrasted to numerous failures among the too many towns founded by competing railroads in the Red River Valley, its accomplishments paled in comparison to those of its rival. For a century and more Fargo has stayed as it began, the distribution center for a large agricultural area. It enjoyed expansion and prosperity despite loss of rural population and an out-migration from its hinterland that has been going on since the 1920s. By 1990, North Dakota was the only state with fewer people than it had seven decades earlier. Contrary to what pioneer boosters expected, Fargo has grown while farms and farmers decreased.[2]

As created by wealth-seeking railroad corporations, the twin cities became communities of moneymaking families shaped by what historian Sam Bass Warner called "the tradition of privatism." Individuals pursued happiness by seeking wealth and the independence that it brought. They built a community that maintained order among moneymakers and allowed opportunities to all because that determined both private and public success. According to this tradition, private entrepreneurial activity and not municipal measures determined urban growth. Churches and schools reflected and perpetuated the culture of privatism. Railroad mangers helped found these institutions by issuing passes to missionaries and educators, donating or selling lots at discounts, and shipping construction materials at reduced rates. Old American and immigrant Protestant congregations preached individual salvation and emphasized individual morality, expecting the elimination thereby of such social problems as injustice, crime, and poverty. North Dakota Catholic bishop John Shanley mirrored Protestants by calling for greater temperance, industry, and respectability among his flock. Public and private schools inculcated a common creed of individualism, self-help, and patriotism to children of every class, religion, and ethnicity. The community believed that arming each pupil with the knowledge and values essential to individual success ensured his or her self-reliance thereafter.[3]

Privatism complicated urban improvements by compelling the propertied to choose between safety and savings. Initially, owners chose savings. Accumulated waste, polluted water, and epidemic diseases altered public consciousness in time. Citizens then decided that safety justified taxation for public sanitation. Yet worries about costs slowed progress. Fargo delayed a filtration plant until 1906 and Moorhead waited another decade before it developed a safe and efficient water system. Sewage disposal plants took even longer. When western urban services finally improved, eastern municipalities provided the techniques and technology.[4]

Many nationalities and races peopled Moorhead and Fargo. The corporate managerial and dual city commercial elite shared a booster ideology that committed them to accepting most ethnic groups, which expanded population and furthered growth. Boosters especially prized Norwegians, Swedes, and Germans because these Protestant Anglo-Saxons shared the essential Victorian middle-class values of piety, character, and respectability with old-stock Americans. Relatively rapid assimilation of these European newcomers confirmed the booster strategy for community building. The small urban population ensured constant face-to-face contact between nationalities in business and politics. Annual community celebrations of St. Patrick's Day and Norwegian independence eased the acceptance of Catholics and Scandinavians by diminishing their otherness. Civic freedom facilitated the development of dual and complementary loyalties to their new homeland and to ethnic communities. Immigrants embraced American democratic and business opportunities while retaining their traditional religion, language, and culture. Catholics and Jews won some acceptance for their economic contributions, but encountered hostility toward their religions, racial traits, and often lower-class status. Racism limited numbers of African Americans, Native Americans, and Asians in the twin cities.

Railroads enabled the dual city middle class to enjoy and display eastern material culture and genteel refinement. The Comstock mansion and Castle Tyler set the standard emulated by others within their means. According to the cult of domesticity, naturally virtuous women managed these house-

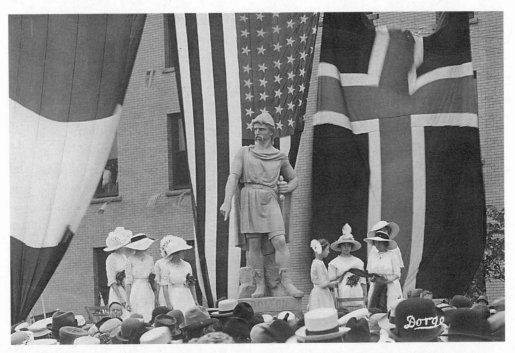

French, American, and Norwegian flags at the Rollo statue dedication in 1912 symbolized ethnic harmony in Fargo. Courtesy Institute for Regional Studies, North Dakota State University, Fargo (51.50.7).

holds, reared children, upheld the markers of social status, and provided a haven from the ruthless business world. Women's civic work made home and domesticity the keystone of associational life in the twin cites. Women founded libraries and aided the poor. They assisted the YMCA in providing an attractive Christian and homelike atmosphere that kept young men from the saloon. They backed the WCTU demand for saving home and family by the abolition of liquor. The more radical became suffragettes, arguing that the female vote would morally improve municipality, state, and nation. Numerous middle-class men joined fraternal societies and other voluntary associations, gaining the tangible benefits of business contacts, life or health insurance, and charity. By establishing fraternal orders, reform societies, schools, churches, homes, and families, men and women of the emerging middle class socialized the young in the Victorian moral code, spread these virtues throughout society, and thereby established middle-class moral order in both cities.

Railroad corporations made available the goods that created the material environment of the bourgeois moral order. Yet the railroads contributed to other activities that tested middle-class hegemony. Seasonal workers, saloons, gambling dens, houses of ill fame, easy divorce, strikes, and unions contested fundamental moral assumptions. Harvest hands by the hundred, accompanied by parasitical thieves, arrived illegally by rail each autumn. Temperance crusaders blamed liquor for the ensuing turmoil. Drunkenness increased, as did disorderly conduct, theft, assault, and murder. Liquor dealers and madams bribed police and evaded prosecution. Some city officials chose prosperity over purity. They looked the other way so long as sin paid its way. A similar attitude made Fargo into a lucrative divorce mill. Businesses trading in vice called individualism into question. Should sinful individuals be restrained? Purists, refusing to compromise with evil, said yes. They demanded prohibition of saloons and prostitution, easy divorce, and gambling. Others said vices could not be banished until all sinners voluntarily gave them up. Purists eventually claimed a partial victory. They made divorce more difficult in North Dakota. They closed bars and brothels in each city, but that did not end either prostitution or drinking. They attained merely a semblance of order imposed on tramps and transient laborers.

Middle-class residents approved only those workers who adopted the bourgeois moral ethos. They accepted labor organizations that acted like fraternal lodges. Yet the middle class condemned workers when they formed unions that adopted the strike as a weapon and engaged in violence against property. Anxieties understandably increased as the railroads brought Coxeyites, organized labor, and strikes into the region. Such collective action challenged the economic individualism of small producers. Yet businessmen were not always hostile. Many sympathized with local members of the ARU in their strike against James J. Hill and the powerful Great Northern. They adopted a neutral stance when workers stuck the Northern Pacific because that corporation employed so many men in the city. Merchants, who equated more wage earners with more sales, backed laborers in their campaign for jobs from local contractors.

Moorhead and Fargo had many similarities. Both originated as railroad towns, bound by steel rails to national and international markets on which they depended for prosperity and the good things of life. Ethnically and religiously diverse populations inhabited both. Both embraced privatism and relied on voluntary societies for communal tasks. Each developed parallel institutions—homes, families, churches, schools, and associations—to establish a middle-class moral order. Yet each remained a "wet" city until forced to become "dry" by an external government. North Dakota entered the Union as a dry state in 1889 and Minnesota adopted "county option" in 1915. The twin cities shared metropolitan aspirations. Both battled privatism in creating honest municipal government and financing efficient services that improved the well-being of middle- and working-class families. Services also created jobs for resident married workers and promoted economic growth for businessmen.

Apart from these equivalences, the twin cities generally carried on separate existences. The municipalities had held joint July Fourth observances in the early years and committees from each had met in building the Red River bridges. Pastors gathered monthly in the Fargo-Moorhead Ministerial Association and several congregations from each town at times held union Sunday school excursions to Detroit Lake. Yet, other institutions and associations functioned separately for the most part. Each community usually conducted its own holiday celebrations, revivals, fraternal events, and other activities independently until the mid-twentieth century. Many dual city differences stemmed from Fargo being larger, wealthier, and the gateway to its state. It created a professional fire department. It laid more miles of paved streets, and improved sewer lines. Although Moorhead had several large homes, Fargo had three or four elite neighborhoods that sought exclusivity despite lesser dwellings in their midst. In addition, the Dakota metropolis had an orphanage, a children's home, and a home for unwed mothers. Its rival's small size and its relatively low rank among Minnesota cities prevented it from acquiring comparable institutions. Smaller Moorhead's higher percentage of foreign-born citizens, however, did result in its electing more ethnic mayors and aldermen than its larger neighbor.

Civic-minded businessmen generally dominated the municipal governments in each city after its incorporation. Such men governed by these precepts: what benefited commerce aided the city; pursuit of private interest best served the public; and municipal contracts awarded to local builders created jobs that fueled trade. Aldermen and mayors established rudimentary services, which attracted settlers and promoted growth. Excessive spending and unchecked vice provoked demands for officials who backed fiscal responsibility, moral rectitude, and professional services. These efforts essentially succeeded. By 1900, the twin cities had established responsible governments, taken on a metropolitan appearance, and numbered just over thirteen thousand inhabitants. Armed with better budgeting, civic leaders delivered modern urban services—paved streets and sidewalks, electric lights and a street railway, municipal water plants and sewer systems. These institutions were sufficiently mature to accommodate population growth that tripled by the 1930s and tripled again by the end of the twentieth century.

Swedish-born Fargo mayor J. A. Johnson and Swedish-born Moorhead alderman Henry Johnson typified the municipal progressives who furthered institutional maturity in the dual city. The mayor and other reformers battled for control of Fargo against the Republican "Old Gang." The alderman, a

Normal School history professor and Congregationalist, delivered a lecture at his church in the spirit of English scholar James Bryce on the "conspicuous failure" of Moorhead and U.S. city government. His frank talk shocked his audience, causing him to reflect about how cultivated ignorance among the respectable permitted corruption. Both men were "evangelistic modernizers" who upheld Christian morality while they applied scientific expertise to solve political and social problems. Both crusaded against vice at the same time that they battled for honest and efficient government. The enthusiasm created by state and national progressivism often sustained their local efforts.[5]

North Dakota progressivism formed in opposition to Boss Alexander McKenzie's machine that dominated the Republican Party and state government from 1890 until 1906. The "Revolution of 1906" ended McKenzie's reign by electing Democrat John Burke as governor. He and his legislative allies extended democracy by establishing primary elections; initiative, referendum, and recall; the commission form of government; and measures against corrupt practices. They also enacted pure food and drug laws; outlawed child labor; founded a juvenile court system; and regulated railroads, banks, and insurance companies. At the same time, the Minnesota progressive coalition of Yankee and Scandinavian reformers enacted a similar legislative program as they battled against political corruption and the liquor interests. National progressives advanced a search for order by fostering rational administration, scientific expertise, executive direction, and the cooperation of affected groups. As progressivism faded by the 1920s, according to historian Robert Wiebe, it left behind an emerging bureaucratic web that became more elaborate throughout the ensuing century.[6]

Mayor J. A. Johnson played the role of moral crusader during his first term in the mid-1880s. He suspended the police chief, who did not shut saloons on Sunday or stop gambling. He mandated moral decency and midnight closing by the vaudeville theaters. He decided that prostitution could not be eradicated and adopted a policy of regulation. He concentrated soiled doves in a red-light district under police surveillance and subjected them to monthly fines.[7]

Returned to office for three terms a decade later, Johnson furthered civic reforms. As president of the North Dakota Tax League, he battled for equal and just assessment of all property against the McKenzie Machine. He overcame the railroad lobby in the North Dakota legislature, winning a retroactive tax payment, and he obtained a higher assessment from the state board of equalization than that set by the Cass County commissioners. Fargo soon joined the National Municipal League that Johnson helped organize. He promoted the North Dakota League and served as its president. He headed the American body and addressed the national convention several times. Describing his North Dakota legislative proposals, Johnson asserted: "What all cities need are laws that will make it impossible to form rings . . . to control them. . . . One of the best safeguards . . . [is] uniformity of laws, rigidly enforced." He commended the North Dakota Special Assessments Law that enabled Fargo to pave streets and construct sewers. He backed the movement for municipal ownership headed by Cleveland mayor Tom Johnson and William Randolph Hearst. He praised Fargo's investment in the Municipal Water Works, which paid for itself. It cut private rates by 60 percent and reduced fire protection costs.[8]

Although Johnson at times battled railroad corporations in advancing municipal reform, he worked with them on other occasions. Johnson knew that the railroads had aided reconstruction after the Fargo fire by 50 percent rate reductions on building materials. He tapped them again by requesting special round-trip fares for the thousands who attended the annual Fargo Fire Festival from within a two hundred-mile radius. Other twin city mayors made similar arrangements for other fetes, conventions, and fraternal gatherings. The new Northern Pacific depot, negotiated by Johnson, gave Fargo a more metropolitan appearance. The railroads also enabled attendance by Johnson and other dual city officials at state and national Municipal League conferences. Participating in these meetings better informed civic leaders about improving their communities through more professional public administration.

Johnson documented the value of progressive reforms. For example, the prohibition law and its strict enforcement lowered the crime rate. Nonpartisan boards applying sound economic principles reduced Fargo's tax rate and per capita indebtedness. As a consequence, population grew and business boomed. In 1899, trade totaled more than $1.5 million and the banks cleared almost $18 million. Citing prices paid for asphalt, vitrified brick, and sandstone by Minneapolis, Moorhead, and Grand Forks, Johnson maintained that Fargo had spent less on these materials than other cities during his three terms as mayor.[9]

Narrowly defeated in the 1902 and 1904 elections, Johnson still actively worked for progressive reforms. He attacked the meat trust and the elevator ring for their large profits and monopolistic practices. He worked for the primary election law. Elected to his fifth term in 1906 by a large margin, Mayor Johnson cracked down on gambling and bordellos. The police busted prostitutes, raided gambling joints, and arrested drunks coming from Moorhead. Citizens rallied in support by organizing a Civic Improvement League and electing Helen deLendrecie as president. Johnson responded to the league's pressure and attempted to close the red-light district. At the same time, he promoted Fargo, which he called the "biggest little city in the world." His detailing of the miles of electric railway, paved streets, water mains, and sewers in his last speech documented institutional maturity and the achievement of metropolitan dreams. He attributed these gains to strict antiliquor laws and recent antiprostitution efforts.[10]

Formation of the nonpartisan and nonsectarian Civic Federation in 1895 expressed the Moorhead impulse toward progressive reform. It proposed to investigate complaints, compel law enforcement against vice, and secure honest, economical administration by nominating able candidates. A few years later, Henry Johnson won a council seat. His autobiography clearly describes progressive assumptions. First, reformers researched the problems of government. Johnson's committee concluded that the Electric Light and Water Plant had not been paid for and that the cost—estimated at between $40,000 and $65,000—could not be determined exactly. The city recorder's records revealed a $14,000 discrepancy. Further research disclosed that the plant had not charged saloons for the electricity used, had not listed some electric customers, and had not collected from others. The plant superintendent had not reported all city expenses in wiring houses for lights. Second, progressives promoted honest government with investigation-based conclusions. Johnson's revelations forced resignations of both the superintendent and the city recorder. Third, his progressive desire for efficiency at times exceeded his humanitarianism. As chairman of the Committee on the Poor, Johnson selected only those deserving relief. He interviewed every applicant and required two committee members to call on each one at home. His committee thereby cut expenditures for relief far below those of previous administrations.[11]

Johnson's desire for efficiency committed him to endorsing Mayor Jacob Kiefer for reelection. Kiefer's honest administration had yielded concrete results by reducing debt, increasing light and water collections, and cutting expenditures for relief, police, streets, light, and water. Yet progressive frugality in aiding the needy annoyed many. Businessmen complained about loss of sales; applicants criticized the red tape; and sentimentalists deplored not "caring for the poor in our midst." When an applicant died after being denied hospitalization, even Johnson wondered if his concern for economy had exceeded humanity in administering assistance to the poor.[12]

The Moorhead progressive impulse continued into the twentieth century. Reformers closed the red-light district in 1906. The city joined the Minnesota Municipal League in 1913. Clay County voted dry in 1915 under a recently enacted County Option Law. A women-sponsored civic league urged urban beautification, assisted in cleaning up residential neighborhoods by obtaining teams and wagons from the council, established a public restroom for downtown shoppers, and requested appointing a police matron and visiting nurse. At times, such women's care for everyday concerns clashed with men's drive for economy in government. Fargo women similarly fostered civic housekeeping by working for better schools, juvenile court officers, police matrons, pure foods, and beautification. Dual city female progressives promoted self-cultivation for all by establishing public libraries. They defended home and family by attacking liquor, gambling, and prostitution. They sought suffrage on similar grounds. The vote made mothers more effective civic housekeepers.[13]

These local efforts at building better municipal institutions would not have succeeded without assistance from a national movement. According to scholar Kenneth Fox, the National Municipal League, the U.S. Census Bureau, and university political scientists all contributed to "a well-conceived model of . . . city government" that made change possible. A national coalition of experts and progressives emerged with the formation of the National Municipal League in 1894. It served as a clearinghouse for information. It developed a bureaucratic orientation. It called for scientific investigation to develop the correct principles of local self-government. Social and political scientists played a prominent role in its national conferences. Between 1899 and 1913, a generalized model of strong city government emerged. It called for freeing cities from control by state legislatures. It demanded centralized administration from a strong mayor and department heads. The Census Bureau supported the model by providing comparative statistical reporting and research on revenues, expenditures, and other urban functions. Although reformers backed executive authority, they accepted ward-based councils in large cities. They did not willfully eliminate entirely the "representative principle" from municipal government.[14]

Banishing the Moorhead and Fargo red-light districts in the early twentieth century failed to end the sex trade. As historian Carl Abbott has remarked, a skid-row district on lower Front Street "with cheap hotels, flophouses, missions, bars, brothels and labor exchanges" served transient workers for several more decades. Novelist Louise Erdrich described nearby Northern Pacific Avenue as "the central thoroughfare of the dingy feel-good roll of Indian bars, Western-ware stores, pawn shops and Christian Revival Missions that Fargo was trying to eradicate." Eventually, urban renewal projects from the 1960s onward removed these blighted areas. By 1976, Fargo ranked second in the quality of life among the smaller metropolitan areas.[15]

Mayor J. A. Johnson and alderman Henry Johnson would have applauded these markers of economic and moral progress. It confirmed their earlier efforts to establish good government, commercial prosperity, and a middle-class moral order in the dual city. They likely would not have perceived that people of color, the poor, and transient single males still struggled to find a permanent place. Despite this shortcoming, the institutions and the values they and other founders established had sustained the twin cities of the northern plains for many decades. Indeed, North Dakotans and Minnesotans remain committed to the traditional moral and civic values of the respectable middle class. Like Solomon G. Comstock and other pioneers, they are community-minded folk who are industrious, sober, thrifty, honest, and driven to self-improvement in their private lives. They vote regularly, donate money to charitable causes, and work to build better communities.[16]

Notes

INTRODUCTION

1. *Hon. J. A. Johnson: A Partial Copy of His Letters, Travels and Addresses,* ed. Alice E. Chester and Laura A. Johnson (Fargo: Privately printed, 1908), 246–50, 256, 259, 263.

2. Ibid., 3–4, 8.

3. Throughout the text, Moorhead and Fargo are the twin cities (lowercase) while Minneapolis and St. Paul are the Twin Cities (uppercase).

4. *Red River Star,* October 17, 1874, and August 4, 1876; *Moorhead Weekly News,* September 7, 1882; *Fargo Evening Republican,* January 30, April 13 and 14, and August 10, 1882; *Fargo Daily Argus,* March 1, 1892; *Fargo Daily Forum and Republican,* July 27, 1895. Editors' use of "twin cities" suggests booster ambitions to surpass the larger Twin Cities of Minneapolis and St. Paul.

5. Elwyn B. Robinson, *History of North Dakota* (Lincoln: University of Nebraska Press, 1966), 10–11, and "The Themes of North Dakota History," *North Dakota History* 26 (winter 1959): 6–9, 14–15; D. Jerome Tweton, "Preface to the North Dakota Edition: Elwyn B. Robinson and the Themes of North Dakota," in Elwyn B. Robinson, *History of North Dakota* (Fargo: Institute for Regional Studies–North Dakota State University, 1995), x–xiii. On factors limiting Fargo, see Lawrence H. Larsen and Roger T. Johnson, "Obstacles to Urbanization on the Northern Great Plains of the United States," *North Dakota History* 50 (summer 1983): 17–20, and "A Story That Never Was: North Dakota's Urban Development," *North Dakota History* 47 (fall 1980): 6–8, 10.

6. Lawrence H. Larsen, *The Urban West at the End of the Frontier* (Lawrence: Regents Press of Kansas, 1978), 9–10, 31, 40, 42–43, 49, 100–103, 116; Lawrence H. Larsen and Barbara J. Cottrell, *The Gate City: A History of Omaha,* enlarged ed. (Lincoln: University of Nebraska Press, 1997), 31–32, 69–71, 79f. On population of Great Plains states, see Richard White, *"It's Your Misfortune and None of My Own": A History of the American West* (Norman: University of Oklahoma Press, 1991), 188. In 1900, Kansas had 1,470,495 people, Nebraska 1,066,300, and North Dakota 319,136.

7. On U.S. statistical categories, see Eric H. Monkkonen, *America Becomes Urban: The Development of U.S. Cities and Towns* (Berkeley: University of California Press, 1988), 70, and Blake McKelvey, *The Urbanization of America (1860–1915)* (New Brunswick, N.J.: Rutgers University Press, 1963), vii. On the local metropolitan dream, see *Fargo Evening Republican,* March 29 and July 25, 1882. For the functional definition of city, see Pauline Maier, "Boston and New York in the Eighteenth Century," *Proceedings of the American Antiquarian Society* 91, Part 2 (October 21, 1981): 178–79. I am indebted to colleague Rick Chapman for this citation.

8. Carl Bridenbaugh, *Cities in the Wilderness: The First Century of Urban Life in America, 1625–1742* (New York: Oxford University Press, 1971), ix–x; Richard C. Wade, *The Urban Frontier: Pioneer Life in Early Pittsburgh, Cincinnati, Lexington, Louisville, and St. Louis* (Chicago: University of Chicago Press, 1971), 341–42; Diane Shaw, *City Building on the Eastern Frontier: Sorting the New Nineteenth-Century City* (Baltimore: Johns Hopkins University Press, 2004), 1–5, 10, 12, 14–15, 18.

9. On the need for study of small American cities, see David Ward, *Cities and Immigrants: A Geography of Change in Nineteenth-Century America* (New York: Oxford University Press, 1971), 9, 15, and Monkkonen, *America Becomes Urban*, 123–25. Small cities on the northern plains have been neglected, according to Carroll Van West, *Capitalism on the Frontier: Billings and the Yellowstone Valley in the Nineteenth Century* (Lincoln: University of Nebraska Press, 1993), 4–5. For early-twentieth-century town building on the northern plains, see John C. Hudson, *Plains Country Towns* (Minneapolis: University of Minnesota Press, 1985), and Paula M. Nelson, *After the West Was Won: Homesteaders and Town-Builders in Western South Dakota, 1900–1917* (Iowa City: University of Iowa Press, 1986). In *Poverty and Progress: Social Mobility in a Nineteenth Century City* (New York: Atheneum, 1969), Stephan Thernstrom says small-city history may reveal "the changes wrought by vast impersonal forces." Kathleen Neils Conzen warns against excessively localized national history and suggests attending to what is distinctly local in communal cultures in "Community Studies, Urban History and American Local History," in *The Past before Us: Contemporary Historical Writing in the United States,* ed. Michael Kammen (Ithaca, N.Y. and London: Cornell University Press, 1980), 270–91. For the impact of corporate structures on middle-class values of local communities, see Robert H. Wiebe, *The Search for Order, 1877–1920* (New York: Hill and Wang, 1967), and Olivier Zunz, *Making America Corporate, 1870–1920* (Chicago: University of Chicago Press, 1990). On how metropolitan economy transforms rural hinterlands, see William Cronon, *Nature's Metropolis: Chicago and the Great West* (New York: W. W. Norton, 1991), and Roberta Balstad Miller, *City and Hinterland: A Case Study of Urban Growth and Regional Development* (Westport, Conn.: Greenwood Press, 1979), 154–57.

10. Sam Bass Warner Jr., *The Private City: Philadelphia in Three Periods of Growth* (Philadelphia: University of Pennsylvania Press, 1968), 3–6; Larsen, *Urban West*, xi, 19, 120.

11. Mary Lethert Wingerd, *Claiming the City: Politics, Faith, and the Power of Place in St. Paul* (Ithaca, N.Y.: Cornell University Press, 2001), 2–7, 32. An important, recently published book details the impact of entrepreneurial culture on the Twin Cities: Jocelyn Wills, *Boosters, Hustlers, and Speculators: Entrepreneurial Culture and the Rise of Minneapolis and St. Paul* (St. Paul: Minnesota Historical Society Press, 2005).

1. AT THE CROSSING

1. "Fargo Founded: Thomas H. Canfield's Story," *Record* 1 (December 1895): 9–10. Canfield's letters describe his campaign based on secrecy and duplicity: T. H. Canfield to D. C. Linsley, May 13, 1871, and to George B. Wright, June 29 and July 13, 1871, LS&PS Co. Letterbooks, vol. 68, no. 1, 421–22, 489, 505, LS&PS Company Records, Northern Pacific Railway Company Papers, Minnesota Historical Society, St. Paul. For settlers' accounts, see *Roy Johnson's Red River Valley,* ed. Clarence A. Glasrud (Moorhead: Red River Valley Historical Society, 1982), 256, 287, and "History of Fargo," in *History of the Red River Valley* (Chicago: C. F. Cooper & Company, 1909), 1:487.

2. Memorandum of directors' meeting, Georgetown, Minnesota, August 21, 1871, Roll 2, Frame 113–14, Land Dept. Records, Northern Pacific Railway Company Papers, Minnesota Historical Society. T. H. Canfield to Carrie A. Canfield, August 27, 1871, Thomas Hawley Canfield Papers—Personal Correspondence, Vermont Historical Library, Montpelier. On names, see Mary Ann Williams, *Origins of North Dakota Place Names* (Bismarck: Tribune, 1966), 64, and Warren Upham, *Minnesota Geographic Names: Their Origin and Historic Significance* (St. Paul: Minnesota Historical Society Press, 1920), 117.

3. On capitalism and economic dependence, see William G. Robbins, *Colony and Empire: The Capitalist Transformation of the American West* (Lawrence: University Press of Kansas, 1994), 62–64, 72, 88, 172–73. The incorporation of America is discussed by Alfred D. Chandler, *The Visible Hand: The Managerial Revolution in American Business* (Cambridge: Belknap of Harvard University Press, 1977), 1, 79–80, 124, 188–89; Alan Trachtenberg, *The Incorporation of America: Culture and Society in the Gilded Age* (New York: Hill and Wang, 1982), 3–8, 22–23, 65–67, 115–18; Olivier Zunz, *Making America Corporate, 1870–1920* (Chicago: University of Chicago Press, 1990), 4–10, 12–13, 16, 19, 39–40, 49–50, 54–56, 59–60.

4. The limited capacity of railroads to create wealth and the town negotiations are noted by Sarah H. Gordon in her *Passage to Union: How the Railroads Transformed American Life, 1829–1929* (Chicago: Ivan R. Dee, 1996), 213, 345–46.

5. John Brinckerhoff Jackson, *American Space: The Centennial Years, 1865–1876* (New York: W. W. Norton, 1972), 49–50; Michael G. Michlovic, "The Archeology of the Red River Valley," *Minnesota History* 51 (summer 1988): 55–59, and "The Red River Valley in the Prehistory of the Northern Plains," *Plains Anthropologist* 28:99 (1983): 23–24, 26–29.

6. John Perry Pritchett, *The Red River Valley, 1811–1849: A Regional Study* (New Haven: Yale University Press, 1942), 264, 3–7, 10, 13, 221.

7. Ibid., 41, 46, 89, 107–8, 252–53; Elwyn B. Robinson, *History of North Dakota* (Lincoln: University of Nebraska Press, 1966), 62–63, 74–75; Rhoda R. Gilman, Carolyn Gilman, and Deborah M. Stultz, *Red River Trails: Oxcart Routes between St. Paul and the Selkirk Settlement, 1820–1870* (St. Paul: Minnesota Historical Society Press, 1979), 2–8, 28.

8. Robinson, *History of North Dakota*, 75–76, 78, 80; Pritchett, *Red River Valley*, 14–15; Gilman, Gilman, and Stultz, *Red River Trails*, 5, 10–13; Gerhard Ens, "Dispossession or Adaptation? Migration and Persistence of the Red River Métis, 1835–1890," *Historical Papers* (1988): 123–25, 133.

9. Pritchett, *Red River Valley*, 255; Gilman, Gilman, and Stultz, *Red River Trails*, 14, 16–17, 87.

10. Robinson, *History of North Dakota*, 65; Gilman, Gilman, and Stultz, *Red River Trails*, 6, 17, 21; John Harnsberger and Robert P. Wilkins, "Transportation on the Northern Plains, II: Steamboating North of Fargo," *North Dakota Quarterly* 29 (spring 1961): 57–59.

11. Harnsberger and Wilkins, "Transportation on the Northern Plains, II," 59–63; Gilman, Gilman, and Stultz, *Red River Trails*, 21–22, 24, 42, 70.

12. Stanley N. Murray, "Early Indian Occupation of the Red River Valley," *Heritage Press* 20 (July/August 1996): 13–14; Gilman, Gilman, and Stultz, *Red River Trails*, 17, 23.

13. Upham, *Minnesota Geographic Names*, 6; Tim Holzkamm and Dean Dormanen, *Fargo Historic Context Study* (Fargo: Historic Preservation Commission, 1993), 16–17.

14. Robert P. Wilkins and Wynona Huchette Wilkins, *North Dakota: A Bicentennial History* (New York: W. W. Norton, 1977), 51; Gilman, Gilman, and Stultz, *Red River Trails*, 23–26, 87;

Robinson, *History of North Dakota*, 101–2; John L. Harnsberger, *Jay Cooke and Minnesota: The Formative Years of the Northern Pacific Railroad, 1868–1873* (New York: Arno Press, 1981), 178–83; Claire Strom, *Profiting from The Plains: The Great Northern Railway and Corporate Development of the American West* (Seattle: University of Washington Press, 2003), 14–15.

15. The newspaper is quoted in Gordon L. Iseminger, "*Land and Emigration*: A Northern Pacific Company Newspaper," *North Dakota Quarterly* 49 (summer 1981): 72; Harnsberger, *Jay Cooke and Minnesota*, 52–53, 56–58, 65, 175.

16. Edward Chase Kirkland, *Industry Comes of Age: Business, Labor, and Public Policy, 1860–1897* (Chicago: Quadrangle Paperback, 1967), 20–21, 70–71, 220–21; Henrietta Melia Larson, *Jay Cooke, Private Banker* (Cambridge: Harvard University Press, 1936), 14, 35, 122, 169, 191–93, 249–53, 329–31, 333–34; Harnsberger, *Jay Cooke and Minnesota*, 70–71.

17. John Harnsberger, "Railroads to the Northern Plains: 1870–1872," *North Dakota Quarterly* 27 (summer 1959): 53–54; John Harnsberger and Robert P. Wilkins, "Transportation on the Northern Plains, III: The Railroads Arrive," *North Dakota Quarterly* 29 (summer 1961): 83; Larson, *Jay Cooke*, 335–36, 338, 369–70; Robin W. Winks, *Frederick Billings: A Life* (New York: Oxford University Press, 1991), 205.

18. Stanley N. Murray, *The Valley Comes of Age* (Fargo: North Dakota Institute for Regional Studies, 1967), 65; John Lee Coulter, "Marketing Agricultural Lands in Minnesota and North Dakota," *American Economic Review* 2 (June 1912): 288–89; B. F. Wade and Jonathan R. Wheat to Willis Drummond, June 22, 1872, Roll 8, Frames 152–54, Northern Pacific Land Dept. Records; John Mack Faragher, *Sugar Creek: Life on the Illinois Prairie* (New Haven: Yale University Press, 1986), 41–42.

19. Winks, *Frederick Billings*, 191, 198–99; Harnsberger, *Jay Cooke and Minnesota*, 244, 311; Murray, *Valley Comes of Age*, 67–68; James B. Hedges, "The Colonization Work of the Northern Pacific Railroad," *Journal of American History* 13 (December 1926): 324–26.

20. Eugene V. Smalley, *History of the Northern Pacific Railroad* (New York: G. P. Putnam's Sons, 1883), 165; *Life of Thomas Hawley Canfield* (Burlington, Vt., 1889), 33–36; Harnsberger, *Jay Cooke and Minnesota*, 83–84, and "Land Speculation, Promotion and Failure: The Northern Pacific Railroad, 1870–1873," *Journal of the West* 9 (January 1970): 35–36; Winks, *Frederick Billings*, 203.

21. Harnsberger, *Jay Cooke and Minnesota*, 83–86, 89, and "Land Speculation, Promotion and Failure," 35–37; Winks, *Frederick Billings*, 203. Strom, *Profiting from the Plains*, 6–7, states that many opposed awarding federal land grants to large corporations. They believed public land should be reserved for individual profit.

22. Letters Received, June 16–20, 1872, Roll 38, Frame 31; James B. Power to George B. Hibbard, April 19 and 23, 1873, and to W. A. Howard, April 21, 1873, Roll 11, Frames, 215–18, 255–57, and 296–97; W. A. Howard to James B. Power, April 19, 1873, Roll 32, Frame 281; George Hibbard to W. A. Howard, August 1873, Roll 12, Frames 160–62, Northern Pacific Land Dept. Records. Canfield may have been inefficient, but buying privately held land required negotiating with widely scattered owners. It took time to identify and contact owners. Northern Pacific directors changing location of the line west of present-day Detroit Lakes further complicated his work. On these points, see T. H. Canfield to Jay Cooke, September 22, 1870, and August 21, 1871, LS&PS Co. Letterbooks, vol. 68, no. 1, 98, 566; T. H. Canfield to Carrie A. Canfield, August 21, 1870, Canfield Papers—Personal Correspondence; T. H. Canfield to F. E. Woodbridge, September 25, 1871, LS&PS Co. Letterbooks, vol. 67, 272–73.

23. Frederick Billings to Jay Cooke, November 17, 1871, Roll 15, Frames 446–48 and Meeting of Land Committee, April 16, 1890, Land Committee Minutes, vol. 32, 292–93, Box 8, Northern Pacific Land Dept. Records; T. H. Canfield to Frederick Billings, May 1, 1873, LS&PS Co. Letterbooks, vol. 71, no. 4, 349–50; Thomas Hawley Canfield Report, September 11, 1873, and Executive Committee Meeting, August 12, September 17 and 30, 1873, Canfield Papers—Business Correspondence; George Stark to C. B. Wright, June 13, 1876, LS&PS Co. Letterbooks, vol. 73, no. 6, 303.

24. Harnsberger, "Land Speculation, Promotion and Failure," 45; George Stark to William Rice, March 5, 1878, LS&PS Co. Letterbooks, vol. 74, no. 7, 163.

25. Augustus J. Veenendahl Jr., *Slow Train to Paradise: How Dutch Investment Helped Build American Railroads* (Stanford, Calif.: Stanford University Press, 1996), 63; A. B. Nettleton to Frederick Billings, August 31, 1872, Roll 8, Frames 141–43, Northern Pacific Land Dept. Records; Harnsberger, *Jay Cooke and Minnesota*, 76–79.

26. Richard White, "Information, Markets and Corruption: Transcontinental Railroads in the Gilded Age," *Journal of American History* 90 (June 2003): 29–30; Harnsberger, *Jay Cooke and Minnesota*, 81–85, 89–90, 134–36, 138–39, 313–17, 322–24, 327–28, 336. What White says about Cooke's ethically dubious decisions and Harnsberger about corruption is corroborated in Larson's biography, *Jay Cooke*, 349, 351–53, 376–80, 387. According to Veenendahl, *Slow Train to Paradise,* 113, construction companies formed by railroad promoters profited while debt bankrupted the road.

27. Rendig Fels, *American Business Cycles, 1865–1897* (Chapel Hill: University of North Carolina Press, 1959), 112; Veenendahl, *Slow Train to Paradise,* 111, 175; White, "Information, Markets and Corruption," 37–39; Harnsberger, *Jay Cooke and Minnesota,* 321–22. Also see Mark Van Rhyn, "An American Warrior: Thomas Lafayette Rosser, 1836–1910" (master's thesis, University of Nebraska–Lincoln, 1998), 96, 101–2, 128–29. Cooke's faith in management reform, the failure of Northern Pacific managers to attend to details, and the Northern Pacific's "total absence of sound system" are discussed in Larson, *Jay Cooke,* 373, 375–76, 382, 405–6. Also see Zunz, *Making America Corporate,* 59–60.

28. Harnsberger, "Land Speculation, Promotion and Failure," 37; John C. Hudson, *Plains Country Towns* (Minneapolis: University of Minnesota Press, 1985), 6, 10–11, 38, 42, 48, 54, 71, 120, 130. Also see John W. Reps, *Cities of the American West: A History of Frontier Urban Planning* (Princeton, N.J.: Princeton University Press, 1979), 525, 535, 544, 547.

29. *Red River Gazette,* July 4, 1872.

30. Hudson, in *Plains Country Towns,* 87–89, describes this standard design. Fargo's original 240–acre site oriented toward the track on the south side deviated somewhat after private parties platted the north side and Broadway became a principal business street perpendicular to the track. The LS&PS nonstandardized symmetric Moorhead plan became a half-symmetric town with Front as the principal business street. See Tom Schmiedeler, "Civic Geometry: Frontier Forms of Minnesota County Seats," *Minnesota History* 57 (fall 2001): 340. Thomas White Harvey says that grid-shaped plans often oriented toward the track and seldom followed the cardinal directions of section lines. Later additions laid out in cardinal directions created wedge-shaped blocks. LS&PS deviated with inadequate right-of-way. See Harvey, "The Making of Railroad Towns in Minnesota's Red River Valley" (master's thesis, Pennsylvania State University, 1982), 75, 79, 83, 85, 87–90.

31. On the role of Yankees, see John Hudson, "Towns of the Western Railroads," *Great Plains Quarterly* 21 (winter 1982): 45–46, 51. Also see *Life of Thomas Hawley Canfield*, 9–16, and excerpts from this autobiography published in "Vermonters: Thomas Hawley Canfield," *Vermont Quarterly* 14 (July 1946): 102–14. "Thomas Hawley Canfield," in *Illustrated Album of Biography* (Chicago: Alden, Ogle & Company, 1889), 800, 834–35, is a lengthy, laudatory account that mirrors his autobiography. C. B. Wright to George Stark, July 26, 1878, Box 14, Northern Pacific Secretary Records, urges scrutiny of Canfield's demanding advances and drawbacks on his wood contracts. Statement of Assets and Liabilities of Thomas H. Canfield, October 20, 1893, Box 2, Canfield Papers. T. H. Canfield to Willis Drummond, March 31, 1871, LS&PS Co. Letterbooks, vol. 68, no. 1, 309–10, states his temperance agenda.

32. T. H. Canfield to George B. Wright, June 21, 1871, and to Joseph E. Turner, September 15, 1871, LS&PS Co. Letterbooks, vol. 68, no. 1, 473 and 576; "Andrew Holes," in *Illustrated Album of Biography*, 169–70; George B. Winship, "Forty Years of Development in the Red River Valley," in *History of the Red River Valley*, 1:85; T. H. Canfield to Governor Smith, October 18, 1871, Roll 12, Frame 342, Northern Pacific Secretary Records; *Red River Gazette*, July 4, 1872; *A Century Together: A History of Fargo, North Dakota and Moorhead, Minnesota* (Fargo-Moorhead: Centennial Corporation, 1975), 136–37.

33. Benjamin F. Mackall, "Early Days in Moorhead," 1933 address, Northwest Minnesota Historical Center, Minnesota State University, Moorhead; Rev. O. H. Elmer diary, October 20, 1871, typed copy, Clay County Historical Society Archives, Moorhead.

34. Thomas H. Canfield to A. Holes, February 5, 1874, and to L. P. White, March 4, 1874, LS&PS Co. Letterbooks, vol. 72, no. 5, 2, 40–41; T. H. Canfield to J. W. Taylor, January 16, 1873, LS&PS Co. Letterbooks, vol. 71, no. 4, 73.

35. T. H. Canfield to Gentlemen, March 21, 1871, Canfield Papers—Business Correspondence; T. H. Canfield to J. W. Taylor, June 13, July 13, November 25, and December 11, 1872, LS&PS Co. Letterbooks, vol. 70, no. 3, 188, 289, 546, and vol. 71, no. 4, 1; T. H. Canfield to L. P. White, March 31, 1874, and P. O. Ingebricksten, April 1, 1874, LS&PS Co. Letterbooks, vol. 72, no. 5, 121–22, 124; T. H. Canfield to Carrie Canfield, June 24, 1875, Canfield Papers—Personal Correspondence; Lyman P. White to Thomas H. Canfield, April 23 and August 6, 1875, LS&PS Co. Letterbooks, vol. 78.

36. T. H. Canfield to J. H. Sharp, May 2, 1873, and to Andrew Holes, December 11, 1873, LS&PS Co. Letterbooks, vol. 71, no. 4, 341; T. H. Canfield to L. P. White, June 27, 1874, LS&PS Letterpress Books, vol. 72, no. 5, 260.

37. *Red River Star*, March 7, 1874; Thomas H. Canfield to A. Holes, February 5, March 10 and 27, 1874, and to L. P. White, March 27, 1874, LS&PS Co. Letterbooks, vol. 72, no. 5, 3, 68, 108–11; Lyman P. White to George Follett, February 11, 1886, LS&PS Co. Letterbooks, vol. 81; *A Century Together*, 136–37; Henry Johnson, *The Other Side of Main Street: A History Teacher from Sauk Centre* (New York: Columbia University Press, 1943), 119.

38. Hudson, "Towns of the Western Railroads," 46; Lyman P. White to Thomas H. Canfield, April 23, 1875, LS&PS Co. Letterbooks, vol. 78; Thomas H. Canfield to W. B. Nickles, N. K. Hubbard, and others, March 11, 1874, LS&PS Co. Letterbooks, vol. 72, no. 5, 76–77.

39. T. H. Canfield to John W. Taylor, April 3, 1872, Letterbooks, vol. 70, no. 3, 15; T. F. Oakes to R. L. Belknap, October 11, 1881 and Land Committee Board of Directors, July 18, 1889, and January 16, 1890, Box 23 and 32, Northern Pacific Secretary Reports.

40. *Moorhead Weekly News,* October 25, 1894; T. H. Canfield to L. P. White, March 11, 1874, LS&PS Co. Letterbooks, vol. 72, no. 5, 67; T. H. Canfield to J. W. Taylor, February 2, 7 and 29, 1872, LS&PS Co. Letterbooks, vol. 69, no. 2, 282, 348, and 432; *Red River Gazette,* July 4, 1872; Lyman P. White to Thomas H. Canfield, January 19 and April 14, 1875, and to George Follett, June 5, 1875, and April 10, 1877, LS&PS Co. Letterbooks, vol. 78.

41. Lyman P. White to Thomas H. Canfield, April 14, 1875, and to George Follett, January 31 and March 24, 1880, LS&PS Co. Letterbooks, vol. 78 and 80; Thomas H. Canfield to A. Holes, February 5 and March 4, 1874, and to L. P. White and H. A. Bruns, March 4, 1874, LS&PS Co. Letterbooks, vol. 72, no. 5, 3, 37–38, 42.

42. Lyman P. White to George P. Follett, November 15, 1877, LS&PS Co. Letterbooks, vol. 78; George Stark to L. P. White, November 22, 1877, and to Bruns and Finkle, December 12, 1877, LS&PS Co. Letterbooks, vol. 74, no. 7, 87, 101–4; Bruns and Finkle to Grandin Brothers, December 13, 1877, and J. L. Grandin to George Stark, December 20, 1877, Box 14, Northern Pacific Secretary Records; *Fargo Times,* October 18, 1879, and February 5, 1880.

43. Zunz, *Making America Corporate,* 4–5, 8–9, 68–69, posits a third explanation in contrast to manipulation by the power elite or functional management behavior.

44. T. H. Canfield to W. B. Nickles, February 24, 1874, LS&PS Co. letterbooks, vol. 72, no. 5, 18; *Red River Star,* July 6, 1872. On booster spirit as a substantial newspaper activity, see Robert R. Dykstra, *The Cattle Towns* (Lincoln: University of Nebraska Press, 1983), 149–51.

45. T. H. Canfield to George W. Sweet, January 4, 1872, LS&PS Co. Letterbooks, vol. 69, no. 2, 124; George Follett to W. B. Nickles and to J. W. Taylor, August 20, 1872, LS&PS Co. Letterbooks, vol. 70, no. 3, 385–86; T. H. Canfield to W. B. Nickles, April 21, 1873, LS&PS Co. Letterbooks, vol. 71, no. 4, 294–96; *Red River Star,* August 2, 1873.

46. T. H. Canfield to W. B. Nickles, February 25, 1874, LS&PS Co. Letterbooks, vol. 72, no. 5, 18; *Red River Star,* March 7 and August 15, 1874, May 22, October 9, and November 6, 1875, and July 22, 1876.

47. Edward W. Nolan, *Northern Pacific Views: The Railroad Photography of F. Jay Haynes* (Helena: Montana Historical Society Press, 1983), 3–6, 136, 141; *Moorhead Advocate,* September 15, 1877; *Clay County Advocate,* April 24 and May 20, 1880; Diane Shaw, *City Building on the Eastern Frontier: Sorting the New Nineteenth-Century City* (Baltimore: Johns Hopkins University Press, 2004), 20, 152–55.

48. *Red River Star,* August 2 and 9, 1873, and February 7, 1874; *Red River Gazette,* July 4, 1872; Thomas H. Canfield to Andrew Holes, March 10, 1874, and to L. P. White, March 11, 1874, LS&PS Co. Letterbooks, vol. 72, no. 5, 67–69. On local views that LS&PS Company lot prices hurt Moorhead, see *Moorhead: The Key City of the Red River Valley* (St. Paul: Northwestern Publishing Company, 1882), 8–9.

49. *Red River Gazette,* January 17, 1873; George B. Wright to Thomas H. Canfield, December 2, 1872, Canfield Papers—Business Correspondence.

50. T. H. Canfield to [Governor Smith], October 18, 1871, Roll 12, Frames 339–42, Northern Pacific Secretary Records; T. H. Canfield to John W. Taylor, September 26 and October 26, 1871, LS&PS Co. Letterbooks, vol. 68, no. 1, 600–601; T. H. Canfield to G. B. Wright, June 24, 1873, LS&PS Co. Letterbooks, vol. 71, no. 4, 440–41; T. H. Canfield to L. P. White, February 24 and June 4, 1874, LS&PS Co. Letterbooks, vol. 72, no. 5, 21, 231.

51. George Stark to L. P. White, December 17, 1877, LS&PS Co. Letterbooks, vol. 74, no. 7,

110; L. P. White to George Follet, May 17 and October 8, 1878, LS&PS Co. Letterbooks, vol. 78–79.

52. *Red River Star,* August 15, 1874; T. H. Canfield to H. A. Bruns, February 26, 1873, LS&PS Co. Letterbooks, vol. 71, no. 4, 218; T. H. Canfield to L. P. White, March 31 and May 28, 1874, LS&PS Co. Letterbooks, vol. 72, no. 5, 124 and 208; L. P. White to George Stark, December 9, 1876, and to George Follett, September 23, 1877, and March 9, 1878, LS&PS Co. Letterbooks, vol. 78; George Follett to L. P. White, September 28, 1877, LS&PS Co. Letterbooks, vol. 74, no. 7, 49–50; *Moorhead Weekly News,* July 13, 1882.

53. *Red River Star,* May 29 and July 17, 1875; Lyman P. White to George Follett, February 3, 1879, LS&PS Co. Letterbooks, vol. 79; Gary Anderson, "Moorhead vs. Fargo: A Study of Economic Rivalry and Urban Development in the Red River Valley of the North," *North Dakota Quarterly* 42 (autumn 1974): 68.

54. *Red River Star,* July 26, 1873, March 27 and May 1, 1875, and April 22, 1876; *Moorhead Advocate,* August 25, 1877, and March 23, 1878; Moorhead City Council Minutes, June 25, 1878, 83; *Clay County Advocate,* September 14 and October 12, 1878, November 11, 1879; *Moorhead Advocate,* September 9, 1880; *Moorhead Weekly News,* March 11, 1886.

55. James B. Power, "Bits of History Connected with the Early Days of the Northern Pacific Railway and the Organization of Its Land Department," in *Collections of the State Historical Society of North Dakota* (Bismarck: Tribune, State Printers, 1910), 3:344–45, 347; Biographical Material, Folder 1, Box 1, James B. Power Papers, Institute for Regional Studies, North Dakota State University, Fargo; William A. Howard to James B. Power, December 18, 1872, Roll 25, Frames 106–7; James B. Power to William A. Howard, November 25, 1873, Roll 12, Frames 610–11, Northern Pacific Land Dept. Records; Robinson, *History of North Dakota,* 132; Winks, *Frederick Billings,* 209; Hiram M. Drache, *Day of the Bonanza* (Fargo: North Dakota Institute for Regional Studies, 1964), 34, 39–40.

56. James B. Power to editors, *Country Gentleman,* May 10, 1877, editor, *Pioneer Press,* May 8, 1877, editor, *New York Tribune,* May 10, 1877, Folder 5, Box 1; James B. Power to G. W. Cass, May 26, 1876, and March 14, 1878, and to Frederick Billings, August 4, 1876, Folder 4 and 6, Box 1, Power Papers; Murray, *Valley Comes of Age,* 108–9; Drache, *Bonanza,* 43–45; James B. Power to George Stark, September 11, 1876, Roll 35, Frames 271–75, Northern Pacific Secretary Records; *Fargo Times,* April 12, 1879.

57. "Fargo Founded: Thomas H. Canfield's Story," *Record* 1 (December 1895): 10; *Fargo Forum,* April 11, 1935; "History of Fargo," 1:487–88; T. H. Canfield to [Governor Smith], October 18, 1871, Roll 12, Frames 339–42, Northern Pacific Secretary Records.

58. Glasrud, *Roy Johnson's Red River Valley,* 278; Thomas H. Canfield Report, September 11, 1873, Canfield Papers—Business Correspondence; T. H. Canfield to George B. Wright, May 2, 1873, LS&PS Co. Letterbooks, vol. 71, no. 4, 345–46; James B. Power to Frederick Billings, July 29, 1880, Box 18, Northern Pacific Secretary Records.

59. Winship, "Forty Years," and "History of Fargo," 1:85, 487–88; Glasrud, *Roy Johnson's Red River Valley,* 336; *Fargo Forum,* January 18, 1927, and April 11, 1935; James B. Power to Frederick Billings, July 29, 1880, Box 18, Northern Pacific Secretary Records; Notes on Original Town Site, Box 29, Folder 1 and 4, Roy P. Johnson/Louis Pfaller Collection, North Dakota State Historical Library Archives, Bismarck.

60. Glasrud, *Roy Johnson's Red River Valley,* 257, 263–64, 267–68; T. H. Canfield to John W.

Taylor, December 20, 1871, LS&PS Co. Letterbooks, vol. 69, no. 2, 80; T. H. Canfield to John W. Taylor and George B. Wright, October 26, 1871, and to Joseph E. Turner, November 2, 1871, LS&PS Co. Letterbooks, vol. 68, no. 1, 646–47, 650–51, 674; Frederick Billings to A. B. Nettleton, February 14, 1872, and to George B. Wright, May 9, 1872, Roll 16, Frames 184–86, 454–55, and George B. Wright to Frederick Billings, May 25, 1872, Roll 6, Frames 324–26, Northern Pacific Land Dept. Records.

61. Glasrud, *Roy Johnson's Red River Valley*, 255, 257, 270; "History of Fargo," 1:490–91; Harnsberger, *Jay Cooke and Minnesota*, 86–88.

62. Glasrud, *Roy Johnson's Red River Valley*, 267–68, 270, 272, 277–78; "History of Fargo," 1:491–92; Harnsberger, *Jay Cooke and Minnesota*, 88–89. On the St. Paul press debate, see George I. Foster Scrapbook, 1871–74, Box 1, Folder 9, Institute for Regional Studies.

63. Glasrud, *Roy Johnson's Red River Valley*, 314; Fred Adelbert Bill et al., *Life on the Red River of the North, 1857–1887* (Baltimore: Wirth Brothers, 1947), 98. The pervasive memories of the Fargo mire shared by several early residents are found in Angela Boleyn, *Quarter Sections and Wide Horizons* (Bismarck: North Dakota State Library, 1978), 76, 248, 298, 329. On local opinion regarding town-site development policies, see *Red River Gazette*, June 5, 1873; *Fargo Express*, June 14, 1873; James B. Power to A. Wackerhagen, November 26, 1873, Roll 12, Frame 624, Northern Pacific Land Dept. Records, and to Frederick Billings, July 29, 1880, Box 18, Northern Pacific Secretary Records.

64. *Fargo Express*, August 6, 1874; "North Dakota Town Lots—Fargo," Box 3, and Board of Directors Minutes, September 22, 1879, vol. 31, 238–39, Box 8, Northern Pacific Land Dept. Records; James B. Power to Frederick Billings, July 15 and November 6, 1880, Box 18 and 19, and Annual Report, 1878, Box 1, Northern Pacific Secretary Records.

65. D. H. Mason to George Stark, July 13, 1876, Roll 35, Frame 30, Northern Pacific Secretary Records; Meeting of the Land Committee, January 15 and June 18, 1884, Minutes of the Land Committee, vol. 31 and 32, Box 8, Northern Pacific Land Dept. Records; J. B. Power to A. Wackerhagen, November 17, 1874, Roll 13, Frame 665, Northern Pacific Land Dept. Records; Hiram M. Drache, "The Economic Aspects of the Northern Pacific Railroad in North Dakota," *North Dakota History* 34 (fall 1967): 326–27; H. Roger Grant, "The Standardized Railroad Station on the Great Plains, 1870–1920," in *The Great Plains: Environment and Culture*, ed. Brian W. Blouet and Frederick C. Luebke (Lincoln: University of Nebraska Press, 1977), 119, 122.

66. Anderson, "Moorhead vs. Fargo," 75–76; Board of Director Resolutions, September 12, 1871, Roll 12, Frame 39, Northern Pacific Secretary Records; A. A. White to George Stark, January 5, 1878, and C. C. Sanborn to George Stark, February 16, 1878, Box 14, Northern Pacific Secretary Records; J. N. Tyner to C. B. Wright, September 2, 1875, Roll 30, Frame 277, Northern Pacific Secretary Records; T. J. Brady to George Stark, September 16, 1876, Roll 35, Frames 295–96, Northern Pacific Secretary Records; H. E. Sargent to Frederick Billings, Box 16, Northern Pacific Secretary Records; Drache, "Economic Aspects of the Northern Pacific Railroad," 327, 361–65.

67. James B. Power to J. A. Johnson, April 4, 1899, Folder 3, Box 4, Power Papers; "History of Fargo," 1:492–93; Fargo City Council Minutes, November 25, 1878, vol. 1, 121, August 4, 1879, and June 14, 1881, vol. 2, 13–14, 155, Institute for Regional Studies; *Second Annual Report of the Chamber of Commerce of Fargo, North Dakota, 1880–1881* (Fargo: Dakota Argus, 1881), 30; *Fargo Forum and Daily Republican*, August 21, 1893.

68. E. S. Tyler, et al. to the President and Board of Directors, February 1879, and H. E. Sargent

to F. Billings, February 5, 1879, Box 14, and July 1 and 11, 1879, Box 15, Northern Pacific Secretary Records; Drache, "Economic Aspects of the Northern Pacific," 353–54.

69. S. G. Comstock to Frederick Billings, June 25, 1879, George Stark to Frederick Billings, June 13, 1879, and T. H. Canfield to Frederick Billings, June 26, 1879, Box 15, Northern Pacific Secretary Records; W. A. Kindred to Frederick Billings, June 25, 1879, Box 15, Northern Pacific Secretary Records; H. E. Sargent to Frederick Billings, June 25, July 15 and 17, Box 15, Northern Pacific Secretary Records; *Clay County Advocate,* March 13 and October 28, 1880.

70. *Fargo Evening Republican,* February 20, 1882; *Fargo Express,* August 6, 1874; *Northern Pacific Mirror,* November 21, 1874, February 27 and May 15, 1875; *Clay County Advocate,* January 11, 1879; James B. Power to C. B. Wright, October 12, 1877, Box 13, Northern Pacific Secretary Records; Melva Moline, *The Forum: First Hundred Years* (Fargo: Moline, 1879), 3; Robinson, *History of North Dakota,* 316.

71. Sig Mickelson, *The Northern Pacific Railroad and the Selling of the West: A Nineteenth-Century Public Relations Venture* (Sioux Falls: Center of Western Studies, 1993), 31–32, 44, 93, 98, 100, 112–13; *Fargo Times,* September 18, 1875; *Fargo Daily Times,* February 1 and April 12, 1879; James B. Power to George Stark, September 11, 1879, Box 16, Northern Pacific Secretary Records.

72. Mickelson, *Northern Pacific Railroad,* 16–20, 135–36; *Fargo Times,* September 18, 1875, and August 2, 1879; *Fargo Daily Times,* February 1, 1879; *Red River Star,* October 4, 1873; *Clay County Advocate,* April 3, 1880; *Moorhead Advocate,* September 23, 1880; Annual Report, 1883, 38–39, Box 1, Northern Pacific Secretary Records.

73. Drache, *Bonanza,* 46, 49, 68–69, 72; Murray, *Valley Comes of Age,* 108–9. On North Dakota railroad colonization policy, see Hedges, "Colonization Work of the Northern Pacific Railroad," 327–34, 340; Ross R. Cotroneo, "Northern Pacific Officials and the Disposition of the Railroad's Land Grant in North Dakota After 1888," *North Dakota History* 37 (spring 1970): 79, and "Reserving the Subsurface: The Mineral Lands Policy of the Northern Pacific Railway, 1900–1954," *North Dakota History* 40.3 (1970): 16.

74. Drache, *Bonanza,* 57–58; James B. Power to C. F. Kindred, December 14, 1880, to A. H. Barney, January 11, 1881, and to W. Bros, August 19, 1881, Folder 2, Box 2, Power Papers.

75. Ronald Howell Ridgley, "Railroads and the Development of the Dakotas, 1872–1914" (Ph.D. dissertation, Indiana University, 1967), 160, 169ff., 183–87.

76. James B. Power to Frederick Billings, July 29 and August 10, 1880, Box 18, Northern Pacific Secretary Records. Winks, *Frederick Billings,* 256–57, says that the Northern Pacific and other western railroads used varied town-site strategies depending on time and place. The Northern Pacific may have accepted Power's strategy because it did not expect an early rival west of Fargo. Hedges, "Colonization Work of the Northern Pacific Railroad," 336–37, reports two Northern Pacific plans in 1883 for new west-river Dakota towns: (1) total ownership and management of lot sales; or (2) half interest and private parties sold lots.

2. BOOSTER DREAMS

1. *Illustrated Album of Biography of the Famous Valley of the Red River of the North and Park Regions* (Chicago: Alden, Ogle & Co., 1889), 703; *Minneapolis Journal,* June 19, 1910.

2. Frederick Jackson Turner, *The Frontier in American History* (New York: Henry Holt and

Company, 1920), 38 and 268; William Cronon, *Nature's Metropolis: Chicago and the Great West* (New York: W. W. Norton, 1991), 150; Richard White, *"It's Your Misfortune and None of My Own": A History of the American West* (Norman: University of Oklahoma Press, 1991), 285; Patricia Nelson Limerick, *The Legacy of Conquest: The Unbroken Past of the American West* (New York: W. W. Norton, 1987), 124–25.

3. *Illustrated Album of Biography*, 703–4; *Minnesota Historical Society Collections—Minnesota Biographies, 1655–1912* 14 (1912), 86; *Moorhead Weekly News*, March 11, 1886, and October 25, 1894. Also see *Roy Johnson's Red River Valley*, ed. Clarence A. Glasrud (Moorhead: Red River Valley Historical Society, 1982), 329–30, 287, and *A Century Together: A History of Fargo, North Dakota, and Moorhead, Minnesota* (Fargo-Moorhead: Centennial Corporation, 1975), 138–39.

4. Donald S. Lilleboe, "Steam Navigation on the Red River of the North, 1859–1881" (master's thesis, University of North Dakota, 1977), 70, 73–74; *A Century Together*, 22–23; Ralph W. Hidy et al., *The Great Northern Railway: A History* (Boston: Harvard Business School Press, 1988), 22; Frank M. Painter, "Romance on the Red River," *Fargo Daily Courier-News*, May 28 and June 11, 1916.

5. Lilleboe, "Steam Navigation," 81–82: *A Century Together*, 22; Glasrud, *Roy Johnson's Red River Valley*, 383–85; Albro Martin, *James J. Hill and the Opening of the Northwest* (New York: Oxford University Press, 1976), 84–85; Painter, "Romance"; *Fargo Daily Courier-News*, June 18, 1916; *Red River Star*, February 6 and October 2, 1875.

6. Stanley N. Murray, *The Valley Comes of Age* (Fargo: North Dakota Institute for Regional Studies, 1967), 81, 83, 94; Glasrud, *Roy Johnson's Red River Valley*, 354, 384; Gary Anderson, "Moorhead vs. Fargo: A Study of Economic Rivalry and Urban Development in the Red River Valley of the North," *North Dakota Quarterly* 42 (autumn 1974): 63; *Clay County Advocate*, April 26, 1879, and February 7, 1880; *Red River Gazette*, April 3 and May 29, 1873; *Red River Star*, July 26, 1873, June 5 and 19, 1875.

7. H. E. Towne to George Stark and W. S. Alexander to George Stark, November 9, 1875, Roll 32, Frames 81–82 and 86–87, G. C. Sanborn to George Stark, September 1, 1876, Roll 35, Frames 241–42, Secretary Records, Northern Pacific Railway Company Papers, Minnesota Historical Society, St. Paul; Mark Peihl, "Steamboating on the Red!" *Clay County Historical Society* [hereafter, *CCHS*] *Newsletter*, 18 (March/April 1995): 7; *Red River Star*, May 13, 1876.

8. *Red River Star*, January 17, 1874, and January 29, 1876; John Harnsberger and Robert P. Wilkins, "Transportation on the Northern Plains, IV: Minneapolis, Manitoba and Monopoly," *North Dakota Quarterly* 29 (autumn 1961): 101–3; *Red River Star*, October 3 and 10, 1874, and May 15, 1875.

9. Lilleboe, "Steam Navigation," 89; Peihl, "Steamboating on the Red!" 7; *A Century Together*, 22; *Moorhead Advocate*, November 10, 1877; *Clay County Advocate*, May 20, 1880; *Moorhead Weekly News*, May 7, 1885; H. T. Alsop, "Sketch," January 20, 1940, Alsop Brothers Freight Line Papers, Minnesota Historical Society; *Second Annual Report of the Chamber of Commerce of Fargo, North Dakota, 1880–1881* (Fargo: Argus Printing Company, 1881), 43; *Fargo Sunday Argus*, June 17, 1883; *Moorhead Weekly News*, June 25, 1885, April 28, 1887, May 3, 1888.

10. Quoted in Fred Adelbert Bill et al., *Life on the Red River of the North, 1857 to 1887* (Baltimore: Wirth Brothers, 1947), 109; *A Century Together*, 23; *Red River Star*, November 1, 1873, November 13, 1875, and July 24, 1876; *Clay County Advocate*, August 17, 1878, and April 19, 1879; *Moorhead Weekly News*, October 4, 1883, and August 5, 1886.

11. Lilleboe, "Steam Navigation," 71–72, 103ff., 112–13, 124; *Red River Star,* January 25, April 5, and August 9, 1873, and April 8, 1876; *Moorhead Advocate,* December 15, 1877; *Clay County Advocate,* May 17, October 25, and November 29, 1879, and March 27, 1880; *Moorhead Weekly News,* July 27 and August 10, 1882.

12. *Moorhead Weekly News,* July 27 and August 17, 1882; February 7 and 14, December 11, 1884; December 31, 1885, and May 26, 1892; Edward Chase Kirkland, *Industry Comes of Age: Business, Labor and Public Policy, 1860–1897* (Chicago: Quadrangle Paperback, 1967), 104–5.

13. Carl Abbott, *Boosters and Businessmen: Popular Economic Thought and Urban Growth in the Antebellum Middle West* (Westport, Conn.: Greenwood Press, 1981), 4–6, 112–13, 121–22, 126; Carroll Van West, *Capitalism on the Frontier: Billings and the Yellowstone Valley in the Nineteenth Century* (Lincoln: University of Nebraska Press, 1993), 147–49; Eric H. Monkkonen, *America Becomes Urban: The Development of U.S. Cities and Towns, 1790–1980* (Berkeley: University of California Press, 1988), 83. For local expressions of the need for an iron foundry and other manufacturing as well as the essential bounty of rich agricultural lands, see *Moorhead Advocate,* December 29, 1877, and September 23, 1880.

14. *Red River Star,* April 26, May 24, and August 9, 1873, October 3, 1874, June 5, 1875, and February 12, 1876; *Clay County Advocate,* January 4 and 11, 1879; *Daily Argonaut,* January 15, 1882; *Moorhead Weekly News,* August 4, 1898.

15. *Red River Star,* February 14, 1874; *Clay County Advocate,* May 20, 1880.

16. *Moorhead Weekly News,* August 17 and 24, 1882, August 2, 1883; *A Century Together,* 143.

17. Lewis E. Atherton, *The Frontier Merchant in Mid-America* (Columbia: University of Missouri Press, 1971), 9, 16–21, 30–33, 53, 163–64, and *Main Street on the Middle Border* (Chicago: Quadrangle Paperback, 1966), 54. For more recent interpretations by "new western historians" on merchants and entrepreneurial activity, see Rodman W. Paul, *The Far West and the Great West and the Great Plains in Transition, 1859–1900* (New York: Harper & Row, 1988), 60–61; Cronon, *Nature's Metropolis,* 34–35, 47, 319, 321–23, 326; Limerick, *Legacy of Conquest,* 62–63, 67, 76–77; White, *"It's Your Misfortune,"* 417.

18. *Red River Star,* July 5, 1873, July 4, 1874, and July 3, 1875; *Moorhead Weekly News,* September 6, 1883, February 16 and March 23, 1893; *Clay County Advocate,* August 16, 1879; *Moorhead Advocate,* August 25 and December 8, 1877.

19. *A Century Together,* 140; *Illustrated Album of Biography,* 704; *Red River Star,* July 6, 1872; *Moorhead Advocate,* June 9 and September 15, 1877, March 9, 1878; *Clay County Advocate,* June 1 and 29, 1878; *Fargo Times,* March 29, 1879; Bruns and Finkle to J. J. Hill, November 21, 1874, James J. Hill Correspondence, Box 2, Great Northern Railway Company Records Minnesota Historical Society; R. G. Dun Company Collection, Minnesota, vol. 2, Clay County, 3, R. G. Dun Records, Baker Library, Harvard University.

20. Glasrud, *Roy Johnson's Red River Valley,* 424; *Red River Star,* February 14, May 23, October 3 and 17, 1874; Thomas H. Canfield to H. A. Bruns, March 4, 1874, LS&PS Co. Letterbooks, vol. 72, no. 5, 37, Northern Pacific Papers; *Illustrated Album of Biography,* 704; *A Century Together,* 142.

21. R. G. Dun and Company Collection, Minnesota, vol. 2, Clay County, 9; *Red River Star,* December 5, 1874, and September 18, 1875; *Moorhead Advocate,* August 18 and November 10, 1877; *Clay County Advocate,* October 14, 1880; *Moorhead Weekly News,* June 21 and September 13, 1883, April 10 and May 22, 1884, January 22, 1885, April 29, 1886, March 24, May 19, and August 11, 1887; Glasrud, *Roy Johnson's Red River Valley,* 424.

22. John Turner and C. R. Semling, *History of Clay and Norman Counties* (Indianapolis: B. F. Brown, 1918), 1:264; George Stark to Bruns and Finkle, December 12, 1877, LS&PS Co. Letterbooks, vol. 74, no. 7, 101–2; *Clay County Advocate,* June 29, 1878, and August 9, 1879; *Fargo Times,* November 15, 1879.

23. *Clay County Advocate,* March 22, 1879; *Fargo Times,* March 29, 1879; *Fargo Weekly Argus,* February 18, 1880; and *Moorhead Weekly News,* March 11, 1886; Solomon Gilman Comstock, "Memoir," *Red River Valley Historian* (winter 1974–75): 4. The large scale of the supply business in terms of dollars, goods, and retailers is documented in a surviving fragment of a Bruns letterbook, February–April 1882, located at the Clay County Historical Society Archives, Moorhead.

24. *A Century Together,* 142–43, 200; *Moorhead Advocate,* December 16, 1880; *Fargo Daily Argus,* February 4 and 18, 1881; *Fargo Sunday Argus,* March 18, 1883; *Moorhead Weekly News,* April 11, 1889, and October 25, 1894. On frontier banking, see Keith Bryant Jr., "Entering Global Economy," in *The Oxford History of the American West,* ed. Clyde A. Milner II et al. (New York: Oxford University Press, 1994), 229, and Henry C. Klassen, "New Banks in New Societies: The Conrads in Fort Benton, Great Falls, and Kalispell," Northern Great Plains History Conference, September 28–October 1, 1994.

25. Turner and Semling, *History of Clay and Norman Counties,* 1:230.

26. Atherton, *Frontier Merchant in Mid-America,* 15–16; Turner and Semling, *History of Clay and Norman Counties,* 1:217, 225–26; *Fargo and Moorhead City Directory, 1900* (St. Paul: Pettibone Directory Company, 1900), 288–97.

27. Kirkland, *Industry Comes of Age,* 255–56; *A Century Together,* 152–53; Mark Peihl, "Cream-Colored Bricks That Built a Town," *CCHS Newsletter* 15 (March/April 1992): 3–5; *Clay County Advocate,* June 15, 1878; *Moorhead Weekly News,* May 4, 1882, October 20, 1887, and February 1, 1900.

28. *Moorhead Weekly News,* November 9, 1882, June 21, 1883, April 2, 1885, March 17, 1892, October 12, 1893, October 31, 1895, August 13, 1896, and August 2, 1900.

29. *A Century Together,* 146–47, 150–52; Moorhead Board of Trade, *The Valley of the Red River of the North, and the City of Moorhead, Minnesota* (Cleveland: J. B. Savage, 1883), 21; *Moorhead Weekly News,* January 19, February 9, and March 23, 1893, and October 17, 1895.

30. *A Century Together,* 220; *Red River Star,* July 25, 1874, January 15 and February 26, 1876; *Moorhead Advocate,* October 13, 1877; *Moorhead Weekly News,* May 16 and July 18, 1889.

31. *A Century Together,* 222; *Moorhead Advocate,* September 15, 1877; *Clay County Advocate,* June 24, 1880; *Moorhead Weekly News,* September 7, 1882, May 29 and August 21, 1884, May 12, 1887, and April 26, 1894; Rev. O. H. Elmer Diary, November 10, 1880, typed manuscript copy, Clay County Historical Society Archives, Moorhead; *Red River Star,* October 11, 1873, and July 17, 1875; Murray, *Valley Comes of Age,* 161–62.

32. Augustus J. Veenendahl Jr., *Slow Train to Paradise: How Dutch Investment Helped Build American Railroads* (Stanford, Calif.: Stanford University Press, 1996), 138–39; Gregory C. Harness, "Solomon Gilman Comstock: Prairie Lawyer, Legislator and Businessman" (master's thesis, Moorhead State College, 1976), 12, 14, 18–21, 97–98; Comstock, "Memoir," 4; Ada Louise Comstock, "Some Memories of Her Life Up to 1943," Carton 2, Ada Louise Comstock Notestein Papers, Schlesinger Library, Radcliffe College, Cambridge; Comstock and White to J. J. Hill, April 8, 1892, Box 21, Correspondence, Solomon G. Comstock Papers, Northwest Minnesota Historical Center, Minnesota State University, Moorhead.

33. Murray, *Valley Comes of Age,* 60–61; S. G. Comstock to J. J. Hill, May 12 and November 23, 1879, and October 21 and 23, 1880, Box 3, James J. Hill Correspondence, Great Northern Records.

34. S. G. Comstock to J. J. Hill, October 21 and 23, 1880, Box 3, James J. Hill Correspondence, Great Northern Records; A. B. Stickney to S. G. Comstock, June 15, 1880, Box 4, Correspondence, Comstock Papers; *Clay County Advocate,* November 4 and December 16, 1880; Mark Peihl, "Railroad War in 1880," *CCHS Newsletter* 18 (November/December 1995): 9–10.

35. Martin, *James J. Hill,* 225, 286; Elwyn B. Robinson, *History of North Dakota* (Lincoln: University of Nebraska Press, 1966), 142–43; H. E. Sargent to Frederick Billings, April 8, 1881, and T. F. Oakes to H. Villard, June 3, 1881, Box 21; Memorandum of Proposed Agreement between Northern Pacific and SPMM, July 23, 1881, and H. Haupt to T. F. Oakes, September 22, 1881, Box 22; T. F. Oakes to H. Haupt, March 4, 1882, and H. Haupt to A. Manvel, March 16, 1882, Box 25, Northern Pacific Secretary Records.

36. Robert P. Wilkins and Wynona Huchette Wilkins, *North Dakota: A Bicentennial History* (New York: W. W. Norton, 1977), 52; Michael P. Malone, *James J. Hill: Empire Builder of the Northwest* (Norman: University of Oklahoma Press, 1996), 90; *Moorhead Advocate,* September 9, 1880; *Moorhead Weekly Argonaut,* February 3, 1881; *Daily Argonaut,* January 10 and March 4, 1882; *Moorhead Weekly News,* May 31 and June 7, 1883, April 9 and June 25, 1885.

37. *Fargo and Moorhead City Directory, 1884* (Fargo: G. E. Nichols and R. W. Bliss, 1884), 242; *Moorhead Weekly Argonaut,* January 13, 1881; *Moorhead Weekly News,* July 19, 1888.

38. S. G. Comstock to J. J. Hill, October 23, 1880, Box 3, and A. J. Harwood to J. J. Hill, January 9 and February 21, 1882, Box 6, James J. Hill Correspondence, Great Northern Records; A. B. Stickney to S. G. Comstock, June 15, 1880, Box 4, J. J. Hill to S. G. Comstock, August 30, 1881, Box 5, A. Manvel to S. G. Comstock, June 24 and August 10, 1882, Box 6, D. A. McKinley to S. G. Comstock, November 20 and December 3 and 5, 1883, Box 6, and "Minutes of Meetings of Board of Directors of Minnesota and Dakota Northern Railroad Company," vol. 48, Box 71, Comstock Papers. Also see Glasrud, *Roy Johnson's Red River Valley,* 284; Harness, "Solomon Gilman Comstock: Prairie Lawyer," 129–30, 101, 103–4; *Clay Country Advocate,* February 8, 1879; *Moorhead Weekly News,* October 25, 1883, and November 29, 1888; Elmer Diary, August 22, 1884.

39. Merchant Bank loans to Bruns were reported in the *Moorhead Weekly News,* February 18, 1892; S. G. Comstock to J. J. Hill, November 27, 1880, Box 3, and H. A. Bruns to J. J. Hill, July 18, 1881, Box 2, James J. Hill Correspondence, Great Northern Records; *Moorhead Advocate,* December 23, 1880; *Moorhead: The Key City of the Red River Valley* (St. Paul: Northwestern Publishing Company, 1882), 6, 12–13, 90–93; Moorhead Board of Trade, *Valley of the Red River of the North,* 34–35; *Daily Argonaut,* January 9, 15, 17, and 18, 1882; *Moorhead Weekly News,* May 7, 1885; *A Century Together,* 156–57, 201.

40. Moorhead Board of Trade, *Valley of the Red River of the North,* 20–22; *Daily Argonaut,* February 9, 10, and 11, 1882.

41. *Fargo Daily Argus,* January 28, 1881; *Fargo Evening Republican,* April 7, 1882; "Articles of Incorporation of the Moorhead Foundry, Car and Agricultural Works," vol. 49, Box 71, Comstock Papers; Harness, "Solomon Gilman Comstock: Prairie Lawyer," 137–38; *A Century Together,* 218; Moorhead Board of Trade, *Valley of the Red River of the North,* 22, 24; *Moorhead Weekly News,* April 13, August 10 and 24, September 7, and December 21, 1882; October 25 and November 15, 1883; July 10, 1884; February 19, March 26, and May 28, 1885; Elmer Diary, May 4, 1885.

42. *A Century Together,* 218; *Moorhead Weekly News,* June 10 and August 5, 1886, and January 14, 1892.

43. *Clay County Advocate,* February 8, 1879, March 6 and 13, 1880; *Moorhead Weekly Argonaut,* February 17, 1881; *Moorhead Weekly News,* January 3, March 27, and September 11, 1884, April 2, 1885, April 22, 1886, and March 17, 1887; Martin, *James J. Hill,* 285–86. On the strategy of hinterland development, see Russell S. Kirby, "Nineteenth-Century Patterns of Railroad Development on the Great Plains," *Great Plains Quarterly* 3 (summer 1983): 158–59, 166.

44. S. G. Comstock to J. J. Hill, April 16 and July 19, 1880, August 2 and September 15, 1881, and October 11, 1883, Box 3, James J. Hill Correspondence, Great Northern Records; Glasrud, *Roy Johnson's Red River Valley,* 302.

45. S. G. Comstock to J. J. Hill, March 8 and 26, 1881, January 9 and October 15, 1884, March 12 and April 14, 1887, Box 3, James J. Hill Correspondence, Great Northern Records; A. Manvel to S. G. Comstock, August 11, 1887, Box 11, Correspondence, Comstock Papers; *Moorhead Weekly News,* March 27, 1884, September 11, 1884, April 2, 1885, April 22, 1886, March 17 and April 21, 1887. On town sites, see Thomas White Harvey, "The Making of Railroad Towns in Minnesota's Red River Valley" (master's thesis, Pennsylvania State University, 1982), 56–59.

46. S. G. Comstock to J. J. Hill, March 5, 1880, August 31, 1881, January 26, 1882, and July 7, 1883, Box 3, James J. Hill Correspondence, Great Northern Records; "Minutes of Meetings of Board of Directors of Minnesota and Dakota Northern Railroad Company," January 25, 1882, and November 20, 1883, vol. 48, Box 71, and "History of the Minnesota and Dakota Northern Railroad Company," Office of the Comptroller, March 1946, Box 71, Comstock Papers.

47. S. G. Comstock to J. J. Hill, April 15, May 4, and June 2, 1882, Box 3, James J. Hill Correspondence, Great Northern Records; H. Haupt to T. F. Oakes, November 23, 1881, Box 24, J. L. Grandin and Oliver Dalrymple to T. F. Oakes, March 1, 1882, and A. Anderson to T. F. Oakes, April 19, 1882, Box 25, Northern Pacific Secretary Records.

48. *Moorhead Weekly Argonaut,* January 13 and December 23, 1881; *Daily Argonaut,* January 12 and 14, February 25, and August 10, 1882; *Moorhead Weekly News,* August 10, 1882.

49. Rendig Fels, *American Business Cycles, 1865–1897* (Chapel Hill: University of North Carolina Press, 1959), 128–29; Robinson, *History of North Dakota,* 151, 153–54; *Moorhead Weekly News,* April 6, 1899.

50. "Jas. Douglass" and "Mrs. Wilhelmina Douglas," R. G. Dun Company Collection, Minnesota, vol. 2, Clay County, 1872–79, 1, 12, and 21; Mark Peihl, "Endangered: Moorhead's Historic Kassenborg Block and Douglas House," *CCHS Newsletter* 26 (November/December 2003): 10–12, 15.

51. "John Erickson," R. G. Dun Company Collection, Minnesota, vol. 2, Clay County, 1873–76, 6 and 14; *Moorhead Weekly News,* January 18, 1900.

52. *Moorhead Weekly News,* January 10, 1884.

53. F. Jay Haynes to Lily [Haynes], [December] 1877, Box 1, Folder 6, L. S. Haynes Collection, Montana State University, Bozeman; *Illustrated Album of Biography,* 706; *Moorhead Weekly News,* April 30, 1885; *Moorhead Daily News,* May 14, 1954; *Minneapolis Journal,* June 19, 1910; *Fargo Daily Republican,* November 27, 1882; *Fargo Sunday Argus,* May 6, 1883, and December 4, 1887.

54. Hidy et al., *Great Northern Railway,* 49; Memorandum of Financial Condition of H. A. Bruns, April 30, 1890, General Correspondence, James J. Hill Papers, Hill Library, St. Paul; *Fargo Sunday Argus,* April 15, 1888. Grand Pacific Hotel nightly registrations ranging from seventeen

to forty-three were reported in the *Moorhead Daily News* between February 8 and May 9, 1892. Population figures are from *Moorhead Weekly News,* January 25, 1883, and *A Century Together,* 44.

55. *Moorhead Weekly News,* April 21, 1887, and February 23, 1888; Henry A. Bruns and Matilda Bruns, July 12, 1888, Warranty Deed to St. Paul Trust Company, Moorhead Properties, 1888–1921, Hill Papers; Malone, *James J. Hill,* 91–92; *Fargo Sunday Argus,* September 4 and October 16, 1887, and May 6, 1888. On February 18, 1892, the *Moorhead Weekly News* reported that Bruns had earlier raised an additional seventy thousand dollars for the Merchants Bank.

56. Memorandum on Financial Condition of H. A. Bruns, April 30, 1890, General Correspondence, Hill Papers.

57. *Minneapolis Journal,* June 19, 1910; Fels, *American Business Cycles,* 212, 218, 220–22, 224–25.

58. *Moorhead Weekly News,* February 11 and 18, and March 3, 1892; April 23 and May 14, 1896; *Moorhead Daily News,* February 8, 9, 11, 12, 13, 18, and July 18, 1892. Bruns protected himself instead of the depositors and failed to avert the Merchants Bank disaster, according to W. J. Hahn to S. G. Comstock, December 30, 1891, Box 21, Comstock Papers.

59. "Judgment in Case of J. J. Hill against H. A. Bruns," May 21, 1892, District Court, Clay County, Moorhead Properties, 1888–1921; H. A. Bruns to W. A. Stephens, November 11, 1892, General Correspondence; Agreement between J. J. Hill and H. A. Bruns and Wife, December 20, 1892 and J. J. Hill to Henry A. and Matilda Bruns, June 10, 1893, Moorhead Properties, 1891–1921, Hill Papers.

60. Examination of Grand Pacific Hotel, March 9, 1893, Circular Letter, March 30, 1893, and Accounts of John A. Baker, Box 2, Agreement with John A. Baker, September 15, 1893, Box 3, Moorhead Properties, 1891–1921, Hill Papers; Baker's failure to pay rent is stated in W. A. Stephens to S. G. Comstock, July 21, 1894, Box 23, Comstock Papers; *Moorhead Weekly News,* September 28, 1893, and September 19, 1895.

61. S. G. Comstock to J. J. Hill, June 8, 1893, General Correspondence, and S. G. Comstock to J. J. Hill, April 30 and May 2, 1896, Moorhead Properties, 1888–1902, Hill Papers; Moorhead City Council Minutes, April 16, 1896. Hill expressed his attitudes in telegrams to S. G. Comstock, May 1 and 2, 1896, Box 24, Comstock Papers.

62. David McCoy to M. C. Healion, July 7, 1896, Moorhead Properties, 1888–1902, Hill Papers; *Moorhead Weekly News,* October 31, 1895, May 7 and 21, 1896.

63. H. C. Eller to M. C. Healion, September 18, 1896, Moorhead Properties, Box 3, Hill Papers; *Moorhead Weekly News,* March 11, 1886, February 11, 1892, and October 25, 1894.

64. *Minneapolis Journal,* June 19, 1910; James Oliver Robertson, *America's Business* (New York: Hill and Wang, 1985), 144–45; Malone, *James J. Hill,* 78.

65. *Minneapolis Journal,* June 19, 1910; *Moorhead Weekly News,* October 25, 1894.

66. White, "It's Your Misfortune," 285 and 417; Cronon, *Nature's Metropolis,* 321–23.

67. "John Kurtz," "Kurtz and Mackall Drug," "J. H. Sharp," and "F. Jay Haynes," R. G. Dun Company Collection, Minnesota, vol. 2, Clay County, 1875–79, 2, 5, and 7; F. Jay Haynes to Lily S. Haynes, November 27, 1877, and [January 1878?], Box 1, Haynes Collection.

68. S. G. Comstock to Ada Louise Comstock, January 25, 1910, Folder 58, Notestein Papers.

69. Harness, "Solomon Gilman Comstock," 4–6, 142–43; Sarah Bell Comstock to Ada Louise Comstock, June 21, 1933, Carton 2, Folder 64, Notestein Papers; Clara Gilman to Solomon G. Comstock, June 12, 1889, Comstock Letter File, Box 15, Comstock Papers.

70. *Moorhead Weekly News,* October 26, 1882.

71. *Moorhead Weekly News,* December 6, 1888, October 10, 1889, January 12 and 19, 1899; Christine Hagen Stafne, "Pioneering in the Red River Valley," Typescript, 1943, 91, Northwest Minnesota Historical Center.

72. *Moorhead Weekly News,* August 8, 1889.

73. *Minneapolis Journal,* June 19, 1910.

74. Thomas C. Kurtz to S. G. Comstock, April 2, 1880, Correspondence, Comstock Papers; *Clay County Advocate,* March 20 and June 24, 1880; *Fargo and Moorhead City Directory, 1900,* 288–97.

3. Boomtown on the Prairie

1. Tim Holzkamm and Dean Dormanen, *Fargo Historic Context Study* (Fargo: Historic Preservation Commission, 1993), 23, 35–36; Leonard K. Eaton, *Gateway Cities and Other Essays* (Ames: Iowa State University Press, 1989), xiv, 8; William Cronon, *Nature's Metropolis: Chicago and the Great West* (New York: W. W. Norton, 1991), 376–77; Lawrence H. Larsen and Robert T. Johnson, "A Story That Never Was: North Dakota's Urban Development," *North Dakota History* 47 (fall 1980): 8–9; *Fargo Forum and Daily Republican,* July 19, 1907. A stimulating discussion of how gateways connected the eastern industrial core with the resource-producing Great Plains is provided by Carl Abbott in "Frontiers and Sections: Cities and Regions in American Growth," *American Quarterly* 37 (1985): 395–410. Abbott suggests that cities fostered the development of regions and integrated them into the national economy.

2. Donald S. Lilleboe, "Steam Navigation on the Red River of the North, 1859–1881" (master's thesis, University of North Dakota, 1977), 87–88, 98–99, 102–3, 109, 111, 123, 126.

3. Carl Abbott, *Boosters and Businessmen: Popular Economic Thought and Urban Growth in the Antebellum Middle West* (Westport, Conn.: Greenwood Press, 1981), 4–6, 14, 112–13, 121–22, and 126. Several historians discuss railroad, town, and business promotion. See, for example, Paula M. Nelson, *After the West Was Won: Homesteaders and Town-Builders in Western South Dakota, 1900–1917* (Iowa City: University of Iowa Press, 1986), 82–85, 171; Richard Lingeman, *Small Town America: A Narrative History, 1620–the Present* (New York: G. P. Putnam's Sons, 1980), 240; David Dary, *Entrepreneurs of the Old West* (New York: Alfred A. Knopf, 1986), 232, 252–53.

4. Newspapers quoted in Gary C. Anderson, "Paradise in Fargo," *Red River Valley Historian* (winter 1976): 24–29. Also see Dary, *Entrepreneurs of the Old West,* 233, and William E. Lass, "The Eden of the West," *Minnesota History* 56 (winter 1998–99): 204 and 211.

5. Robert P. Wilkins and Wynona Huchette Wilkins, *North Dakota: A Bicentennial History* (New York: W. W. Norton, 1977), 76–78, 84; Hiram M. Drache, *Day of the Bonanza* (Fargo: North Dakota Institute for Regional Studies, 1964), 12, 87 n; *Clay County Advocate,* September 7, 1878; *Fargo Times,* December 27, 1879.

6. Henry J. Winser to Henry Villard, August 24, 1882, Box 26, Secretary Records, Northern Pacific Railway Company Papers, Minnesota Historical Society, St. Paul; Stanley N. Murray, *The Valley Comes of Age* (Fargo: North Dakota Institute for Regional Studies, 1967), 92, 94, 141; Drache, *Bonanza,* 6, 25, 29.

7. Henry J. Winser to Henry Villard, August 24, 1882, Box 26, and Northern Pacific Railway Company Annual Report, 1882, 62, Box 1, Northern Pacific Secretary Records; *Fargo Sunday*

Argus, May 20, September 30, and December 30, 1883; Hiram M. Drache, "The Economic Aspects of the Northern Pacific Railroad in North Dakota," *North Dakota History* 34 (fall 1967): 329–30, 332, 334, 336–37, 361–65, 367; *Fargo Daily Republican,* November 20, 1882.

8. E. J. Cooley, *The Boom of a Western City* (Boston: Lee and Shephard Publishers, 1897). On the success and failure of small-town businessmen, see Lingeman, *Small Town America,* 155–57.

9. *Roy Johnson's Red River Valley,* ed. Clarence A. Glasrud (Moorhead: Red River Valley Historical Society, 1982), 286–91; "J. B. Chapin," R. G. Dun Company Collection, vol. 2, Western Territory, 133, Baker Library, Harvard University; *Red River Star,* April 5, 1873.

10. Glasrud, *Roy Johnson's Red River Valley,* 291, 294; "J. B. Chapin," R. G. Dun Company Collection, vol. 2, Western Territory, 133; *Fargo Times,* December 13, 1879. On "blocks" as speculation, see Lingeman, *Small Town America,* 152–53.

11. Glasrud, *Roy Johnson's Red River Valley,* 295, 298–99; *Fargo Times,* May 24, June 21, and October 4, 1879.

12. Glasrud, *Roy Johnson's Red River Valley,* 296, 306–9; "Peter A. Goodman and W. A. Yerxa," R. G. Dun Company Collection, vol. 2, Western Territory, 214; *Fargo Forum,* January 18, 1927.

13. *A Century Together: A History of Fargo, North Dakota, and Moorhead, Minnesota* (Fargo-Moorhead: Centennial Corporation, 1975), 88; Melva Moline, *The Forum: The First Hundred Years* (Fargo: Moline, 1979), 22 and 25.

14. Moline, *The Forum,* 25, 32, 81; *Fargo Sunday Argus,* June 19, 1881, and February 25, March 18, and June 10, 1883; Nelson, *After the West Was Won,* 90 and 95.

15. Moline, *The Forum,* 30, 50; A. W. Edwards to James J. Hill, October 5 and 25, 1881, and October 30, November 16 and 26, 1882, General Correspondence, James J. Hill Papers, James J. Hill Library, St. Paul; *Fargo Daily Argus,* April 4, 1886, January 14, and September 4, 1891; Albro Martin, *James J. Hill and the Opening of the Northwest* (New York: Oxford University Press, 1976), 428; *Fargo Forum,* February 21, 1930.

16. Moline, *The Forum,* 51, 59–60; John P. Edwards, "Reminiscence" (n.d.), Major Alanson W. Edwards Family Papers, Institute for Regional Studies, North Dakota State University, Fargo; *Fargo Forum and Daily Republican,* November 17, 1894, August 3 and November 17, 1896.

17. Carroll Van West, *Capitalism on the Frontier: Billings and the Yellowstone Valley in the Nineteenth Century* (Lincoln: University of Nebraska Press, 1993), 147–49.

18. Robert H. Wiebe, *The Search for Order, 1877–1920* (New York: Hill and Wang, 1967), 12–15, 47–49, 112, 145–47.

19. *Fargo Times,* November 29, 1879, January 15, March 4 and 11, April 8 and 22, June 10, 1880; A. W. Edwards to [General Wilkinson?], March 29, 1880, Box 17, Northern Pacific Secretary Records; Mark Peihl, "Haynes Photos among Earliest in Clay County," *CCHS Newsletter,* 14 (November/December 1993): 7.

20. *Second Annual Report of the Chamber of Commerce of Fargo, 1880–1881* (Fargo: Argus, 1881), 15–16, 18–19, 33–34, 42, 44–45, 47, 49–60.

21. Ibid., 26–27. On standard time, see *Fargo Sunday Argus,* December 2, 1883. On expanding telephone service, see *A Century Together,* 116; *Fargo Sunday Argus,* July 18, 1886; *Fargo Forum and Daily Republican,* March 3, 1896, November 11, 1897, and March 21, 1899.

22. Charles N. Glaab, *Kansas City and the Railroads: Community Policy in the Growth of a Regional Metropolis* (Madison: State Historical Society of Wisconsin, 1962), viii, 56, 121–23, 168–69, 173–74, 178, 192; John Hudson, *Plains Country Towns* (Minneapolis: University of Minnesota

Press, 1985), 164–65; Drache, "Economic Aspects of Northern Pacific," 346; *Fargo Times,* April 22, 1880; *Fargo Sunday Argus,* January 30 and April 24, 1881.

23. A. J. Harwood to J. J. Hill, January 9 and February 21, 1882, Box 6, James J. Hill Correspondence, Great Northern Railway Company Records, Minnesota Historical Society; *Fargo Daily Republican,* February 22 and August 22, 1882; *Fargo Sunday Argus,* December 2, 1883. On Yerkes's Fargo career, see Richard E. Blair, "A Multi-Millionaire in Fargo! A History: The Story of Charles T. Yerkes Jr. and the Fargo and Southern Railroad" (master's thesis, North Dakota State University, 1961), 1–11, 19–27. Yerkes erected the "Time Block" at Broadway and Second Avenue North and as president of the Fargo Agricultural Society planned an ambitious expositional fair that drowned in rain and red ink in September 1881.

24. Glasrud, *Roy Johnson's Red River Valley,* 284: *Fargo Sunday Argus,* January 21, 1883; F. R. Delano to Frederick Billings, September 18 and October 1, 1880, Box 19, Northern Pacific Secretary Records; *Fargo Sunday Argus,* February 27, 1881, and *Fargo Evening Republican,* March 1, 1882. On Hill's strategy for developing a "city-hinterland symbiosis," see Claire Strom, *Profiting from the Plains: The Great Northern Railway and Corporate Development of the American West* (Seattle: University of Washington Press, 2003), 16–18.

25. *Fargo Times,* April 8, 1880; Glasrud, *Roy Johnson's Red River Valley,* 302; *Fargo Sunday Argus,* October 23, 1881, July 8 and December 2, 1883. According to Blair, "A Multi-Millionaire in Fargo!" 30, Yerkes became the largest stockholder in the Fargo and Southern.

26. Glasrud, *Roy Johnson's Red River Valley,* 281, 302; *Fargo Daily Argus,* May 20, 1884, and June 17, 1885; *Moorhead Weekly News,* June 26 and August 21, 1884.

27. Elwyn B. Robinson, *History of North Dakota* (Lincoln: University of Nebraska Press, 1966), 135–36; William E. Lass, *Minnesota: A Bicentennial History* (New York: W. W. Norton, 1977), 136–37; Mildred Hartsough, *The Twin Cities as a Metropolitan Market: A Regional Study of the Economic Development of Minneapolis-St. Paul* (Minneapolis: University of Minnesota Press, 1925), 54–55, 133–34.

28. Robinson, *History of North Dakota,* 247–48, 273–76.

29. David B. Danbom, *"Our Purpose Is to Serve": The First Century of the North Dakota Agricultural Experiment Station* (Fargo: North Dakota Institute for Regional Studies, 1990), 7, 9–10, 18–21.

30. David B. Danbom, "Politics, Science and the Changing Nature of Research at the North Dakota Agricultural Experiment Station, 1900–1930," *North Dakota History* 56 (summer 1989): 24–29; Murray, *Valley Comes of Age,* 175–76, 188.

31. Hiram M. Drache, *The Challenge of the Prairie: Life and Times of the Red River Valley* (Fargo: North Dakota Institute for Regional Studies, 1970), 116; James B. Power, Letterpress Book, March 10, 1885, to October 10, 1890, and January 25, 1887, to April 16, 1891; J. B. Power to Fargo Packing Co., April 27, 1899, and to Rusch and Smith, May 2, 1899, Box 5, Folder 3; James B. Power to W. H. Gross, May 31, 1899, and to L. A. Huntoon, July 24, 1899, Box 5, Folder 3; James B. Power to Greenleaf–Tenney and to D. B. Shotwell, November 17, 1891, Box 5, Folder 2; James B. Power to George Power, September 7, 1894, Box 8, Folder 5, James B. Power Papers, Institute for Regional Studies.

32. J. B. Power to George Power, April 17 and June 20, 1893, and to Clark and Barclay, June 10, 1893, Box 7, Folder 15 and 17; J. B. Power to George Power, August 22, 1894, Box 4, Folder 1, Power Papers.

33. Stanley N. Murray, "Railroads and the Agricultural Development of the Red River Valley," *Agricultural History* 21 (October 1957): 65–66; Danbom, *"Our Purpose Is to Serve,"* 24–25; James B. Power to J. W. Kjilgaard, August 24, 1894, Box 8, Folder 5; James B. Power, "Combination of Wheat and Livestock," Box 6, Folder 23; Northwestern Stock-Breeders' Association Pamphlet, February 20, 1900, and to J. A. Johnson, May 4, 1899, Box 1, Folder 2; James B. Power to E. J. Jennings, February 24, 1899, Box 4, Folder 3; J. B. Power to J. T. Davlin, January 14, 1904, Box 5, Folder 3, all located in Power Papers.

34. *Fargo Daily Argus,* March 4, April 1, and October 20, 1891.

35. *Fargo Forum and Daily Republican,* March 25, May 13, 18, and 20, August 30, November 21, and December 19, 1895; January 24, 1900; *A Century Together,* 117.

36. A. T. Andreas, *Andreas' Historical Atlas of Dakota* (Chicago: A. T. Andreas, 1884), 185. On how railroads shaped urban physical form, see Thomas White Harvey, "The Making of Railroad Towns in Minnesota's Red River Valley" (master's thesis, Pennsylvania State University, 1982), 164, 177, 223–24. Northern Pacific influence on the Fargo cityscape can be seen in the *Sanborn Fire Insurance Map: Fargo, North Dakota, 1901* (Teaneck, N.J.: Chadwyck-Healey, 1983) and the *Fargo and Moorhead City Directory, 1901* (St. Paul: Pettibone Directory Company, 1900), 196–97, 203–7, 213, 216–17, 219. The Northern Pacific carried two-thirds of Fargo's trade, according to the *Fargo Forum and Daily Republican,* November 29, 1897.

37. *Sanborn Fire Insurance Map, 1901; Fargo and Moorhead City Directory, 1901,* 217.

38. *Fargo Forum and Daily Republican,* July 19, 1907, October 2 and 4, 1909; *Record* 5 (October 1899): 22. For an attempt by city leaders to tap the hinterland, see *Fargo Forum and Daily Republican,* November 29, 1897.

39. Harvey, "The Making of Railroad Towns," 173, 176–77; *The Leading Industries of Fargo, Dakota* (Chicago: Reed & Company, 1881), 99–101; Henry J. Winser to Henry Villard, August 17, 1882, Box 26, Northern Pacific Secretary Records; *Fargo Sunday Argus,* August 29, 1886, and July 15, 1888.

40. Harvey, "The Making of Railroad Towns," 177; John Hudson, "The Plains Country Town," in *The Great Plains: Environment and Culture,* ed. Brian W. Blouet and Frederick C. Luebke (Lincoln: University of Nebraska Press, 1979), 112; *Fargo and Moorhead City Directory, 1900,* 211; *Record* 1 (May 1895): 35; *Fargo Times,* October 18 and November 15, 1879; *Second Annual Report of the Chamber of Commerce of Fargo,* 42, 48.

41. Hudson, "The Plains Country Town," 101–2; Nelson, *After the West Was Won,* 89, 98–99.

42. *Leading Industries of Fargo, Dakota,* 6–8, 70–71; *Moorhead Weekly News,* May 12, 1887.

43. Benjamin J. Klebaner, *American Commercial Banking: A History* (Boston: Twayne Publishers, 1990), 64, 67–70, 82, 92; *History of the Red River Valley* (Chicago: C. F. Cooper & Company, 1909), 1:505–6; *Fargo Sunday Argus,* July 15, 1888; *Fargo Forum and Daily Republican,* October 11, 1897; Hartsough, *Twin Cities,* 193.

44. *Fargo Daily Republican,* August 30 and September 6, 1882; *Fargo Daily Argus,* November 3, 1891.

45. Henry J. Winser, Report on Manufacturers, August 19, 1882, Box 26, Northern Pacific Secretary Records.

46. Frank E. Vyzralik, "Brick-making in North Dakota, 1868–1898," *North Dakota History* 65 (spring/summer 1998): 34; *Fargo Sunday Argus,* June 5, 1881, and June 10, 1884.

47. "F. N. Whitman," R. G. Dun Company Collection, vol. 2, Western Territory, 125; *North-*

ern Pacific Mirror, October 14, 1874; "Memories of Charles E. Bristol of Events in Fargo, Dakota Territory from 1881 to 1890," 1–2, 5, Institute for Regional Studies; *Fargo and Moorhead City Directory,* 1900, 199 and 206.

48. *Fargo Daily Republican,* May 16 and 27, July 4, 1882; *Moorhead Weekly News,* January 10 and May 1, 1884; *Fargo Sunday Argus,* November 18, 1883.

49. *Fargo Sunday Argus,* February 13, 1881; Henry J. Winser, Report on Flouring Mills and Elevators, August 17, 1882, Box 26, Northern Pacific Secretary Records; *Moorhead Weekly News,* February 5, 1885; *Fargo Daily Argus,* December 11, 1890; *Fargo Forum and Daily Republican,* October 16, 1896; Holzkamm and Dormanen, *Fargo Historic Context Study,* 61; Alfred D. Chandler Jr., *The Visible Hand: The Managerial Revolution in American Business* (Cambridge: Harvard University Press, 1977), 250–51, 253, 294–95.

50. *Fargo Forum and Daily Republican,* June 18 and September 28, 1897, January 15, 1898; *Record,* 4 (December 1898).

51. *Fargo Forum and Daily Republican,* February 22 and July 17, 1896; *Record* 4 (December 1898); Fred A. Shannon, *The Farmer's Last Frontier: Agriculture, 1860–1897* (New York: Harper Torchbook, 1968), 234–36.

52. *Fargo Forum and Daily Republican,* May 24, 1900; Mary Ann Williams, *Origins of North Dakota Place Names* (Bismarck: Tribune, 1966), 72–73; Hartsough, *Twin Cities,* 187.

53. *Fargo Daily Republican,* March 10, 11, and 29, April 3, June 1, 6, and 15, July 15, 1882.

54. H. Haupt to James B. Williams, September 28, 1882, Box 26, and John H. Ames to James B. Williams, December 15, 1882, Box 27, Northern Pacific Secretary Records; *Fargo Daily Argus,* November 4, 1885, April 11 and September 19, 1886; *Fargo Forum and Daily Republican,* December 6, 1897; Richard White, *"It's Your Misfortune and None of My Own": A History of the American West* (Norman: University of Oklahoma Press, 1991), 273.

55. In the early 1880s, 40 percent of Fargo business houses engaged in selling goods. The percentage is based on counting and categorizing index listings in the *Fargo City Directory, 1883* (Fargo: G. E. Nichols, 1883), 198–200. Numbers are not available for 1900, but retail always played a significant role in the city economy. In 1930, for example, retail stores employed almost 20 percent of those employed and had 9 percent of the state's retail sales despite having only 4 percent of the population, according to David Danbom, *Going It Alone: Fargo Grapples with the Great Depression* (St. Paul: Minnesota Historical Society Press, 2005), 13. On changes in merchandising, see Ann Satterthwaite, *Going Shopping: Consumer Choices and Community Consequences* (New Haven: Yale University Press, 2001), 26–27, 39, 63, 82, 126, 134–45, and Jessica Sewell, "Gender, Imagination and Experience in the Early-Twentieth-Century American Downtown," in *Everyday America: Cultural Landscape Studies after J. B. Jackson,* ed. Chris Wilson and Paul Groth (Berkeley: University of California Press, 2003), 241, 244–47. On retail stores and "female space," also see Diane Shaw, *City Building on the Eastern Frontier: Sorting the New Nineteenth-Century City* (Baltimore: Johns Hopkins University Press, 2004), 112.

56. John Hudson discusses factors contributing to fluidity and persistence in *Plains Country Towns,* 106–10. Also see Nelson, *After the West Was Won,* 89–90.

57. "N. K. Hubbard," *Record* 1 (December 1895): 14; "N. K. Hubbard & Co.," R. G. Dun Company Collection, Minnesota, vol. 2, Clay County, 5; *Red River Star,* April 3, 1875; *Fargo Express,* June 25, 1874; *Fargo Times,* March 15, 1879.

58. *Fargo Express,* June 25, 1874; *Northern Pacific Mirror,* October 14, 1874, and May 15, 1875;

"N. K. Hubbard," *Record* 1 (December 1895): 14; *Fargo Forum and Daily Republican,* August 21, 1923.

59. *Record* 4 (December 1898); *Fargo Forum,* November 3, 1929; Patricia S. Hull, "Pioneers in Merchandising," *Red River Valley Historian* 4–5 (1970–71): 24.

60. *Fargo Forum,* June 19, 1955; Hull, "Pioneers in Merchandising," 24, 26; *Fargo Sunday Argus,* November 10, 1889. Novelist Larry Woiwode depicts a trip to Fargo for a graduation suit in *Beyond the Bedroom Wall: A Family Album* (New York: Farrar, Straus and Giroux, 1975), 45.

61. *Fargo Forum and Daily Republican,* September 1, 1894, August 27, 1901, May 3, 1909, November 3, 1929, and June 19, 1955; Hull, "Pioneers in Merchandising," 26; Sewell, "Gender, Imagination and Experience," 246–47; Shaw, *City Building,* 87.

62. Hull, "Pioneers in Merchandising," 26; Satterthwaite, *Going Shopping,* 83; *Record* 4 (December 1898); *Fargo Forum and Daily Republican,* April 12, 1899.

63. *A Century Together,* 39, 41; Roy P. Johnson, "Fargo's Landmark Gives Way to Civic Center" (undated newspaper clipping), Fargo, North Dakota, Historical Collections, Institute for Regional Studies; *Fargo Sanborn Fire Insurance Map,* 1901. I am indebted to geographer Paul Groth for suggestions that shaped this paragraph and this section.

64. *Leading Industries of Fargo,* 105.

65. The mercantile model of development, wholesaling as a shaping force, and types of wholesaling are discussed in James E. Vance, *The Merchant's World: The Geography of Wholesaling* (Englewood Cliffs, N.J.: Prentice Hall, 1970), 27–33, 80–81, 85, 92, 98–100, 158, 166–67. I am indebted to Paul Groth for this citation and for emphasizing the importance of the wholesale trade. On "intelligence flows" and wholesaling, see Shaw, *City Building,* 131. According to Danbom, *Going It Alone,* 6, 13–14, nearly 1,200 Fargoans worked in wholesale and the city did 16 percent of the state's wholesale trade by 1930. Also see White, "It's Your Misfortune," 273; *Fargo and Moorhead City Directory,* 1900, 195–96, 205–6; *Fargo Forum and Daily Republican,* November 17, 1894; Eaton, *Gateway Cities,* 120.

66. *A Century Together,* 106–7; *Fargo Times,* March 15 and December 20, 1879; January 3, March 18, and April 8, 1880; *Fargo Daily Republican,* November 4, 1882; Chandler, *The Visible Hand,* 306, 402–3, 409.

67. Olivier Zunz, *Making America Corporate, 1870–1920* (Chicago: University of Chicago Press, 1990), 13, 39, 151, 154, 156, 160–66, 171–73. George A. Freudeureich, Report on Fargo, DT, June 23, 1877, McCormick Harvesting Machine Company Papers, Incoming Correspondence and Reports, Reel 199, P91–3921, State Historical Society of Wisconsin, Madison.

68. George A. Freudeureich to C. H. and L. J. McCormick, July 27, 1877, McCormick Harvesting Machine Company Papers, Series 2X, Reels 199, 91–3921 and 211, P91–1933; Murray, *Valley Comes of Age,* 140; *Fargo Times,* August 16, 1879.

69. George A. Freudeureich to C. H. and L. J. McCormick, August 6, 1877, McCormick Harvesting Machine Company Papers, Series 2X, Reels 199, 91–3921 and 211, P91–1933.

70. J. R. McLaughlin to C. H. and J. L. McCormick, February 24, 1878, McCormick Harvesting Machine Company Papers, Series 2X, Reel 223, P91–3945; George A. Freudeureich to C. H. and L. J. McCormick, April 10, June 3, 4, and 6, 1878, McCormick Harvesting Machine Company Papers, Series 2X, Reel 221, P91–3943; *Fargo Sunday Argus,* August 19, 1883.

71. Collections, Dakota Territory, 1880–85, McCormick Harvesting Machine Company Papers, Series 3X, Reels 32, P92–8535 and 33, P92–8535; 1900 Reports–Fargo, ND, McCormick

Harvesting Machine Company Papers, Series 2X, Reel 380, P93–602 and 621; McCormick Harvesting Machine Company to Local Collecting Agents, August 31, 1900, and J. C. Sheldon to McCormick Harvesting Machine Company, September 3, 1900, McCormick Harvesting Machine Company Papers, Series 2X, Reel 374, P93–596.

72. *A Century Together,* 106–7; *Fargo Daily Argus,* September 27, 1892; *Fargo Forum and Daily Republican,* October 31, 1893, May 28, 1894, July 27, 1895, January 11, 1896, and December 10, 1897.

73. Chandler, *The Visible Hand,* 217–18; Cronon, *Nature's Metropolis,* 327, 330–31; Hartsough, *Twin Cities,* 173, 181, 186–87.

74. *Fargo Sunday Argus,* June 12, 1881, November 18 and December 30, 1883; *Fargo Daily Republican,* May 5, September 27, and November 22, 1882.

75. *Fargo Sunday Argus,* March 20, April 10, May 8, and July 24, 1887; *Green Pastures and Vast Wheat Fields: A Sketch* (Fargo: Republican Steam Printing House, 1888), 39; *Moorhead Weekly News,* July 21, 1887.

76. *Record* 1 (December 1895): 45, and (May 1895): 34, 1 (February/March 1896): 24, and 4 (December 1898); *Fargo Daily Forum and Republican,* September 18 and December 3, 1895, March 5 and 26, April 3, and November 30, 1896, November 30, 1897, and November 10, 1899.

77. *Fargo Forum and Daily Republican,* January 13, 1900.

78. Holzkamm and Dormanen, *Fargo Historic Context Study,* 58–61; Glasrud, *Roy Johnson's Red River Valley,* 283–84; *Fargo Forum and Daily Republican,* July 19, 1907.

4. OLD AND NEW AMERICANS

1. Julie Roy Jeffrey, *Frontier Women: The Trans-Mississippi West, 1840–1880* (New York: Hill and Wang, 1979), 96–97, 106; Richard White, *"It's Your Misfortune and None of My Own": A History of the American West* (Norman: University of Oklahoma Press, 1991), 302, 307–9, 315.

2. Martin E. Marty, *Righteous Empire: The Protestant Experience in America* (New York: Dial Press, 1970), 129, 174–75; White, *"It's Your Misfortune,"* 309–11; Sydney E. Ahlstrom, *A Religious History of the American People,* 2d ed. (New Haven: Yale University Press, 2004), 740–41; Winthrop S. Hudson, *Religion in America* (New York: Charles Scribner's Sons, 1965), 227–28.

3. Lawrence H. Larsen, *The Urban West at the End of the Frontier* (Lawrence: Regents Press of Kansas, 1978), 25; U.S. Census, *Twelfth Census of the United States,* vol. 1, *Population* (Washington: U.S. Census Office, 1901), 588, 595, 662, 671, 763, 765, 732–35, 806–7; Sig Mickelson, *The Northern Pacific Railroad and the Selling of the West: A Nineteenth-Century Public Relations Venture* (Sioux Falls: Center for Western Studies, 1993), 152; Henry Johnson, *The Other Side of Main Street: A History Teacher from Sauk Centre* (New York: Columbia University Press, 1943), 117.

4. *Fargo Daily Republican,* January 14, 1882; *Fargo Sunday Argus,* April 22, 1883; *Sanborn Fire Insurance Map: Fargo, North Dakota, 1901* (Teaneck, N.J.: Chadwyck-Healey, 1983); John Turner and C. R. Semling, *History of Clay and Norman Counties* (Indianapolis: B. F. Brown, 1918), 1:199–211; *A Century Together: A History of Fargo, North Dakota, and Moorhead, Minnesota* (Fargo-Moorhead: Centennial Corporation, 1975), 76.

5. Only a third of the state's population were church members, according to Elwyn B. Robinson, *History of North Dakota* (Lincoln: University of Nebraska Press, 1966), 295; *Fargo Sunday Argus,* July 15, 1888; White, *"It's Your Misfortune,"* 311.

6. *Roy Johnson's Red River Valley,* ed. Clarence A. Glasrud (Moorhead: Red River Valley Historical Society, 1982), 427; William C. Sherman and Playford V. Thorson, eds., *Plains Folk: North Dakota's Ethnic History* (Fargo: North Dakota Institute for Regional Studies, 1988), 59. For a discussion of Yankee distinctiveness, see Andrew R. L. Cayton and Peter S. Onuf, *The Midwest and the Nation: Rethinking the History of an American Region* (Bloomington: Indiana University Press, 1990), 50, and Don Harrison Doyle, *The Social Order of a Frontier Community: Jacksonville, Illinois, 1825–1870* (Urbana: University of Illinois Press, 1978), 122–23. Doyle also stresses booster ideology as an integrative force between otherwise competing groups.

7. F. M. Wood to Robert Harris, June 28, 1887, Box 31, and H. C. Simmons to Robert Harris, September 25, 1884, Box 30, Secretary Records, Northern Pacific Railway Company Papers, Minnesota Historical Society, St. Paul.

8. *A Century Together,* 71, 186; *Red River Star,* January 25, 1873; William H. White, "History of Methodism in North Dakota," in *Collections of the State Historical Society of North Dakota* (Bismarck: Tribune, State Printers, 1906), 1:310–11.

9. *Fargo Daily Republican,* May 1, July 28, and December 5, 1882; *Fargo Sunday Argus,* July 22, 1883, and July 18, 1886; *Fargo Forum and Daily Republican,* March 4, June 18, and November 12, 1895, March 18, 1896, September 11, 1899; Ellen J. Cooley, *The Boom of a Western City* (Boston: Lee and Shephard Publishers, 1897), 44–45.

10. Rowland Berthoff, *An Unsettled People: Social Order and Disorder in American History* (New York: Harper & Row, 1971), 252–53; *First Presbyterian Church, Moorhead, Minnesota* (n.p.; n.d.), 10–13; *Moorhead Advocate,* September 1, 1877; *Clay County Advocate,* December 28, 1878. Local church histories indicate mission support, and Robinson, *History of North Dakota,* 296–97, recounts dependence on outside aid by American Protestant churches in North Dakota.

11. *Fargo Daily Argus,* September 3, 1892; Marty, *Righteous Empire,* 166–67, 173–74.

12. *First Presbyterian Church: 75th Anniversary, 1877–1952* (Fargo: First Presbyterian Church, 1977), 11, 17; *First Congregational Church: Celebrating Our Hundredth Anniversary, 1881–1981* (Fargo: First Congregational, 1981), 3; *First Congregational Church, Fargo, ND: Twenty-fifth Anniversary, 1881–1906* (n.p.; n.d.), 15; *St. Mark's 75th Anniversary, 1887–1962* (Fargo: St. Mark's Lutheran, 1962), 1–2.

13. *Fargo Daily Argus,* September 3, 1892; Marty, *Righteous Empire,* 75–76. Moorhead church histories refer to Sunday schools. The Fargo Methodist Sunday school preceded the church, according to White, "History of Methodism in North Dakota," 1:311. Ahlstrom, *Religious History,* 741, suggests that Sunday school may have been valued more than worship.

14. Ahlstrom, *Religious History,* 858; Hudson, *Religion in America,* 411; White, "History of Methodism in North Dakota," 1:317; *Fargo Forum and Daily Republican,* May 17 and September 19, 1893, January 24, 1895, June 6, September 2, and December 5, 1896. Church histories refer to several youth fellowships.

15. *First Presbyterian Church: 75th Anniversary,* 68–69; Bill G. Reid, *The First Presbyterian Church of Fargo, North Dakota: A Centennial History, 1877–1977* (Fargo: First Presbyterian Church, 1977), 8–9; White, "History of Methodism in North Dakota," 1:316; *Clay County Advocate,* August 24 and December 7, 1878; *Fargo Daily Republican,* November 23 and December 9, 1882; *Fargo Daily Argus,* April 22, 1884; *Fargo Forum,* November 4, 1893.

16. Marty, *Righteous Empire,* 174, 176; Ahlstrom, *Religious History,* 864–65; Hudson, *Religion in America,* 296–98, 318–22; *First Presbyterian Church: 75th Anniversary,* 68; White, "His-

tory of Methodism in North Dakota," 1:317; *Fargo Sunday Argus,* March 6, 1887, and January 6, 1889.

17. *Red River Star,* August 16, 1873; *Fargo Express,* April 30, 1874; Pollock is quoted in *75th Anniversary of First Methodist Church* (Fargo: First Methodist Church, 1949), 3; *A Century Together,* 71; White, "History of Methodism in North Dakota," 1:315; Clement A. Lounsberry, "Biographical: William H. White," in *North Dakota History and People* (Chicago: S. J. Clarke Publishing Company, 1917), 2:5–7; Marty, *Righteous Empire,* 110, 148–149, 153.

18. Marty, *Righteous Empire,* 172; Richard L. Bushman, *The Refinement of America: Persons, Houses, Cities* (New York: Alfred A. Knopf, 1992), 313, 352; Cora Vere, *One Hundred Years of the Episcopal Church* (Fargo-Moorhead: Centennial Committee, 1972), 6, 8; A. W. McNair, *Parish History of Gethsemane Cathedral, 1872–1947* (Fargo: Gethsemane, 1948), 5. Architectural details are from Norene A. Roberts, *Fargo's Heritage* (Fargo: Fargo Heritage Society, 1983), 38, and Ronald L. Ramsey, ed., *Fargo-Moorhead: A Guide to Historic Architecture* (Fargo: Plains Architectural Heritage Foundation and FM Board of Realtors, 1975), 8–9, 40, 43, 49, 68–69. *Fargo Forum and Daily Republican,* December 24, 1896.

19. Berthoff, *An Unsettled People,* 243–45; Doyle, *Social Order of a Frontier Community,* 169, 178.

20. *Fargo Daily Argus,* March 11, 18, and 25, April 1, 1885; *Moorhead Weekly News,* April 9, 1885.

21. *Fargo Forum,* October 31, 1893; *Moorhead Weekly News,* November 2, 23, and 30, 1893.

22. *Fargo Forum and Daily Republican,* August 18 and 23, November 16, 17, and 18, 1897, October 27, 1899; *Moorhead Weekly News,* November 2, 1899.

23. *Moorhead Weekly News,* April 9, 1885; *Fargo Daily Argus,* April 8, 1884, and April 22, 1885; Jay P. Dolan, *The American Catholic Experience: A History from Colonial Times to the Present* (New York: Doubleday, 1985), 219, 226–27; James S. Olson, *Catholic Immigrants in America* (Chicago: Nelson-Hall, 1987), 198–99.

24. Marty, *Righteous Empire,* 178, 187. For Congregationalist stands on these issues, see *Fargo Daily Republican,* October 18, 1882; *Fargo Sunday Argus,* March 4, 1883; *Fargo Forum and Daily Republican,* May 27, 1895.

25. Berthoff, *An Unsettled People,* 260–61, 439–40; Lewis Atherton, *Main Street on the Middle Border* (Chicago: Quadrangle Paperback, 1966), 65, 67–70, 79.

26. White, *"It's Your Misfortune,"* 314; Jeffrey, *Frontier Women,* 12, 90, 94.

27. *A Century Together,* 63–64; *Fargo Sunday Argus,* June 10, 1883, June 26, 1886, June 19, 1887, June 24, 1888; *Fargo Daily Republican,* November 17, 1882; *Fargo Forum and Daily Republican,* October 5, 1895; *Record* 1 (December 1895): iv–v; *Manual of the Public Schools of Fargo* (Fargo: Argus Co. Printers, 1885), Box 13, and Board of Education Minutes, March 7, 1900, 273–74, Box 3, Fargo Public School Records, Institute for Regional Studies, North Dakota State University, Fargo. On special day observances and other forms of moral instruction, see Ellen M. Litwicki, *America's Public Holidays, 1865–1920* (Washington, D.C.: Smithsonian Institution Press, 2000), 155; North Dakota Superintendent of Public Instruction, *Biennial Report, 1888–1890* (Bismarck: North Dakota Department of Public Instruction, 1890), 27–28, 155; North Dakota, *Biennial Report, 1890–1892,* 22–23, 561, 593; North Dakota, *Biennial Report, 1892–1894,* 26–27, and North Dakota, *Biennial Report, 1900–1902,* 23, 31–83.

28. *Fargo Forum and Daily Republican,* October 5, 1895; *Fargo Daily Republican,* January 27,

August 22, and December 14, 1882; *Fargo Sunday Argus,* May 6, 1883; *Fargo Daily Argus,* November 19, 1884; *Manual of the Public Schools of Fargo,* 10–12.

29. Angela Boleyn, *Quarter Sections and Wide Horizons* (Bismarck: North Dakota State Library, 1978), 295–96.

30. *A Century Together,* 174, 176–78; *Red River Star,* April 12, June 14, and September 20, 1873; January 17, May 16, and August 29, 1874; *Fargo Times,* October 4, 1879, and April 1, 1880; *Clay County Advocate,* February 7 and April 3, 1880; *Fargo and Moorhead City Directory, 1885* (Fargo: R. W. Bliss, 1885), 229.

31. Daniel J. Boorstin, *The Americans: The National Experience* (New York: Vintage Books, 1967), 152–55, 158–60; Jeffrey, *Frontier Women,* 195.

32. A. W. Edwards to Frederick Billings, January 25, 1881, Box 20, Northern Pacific Secretary Records; *Fargo Daily Republican,* April 12, 14, and 25, July 19 and 20, 1882; *Fargo Sunday Argus,* November 11, 1883, and October 2, 1887; *Moorhead Weekly News,* May 3, 1888, April 20 and 27 and July 20, 1882.

33. *A Century Together,* 175–76; Gregory Harness, "Solomon Gilman Comstock: Portrait of a Pioneer," *Red River Valley Historian* (winter 1974–75): 8–9, and "Solomon Gillman Comstock: Prairie Lawyer, Legislator and Businessman" (master's thesis, Moorhead State College, 1976), 135–36; *Moorhead Weekly News,* April 20, 1882, and February 1, 1883; Thomas Dickey to T. F. Oakes, July 29, 1883, Box 28, Northern Pacific Secretary Records.

34. Julian Bjornson, "The Fargo College," 1–5, Fargo College Collection SC 1133, Institute for Regional Studies, North Dakota State University, Fargo.

35. Ibid., 6–8; Frederick E. Stratton, "Early History of Fargo College," chapter 2, 2–3; chapter 3, 1–3, Box 2, Frederick E. Stratton Papers, Institute for Regional Studies; *Fargo Sunday Argus,* December 29, 1889.

36. Stratton, "Fargo College," chapter 5, 1–2; chapter 10, 7–8, 18, 24.

37. Ibid., chapter 8, 1, 10–11; *Fargo Daily Argus,* October 8, 1890; Robinson, *History of North Dakota,* 694. Marty, *Righteous Empire,* 23, and Hudson, *Religion in America,* 320, 321, discuss Anglo-Saxon Protestant ideology.

38. Stratton, "Fargo College," chapter 4, 3; *Fargo Forum and Daily Republican,* January 18, 1897, October 28, 1893, March 18, 22, 23, November 22, 1895.

39. *Fargo Daily Argus,* June 23, 1891; *Fargo Forum and Daily Republican,* February 27 and June 13, 1896.

40. H. C. Simmons to O. G. Barnes, December 19, 1894, Box 1, O. G. Barnes Papers, Institute for Regional Studies; Stratton, "Fargo College," chapter 9, 6; chapter 11, 13–14; *Fargo Forum and Daily Republican,* September 15, 1897.

41. Bjornson, "The Fargo College," 10–12; George E. Perley to R. M. Pollock, March 26, 1903, and A. A. Miller to R. M. Pollock, April 4, 1903, Box 1, R.M. Pollock Papers, Institute for Regional Studies.

42. Solomon Gilman Comstock, "Memoir," *Red River Valley Historian* (winter 1974–75): 5; *A Century Together,* 180–81; R. M. Probstfield to Brandborg, January 29, 1894, Box 1, R. M. Probstfield Papers, Northwest Minnesota Historical Center, Minnesota State University, Moorhead.

43. William C. Hunter, *Beacon across the Prairie: North Dakota's Land-Grant College* (Fargo: North Dakota Institute for Regional Studies, 1961), 6–7, 10, 14–15, 24, 35; *A Century Together,* 67–68.

44. Litwicki, *America's Public Holidays,* 1–3, 144–45, 147, 151–53; Doyle, *Social Order of a Frontier Community,* 141–42, 228–29; Michael Kammen, *Mystic Chords of Memory: The Transformation of Tradition in American Culture* (New York: Vintage Books, 1993), 255–56.

45. *Fargo Express,* June 28 and July 12, 1873, July 5, 1879; *Clay County Advocate,* June 21, 1879.

46. *Fargo Daily Republican,* July 5, 1882; *Fargo Sunday Argus,* July 8, 1883, July 6, 1885, and July 3, 1887.

47. *Fargo Daily Argus,* July 4, 1890, and July 5, 1892; *Fargo Forum and Daily Republican,* July 5, 1893, July 5, 1894, July 1, 5, and 6, 1895.

48. *Fargo Forum and Daily Republican,* July 6, 1896, July 4, 1898, July 3, 1899.

49. Kammen, *Mystic Chords of Memory,* 207–8, 210–12, 219–20; *Fargo Daily Republican,* October 23, November 21, 1882; *Fargo Forum and Daily Republican,* November 19, December 18 and 21, 1894.

50. Elizabeth H. Pleck, *Celebrating the Family: Ethnicity, Consumer Culture, and Family Rituals* (Cambridge: Harvard University Press, 2000), 21–22, 27–28, 30; *Fargo Daily Republican,* November 29 and December 1, 1882; *Fargo Forum and Daily Republican,* November 29, 1894, November 26, 1897, and November 25, 1898.

51. On booster community building, see Boorstin, *The Americans,* 113–68 and Doyle, *Social Order of a Frontier Community,* 62, 91, 122–23. For a booster editorial on Norwegian Independence Day, see *Fargo Daily Republican,* May 18, 1882. Doyle, *Social Order of a Frontier Community,* 7–10, summarizes the debate regarding consensus and conflict in frontier communities. On race preference, see Matthew Frye Jacobson, *Whiteness of a Different Color: European Immigrants and the Alchemy of Race* (Cambridge: Harvard University Press, 1998), 69, 75. By 1930 in Fargo, "dwindling immigration and continuing assimilation—especially of young people—had reduced [ethnic] divisions substantially," according to David B. Danbom, *Going It Alone: Fargo Grapples with the Great Depression* (St. Paul: Minnesota Historical Society Press, 2005), 8. The 1930 census reported the city's population as more than 90 percent white and only 13 percent foreign-born.

52. For this analysis, I am indebted to Doyle, *Social Order of a Frontier Community,* 154–55.

53. Jon Gjerde, *The Minds of West: Ethnocultural Evolution of the Rural Middle West, 1830–1917* (Chapel Hill: University of North Carolina Press, 1997), 59–60, 73–75, 247–49, 252, 263, 268–70, 272, 278.

54. Christine Hagen Stafne, "Pioneering in the Red River Valley" (typescript, 1943, Northwest Minnesota Historical Center), 27–28, 37, 40, 42.

55. Ibid., 62–63, 66–67, 80. Also see Playford V. Thorson, "North Dakota Norwegian-American Statuary," *North Dakota Quarterly* 49 (autumn 1981): 79–88.

56. Cooley, *Boom of a Western City,* 46; Edith S. Moll, "Moorhead, MN: Frontier Town, 1871–1915" (master's thesis, North Dakota Agricultural College, 1957), 83, 86; Gary C. Anderson, "Paradise in Fargo," *Red River Valley Historian* (winter 1975–76): 27, 31; *Fargo Times,* April 12, 1879; *Clay County Advocate,* May 1, 1880; *Fargo Sunday Argus,* February 6, 1881; *Moorhead Weekly News,* May 1, 1884, and September 1, 1892; *Fargo Forum,* December 9, 1892.

57. Gertrude Knutson, *A Centennial History of Trinity Lutheran Church, Moorhead, Minnesota* (Moorhead: Trinity Lutheran Church, 1982), 34–35; Kathleen Neils Conzen, "Historical Approaches to the Study of Rural Ethnic Communities," in *Ethnicity on the Great Plains,* ed. Frederick C. Luebke (Lincoln: University of Nebraska Press, 1980), 4–10; Robert C. Ostergren, *A*

Community Transplanted: The Trans-Atlantic Experience of a Swedish Immigrant Settlement in the Upper Middle West, 1835–1915 (Madison: University of Wisconsin Press, 1988), 168, 181, 210–11.

58. Odd Sverre Lovoll, *The Promise of America: A History of the Norwegian-American People* (Minneapolis: Norwegian-American Historical Association, 1984), 173; *Pontoppidan Lutheran Church: Seventy-fifth Anniversary, 1877–1952* (Fargo: Pontoppidan Lutheran Church, 1952), 5, 21; Mrs. Julian P. Melberg, "History of Trinity Sunday School," in *Trinity Church: Fiftieth Anniversary, 1882–1932* (Moorhead: Trinity Lutheran Church, 1932), 16–17; *A Century Together*, 75. Also see Robinson, *History of North Dakota*, 294 and 296: In 1890, Lutherans made up 26 percent of sixty-four thousand North Dakota Christians. Scandinavian Lutherans divided into eleven synods among five national groups.

59. *Seventy-fifth Anniversary, First Lutheran Church* (Fargo: First Lutheran Church, 1947), 6–7; *Fargo Forum and Daily Republican*, May 25, 1895; *Pontoppidan Lutheran Church: Seventy-fifth Anniversary*, 4–9; Herman C. Nordlie, "History of Trinity Lutheran Church in Moorhead, Minnesota" (typed manuscript, 1958[?]), [2, 4–5]; Knutson, *Centennial History of Trinity Lutheran Church*, 9–10.

60. *Pontoppidan Lutheran Church: Seventy-fifth Anniversary*, 6, 9–10; Sherman and Thorson, *Plains Folk*, 192–93; Lovoll, *Promise of America*, 174.

61. *Pontoppidan Lutheran Church: Seventy-fifth Anniversary*, 21–22; *Seventy-fifth Anniversary, First Lutheran Church*, 11; Mrs. J. H. Hjelmstad, "History of Trinity Ladies' Aid and Missionary Society," in *Trinity Church: Fiftieth Anniversary*, 13–15; Erik Luther Williamson, "'Doing What Had to Be Done': Norwegian Lutheran Ladies Aid Societies of North Dakota," *North Dakota History* 57 (spring 1990): 3–4, 6–8, 10–12.

62. E. Clifford Nelson, *The Lutheran Church among Norwegian-Americans: A History of the Evangelical Lutheran Church*, vol. 2, 1890–1959 (Minneapolis: Augsburg Publishing, 1960), 243–45, 99–103; Knutson, *Centennial History of Trinity Lutheran Church*, 10, 35; *Fargo Forum and Daily Republican*, November 8 and 14, 1899; Melberg, "History of Trinity Sunday School," 18; *Pontoppidan Lutheran Church: Seventy-fifth Anniversary*, 15.

63. *A Century Together*, 74; Clara Byers Scrapbook, Institute for Regional Studies; *Fargo Sunday Argus*, July 3, 1887, July 15, 1888, and November 24, 1889; *Fargo Forum and Daily Republican*, May 8, 1895.

64. *Fargo Sunday Argus*, October 9, 1887; *A Booklet to Commemorate the Centennial Celebration of Bethel Evangelical Free Church, Fargo, ND* (Fargo: Bethel Evangelical Free Church, 1992), 1–3.

65. Robinson, *History of North Dakota*, 317; *Red River Star*, April 17 to May 15, 1875; *Fargo Times*, April 5 and May 10, 1879; *Fargo Sunday Argus*, November 20, 1881; *Record* 3 (November 1897): 102; *Daily Argonaut*, January 15, 1882; *Moorhead Weekly News*, April 5, 1894, April 4 and September 26, 1895; H. L. Shirley to R. M. Probstfield, May 20, 1894, Box 1, Probstfield Papers.

66. Ronald L. Ramsey, *An Historic Sites Inventory* (Fargo: n.p., 1979), 47; A. T. Andreas, *Andreas' Historical Atlas of Dakota* (Chicago: A. T. Andreas, 1884), 243–47; *Fargo Times*, June 28, 1879, and July 1, 1880; *Fargo Daily Republican*, November 20, 1882; *Fargo Daily Argus*, January 14 and February 5, 1881, March 11 and December 30, 1885; *Moorhead Weekly News*, March 1, 1888; *Fargo Sunday Argus*, January 3, 1886; *Fargo Forum*, July 5, 1894.

67. *Fargo Daily Argus*, April 8 and September 1, 1891; Carroll Engelhardt, *On Firm Foundation Grounded: The First Century of Concordia College* (Moorhead: Concordia College, 1991), 21–23.

68. Engelhardt, *On Firm Foundation Grounded,* 24–32.

69. Litwicki, *America's Public Holidays,* 114–15; Orm Øverland, *Immigrant Minds, American Identities: Making the United States Home, 1870–1930* (Urbana and Chicago: University of Illinois Press, 2000), 3, 162; *Red River Star,* July 5, 1873; *Fargo Express,* June 11, 1874; *Northern Pacific Mirror,* May 15, 1875; *Clay County Advocate,* May 24, 1879, and May 20, 1880; *Fargo Times,* May 24, 1879; *Fargo Daily Republican,* May 18, 1882; *Fargo Sunday Argus,* May 15, 1881, May 16, 1886, and May 5, 1889; *Moorhead Weekly News,* May 23, 1889.

70. Litwicki, *America's Public Holidays,* 135; *Moorhead Weekly News,* May 18, 1893, and May 24, 1894; *Fargo Forum and Daily Republican,* May 18, 1899, and May 18, 1900.

71. John Bodnar, *The Transplanted: A History of Immigrants in Urban America* (Bloomington: Indiana University Press, 1985), 205; Carl H. Chrislock, *The Progressive Era in Minnesota, 1899–1918* (St. Paul: Minnesota Historical Society Press, 1971), 33–34; Dora Josephine Gunderson, "The Settlement of Clay County, Minnesota, 1870–1900" (master's thesis, University of Minnesota, 1929), 64–69, 71–72; *Red River Star,* May 31, 1873.

72. Gunderson, "Settlement of Clay County," 74, 77–78, 80–81.

73. *Moorhead Weekly News,* March 1, 1894, and August 11, 1898; Duane Lindberg, "Pastors, Prohibition and Politics: The Role of Norwegian Clergy in the North Dakota Abstinence Movement, 1880–1920," *North Dakota Quarterly* 49 (autumn 1981): 26–31.

74. O. J. Johnson to James B. Williams, March 4 and June 3, 1881, Box 20 and 21, Northern Pacific Secretary Records; Sherman and Thorson, *Plains Folk,* 219; *Moorhead Weekly Argonaut,* February 10, 1881.

75. O. G. Berg, *A History of the Evangelical Lutheran Bethesda Congregation of Moorhead, Minnesota, 1880–1930* (Moorhead: Bethesda, 1930), 8–10, 17–18, 37–42, 65; *A Century Together,* 188; "Rev. J. O. Cavallin," in *Collections of the State Historical Society of North Dakota,* ed. O. G. Libby (Bismarck: Tribune, State Printers, 1910), 3:285–89; *Moorhead Advocate,* December 9, 1880; *Moorhead Weekly News,* July 29, 1886, and May 4, 1893.

76. *Elim Lutheran Church: Remembrances and Records,* ed. Naomi Larson et al. (Fargo: Elim Lutheran Congregation, 1991), 9–14; *A Century Together,* 74–75; *Fargo Daily Argus,* March 31, 1892.

77. *A Century Together,* 74 and 188; Sherman and Thorson, *Plains Folk,* 219; *Moorhead Weekly News,* June 25, 1885, and May 2, 1895; *Fargo and Moorhead City Directory, 1885,* 227–28; *Fargo Daily Argus,* October 13, 1892; *Fargo Forum and Daily Republican,* March 18, 1895, January 8, 1898, and July 3, 1900.

78. *A Century Together,* 174–75; *Moorhead Weekly News,* February 23, May 10, November 1, 1888; January 17 and May 2, 1889; December 8, 1892; Berg, *History of the Evangelical Lutheran Bethesda Congregation,* 19–20.

79. Joy K. Lintelman, *"Likede få job?* Profiles of Swedish Immigrant Employment in Moorhead, Minnesota, 1880–1920," *Hembygden & Världen: Féstskrift till Ulb Beijbom* (Växjö Sweden: Svenska Emigrantinstitutet, 2002), 303–7; *Moorhead Advocate,* January 19, 1878; *Clay County Advocate,* June 24, 1880; Andreas, *Andreas' Historical Atlas,* 243–47; Sherman and Thorson, *Plains Folk,* 219.

80. Lintelman, *"Likede få job?"* 305; Oscar E. Euren interview, July 4 and 8, 1971, Northwest Minnesota Historical Center; Mark Peihl, "Ethnic Settlement Patterns in 1910: Who Settled Where?" *CCHS Newsletter* 22 (July/August 1999): 9, and "Bergquist Cabin Well Hidden," *CCHS Newsletter* 20 (November/December 1997): 6.

81. Glasrud, *Roy Johnson's Red River Valley*, 427; *Fargo Daily Republican*, July 10, 1882; *Fargo Sunday Argus*, January 2, 1887; *Moorhead Weekly News*, May 3, 1888.

82. *Fargo Daily Republican*, April 19 and 29, May 1, June 5, July 25 and 31, August 19, and September 1, 1882; *Fargo Sunday Argus*, April 29, 1883; Robinson, *History of North Dakota*, 317.

83. *A History of the Calvary United Methodist Church: Fargo, ND, 1879–1979* (Fargo: Calvary United Methodist Church, 1879), 5–9; *Fargo Sunday Argus*, May 20, 1888.

84. *Grace Evangelical Lutheran Church: Fargo, ND, 1898–1998* (Fargo: Grace Evangelical Lutheran Church, 1998), 1–7; *A Century Together*, 75; *Fargo Sunday Argus*, December 5, 1886, August 14, 1887, and April 1, 1888; *Fargo Forum*, December 17, 1892; Robinson, *History of North Dakota*, 296, describes German religious divisions: many Roman Catholics, many Lutherans distributed among four Synods, some Mennonites, some Evangelical Association members, some Congregationalists, and some Reformed.

85. Simone de Beauvoir, *The Second Sex*, trans. H. M. Parshley (New York: Vintage Books, 1974), xix–xx.

86. Dolan, *The American Catholic Experience*, 202–3; Jacobson, *Whiteness of a Different Color*, 52, 54, 68–69, 74–75; David R. Roediger and James Barrett, "Inbetween Peoples: Race, Nationality, and the 'New Immigrant' Working Class," in *Colored White: Transcending the Racial Past* (Berkeley: University of California Press, 2002), 141, 146, 148, 149, 164. Danbom, *Going It Alone*, 8–11, thoughtfully discusses evidence of ethnic assimilation as well as racial and religious tensions during the 1930s.

87. Frank J. Richard and Joseph M. DiCola, *The Centennial History of St. Mary's Parish* (Fargo: St. Mary's, 1980), 18–19; *A Century Together*, 186–87; *Clay County Advocate*, September 6, 1879; *Fargo Times*, October 4, 1879.

88. Richard and DiCola, *The Centennial History of St. Mary's Parish*, 20–21, 24–25; Mary R. Brennan, "Bishop John Shanley," in *Collections of the State Historical Society of North Dakota*, 3:681–82; *Fargo Times*, August 19 and 26, September 23, 1880; *Clay County Advocate*, June 15, 1878; *Fargo Daily Republican*, September 19 and 21, 1882; *Fargo Sunday Argus*, November 3, 1889; *Fargo Forum and Daily Republican*, October 29, 1892, October 23, 1894, and November 28, 1896. Catholics composed 48 percent of the sixty-four thousand North Dakota church members in 1890, according to Robinson, *History of North Dakota*, 294.

89. Dolan, *The American Catholic Experience*, 266–67, 276–77; Richard and DiCola, *The Centennial History of St. Mary's Parish*, 52–55; *Fargo Daily Argus*, June 9, 1882, and September 7, 1891.

90. *Fargo Sunday Argus*, October 28, 1888, and August 11, 1891; Richard and DiCola, *The Centennial History of St. Mary's Parish*, 32–36; Brennan, "Bishop John Shanley," 3:680; *Fargo Forum and Republican*, May 30, 1899.

91. *A Century Together*, 72; Dolan, *The American Catholic Experience*, 324–25.

92. Dolan, *The American Catholic Experience*, 155–57, 189–91; *Fargo Sunday Argus*, February 26, 1888, and September 8, 1889; *Fargo Forum and Daily Republican*, November 28, 1896. Danbom, *Going It Alone*, 10–11, finds "mutual wariness and distrust" between Protestants (especially Lutherans) and Catholics in the 1930s.

93. Berthoff, *An Unsettled People*, 418–19; Dolan, *The American Catholic Experience*, 313; Marvin O'Connell, *John Ireland and the American Catholic Church* (St. Paul: Minnesota Historical Society Press, 1988), 262–63; Richard and DiCola, *The Centennial History of St. Mary's Parish*, 29,

31; Brennan, "Bishop John Shanley," 3:678–79; *Fargo Forum and Daily Republican,* February 16, 1897, May 26, 1908, July 17 and August 4, 1909.

94. *Fargo Forum and Daily Republican,* November 23, 1892, January 30, 1893, March 23 and April 18, 1895; O'Connell, *John Ireland,* 107–9, 111, 114, 538 n. 82.

95. *Fargo and Moorhead City Directory, 1900* (St. Paul: Pettibone Directory Company, 1900), 24; *Fargo and Moorhead City Directory, 1904* (St. Paul: Pettibone Company, 1904), 36; Dolan, *The American Catholic Experience,* 257–58, 313, 392; *Fargo Forum and Daily Republican,* December 12, 1904, and September 10, 1909.

96. Øverland, *Immigrant Minds,* 2–3; Doyle, *Social Order of a Frontier Community,* 141–42; Litwicki, *America's Public Holidays,* 134; *Fargo Express,* March 19, 1874; *Fargo Times,* March 22, 1879; *Clay County Advocate,* March 22, 1879; *Moorhead Weekly News,* March 21, 1889; *Fargo Daily Argus,* March 17, 1892; *Fargo Forum and Daily Republican,* March 17 and 21, 1896, and March 18, 1897; O'Connell, *John Ireland,* 104–5.

97. Robert J. Lazar, "From Ethnic Minority to Socio-Economic Elite: A Study of the Jewish Community" (Ph.D. dissertation, University of Minnesota, 1968), 238–39, and "Jewish Communal Life in Fargo, North Dakota: The Formative Years," *North Dakota History* 36 (fall 1969): 348–51, 355; Sherman and Thorson, *Plains Folk,* 400–401, 403–4; *Fargo and Moorhead City Directory, 1900,* 88, 170–71. Danbom, *Going It Alone,* 9–10, discusses Jewish prosperity, acceptance, and apartness in Fargo during the 1930s.

98. Lazar, "Jewish Communal Life," 349–54; Sherman and Thorson, *Plains Folk,* 403.

99. Sherman and Thorson, *Plains Folk,* 381, 384; *Clay County Advocate,* April 5, 1879; *Fargo Sunday Argus,* January 6, 1889, and March 25, 1892.

100. Earl Lewis, "Pioneers of a Different Kind," *Red River Valley Historian* (winter 1978–79): 14–16; *Fargo Forum and Daily Republican,* May 8 and June 11, 1895, August 29, 1899, March 31, 1900; *Fargo Forum,* February 24, 1960.

101. Lewis, "Pioneers of a Different Kind," 16; Sherman and Thorson, *Plains Folk,* 385; *Fargo Forum and Daily Republican,* October 31, 1895, April 3 and 4, 1896; *Fargo Sunday Argus,* October 14, 1888, and January 6, 1889; *Moorhead Weekly News,* July 20 and 27, 1899.

102. Sherman and Thorson, *Plains Folk,* 385–86.

103. Stephanie Abbot Roper, "Anti-Black Prejudice in North Dakota, 1860–1940" (Northern Great Plains History Conference Paper, October 1–3, 1992), 5, 8, 10, in author's possession; *Fargo Weekly Argus,* February 4, 1880; *Fargo Sunday Argus,* November 25, 1888; *Fargo Daily Argus,* February 18, 1891; *Fargo Forum,* December 11 and 15, 1894. Similar negative racial attitudes toward blacks were expressed in the 1930s, according to Danbom, *Going It Alone,* 8–9.

104. *Fargo Sunday Argus,* October 14, 1888; *Fargo Daily Argus,* August 19, 1892; *Fargo Forum and Daily Republican,* August 7 and 27, 1900.

105. *Fargo Express,* June 14 and 21, 1873, and April 30, 1874; *Red River Star,* August 11, 1876; Stafne, "Pioneering in the Red River Valley," 32.

106. *Red River Star,* March 7, 1874; *Clay County Advocate,* April 19, 1879; *Moorhead Weekly News,* January 22, 1885; *Fargo Sunday Argus,* July 31, 1881; Boleyn, *Quarter Sections and Wide Horizons,* 330. On similar negative attitudes expressed toward Native Americans in New York, see Diane Shaw, *City Building on the Eastern Frontier: Sorting the New Nineteenth-Century City* (Baltimore: Johns Hopkins University Press, 2004), 104–6.

107. *Fargo Times*, June 21, August 16, and September 6, 1879; *Clay County Advocate*, August 9, 1879; *Moorhead Weekly News*, January 17 and 31, 1884, and March 22, 1888.

108. Brennan, "Bishop John Shanley," 3:681.

109. Sherman and Thorson, *Plains Folk*, 343; *Fargo City Directory, 1881* (Fargo: Abbot and Nichols, 1881), 68; *Fargo and Moorhead City Directory, 1898–1899* (St. Paul: Pettibone Directory Company, 1897), 95; *Fargo Times*, May 3, June 21, and August 2, 1879; *Moorhead Weekly News*, January 28 and May 27, 1886. The thirty-five Chinese residents of Fargo in 1930 faced similar negative newspaper comment, according to Danbom, *Going It Alone*, 8.

110. Sam Bass Warner Jr., *The Private City: Philadelphia in Three Periods of Growth* (Philadelphia: University of Pennsylvania Press, 1968), 3–4, 111, 117–18, informs my discussion of privatism and public education.

111. Øverland, *Immigrant Minds*, 27.

112. Engelhardt, *On Firm Foundation Grounded*, 103.

5. DOMESTIC VIRTUES

1. Alexis de Tocqueville, *Democracy in America*, ed. J. P. Mayer, trans. George Lawrence (New York: Harper Perennial, 1988), 189, 513–15, 517, 523–24; Paul Boyer, *Urban Masses and Moral Order in America, 1820–1920* (Cambridge: Harvard University Press, 1978), 34, 58, 61, 70, 95. Also see Robert H. Wiebe, *The Search for Order, 1877–1920* (New York: Hill and Wang, 1967), chapters 2 and 3; Don Harrison Doyle, *The Social Order of a Frontier Community: Jacksonville, Illinois, 1825–1879* (Urbana: University of Illinois Press, 1978), 14–15; Karen Halttunen, *Confidence Men and Painted Women: A Study of Middle-Class Culture in America, 1830–1970* (New Haven: Yale University Press, 1982), xvi–xvii, 20–21, 60–61, 90–91, 196–97; Elliott J. Gorn, *The Manly Art: Bare-Knuckle Prize Fighting in America* (Ithaca, N.Y.: Cornell University Press, 1986), 31–32, 66, 108, 121; Richard L. Bushman, *The Refinement of America: Persons, Houses, Cities* (New York: Alfred A. Knopf, 1992), xii–xiii, xv–xviii, 278–79, 281, 313, 352–54, 370, 375, 383, 388–89, 400, 403, 406–7, 410–11, 425, 433–34; Timothy R. Mahoney, *Provincial Lives: Middle-Class Experience in the Antebellum Middle West* (New York: Cambridge University Press, 1999), 81–84, 101, 110–14, 211–12, 260–61.

2. *Red River Star*, September 20, 1873. For discussions of Midwestern middle-class culture, see Andrew R. L. Cayton and Peter S. Onuf, *The Midwest and the Nation: Rethinking the History of an American Region* (Bloomington: Indiana University Press, 1990), 52, 63, 84–85, and Lewis Atherton, *Main Street on the Middle Border* (Chicago: Quadrangle Paperback, 1966), 186–89.

3. Stuart M. Blumin, "Hypothesis of Middle-Class Formation in Nineteenth-Century America: A Critique and Some Proposals," *American Historical Review* 90 (April 1985): 309, 312–13, 330–36, and *The Emergence of the Middle Class: Social Experience in the American City, 1760–1900* (New York: Cambridge University Press, 1989), 12–13, 187, 190–91, 215–18, 297, 304, 307–8.

4. Barbara Miller Solomon, *From Western Prairies to Eastern Commons: A Life in Education, Ada Comstock Notestein, 1876–1973*, ed. Susan Ware (Cambridge: Estate of Barbara Miller Solomon, 1993), 9–10, Schlesinger Library, Radcliffe College, Cambridge; Gregory C. Harness, "Solomon Gilman Comstock: Prairie Lawyer, Legislator and Businessman" (master's thesis, Moorhead State College, 1976), 4, 6, 10, and "Solomon Gilman Comstock: Portrait of a Pioneer," *Red River Valley Historian* (winter 1974–75): 6–7.

5. Solomon, *From Western Prairies to Eastern Commons,* 10–11, 19; Rev. O. H. Elmer Diary, August 23 and December 7, 1877, typed manuscript copy, Clay County Historical Society, Moorhead; *Moorhead Daily News,* June 5, 1933, and January 27, 1941.

6. Solomon, *From Western Prairies to Eastern Commons,* 11–12; Harness, "Solomon Gilman Comstock: Prairie Lawyer," 14, 18–21; Solomon Gilman Comstock, "Memoir," *Red River Valley Historian* (winter 1974–75): 3–4; Henry Johnson, *The Other Side of Main Street: A History Teacher from Sauk Centre* (New York: Columbia University Press, 1943), 118; Solomon G. Comstock to Ada Louise Comstock, October 10, 1919, 88–M193, Carton 2, Folder 59; Ada Louise Comstock Notestein Papers, Schlesinger Library.

7. Solomon, *From Western Prairies to Eastern Commons,* 13, 15; Ellen Gruber Garvey, *The Adman in the Parlor: Magazines and the Gendering of Consumer Culture, 1880s to 1910s* (New York: Oxford University Press, 1996), 18, 80, 83–84, 164–65, 186; Kendra Dillard, "Moorhead's Comstock House: A Story of Restoration," *Minnesota History* 56 (spring 1998): 27–28; Robert Loeffler, "The Comstock House," *Red River Historian* (winter 1974–75): 18.

8. Solomon, *From Western Prairies to Eastern Commons,* 13–15; Sarah Comstock, "Twenty Years of Club Progress," 88–M193, Carton 2, Folder 68, Notestein Papers; Harness, "Solomon Gilman Comstock: Prairie Lawyer," 145.

9. Solomon, *From Western Prairies to Eastern Commons,* 12, 19; Ada Louise Comstock, "Some Memories of Her Life up to 1943," 5, Collected by Roberta Yerkes Blanshard, 78–M59, Carton 2, Notestein Papers; S. G. Comstock to Grace McMillan, March 30, 1890, Letterbook, vol. 6, Solomon G. Comstock Papers, Northwest Minnesota Historical Center, Minnesota State University, Moorhead.

10. Solomon, *From Western Prairies to Eastern Commons,* 13; Ada Comstock, "Some Memories," 4; Dillard, "Moorhead's Comstock House," 20, 23, 25–26, 30–31; Loeffler, "The Comstock House," 19.

11. Solomon, *From Western Prairies to Eastern Commons,* 7–8; Ada Comstock, "Some Memories," 3–4; Ada Louise Comstock Diary, vol. 3, July 25 and August 3, 1904, Notestein Papers. On the movement of respectable women on public streets, see Diane Shaw, *City Building on the Eastern Frontier: Sorting the New Nineteenth-Century City* (Baltimore: Johns Hopkins University Press, 2004), 96–101.

12. Bushman, *The Refinement of America,* xiii, xvii–xviii, 281; Mahoney, *Provincial Lives,* 131, 134; *A Century Together: A History of Fargo, North Dakota, and Moorhead, Minnesota* (Fargo-Moorhead: Centennial Corporation, 1975), 43–45; Tim Holzkamm and Dean Dormanen, *Fargo Historic Context Study* (Fargo: Historic Preservation Commission, 1993), 53–54, 56; *Fargo Sunday Argus,* November 18, 1883; *Fargo Daily Argus,* July 1, 1884; *Fargo Daily Republican,* August 22, October 12, and November 6, 1882. South Eighth Street and North Broadway remained elite neighborhoods in the 1930s, according to David B. Danbom, *Going It Alone: Fargo Grapples with the Great Depression* (St. Paul: Minnesota Historical Society Press, 2005), 4–5.

13. *A Century Together,* 47–48; *Fargo Daily Republican,* November 6, 1882; *Fargo Sunday Argus,* October 22, 1882; *Fargo Daily Argus,* February 14, 1883.

14. On the westward spread of gentility and its effect on middle-class status, see Bushman, *The Refinement of America,* xiii–xviii, 338, 389, 403, 433–34. On less expensive housing, which furthered gentility for many, see Michael J. Doucet and John C. Weaver, "Material Culture and the North American House: The Era of the Common Man, 1870–1920," *Journal of American*

History 72 (December 1985): 561, 563–72, 580–85. On the architecture of middle-class homes, see Gwendolyn Wright, *Moralism and the Model Home: Domestic Architecture and Cultural Conflict in Chicago, 1873–1913* (Chicago: University of Chicago Press, 1980), 4–5, 97–98, and *Building the Dream: A Social History of Housing in America* (New York: Pantheon Books, 1981), 99–102.

15. *Fargo Forum and Daily Republican,* April 19, 1899. For how five immigrant women acquired homes, see Angela Boleyn, *Quarter Sections and Wide Horizons* (Bismarck: North Dakota State Library, 1978), 257, 259, 268, 283, 343–47. Some of these cottages may have been erected by builder-owners, as argued by Olivier Zunz, "Neighborhoods, Homes and the Housing Market," *Michigan History* 66. 6 (1966): 34–35, 39–41, and *The Changing Face of Inequality: Urbanization, Industrial Development, and Immigrants in Detroit, 1880–1920* (Chicago: University of Chicago Press, 1982), chapter 6. Joseph Bigott discusses the pervasiveness of working-class housing in *From Cottage to Bungalow: Houses and the Working Class in Metropolitan Chicago, 1869–1929* (Chicago: University of Chicago Press, 2001), 4–5, 7, 53, 145, 162, 206. *A Century Together,* 113, and Wright, *Building the Dream,* 100, discuss building and loan associations. Danbom, *Going It Alone,* 5, reports that workers still lived in the area north and west of downtown during the 1930s, as well as just north of the water plant on the south side.

16. *Fargo Daily Republican,* October 13, 1882, and *Fargo Daily Argus,* April 13, 1891, suggest seasonal entertainments in developing towns as discussed by Stuart M. Blumin in *The Urban Threshold: Growth and Change in a Nineteenth-Century American Community* (Chicago: University of Chicago Press, 1976). Also see *Red River Star,* August 15, 1874; *Fargo Times,* December 2, 1880; *Fargo Forum and Daily Republican,* July 12 and 15, 1895; Mark Peihl, "Bicycling: The Fad That Didn't Go Away!" *CCHS Newsletter* 14 (May/June 1993): 8–10.

17. Elizabeth H. Pleck, *Celebrating the Family: Ethnicity, Consumer Culture, and Family Rituals* (Cambridge: Harvard University Press, 2000), 147–51. On dancing in the twin cities, see *A Century Together,* 45–46; *Fargo Evening Republican,* February 8, 11, and 18, 1882; *Fargo Daily Argus,* February 11, 1881; *Fargo Sunday Argus,* January 7, November 18 and 29, 1883, November 18, 1885, and October 7, 1888.

18. *Fargo Forum and Daily Republican,* February 23, 1898; L. S. Haynes Diary, June 12, 1885, and January 12, 1887, Box 2, L. S. Haynes Collection, Montana State University, Bozeman.

19. *A Century Together,* 93; *Roy Johnson's Red River Valley,* ed. Clarence A. Glasrud (Moorhead: Red River Valley Historical Society, 1982), 295; *Second Annual Report of the Chamber of Commerce of Fargo, North Dakota, 1880–1881* (Fargo: Daily Argus, 1881), 29; *Fargo Times,* March 29, April 5, and August 2, 1879; *Fargo Evening Republican,* February 7, 13, and 20, 1882; *Fargo Sunday Argus,* August 21, 1881.

20. *Second Annual Report of the Chamber of Commerce of Fargo,* 29; *A Century Together,* 93; Glasrud, *Roy Johnson's Red River Valley,* 295–96; *Fargo Evening Republican,* March 21, 1882; *Fargo Sunday Argus,* December 2, 1883, and October 7, 1888; *Fargo Daily Argus,* November 17, 1891, and March 1, 1892; *Fargo Forum,* December 9, 1892.

21. *A Century Together,* 93: *Fargo Forum,* February 15, 1894, and March 5, 1965; *Fargo Forum and Daily Republican,* May 16, 1898; Fargo Opera House Programs, 1894–99, Box 1, Mary Darrow Wieble Collection, Institute for Regional Studies, North Dakota State University, Fargo.

22. Richard White, *"It's Your Misfortune and None of My Own": A History of the American West* (Norman: University of Oklahoma Press, 1991), 311–12, 315; Julie Roy Jeffrey, *Frontier Women: The Trans-Mississippi West, 1840–1880* (New York: Hill and Wang, 1979), 113, 132–35, 184–85.

23. Cayton and Onuf, *The Midwest and the Nation*, 58; *Red River Star*, February 1, 1873, and December 12, 1874; *Northern Pacific Mirror*, November 21, 1874; *Fargo Daily Republican*, January 11, 1882.

24. Karen J. Blair, *The Clubwoman as Feminist: True Womanhood Redefined, 1868–1914* (New York: Holmes & Meier Publishers, 1980), 4–5, 13, 23, 25, 31, 57, 71.

25. "Historical Sketch," Box 2; Minutes, September 17, 1886, Box 1; President's Annual Report, 1888, 1889, and 1894, Box 4, [all in] Woman's Club of Fargo Records, Institute for Regional Studies; *Fargo Sunday Argus*, February 26, 1888.

26. President's Annual Report, 1898 and 1899, Box 4, Woman's Club of Fargo Records; *Record*, 3 (November 1897): 97–98; Patricia Schroeder, "The Fargo Fortnightly Club: A Study of Clubwomen's Activities" (master's thesis, Moorhead State University, 1983), 1–2, 6, 10–14; Blair, *The Clubwoman as Feminist*, 93, 99, 101, 114–19.

27. *Moorhead Weekly News*, February 25 and March 24, 1892, June 7, 1894, and May 17, 1900; Moorhead City Council Minutes, January 29 and June 6, 1904, October 8, 1906, 339, 361, and 551; Terry L. Shoptaugh, "The Woman's Club and the Moorhead Public Library," 1–4, undated typed manuscript, Northwest Minnesota Historical Center.

28. *Red River Star*, November 27, 1875; *Fargo Times*, December 20, 1879; *Fargo Daily Republican*, October 31 and December 1, 1882; *Fargo Sunday Argus*, May 6, December 9 and 30, 1883, January 31 and June 20, 1886, May 1, 1887, and October 6, 1889; *Fargo Daily Argus*, July 14, 1892; *Fargo Forum and Daily Republican*, November 14, 1895, March 12, 15, and 18, April 3, 1897; Fargo City Council Minutes, March 16 and April 5, 1897, Box 5, Institute for Regional Studies.

29. Fargo City Council Minutes, March 15 and April 2, 1900; *Fargo Forum and Daily Republican*, March 19 and 31, June 14, 1900; President's Annual Reports, 1900, Box 4, Woman's Club of Fargo Records; Roy Johnson Index Fargo City Council Minutes, April 5, 1897, March 15, April 12, and November 5, 1900, April 1, 1901, and February 2, 1903; Lauren L. McCroskey, "'A Mighty Influence': Library Philanthropy in North Dakota during the Carnegie Era," *North Dakota History* 57 (spring 1990): 15, 17–20.

30. Boyer, *Urban Masses*, 157–61; Thomas Bender, *Toward an Urban Vision: Ideas and Institutions in Nineteenth-Century America* (Lexington: University Press of Kentucky, 1975), 153–55.

31. *Moorhead Weekly News*, December 13, 1883, January 10, 1884, February 9, 1887, October 24 and November 7, 1889, November 9, 1893, January 4 and November 8, 1894.

32. *Moorhead Weekly News*, January 17, 1895, and January 23, 1896; Johnson, *The Other Side of Main Street*, 127–28.

33. *Fargo Forum and Daily Republican*, February 16, 1895, states the neighborly charity ideal. Steven R. Hoffbeck discusses North Dakota poor relief in "Prairie Paupers: North Dakota Poor Farms, 1879–1973" (doctor of arts thesis, University of North Dakota, 1992), 34, 37, 43, 45–46, 50. Also see *Fargo Daily Republican*, November 28, 1882; *Fargo Sunday Argus*, January 31 and December 12, 1886, November 24, 1889; Roy Johnson Index Fargo City Council Minutes, January 25, 1887, 18.

34. Hoffbeck, "Prairie Paupers," 38–42, 57, 94; Boyer, *Urban Masses*, 144, 148–52; *Fargo Forum and Daily Republican*, December 4, 1893, March 15, 1894, and February 16, 1895.

35. Hoffbeck, "Prairie Paupers," 48–49; *Fargo Forum and Daily Republican*, April 18 and May 30, 1895, March 26, 1896.

36. *Fargo Forum and Daily Republican*, March 6 and June 25, 1896; February 9, March 5, and April 5, 1897; March 1, 1899, and January 17, 1900.

37. *Fargo Daily Argus*, January 27, 1892; *Fargo Forum and Daily Republican*, October 25, 1893, October 24, 1895, November 17 and December 10 and 23, 1896, March 4, 1899, and February 17, 1900. On the Catholic charity crusade, see Jay P. Dolan, *The American Catholic Experience: A History from Colonial Times to the Present* (New York: Doubleday, 1985), 328–29, 334–35, 343–44. In the late nineteenth century, Catholics and Protestants each focused on individual charity. The American Catholic church did not embrace social justice until after the First World War.

38. Hoffbeck, "Prairie Paupers," 66–68, 112.

39. Sara M. Evans analyzes the connections between domesticity, reform, and suffrage in *Born for Liberty: A History of Women in America* (New York: Free Press, 1989), chapters 6 and 7. Also see Blair, *The Clubwoman as Feminist*, 114, 117; Elwyn B. Robinson, *History of North Dakota* (Lincoln: University of Nebraska Press, 1966), 259; Elizabeth Preston Anderson, Autobiography—"Under the Prairie Wind," 83–84, Box 1, Elizabeth Preston Anderson Papers.

40. Schroeder, *"Fargo Fortnightly Club,"* 14; *Fargo Forum and Daily Republican*, November 13, 15, and 18, 1895, February 6, April 9, 10, and 22, July 8, and October 27, 1896.

41. *Fargo Weekly Argus*, January 14, 1880; Elmer Diary, January 26, 1884; Boyer, *Urban Masses*, 142.

42. Carroll Engelhardt, "Religion, Morality and Citizenship in the Public Schools: Iowa, 1858–1930," in *Ideas in America's Cultures: From Republic to Mass Society*, ed. Hamilton Cravens (Ames: Iowa State University Press, 1982), 45–46, 48–51, 56.

43. Johnson, *The Other Side of Main Street*, 119; Elmer Diary, March 20, 1884; *Fargo Daily Republican*, February 28 and April 25, 1882; *Fargo Daily Argus*, November 19, 1884; *Moorhead Weekly News*, April 28 and December 22, 1892, May 2, 1895.

44. *Red River Star*, October 11, 1873; *Moorhead Weekly News*, June 14, 1883, June 24 and December 23, 1886, August 8 and 29, 1889, December 7, 1899; Fargo City Council Minutes, December 6, 1886, vol. 3, 331.

45. Boyer, *Urban Masses*, 108–17; Howard P. Chudacoff, *Age of the Bachelor: Creating An American Subculture* (Princeton, N.J.: Princeton University Press, 1999), 164–65; Thomas Winter, *Making Men, Making Class: The YMCA and Working Men, 1877–1920* (Chicago: University of Chicago Press, 2002), 3–4, 7, 48, 63, 86–87, 89, 146–47; Jessica I. Elfenbein, *The Making of a Modern City: Philanthropy, Civic Culture, and the Baltimore YMCA* (Gainesville: University Press of Florida, 2001), 4–5, 26–27, 78, 118.

46. *Fargo Times*, August 23 and September 6, 1879; *Fargo Sunday Courier-News*, March 12, 1911; *Fargo Daily Republican*, June 24, November 13 and 14, 1882; *Daily Argonaut*, December 28, 1881; *Moorhead Weekly News*, April 20, 1882, May 7, 1885, and February 6, 1896.

47. *Moorhead Weekly News*, May 4, 1899, May 17 and 31, September 27, October 24, 1900; Chudacoff, *Age of the Bachelor*, 157; Elfenbein, *Making of a Modern City*, 104–6; Winter, *Making Men, Making Class*, 108–11.

48. *Fargo Forum and Daily Republican*, November 11, 1894, May 28, September 25, November 13, 20, 22, and 29, 1895, July 22, 1896, September 29, 1897, and May 12, 1899; Elfenbein, *Making of a Modern City*, 11–12.

49. Gorn, *The Manly Art*, 180; *Fargo Sunday Argus*, February 10, 1889; *Fargo Forum and Daily Republican*, May 18, 1894, November 20, 1895, May 19, 1896, May 25, 1897, March 9 and July 1, 1898.

50. Boyer, *Urban Masses*, 140–41; *Moorhead Weekly News*, May 9, June 27, July 4, October 17, and November 21, 1895, January 30, 1896; *Fargo Forum and Daily Republican*, March 19, 1896.

51. Doyle, *Social Order of a Frontier Community*, 212, 214–15, 226; White, *"It's Your Misfortune*," 361; Norman H. Clark, *Deliver Us from Evil: An Interpretation of American Prohibition* (New York: W. W. Norton, 1976), 62–63; Joseph R. Gusfield, *Symbolic Crusade: Status Politics and the American Temperance Movement* (Urbana: University of Illinois Press, 1976), 4–7, 45–46, 57, 59, 70–71.

52. White, *"It's Your Misfortune*," 361; *Moorhead Advocate*, April 13 and 27, 1878; *Clay County Advocate*, December 2, 9, 16, and 23, 1880; *Fargo Times*, December 9, 1880; *Fargo Daily Argus*, February 4, 1881, and June 25, 1890; *Fargo Sunday Argus*, October 31, 1881, August 14, 1887, and July 1, 1888; *Fargo Daily Republican*, February 13 and July 10, 1882; Elmer Diary, March 15, 1881.

53. For Shanley's position, see *Fargo Forum and Daily Republican*, January 30, 1893. On Scandinavian temperance, see Jon Gjerde, *The Minds of the West: Ethnocultural Evolution in the Rural Middle West, 1830–1917* (Chapel Hill: University of North Carolina Press, 1997), 295; *Fargo Sunday Argus*, July 25 and August 15, 1886; *Fargo Forum and Daily Republican*, June 30 and July 4, 1900; *Moorhead Weekly News*, April 5, 1888, March 3, 1892, November 16 and 23, 1893; Carroll Engelhardt, *On Firm Foundation Grounded: The First Century of Concordia College, 1891–1991* (Moorhead: Concordia College, 1991), 28–29, 62–63.

54. Evans, *Born for Liberty*, 125–29; Gusfield, *Symbolic Crusade*, 72, 83, 85; White, *"It's Your Misfortune*," 361–62; Jeffrey, *Frontier Women*, 185, 189; Clark, *Deliver Us from Evil*, 65, 73–77, 85–87, 90–91; Sydney E. Ahlstrom, *A Religious History of the American People*, 2d ed. (New Haven: Yale University Press, 2004), 863. For an example of direct action by North Dakota Norwegian farm women in contrast to moral suasion of the American-dominated WCTU, see Barbara Handy-Marchello, "Land, Liquor and the Women of Hatton, North Dakota," *North Dakota History* 59 (fall 1992): 23–25.

55. *Moorhead Weekly News*, July 12, 1883, August 27, 1885, October 21, 1886, June 9, 1887, January 25 and June 21, 1894; Moorhead City Council Minutes, January 7, 1884, 207.

56. Bill G. Reid, "Elizabeth Preston Anderson and the Politics of Social Reform," in *The North Dakota Political Tradition*, ed. Thomas W. Howard (Ames: Iowa State University Press, 1981), 189; *Fargo Times*, September 2, 1880; *Fargo Daily Republican*, August 31, December 4, 1882; *Fargo Sunday Argus*, January 2 and February 27, 1887, June 24 and August 19, 1888, January 27, 1889; *Moorhead Weekly News*, June 30, 1887; Fargo City Council Minutes, December 3, 1888, vol. 3, 603.

57. *Fargo Sunday Argus*, October 20, 1889; Elizabeth Preston, "Prohibition" (1889), Speeches, Box 1, and "Under the Prairie Winds," 25–26, 77, Elizabeth Preston Anderson Papers; Reid, "Elizabeth Preston Anderson," 188–90, 192–94.

58. Robinson, *History of North Dakota*, 258–59; *Fargo Daily Argus*, May 27, 1885, and July 11, 1890; *Moorhead Weekly News*, October 27, 1887, and March 8, 1888.

59. Anderson, "Under the Prairie Winds," 81, 83, 86–87, 97–98; Frances Willard to E. Preston, November 27, 1894; Elizabeth Preston to Katharine Stevenson, February 18, 1898, [all in] Elizabeth Preston Anderson Papers; Reid, "Elizabeth Preston Anderson," 194–99.

60. *Moorhead Weekly News*, February 14, 1895; Melva Moline, *The Forum: First Hundred Years* (Fargo: Moline, 1979), 38, 73–74; *Fargo Forum and Daily Republican*, March 25, 29, and 30, 1895, February 3 and May 21, 1897, January 11, 1898, and December 18, 1899.

61. *Fargo and Moorhead City Directory, 1900* (St. Paul: Pettibone Directory Co., 1900), 23–28, 225–27; Lynn Dumenil, *Freemasonry and American Culture, 1880–1930* (Princeton, N.J.: Princeton University Press, 1984), xi; Rowland Berthoff, *An Unsettled People: Social Order and Disorder in American History* (New York: Harper & Row, 1971), 445, 447; Chudacoff, *Age of the Bachelor,* 152–53. For explanations that connect fraternalism to middle-class moral order, see Berthoff, *An Unsettled People,* 254, 274; Doyle, *Social Order of a Frontier Community,* 178–80, 187, 190, 192–93; Mark C. Carnes, *Secret Ritual and Manhood in Victorian America* (New Haven: Yale University Press, 1989), 2–4, 31–32; David T. Beito, *From Mutual Aid to the Welfare State: Fraternal Societies and Social Services, 1890–1967* (Chapel Hill: University of North Carolina Press, 2000), 27–31, 44–45. For a recent revisionist interpretation that stresses competitive voluntarism, self-segregation, and insurance benefits, see Jason Kaufman, *For the Common Good? American Civic Life and the Golden Age of Fraternity* (New York: Oxford University Press, 2002), 3, 5, 8, 144, 161, 178, 188. He concludes that fraternalism poorly formed social capital.

62. Dumenil, *Freemasonry and American Culture,* xi–xiii, 219; Catherine McNicol Stock, *Main Street in Crisis: The Great Depression and the Old Middle Class on the Northern Plains* (Chapel Hill: University of North Carolina Press, 1992), 60, 170–72, 184; *Semi-Centennial Anniversary, 1883–1933* (Fargo: *Keystone Chapter No. 5,* 1933), 1; Harold Sackett Pond, *Masonry in North Dakota, 1804–1964* (Grafton: Record Printers, 1964), 61; John Turner and C. R. Semling, *History of Clay and Norman Counties* (Indianapolis: B. F. Brown, 1918), 1:250; *Red River Star,* April 1, 1876.

63. Carnes, *Secret Ritual,* 5; *Souvenir of Masonic Temple, Fargo, ND* (Fargo: Walker Brothers and Hardy, 1903), 4, 8, 10, 44–52; Pond, *Masonry in North Dakota,* 98.

64. Chudacoff, *Age of the Bachelor,* 153–54; Carnes, *Secret Ritual,* 14, 60–63, 75–79, 114–16, 120, 126, 149–50.

65. Carnes, *Secret Ritual,* 81, 84–88; Mary Ann Clawson, "Nineteenth-Century Women's Auxiliaries and Fraternal Orders," *Signs: Journal of Women in Culture and Society* 12 (autumn 1986): 45–46, 50–52; Turner and Semling, *History of Clay and Norman Counties,* 1:251; *Fargo Forum and Daily Republican,* December 16, 1893, October 12, 1894, and June 20, 1895; *Souvenir of Masonic Temple, Fargo, ND,* 48.

66. Dumenil, *Freemasonry and American Culture,* 220–21; Beito, *From Mutual Aid to the Welfare State,* 3, 7–8, 10, 14–15, 19, 49, 62; George Emery and J. C. Herbert Emery, *A Young Man's Benefit: The Independent Order of Odd Fellows and Sickness Insurance in the United States and Canada, 1860–1929* (Montreal and Kingston: McGill-Queen's University Press, 1999), 3, 46, 65–66; *Fargo Daily Republican,* May 2, 1882; *Fargo Sunday Argus,* October 20, 1889; *Fargo Forum,* November 8, 1892, and February 1, 1894; Turner and Semling, *History of Clay and Norman Counties,* 1:251.

67. Dumenil, *Freemasonry and American Culture,* 220; Beito, *From Mutual Aid to the Welfare State,* 12; Carnes, *Secret Ritual,* 9; Berthoff, *An Unsettled People,* 446; Turner and Semling, *History of Clay and Norman Counties,* 1:256; *Moorhead Advocate,* May 11, 1878; *Fargo Daily Republican,* September 27, 1882; *Fargo Forum and Daily Republican,* September 4 and December 19, 1894, November 19, 1895, February 5, 1896.

68. Carnes, *Secret Ritual,* 8; Berthoff, *An Unsettled People,* 446; Roy Johnson, "The Boys in Blue," *Fargo Forum,* undated clipping, North Dakota Masonic Collection, Institute for Regional Studies; *Fargo Forum and Daily Republican,* December 17, 1894; GAR Meeting Minutes, January 1, June 18, and October 15, 1900, Box 1, GAR Papers and WRC Meeting Minutes, June 19, 1893, and September 3, 1894, Box 1, Woman's Relief Corps Records, Institute for Regional Studies.

69. Richard Lingeman, *Small Town America: A Narrative History, 1620 to the Present* (New York: G. P. Putnam's Sons, 1980), 318–19; Ellen M. Litwicki, *America's Public Holidays, 1865–1920* (Washington, D.C.: Smithsonian Institution Press, 2000), 11–14, 24–26; Michael Kammen, *Mystic Chords of Memory: The Transformation of Tradition in American Culture* (New York: Vintage Books, 1993), 104–6; *Fargo Sunday Argus,* May 29, 1887; *Fargo Forum and Daily Republican,* May 21 and 30, 1894, May 30, 1895, May 24, 1897, May 30, 1898, May 29, 1899.

70. WRC Meeting Minutes, May 21, 1894, February 4, 1895, March 2 and October 5, 1896, Box 1, Woman's Relief Corps Records; *Fargo Forum and Daily Republican,* March 19, 1895.

71. Thomas White Harvey, "The Making of Railroad Towns in Minnesota's Red River Valley" (master's thesis, Pennsylvania State University, 1982), 186, 189.

72. Sam Bass Warner Jr., *The Private City: Philadelphia in Three Periods of Growth* (Philadelphia: University of Pennsylvania Press, 1968), 3–4.

73. White, *"It's Your Misfortune,"* 317–18, 325.

6. VAGABONDS, WORKERS, AND PURVEYORS OF VICE

1. The quotation is from Rowland Berthoff, *An Unsettled People: Social Order and Disorder in American History* (New York: Harper & Row, 1971), 232; also see 219, 222–25, 331–33, and 427. Julie Roy Jeffrey, *Frontier Women: The Trans-Mississippi West, 1840–1880* (New York: Hill and Wang, 1979), 4, 6–7, 10, 12–13, 24, 79, 80–84.

2. For the local struggle between middle-class order and working-class disorder, see Solomon Gilman Comstock, "Memoir," *Red River Valley Historian* (winter 1974–75): 4; Rev. O. H. Elmer Diary, October 22 and December 17, 1871, November 25 and 29, December 7, 1872, typed manuscript copy, Clay County Historical Society, Moorhead. On the same contest in other western cities, see Lawrence H. Larsen and Barbara J. Cottrell, *The Gate City: A History of Omaha,* enlarged ed. (Lincoln: University of Nebraska Press, 1997), 90–91, 94–97; Robert R. Dykstra, *The Cattle Towns* (Lincoln: University of Nebraska Press, 1983), 242, 253.

3. Arthur Meier Schlesinger, *The Rise of the City, 1878–1898* (New York: Macmillan, 1933), 117–19; Berthoff, *An Unsettled People,* 331–32; Todd DePastino, *Citizen Hobo: How a Century of Homelessness Shaped America* (Chicago: University of Chicago Press, 2003), 5, 8–10, 12–15, 17; Kenneth L. Kusmer, "The Underclass in Historical Perspective: Tramps and Vagrants in Urban America, 1870–1930," in *On Being Homeless: Historical Perspectives,* ed. Rick Beard (New York: Museum of the City of New York, 1987), 21–23, and *Down and Out, on the Road: The Homeless in American History* (New York: Oxford University Press, 2002), 110, 112–13, 116–20, 140–41.

4. Frank Tobias Higbie, *Indispensable Outcasts: Hobo Workers and Community in the American Midwest, 1880–1930* (Urbana: University of Illinois Press, 2003), 2–5, 41–42, and "Indispensable Outcasts: Harvest Laborers in the Wheat Fields of the Middle West, 1890–1925," *Labor History* 38 (fall 1997): 393–94; Thomas D. Isern, *Bull Threshers and Bindlestiffs: Harvesting and Threshing on the North American Plains* (Lawrence: University Press of Kansas, 1975), 137; Kusmer, *Down and Out,* 126. On the origins of Red River Valley harvest hands, see *Fargo Forum and Daily Republican,* March 19, 1896. Hobo life and lodgings are described in a classic sociological study by Nels Anderson, *The Hobo: The Sociology of the Homeless Man* (Chicago: University of Chicago Press, 1961), 27, 29–31, 40–41, 61, 142, 149, 150, 167, 261–62, and in a work by

geographer Paul Groth, *Living Downtown: The History of Residential Hotels in the United States* (Berkeley: University of California Press, 1994), 23–24, 120–21, 140–41, 151–52, 160.

5. Isern, *Bull Threshers and Bindlestiffs*, 149–50; *Fargo Forum and Daily Republican*, July 11, 1895, August 19, 1898, and April 18, 1899; *Moorhead Weekly News*, July 26, 1900.

6. Isern, *Bull Threshers and Bindlestiffs*, 160; "Higbie, "Indispensable Outcasts," 399–400; Kusmer, *Down and Out*, 60–62, 64–66; *Moorhead Weekly News*, August 5, 1886.

7. DePastino, *Citizen Hobo*, 70, 79–80; *Moorhead Weekly News*, August 9, 1888; *Fargo Forum*, May 22 and August 17, 1894.

8. Higbie, "Indispensable Outcasts," 409–12 and *Indispensable Outcasts*, 42; H. E. Berggren, "Notes on My Journey to America in 1893 and Finding Work in the New Land," *Swedish American Historical Quarterly* 42 (July 1991): 148–57. Colleague Joy Lintelman alerted me to this article.

9. Kusmer, *Down and Out*, 51, 57–58, 74; *Clay County Advocate*, April 26, 1879, and April 10, 1880; *Fargo Times*, April 19, July 12, and August 2, 1879, August 5, 1880.

10. DePastino, *Citizen Hobo*, 22; *Fargo Daily Argus*, August 5, 1885; *Moorhead Weekly News*, August 1, 1895 and September 14, 1899; Moorhead City Council Minutes, August 2, 1897, 364–65; *Fargo Forum*, August 3, 1894.

11. Knut Hamsun, "On the Prairie: A Sketch of the Red River Valley," *Minnesota History* 13 (September 1961): 268; *Moorhead Weekly News*, September 27, 1888, September 26, 1895, and August 25, 1898; *Fargo Forum and Daily Republican*, August 3, 1898.

12. An 1885 state census lists 159 railroad employees who are mostly laborers. See *Dakota Territory, 1885 Census*, HA 631 1885 .D34, Institute for Regional Studies, North Dakota State University, Fargo; William H. Hunt and Randell Hunt, *The City of Fargo, Its History and Census* (January 1, 1879), 30–31; *Fargo Express*, June 18, 1874; D. Jerome Tweton, *In the Union There Is Strength: The North Dakota Labor Movement and the United Brotherhood of Carpenters and Joiners* (Grand Forks: North Dakota Carpenter Craftsman Heritage Society, 1982), 27; Shelton Stromquist, *A Generation of Boomers: The Pattern of Railroad Labor Conflict in Nineteenth-Century America* (Urbana: University of Illinois Press, 1987), 106–9; Thomas Winter, *Making Men, Making Class: The YMCA and Working Men, 1877–1920* (Chicago: University of Chicago Press, 2002), 67–68; Richard White, *"It's Your Misfortune and None of My Own": A History of the American West* (Norman: University of Oklahoma Press, 1991), 289.

13. *Fargo Express*, June 18, 1874; *Fargo Sunday Argus*, February 21, 1886, December 2, 1888, and July 7, 1889; *Fargo Daily Argus*, August 19, 1884; *Fargo Forum*, November 19, 1892, and December 1, 1893.

14. Stromquist, *A Generation of Boomers*, 102–5, 117, 122–23, 138.

15. *Moorhead Advocate*, July 28 and August 11, 1877; DePastino, *Citizen Hobo*, 24; Kusmer, *Down and Out*, 44–45, 47–48.

16. Richard Hofstadter, *The Age of Reform: From Bryan to FDR* (New York: Vintage Books, 1955), 64, 121–22; Herbert G. Gutman, *Work, Culture and Society in Industrializing America: Essays in American Working-Class and Social History* (New York: Vintage Books, 1977), 48–51; *Moorhead Weekly News*, August 2, 1883, January 10, 1884, March 24, 1892, and August 31, 1893.

17. *Fargo Daily Argus*, July 19, August 19, and 27, 1892.

18. Carlos A. Schwantes, *Coxey's Army: An American Odyssey* (Lincoln: University of Nebraska Press, 1985), 1–2, 8–12; DePastino, *Citizen Hobo*, 60, 64.

19. *Fargo Forum*, May 1, 2, and 3, 1894; *Moorhead Weekly News*, May 3, 1894; Schwantes, *Coxey's Army*, 261–62, 265, 267.

20. Schwantes, *Coxey's Army*, 56, 235, 239–40, 245, 269; *Fargo Forum and Daily Republican*, June 7, 8, and 12, 1894; *Moorhead Weekly News*, June 14, 1894.

21. *Fargo Forum and Daily Republican*, June 15 and 16, 1894; Schwantes, *Coxey's Army*, 240, 243–45, 257, 266.

22. *Fargo Forum and Daily Republican*, June 26, 1894; *Moorhead Weekly News*, June 28, 1894; Schwantes, *Coxey's Army*, 12, 254–56, 271–72, 275.

23. *Moorhead Weekly News*, April 19 and 26, 1894; *Fargo Forum and Daily Republican*, April 19 and 27, 1894; Stromquist, *A Generation of Boomers*, 146; Claire Strom, *Profiting from the Plains: The Great Northern Railway and Corporate Development of the American West* (Seattle: University of Washington Press, 2003), 154; Olivier Zunz, *Making America Corporate, 1870–1920* (Chicago: University of Chicago Press, 1990), 64.

24. *Moorhead Weekly News*, May 3, 1894; *Fargo Forum and Daily Republican*, May 2 and 4, June 5, 1894; M. A. Hildreth to W. L. Willard, May 5, 1894, Box 2, Melvin A. Hildreth Papers, Institute for Regional Studies; Albro Martin, *James J. Hill and the Opening of the Northwest* (New York: Oxford University Press, 1976), 415–16.

25. Stanley Buder, *Pullman: An Experiment in Industrial Order and Community Planning, 1880–1930* (New York: Oxford University Press, 1977), 158, 161, 168–70, 179. For an acute analysis of shifting class divisions in two Iowa railroad communities during 1877 and 1888 strikes, see Stromquist, *A Generation of Boomers*, xv, 146, 172–74, 181–82, 186–87.

26. *Fargo Forum and Daily Republican*, June 28 and 29, July 3 and 5, 1894; *Moorhead Weekly News*, June 28, 1894.

27. *Fargo Forum and Daily Republican*, July 7, 9, 10, and 11, 1894.

28. Buder, *Pullman*, 183–85, 187; *Fargo Forum and Daily Republican*, July 12, 13, and 19, 1894; *Moorhead Weekly News*, July 19, 1894; Stromquist, *A Generation of Boomers*, 127.

29. Buder, *Pullman*, 187–88; Mary Lethert Wingerd, *Claiming the City: Politics, Faith, and the Power of Place in St. Paul* (Ithaca, N.Y.: Cornell University Press, 2001), 86–87, 112; Stromquist, *A Generation of Boomers*, 141.

30. *Moorhead Weekly News*, July 26 and August 9, 1894; *Fargo Forum and Daily Republican*, August 8, 1894, and March 5, 1896; *Record*, 1 (May 1895): 34.

31. Edward Chase Kirkland, *Industry Comes of Age: Business, Labor, and Public Policy, 1860–1897* (Chicago: Quadrangle Books, 1967), 369; *Fargo Forum*, May 10, 1941; *Fargo Forum and Daily Republican*, February 26, March 4, 7, and 8, June 3, November 2 and 9, 1895; *Moorhead Weekly News*, March 14 and November 7, 1895.

32. Shelton Stromquist, "The Crisis of 1894 and the Legacies of Producerism," in *The Pullman Strike and the Crisis of the 1890s: Essays in Labor and Politics*, ed. Richard Schneirove, Shelton Stromquist, and Nick Salvatore (Urbana: University of Illinois Press, 1999), 186; Gerald N. Grob, *Workers and Utopia: A Study of Ideological Conflict in the American Labor Movement, 1865–1900* (Chicago: Quadrangle Books, 1969), 148; *Fargo Evening Republican*, March 8, 1882; *Fargo Forum*, December 19, 1892, January 12 and October 31, 1893.

33. Tweton, *In the Union There Is Strength*, 27; Melvyn Dubofsky, *Industrialism and the American Worker, 1865–1920*, 2d ed. (Arlington Heights, Ill.: Harlan Davidson, 1985), 64–65;

Fargo Forum and Daily Republican, July 2, 1894, December 5, 1895, January 2 and April 14, 1896, August 26 and November 4, 1898; *Moorhead Weekly News,* June 25, 1896.

34. *Fargo Forum and Daily Republican,* May 18, July 6, 9, and 24, 1894, August 15, 1895.

35. *Fargo Sunday Argus,* May 6 and 27, 1888; *Moorhead Weekly News,* July 5, 1888; *Fargo Forum and Daily Republican,* December 17, 1892, January 4, 24, and 31, April 4, 1893, May 11 and 13, 1895, April 9, 1896, May 22 and 25, December 31, 1897.

36. *Fargo Forum and Daily Republican,* March 31, April 1, and May 19, 1896; "Fargo Biographies," Newspaper Clippings, North Dakota Masonic File #370 and Roy Johnson's Index Fargo City Council Minutes, July 7, 1886, 18, Institute for Regional Studies.

37. Ellen M. Litwicki, *America's Public Holidays, 1865–1920* (Washington, D.C.: Smithsonian Institution Press, 2000), 73–74, 80–82, 94–95, 97, 100–103, 106, 110–12.

38. *Fargo Daily Argus,* September 1 and 8, 1891, September 5 and 6, 1892; *Fargo Forum and Daily Republican,* September 5, 1893, September 3, 1894, August 17, September 2, 3, and 5, 1895, *Moorhead Weekly News,* September 5, 1895.

39. *Fargo Forum and Daily Republican,* September 5, 1898, and September 4, 1899; Litwicki, *America's Public Holidays,* 74.

40. *Fargo Forum and Daily Republican,* September 23, October 14, 15, and 16, 1896; Dubofsky, *Industrialism and the American Worker,* 71–75.

41. Tweton, *In the Union There Is Strength,* 27–30, 32, and 96; Catherine McNicol Stock, *Main Street in Crisis: The Great Depression and the Old Middle Class on the Northern Plains* (Chapel Hill: University of North Carolina Press, 1992), 9; Dubofsky, *Industrialism and the American Worker,* 65–67, 75. Fargo remained inhospitable to unions during the 1930s, according to David B. Danbom, *Going It Alone: Fargo Grapples with the Great Depression* (St. Paul: Minnesota Historical Society Press, 2005), 144, 155.

42. Norman H. Clark, *Deliver Us from Evil: An Interpretation of American Prohibition* (New York: W. W. Norton, 1976), 4, 12–13, 34, 42–44, 50–58, 66–67; Jeffrey, *Frontier Women,* 184–85; Thomas J. Noel, *The City and the Saloon: Denver, 1858–1916* (Lincoln: University of Nebraska Press, 1982), 79, 81; Perry R. Duis, *The Saloon: Public Drinking in Chicago and Boston, 1880–1920* (Urbana: University of Illinois Press, 1983), 283. I calculated per capita beer consumption from Clark's production figures of 36 million gallons (1850) and 855 million gallons (1890).

43. Howard P. Chudacoff, *Age of the Bachelor: Creating An American Subculture* (Princeton, N.J.: Princeton University Press, 1999), 107, 110, 113, 229–30; DePastino, *Citizen Hobo,* 79–80; Henry Johnson, *The Other Side of Main Street: A History Teacher from Sauk Centre* (New York: Columbia University Press, 1943), 120. For other scholarly treatments of the saloon as a workingman's club, see Madelon Powers, *Faces along the Bar: Lore and Order in the Workingman's Saloon, 1870–1920* (Chicago: University of Chicago Press, 1998), 2–3, 6–7, 227–30; Duis, *The Saloon,* 71, 121; Noel, *The City and the Saloon,* 91.

44. *Fargo and Moorhead City Directory, 1884* (Fargo: G. E. Nichols and R. W. Bliss, 1884), 170 and 225; *Fargo and Moorhead City Directory, 1900* (St. Paul: Pettibone Directory Co., 1900), 295–96; Elliot West, *The Saloon on the Rocky Mountain Mining Frontier* (Lincoln: University of Nebraska Press, 1979), 47, 50, 52–53, 56, 59–62, 96; Duis, *The Saloon,* 78, 83–85, 271–73.

45. *Souvenir: Haas's Midway Café, Moorhead, Minn., 1899; Moorhead Daily News,* September 18, 1897; Noel, *The City and the Saloon,* 23, 31–32.

46. *Atlas of Cass County, 1906* (St. Paul: R. L. Polk & Co., 1906), 121, 123, 125; *A Century*

Together: A History of Fargo, North Dakota and Moorhead, Minnesota (Fargo-Moorhead: Centennial Corporation, 1975), 152; Hiram M. Drache, *The Challenge of the Prairie: Life and Times of Red River Pioneers* (Fargo: North Dakota Institute for Regional Studies, 1970), 280–82; Duis, *The Saloon*, 154, 177; Powers, *Faces along the Bar*, 34, 212.

47. Joseph R. Gusfield, *Symbolic Crusade: Status Politics and the American Temperance Movement* (Urbana: University of Illinois Press, 1976), 4–7.

48. Gregory Harness, "Solomon Gilman Comstock," *Red River Valley Historian* (winter 1974–75): 7; John Turner and C. R. Semling, *History of Clay and Norman Counties* (Indianapolis: B. F. Brown, 1918), 1:271; Edith S. Moll, "Moorhead, MN: Frontier Town, 1871–1915" (master's thesis, North Dakota Agricultural College, 1957), 92, 95, 97, 100–104.

49. Elmer Diary, May 15 and 19, 1873, January 11, 1876, April 9, 1881, May 11, 1884, January 21 and 22, 1886; Moorhead City Council Minutes, May 7 and 26, 1875, 5–8, 19; *Red River Star*, July 17, 1875; *Clay County Advocate*, April 3 and July 1, 1880. From the start, many western communities licensed saloons for revenue and control, according to West, *Saloon on the Rocky Mountain Mining Frontier*, 114.

50. Fargo City Council Minutes, July 10 and August 10, 1875, vol. 1, 11 and 13; *Fargo Times*, November 18 and December 2, 1880.

51. Jeffrey, *Frontier Women*, 134–35, 184–85, West, *Saloon on the Rocky Mountain Mining Frontier*, 132–33, 138, 142; Moorhead City Council Minutes, May 2 and 16, 1881, 8 and 11, April 29, 1884, 251, and April 28, 1887, 429–32; *Moorhead Weekly News*, July 26, 1883, January 17 and February 14, 1884, April 11 and December 26, 1889.

52. Fargo City Council Minutes, November 26, 1883, January 7, July 7, and October 6, 1884, vol. 3, 116, 122, 171, and 200; Roy Johnson Index Fargo City Council Minutes, May 5, September 1, and October 6, 1884, and December 6, 1886, 17–18; *Fargo Sunday Argus*, May 1, August 14, October 9, and November 13, 1887; *Moorhead Weekly News*, November 3 and 10, 1887.

53. *Moorhead Weekly News*, October 13, 1887, March 1, 1888, November 7, 1889; Johnson, *The Other Side of Main Street*, 120.

54. *Moorhead Weekly News*, June 16 and July 7, 1892, March 29 and October 25, 1894, April 7, 1898; Moorhead City Council Minutes, June 29 and July 1, 1892, 216, 218, April 9, 1900, 54.

55. *Moorhead Weekly News*, April 13, 1893, August 9 and 16, 1894, March 5 and April 16, 1896, December 15, 1898, March 29, September 27, October 4 and December 27, 1900; Moorhead City Council Minutes, July 7, 1899, 637, and December 10 and 17, 1900, 126–28.

56. Elwyn B. Robinson, *History of North Dakota* (Lincoln: University of Nebraska Press, 1966), 258–59; *Moorhead Weekly News*, August 11, 1892; Roy Johnson Index Fargo City Council Minutes, February 6, 1893, and April 17, 1894, 19; *Fargo Daily Argus*, November 3, 1891.

57. *Fargo Forum and Daily Republican*, February 9 and November 9, 1893, May 29, June 15, and October 3 and 4, 1894, October 31, 1895.

58. Robinson, *History of North Dakota*, 259; *Moorhead Weekly News*, March 9, 1893.

59. *Fargo Forum*, November 13, 25, and 27, 1893, and February 1, 1894; "Defendant Lars Christianson vs. Plaintiff Cass County," Cass County, North Dakota Court Records, AK, 136, Page 4618, PH No 1001, Institute for Regional Studies.

60. *Fargo Daily Argus*, July 14 and 15, 1891; *Fargo Forum and Daily Republican*, October 10, 1893, June 21, July 26 and 29, November 2, 1895, February 21 and 24, July 14 and 16, 1896.

61. Berthoff, *An Unsettled People*, 429–30; Gusfield, *Symbolic Crusade*, 108–9; Moorhead City

Council Minutes, February 24, 1902, 229, March 2, 1903, 292, May 13 and 17, June 10, 1913, 399, 402, 407, April 10, 1916, 623, July 10, 1916, 5. On liquor and police corruption in the 1930s, see Danbom, *Going It Alone*, 201.

62. Powers, *Faces along the Bar*, 111–13; Ann Fabian, *Card Sharps, Dream Books and Bucket Shops: Gambling in 19th Century America* (Ithaca, N.Y.: Cornell University Press, 1990), 2–5, 10–11, 26, 56.

63. *Moorhead Weekly News*, September 28, October 5 and 12, 1893, January 30 and July 9, 1896, June 15 and 22, 1899; *Fargo Forum and Daily Republican*, September 12, 1893, July 24, 1895, March 22, 1897; *Charter and Ordinances of the City of Fargo, North Dakota* (Fargo: Walker Brothers, 1896), 220–21; Roy Johnson Index Fargo City Council Minutes, August 21, 1906, 21. Danbom, *Going It Alone*, 196, points out the selective enforcement of gambling laws during the 1930s; police did not disturb middle-class gaming, but raided working-class establishments periodically.

64. *Red River Star*, July 5, 1873; *Fargo Daily Argus*, September 20, 1892; *Moorhead Weekly News*, February 1, 1900.

65. Mark Peihl, "Crime and Liquor in Moorhead," *CCHS Newsletter* 23 (January/February 2000): 7, 9; Moorhead City Council Minutes, September 18, October 2, and November 6, 1893, 352, 360, and 368–69; Criminal Calendar A, April 22 to December 3, 1896, in Fargo Justice of the Peace Records, Institute for Regional Studies; *Fargo Forum and Daily Republican*, November 1, 1900.

66. Helen Lefkowitz Horowitz, *Rereading Sex: Battles over Sexual Knowledge and Suppression in Nineteenth-Century America* (New York: Alfred A. Knopf, 2002), 251; Nancy F. Cott, *Public Vows: A History of Marriage and the Nation* (Cambridge: Harvard University Press, 2000), 106–7, 120–24, 130–31, 136–37, 146. For local expressions of alarm about prostitution threatening decency and female virtue, see *Fargo Daily Republican*, September 27, 1882, and *Fargo Forum and Daily Republican*, September 2, 1897.

67. Anne M. Butler, *Daughters of Joy, Sisters of Misery: Prostitutes in the American West, 1865–1890* (Urbana: University of Illinois Press, 1985), xvii, 7–9; Schlesinger, *Rise of the City*, 157–59; Dykstra, *The Cattle Towns*, 104–6, 122, 126–128n, 240, 254–57, 260, 272, 286, 292; Joel Best, *Controlling Vice: Regulating Brothel Prostitution in St. Paul, 1865–1883* (Columbus: Ohio State University Press, 1998), ix, 50–52; Mary P. Ryan, *Civic Wars: Democracy and Public Life in the American City during the Nineteenth Century* (Berkeley: University of California Press, 1997), 53.

68. Lefkowitz Horowitz, *Rereading Sex*, 4–5, 14, 192, 439–440. For other scholarly views on Victorian cultural divisions and the exercise of middle-class power over lower-class sexuality, see Judith R. Walkowitz, *Prostitution and Victorian Society: Women, Class and State* (Cambridge: Cambridge University Press, 1980), vii, 4–5, and Ruth Rosen, *The Lost Sisterhood: Prostitution in America, 1900–1918* (Baltimore: Johns Hopkins University Press, 1982), xi–xv. For a discussion of middle-class male and female pietists and their attack on saloons and brothels in defense of the bourgeois family, see Clark, *Deliver Us from Evil*, 62–67, 73–77, 86–87; Jeffrey, *Frontier Women*, 113, 133–35, 184–85; David J. Pivar, *Purity Crusade: Sexual Morality and Social Control, 1868–1900* (Westport, Conn.: Greenwood Press, 1973), 43, 112–13, 131–32, 140–41, 147, 167, 204, 256.

69. Francine du Plessix Gray, "Splendor and Miseries," *New York Review of Books* 39 (July 16, 1992): 31; Best, *Controlling Vice*, 36–37, 40–44, 47–48, 52–55, 59–61, 71. Scholars supporting Best include Rosen, *The Lost Sisterhood*, xvii, 3, 137, 150, 158, and Walkowitz, *Prostitution and Victo-*

rian Society, 15–16, who states that most prostitutes in Victorian England engaged in the trade for economic reasons and were "the unskilled daughters of the unskilled classes." For a more negative view, see Butler, *Daughters of Joy,* 26–28, 33, 38–39, 43–45, 68–69. Local evidence of self-destructive lives is found in *Clay County Advocate,* August 22, 1878; *Fargo Daily Republican,* November 2, 1882; *Moorhead Weekly News,* June 3, 1886, and November 21, 1895. Fargo-Moorhead prostitutes shared some of the characteristics described by Best. Evidence gathered by Clay County Historical Society archivist Mark Peihl from the *Minnesota State Census, 1895* shows that five madams ranged in age from thirty-two to thirty-eight years; their ten prostitutes ranged in age from twenty to twenty-four years. Two of the houses had four prostitutes; one had two; and one madam lived alone. All were American-born from New York and five Midwestern states. The city directory also shows small Moorhead houses: in 1893, three madams had eight "boarders"; in 1896–97, four madams claimed eleven inmates. The *Moorhead Weekly News,* August 2, 1882, reported that four Fargo madams and nineteen females paid a "tax" of $195 to Judge Roberts. Census data for Fargo "sports" lists 25, 31, and 35 years as ages of three madams. One house had five "boarders," the other had two, and one madam lived alone. The seven "boarders," all white and American-born, ranged in age from 17 to 25 years. See *Dakota Territory, 1885 Census,* page 8, HA 631 1885 .D34. An enumeration in June 1900 lists madam Malvina (Massey) Rae, a housekeeper, occupying her house at 217 Second Avenue North. Housekeeper Maude Lindstrom, housekeeper G. Upton, and bartender James Morrison rented the former houses of ill fame at 115, 119, and 121 Third Street North, respectively. An anti-vice campaign likely had closed the brothels for a time. The 1910 federal census for the same neighborhood reveals three madams with ten inmates in their houses. Ages ranged from nineteen to fifty-five with six at twenty-something. The thirteen native-born women included five whites, five blacks, and three mulattoes. A thirty-four-year-old black madam lived alone. See *United States Census: North Dakota, 1900 and 1910,* Microfilm HA 561 1900 .U51970 and HA 561.5 1910 .U51982, Institute for Regional Studies. Fargo-Moorhead prostitutes moved frequently. Four new inmates in 1897 replaced the six boarders earlier listed at madam Raymond's house. Moorhead madams Helen MacIntyre and Anna Faust also managed Fargo houses.

70. Butler, *Daughters of Joy,* xvii–xviii, 2–4, 10–11, 13–16, 51, 53, 55–56, 60–61; White, "It's Your Misfortune," 305.

71. DePastino, *Citizen Hobo,* 84–85; Chudacoff, *Age of the Bachelor,* 14; *Fargo Weekly Argus,* February 18, 1880; *Fargo Daily Republican,* September 1 and October 23, 1882; *Fargo Forum and Daily Republican,* January 12 and September 18, 1895, February 14, 1896, August 31, 1897, and October 31, 1898; *Mary E. Stephens v. Alfred L. Stephens,* April 14, 1884, Cass County Civil Court Cases #30–2113.

72. Mark Peihl, "A Bird's-eye View of Moorhead in 1882," *CCHS Newsletter* 24 (July/August 2001): 10. According to Peihl, Kittie Raymond appeared on the Clay County tax lists in 1885 and disappeared in 1904. Peihl also researched mechanics' liens, documenting the seasonal sex trade. Madams employed carpenters in the winter to repair their property. The workmen placed a lien on the house until madams paid the bill, usually at the end of harvest. Also see Harness, "Solomon Gilman Comstock," 7; Moll, "Moorhead, MN," 96; *Fargo Sunday Argus,* February 20, 1881; *Fargo Daily Republican,* November 2 and December 5, 1882; Tim Holzkamm and Dean Dormanen, *Fargo Historic Context Study* (Fargo: Historic Preservation Commission, 1993), 51. *Sanborn Fire Insurance Map: Fargo, Dakota Territory* (Teaneck, N.J.: Chadwyck-Healey, 1983)

shows three female boardinghouses at 117, 118, and 119 Third Street North in 1884. The *Fargo and Moorhead City Directory, 1884* does not list the women who owned or boarded at these addresses. I could not find any women listed at these addresses in the June 1885 census enumeration. The "sports" enumerated are living at three houses without numbers on First Street, which did not exist on the North Side in "the flat." See *Dakota Territory, 1885 Census,* page 8, HA 631 1885 .D34. After the Fargo council in 1890 concentrated brothels in this area, *Sanborn Fire Insurance Map: Fargo, North Dakota* in 1892 displays six female boardinghouses at 115, 117, 118, 119, 121, and 201 Third Street North. The Scandinavian Church at 67 Fourth Street North and the Norwegian Lutheran Church at 421 Third Street North show Norwegians and Swedes living near the brothels. *Sanborn Fire Insurance Map: Fargo, North Dakota* in 1896 indicates a Norwegian Baptist Church at 123 Fourth Street North and a Norwegian Congregational Church at 223 Fourth Street North.

73. The Frank Pearson and Matilda Roberts recollections were published in the *Fargo Forum,* January 18, 1927, February 20 and June 22, 1930. Those of Alicia Baker Spaulding appeared in Angela Boleyn, *Quarter Sections and Wide Horizons* (Bismarck: North Dakota State Library, 1978), 300. Also see *Moorhead Weekly News,* October 23, 1884. Walkowitz, *Prostitution and Victorian Society,* 25–26, argues that dress marked membership in a female peer group and that a female subculture distinguished nineteenth-century prostitution in England. Although twin city prostitutes dressed distinctively, it does not demonstrate conclusively they shared a female subculture. On prostitution in concert saloons and music halls, see Lefkowitz Horowitz, *Rereading Sex,* 321, and Chudacoff, *Age of the Bachelor,* 133–34.

74. *Fargo Sunday Argus,* February 20 and March 13, 1881; Best, *Controlling Vice,* 16–17; Melva Moline, *The Forum: First Hundred Years* (Fargo: Moline, 1979), 38; Fargo City Council Minutes, November 4 and 11, 1885, 267–68, and August 1 and September 12, 1887, vol. 3, 414 and 432.

75. Fargo City Council Minutes, August 4 and October 6, 1890, 264 and 290, April 6, 1891, 340, June 5 and September 5, 1893, 44; *Fargo Daily Argus,* April 7, 1891; *Fargo Forum,* June 6, 1893, June 5, 1894; Moline, *The Forum,* 72–73. For arguments made by Fargo mayor J. A. Johnson and Moorhead mayor Jacob Kiefer on the advantages of control by regulation, see J. A. Johnson to A. E. Wood, June 5, 1885, J. A. Johnson Papers M491, Reel 1, Minnesota Historical Society, St. Paul, and Johnson, *The Other Side of Main Street,* 130. Walkowitz, *Prostitution and Victorian Society,* 15, notes similar regulation, segregation, and accommodation in England.

76. Fargo City Council Minutes, February 12 and 28, 1896, 454 and 466; "Houses of Ill Fame," in *Charter and Ordinances of the City of Fargo,* 221–23; Moline, *The Forum,* 73; M. A. Hildreth to Mayor E. H. Smith and Council, April 2, 1894, Box 2, Hildreth Papers. Monthly payments are recorded from April until December in Fargo Justice of the Peace Records, 1896, Book A—Criminal Calendar. The madams included Clara "Cad" Devine, Anna Faust, Rosa Gray, Malvina Massey, Helen McIntyre, and Sally Campbell. Pearl Gould, who kept a bordello at 321 Third Street North, did not appear for several months. Once charged, she also paid by installments. Madam Clara Morton did not appear in these records. Throughout the 1880s, newspapers reported arrests and fines of prostitutes, who were released and told "to go and sin again." In one court session "the frail denizens of the 'the flat'" paid $380 to the treasury. Another account stated that the city received $3,000 annually from eight madams who paid $32 monthly. See *Fargo Weekly Times,* December 9, 1880; *Fargo Daily Republican,* December 5, 1882; *Moorhead Weekly News,* November 24, 1887. On the official and unofficial licensing of prostitution through selective

enforcement and fines, see Pivar, *Purity Crusader,* 147; Rosen, *The Lost Sisterhood,* 4–5; Best, *Controlling Vice,* 3–5, 10, 19–20, 31–32, 34, 79–80, 83.

77. Penalties for streetwalking and keeping rooms for immoral purpose are recorded from April until December in Fargo Justice of the Peace Records, 1896, Book A—Criminal Calendar. The advantages of control through regulation are discussed by Best, *Controlling Vice,* 98–99, 137. Butler, *Daughters of Joy,* 76–77, 85, and 100–101, points out that revenue, bribery, and personal sexual favors motivated regulation. Self-interest dictated that madams cooperate with authorities.

78. *Moorhead Advocate,* July 7, 1877; Moorhead City Council Minutes, May 2, 1881, 8; *Moorhead Weekly News,* March 25, 1886.

79. For information about Moorhead monthly fines, I am indebted to Clay County Historical Society archivist Mark Peihl, who researched the municipal court dockets, Judge Daniel Titus, vol. 1–3, Clay County Historical Society, Moorhead. The *Fargo Times,* May 24, 1879, and *Clay County Advocate,* November 22, 1879, reported twenty-dollar fines for Samuel and Sarah Griswold, who kept a "house of ill fame" near the Northern Pacific railroad bridge. The judge threatened to punish both severely if arrested again. After the district court subsequently sentenced Samuel Griswold to ten months in jail, the *Clay County Advocate* hoped his conviction would keep other brothels away. It did not. The *Moorhead Weekly News,* July 26, 1883, stated that Chief P. J. Sullivan arrested four soiled doves from a Front Street bordello. After pleading guilty, Lillie, who previously had been fined, paid only fifteen dollars and costs on this occasion; the others paid less. After sin paid its way, all returned to work. *Moorhead Weekly News,* September 28, 1893, and February 2, 1899, told of the E. C. Sprague house being moved to Front Street east—allegedly as a "laundry." Several years later, Chief Thomas L. Murphy charged a colored man and woman for keeping a disorderly house there. When sin could not pay its way, or race was involved, courts imposed alternative punishments. The judge sentenced the man to fifteen days in jail and ordered the woman to leave the city. According to the Moorhead Council Minutes, May 2, 1887, 433, and the *Moorhead Weekly News,* October 5, 1893, the council denied liquor licenses to saloons keeping an "immoral house." The *Moorhead Weekly News,* April 16, 1896, reported that authorities permitted a few to solicit trade through barmaids.

80. According to Best, *Controlling Vice,* 47–48 and 64, Bailey had been an inmate at madam Mary Robinson's St. Paul brothel for several years before she relocated to Moorhead. Her daughter, raised in Missouri and Minnesota convents, did not learn about her mother's work for a long time. *Clay County Advocate,* August 10 and 31, 1878, April 5, 1879; *Fargo Times,* March 8, 1879.

81. Pivar, *Purity Crusade,* 132 and 256; *Clay County Advocate,* August 10, 1878, and *Moorhead Weekly News,* January 11, 1883. Police forcibly subdued Vandecar; they jailed and charged him with assault until Clark's fate could be determined. The sheriff, announcing that he would protect the prisoner, stopped talk of a lynching. After Clark died, Vandecar escaped until recaptured in Wisconsin five years later. The *Fargo Times,* July 1, 1880, and *Clay County Advocate,* July 1, 1880, detailed the trial, divorce, and attempted suicide by madam Harriet B. Burner. In a story titled "An Unfortunate Woman Dies in Disgrace," the *Moorhead Weekly News,* December 4, 1884, reported the death of a prostitute known only as "Alice" in gambler Torrey West's room. Western newspaper coverage of prostitution ranged from "cruel humor to mawkish obituaries," according to Butler, *Daughters of Joy,* 82. In her view, the press did not make any

substantial attempts to awaken community consciousness prior to 1890. Dual city newspapers became active in the 1880s.

82. *Fargo Forum and Daily Republican,* October 30, 1895.

83. Rosen, *The Lost Sisterhood,* 8, 50; Walkowitz, *Prostitution and Victorian Society,* 146–47; *Fargo Forum and Daily Republican,* May 17, 1893, November 10 and 13, 1899; Butler, *Daughters of Joy,* 65–67.

84. On these national trends toward social purity in England and the United States, see Walkowitz, *Prostitution and Victorian Society,* 245–46, 252–56; Best, *Controlling Vice,* 110–14; Rosen, *The Lost Sisterhood,* xvi–xvii, 9–11, 38–39, 46. On vagrancy laws, see Pivar, *Purity Crusade,* 216–17. On the Improvement League and recurring efforts to clean up Fargo, see Moline, *The Forum,* 73; *Fargo Forum and Daily Republican,* August 1 and 7, 1896, and May 13, 1898. Norwegian-born Anne Brandon Johnson's recollections of the purity crusade are found in Boleyn, *Quarter Sections and Wide Horizons,* 412–13. Andrew Johnson, her Swedish born-husband, built the workingman's Central Hotel in 1881. For the next seventy-eight years, carpenters, brick-layers, painters, and farmers, who hauled grain to the nearby elevator, occupied its twenty-three rooms. The federal census in 1900 did not list madams or brothels in the hotel neighbor-hood, indicating that anti-vice campaigns sometimes succeeded temporarily. See, *United States Census: North Dakota, 1900,* Microfilm HA 561 1900 .U51970, *Andrew Johnson et al. v. Malvina Massey et al.* (1904), Third District Court, Cass County, North Dakota #11666/958, and Roy P. Johnson, "Fargo Landmark Gives Way to Civic Center," undated and unidentified newspaper clipping found in Fargo, North Dakota, Historical Collections MSS 414, Buildings—General File, Institute for Regional Studies.

85. *Fargo Forum and Daily Republican,* December 19 and 21, 1898, April 25 and 27, June 1, 1899, October 21, 1904; *Moorhead Daily News,* August 24, 1904, and July 1, 1915.

86. *Moorhead Weekly News,* January 9 and May 7, 1896, May 5, 1898. Based on material supplied by Mark Peihl, progressive mayors William R. Tillotson (1901–03) and Carroll A. Nye (1903–07) cleaned up Moorhead. In 1914, *Sanborn Fire Insurance Map: Moorhead, Minnesota* shows the red-light district destroyed, but press reports reveal ongoing prostitution. The *Moorhead Weekly News,* April 4, 1901, March 17, 1904, May 26, 1904, and February 27, 1908, indicate ongoing attempts to stop streetwalkers.

87. Mark Thomas Connelly, *The Response to Prostitution in the Progressive Era* (Chapel Hill: University of North Carolina Press, 1980), 4–7, 20, 22, 26, 47, 68, 82–83, 139; Best, *Controlling Vice,* 110–14. *Sanborn Fire Insurance Map: Fargo, North Dakota* shows that the former female boarding-houses are labeled "dwellings" by 1916. According to Danbom, *Going It Alone,* 196–98, small houses on lower Front Street housed several African American prostitutes, while white women worked some downtown hotels. Well-publicized cleanup campaigns took place annually.

88. Earl Lewis, "Pioneers of a Different Kind," *Red River Valley Historian* (winter 1978–79): 15; *Moorhead Weekly News,* March 24, 1892; *Fargo Forum and Daily Republican,* November 12 and 14, 1895, July 24, 1896, April 25 and July 6, 1900; Malvina Massey Estate, May 11, 1911, Cass County Court Records. Madam Massey's street addresses are listed in the *Fargo and Moorhead City Directory*: 118 Third Street North (1891), 123 Third Street North (1893), 217 Second Avenue North (1895–96), and 201 Third Street North (1904–10). *Moorhead Weekly News,* March 24, 1892, reported her house destroyed by fire. A colored woman was shot at the Massey house, accord-ing to the *Moorhead Weekly News,* March 10, 1910. "Aged Negress Is Dead," announced the eve-

ning edition of the *Fargo Forum and Daily Republican,* May 4, 1911. She died in a local hospital at seventy-three years of age. She had lived in Fargo for thirty years and three relatives survived. From the *Fargo and Moorhead City Directory,* I can only document her residence in the city for twenty years. In the *United States Census, 1900,* she reported an October 1854 birth date. Ten years later, she claimed to be fifty-one and had one son from her nineteen-year marriage.

89. *Moorhead Weekly News,* July 19, 1894; *Fargo Forum and Daily Republican,* October 21, 1895; *Fargo Sunday Argus,* February 6, 1881; Moline, *The Forum,* 37; Elaine Tyler May, *Great Expectations: Marriage and Divorce in Post-Victorian America* (Chicago: University of Chicago Press, 1980), 5; Robinson, *History of North Dakota,* 259; M. A. Hildreth to Charles O. Willard, February 8, 1894, Box 1, Hildreth Papers. I am indebted to a former student for data and analysis in this paragraph: Rachel Anne Clarens, "Fargo, North Dakota: An 1890s Divorce Mecca" (unpublished history seminar paper, Concordia College, April 2003; in author's possession), 2, 4–6, 8–10, 13, 23.

90. Clarens, "Fargo, North Dakota," 18; *History of the First Baptist Church, Fargo, North Dakota, 1879–1979* (Fargo: First Baptist, 1979), 14; *Fargo Forum and Daily Republican,* August 31, 1896; Moline, *The Forum,* 37; M. A. Hildreth to M. L. Willard, February 5, 1894, Box 1, and to C. L. Hildreth, May 9, 1894, Box 2, Hildreth Papers.

91. *Moorhead Weekly News,* December 6, 1894, January 12 and February 9, 1899; Moline, *The Forum,* 75; Kevin A. Duchschere, "John Shanley: North Dakota's First Catholic Bishop," *North Dakota History* 46 (spring 1979): 9–10; Clark, *Deliver Us from Evil,* 73 and 77; Clarens, "Fargo, North Dakota," 24.

7. BUILDING A BETTER COMMUNITY

1. Frank Pearson's recollections appeared in the *Fargo Forum,* June 22, 1930. The *Fargo Weekly Times,* December 14, 1880, complained about the appearance of a country town. On professional expertise in the expanded and improved municipal services of the 1890s, see Jon C. Teaford, *The Unheralded Triumph: City Government in America, 1870–1900* (Baltimore: Johns Hopkins University Press, 1984), 133, 136–38, 146, 150, 157, 162, 187–88, 198, 205, 213–14, and 219. On booster government, see Robin L. Einhorn, *Property Rules: Political Economy in Chicago, 1833–1872* (Chicago: University of Chicago Press, 1991), 28, 39–40, 49–50, and Eric H. Monkkonen, *America Becomes Urban: The Development of U.S. Cities and Towns, 1780–1980* (Berkeley: University of California Press, 1988), 108, 125, 127, 142.

2. Monkkonen, *America Becomes Urban,* 92–94. Arthur Meier Schlesinger, in *The Rise of the City, 1878–1898* (New York: Macmillan, 1933), 120, recognized that "urban progress was experimental, uneven, often accidental." Yet American municipalities had a creditable record through inventing the necessary technologies for transport, lighting, sanitation, and communication. Teaford, *The Unheralded Triumph,* 6–10, essentially agrees: "American city government did . . . meet these challenges of diversity, growth, and financing with remarkable success." If business leaders, neighborhood shopkeepers, ward politicos, and municipal experts cooperated peacefully, then city governments operated effectively. From the 1880s onward, the service city initiated the emergence of expanded state and federal government power in the United States. In 1902, local government accounted for 58 percent of public expenditures. States and cities regulated personal behavior, business activity, education, health, and safety. Federal supervision of these areas expanded after 1887. For a discussion of these issues, see Ballard C. Campbell, *The*

Growth of American Government: Governance from the Cleveland Era to the Present (Bloomington: Indiana University Press, 1995), 1–7, 14, 16, 18, 29, 32, 59, and 80–81. On services in western cities, see Lawrence H. Larsen and Barbara J. Cottrell, *The Gate City: A History of Omaha,* enlarged ed. (Lincoln: University of Nebraska Press, 1997), 105–7 and Lawrence H. Larsen, *The Urban West at the End of the Frontier* (Lawrence: Regents Press of Kansas, 1978), 60, 71, 110, 120.

3. Monkkonen, *America Becomes Urban,* 112, 123. The seventy-one men elected to Moorhead municipal government in the late nineteenth century included thirty-seven immigrants, according to Alyssa Erickson, "Moorhead Municipal Government and Ethnicity" (undated Concordia College history seminar paper, in author's possession), 3–4. Teaford, *The Unheralded Triumph,* 38–39, states that the ward system enabled ethnic participation as neighborhoods elected countrymen to municipal office.

4. Monkkonen, *America Becomes Urban,* 111, 128–30; *Fargo Express,* July 19, 1873; *A Century Together: A History of Fargo, North Dakota and Moorhead, Minnesota* (Fargo-Moorhead: Centennial Corporation, 1975), 50; Mark Peihl, "County Seat Fight a Bitter Struggle," *CCHS Newsletter* 24 (September/October 2001): 5–6, 10–11.

5. *A Century Together,* 145, 163; *Red River Gazette,* March 6, 1873; *Red River Star,* January 23 and April 10, 1875; Moorhead City Council Meetings, March 24, May 7, and September 25, 1875, 3, 4, 29; January 1, 1881, 142–43, March 21 and 22, 1881, 1–3.

6. Fargo City Council Minutes, April 12, 1875, vol. 1, 1–3, Institute for Regional Studies, North Dakota State University, Fargo; *Northern Pacific Mirror,* November 21, 1874; *Roy Johnson's Red River Valley,* ed. Clarence A. Glasrud (Moorhead: Red River Valley Historical Society, 1982), 318–19, 322.

7. Three generations of urban historians have emphasized different aspects of municipal problems in this period. This paragraph synthesized ideas from the following: Schlesinger, *Rise of the City,* 389; Robert R. Dykstra, *The Cattle Towns* (Lincoln: University of Nebraska Press, 1983), 364–65; Mary P. Ryan, *Civic Wars: Democracy and Public Life in the American City during the Nineteenth Century* (Berkeley: University of California Press, 1997), 16–17, 98.

8. *Fargo Daily Argus,* March 25 and April 8, 1884; *Moorhead Weekly News,* March 22, 1883, and January 17, 1884; *Fargo Sunday Argus,* November 4, 1888, and March 30, 1890. The possible decline of political participation and its significance is discussed by Glenn C. Altschuler and Stuart M. Blumin, *Rude Republic: Americans and Their Politics in the Nineteenth Century* (Princeton, N.J.: Princeton University Press, 2000), 217–19, 225–26, 235, 237–39.

9. Monkkonen, *America Becomes Urban,* 124–25; *Fargo Times,* March 15 and 29, 1879; *Fargo Weekly Argus,* April 7, 1880; *Fargo Daily Argus,* April 6 and 7, 1880, March 29 and 30, April 4 and 5, 1881; Melva Moline, *The Forum: First Hundred Years* (Fargo: Moline, 1979), 18–19.

10. Roy Johnson Index Fargo City Council Minutes, May 18 and June 14, 1881, 8; *Fargo Daily Republican,* September 18, 1882; Glasrud, *Roy Johnson's Red River Valley,* 296, 300–302.

11. *Fargo Times,* January 15 and February 5, 1880; Fargo City Council Minutes, January 8 and February 2, 1880, vol. 2, 35, 38; *Fargo Weekly Argus,* January 28 and February 4, 1880; *Fargo Sunday Argus,* June 26, 1881; *Fargo Evening Republican,* March 13, 1882.

12. Fargo City Council Minutes, October 23, 1880, December 24, 1881, May 12 and June 5, 1882, vol. 2, 100, 190, 248, 252; *Fargo Sunday Argus,* August 21, 1881; *Fargo Daily Republican,* January 12, 1882. On city budgets and bonded indebtedness, see Monkkonen, *America Becomes Urban,* 132, 134, 138.

13. *Fargo Evening Republican,* February 16, March 4, 14, 15, and 31, April 4, 1882. Chapin is quoted in Glasrud, *Roy Johnson's Red River Valley,* 303.

14. Fargo City Council Minutes, August 4 and October 13, 1879, February 9, 1881, May 2 and June 5, 1882, and March 5, 1883, vol. 2, 13, 20, 113–14, 240–41, 251, 324–25; July 16, August 6, October 1, and November 26, 1883, vol. 3, 63, 72, 96, and 115; *Fargo Daily Republican,* May 3, June 6, August 8, 19, and 24, 1882.

15. *Fargo Sunday Argus,* February 13, 1881, April 1, 1883, April 11, 1886, and April 3, 1887; Fargo Mayoral Elections, 1875–1941, compiled by John Bye, Institute for Regional Studies; *Fargo Times,* March 4, 1880; Fargo City Council Minutes, March 16, 1885, vol. 3, 223; Roy Johnson Index Fargo City Council Minutes, January 6 and March 16, 1885, January 25 and April 20, 1887, 9; *Fargo Sunday Republican,* April 3, 1887. Fargo's fiscal record keeping improved relative to its previously inadequate system. On business and booster leadership as well as the structural weaknesses and fiscal shortcomings of municipal government in the 1930s, see David B. Danbom, *Going It Alone: Fargo Grapples with the Great Depression* (St. Paul: Minnesota Historical Society Press, 2005), 7–8, 38–40.

16. *Clay County Advocate,* February 15 and March 29, 1879; Moorhead City Council Minutes, March 5, 1888, 483 and 485; *Fargo Sunday Argus,* February 6, 1881; *Moorhead Weekly Argonaut,* March 2, 1881; *A Century Together,* 163, 169; Einhorn, *Property Rules,* 28.

17. *Fargo Sunday Argus,* February 27, 1881; *Fargo Daily Argus,* March 4, 5, 7, and 16, 1881; *A Century Together,* 158–59; Audrey Zube Jones, *A History of the First Congregational United Church of Christ, 1894–1994* (Moorhead: First Congregational, 1993), 16, 38; *Fargo Evening Republican,* March 18 and 22, 1882; *Moorhead Weekly News,* March 22, 1883.

18. Moorhead City Council Minutes, August 22, 1881, 22; *A Century Together,* 143–44, 168; Morris Fredericks, "Early History of Moorhead in the 1870s and 1880s" (bachelor's thesis, Concordia College, 1926), 18; Edith S. Moll, "Moorhead, MN: Frontier Town, 1871–1915" (master's thesis, North Dakota Agricultural College, 1957), 46–47; David R. Vik, "Early Bridges of Moorhead and Fargo, 1871–1893" (master's thesis, Moorhead State University, 1984), 9 and 12–13; *Red River Star,* June 14, 1873, and January 31, 1874.

19. Vik, "Early Bridges," 14, 38; *Red River Star,* February 13 and March 6, 1875; *Moorhead Advocate,* April 20, 1877; *Clay County Advocate,* January 25, February 1, and June 14, 1879, April 10, 1880.

20. Moorhead City Council Minutes, November 11, 1881, 37; July 18 and 20, 1882, 68–70; August 1 and 7, 1882, 71 and 73; Fargo City Council Minutes, October 31 and November 11, 1881, October 26, 1882, vol. 2, 177, 184, and 296; *Daily Argonaut,* January 19, 1882; *Fargo Daily Republican,* January 13, February 15 and 16, April 27, July 17 and 18, August 2, and October 27, 1882; *Moorhead Weekly News,* April 27, June 15, July 20 and 29, 1882; January 4, 1883.

21. Vik, "Early Bridges," 59; Fargo City Council Minutes, January 15 and February 5, 1883, vol. 2, 316–18, October 13 and November 19 and 26, 1883, vol. 3, 101, 112, 117; Moorhead City Council Minutes, February 10 and March 13, 1883, 104, and February 4, 1884, 216–17; *Moorhead Weekly News,* April 19, October 11 and 25, 1883, February 7, April 17 and 24, 1884; *Fargo Sunday Argus,* December 2, 1883.

22. *Moorhead Weekly News,* February 7 and March 6, 1884; *Fargo Sunday Argus,* December 30, 1883; Vik, "Early Bridges," 64, 71, 78, 84, 90, 99; Moorhead City Council Minutes, February 14, 1884, 216; Roy Johnson Index Fargo City Council Minutes, September 1 and October 6,

1884, September 7, 1885, and July 6, 1887, 1, 8–9; Fargo City Council Minutes, September 7, 1885, vol. 3, 257.

23. *Fargo Daily Argus*, January 2, 1884; Moorhead City Council Minutes, January 2 and 5, 1884, 198 and 204; *Moorhead Weekly News*, January 3 and 10, 1884, July 30, 1885, February 16 and August 4, 1887, February 28, 1889. The *News* alleged that the empty treasury caused Bruns's sudden resignation. Citizen participation remained small as mayoral vote totals ranged from 418 (1884) to 169 (1889). It became difficult to recruit mayoral candidates, according to Mark Peihl, "Moorhead's 1880s (Un)Well," *CCHS Newsletter* 21 (November/December 1998): 5.

24. Moorhead City Council Minutes, March 18, 1887, 415, and March 5, 1888, 483 and 485; *Moorhead Weekly News*, November 24, 1887.

25. Monkkonen, *America Becomes Urban*, 136, 139–41, and 143–44.

26. Ibid., 151–52, 154–55 and 157.

27. Teaford, *The Unheralded Triumph*, 54, 128–29, 283–84, 288, 290, 294–96, and 304–6.

28. Roy Johnson Index Fargo City Council Minutes, March 24, 1890, September 14, 1891, May 2, 1892, August 9, 1893, February 2, May 10, and July 6, 1897, 9–10; *Moorhead Weekly News*, August 25, 1898, and March 15, 1900.

29. Moorhead City Council Minutes, June 27, 1892, 219–21; *Moorhead Weekly News*, May 16, 1895, April 9, May 7, November 12, and December 3, 1896.

30. *Moorhead Weekly News*, February 17 and March 3, 1898, April 13, 1899, March 8 and July 19, 1900; Moorhead City Council Minutes, May 15, 1899, 614–15, November 11, 1919, 195, and January 5, 1920, 203; John Turner and C. R. Semling, *History of Clay and Norman Counties* (Indianapolis: B. F. Brown, 1918), 1:269.

31. *Fargo Forum and Daily Republican*, January 22, June 17, July 2 and 7, August 17 and 18, 1896, July 16, 20, and 31, August 17, 1897, November 15, 1899; Fargo City Council Minutes, July 20, 1896, vol. 5, 1–2.

32. Edward Chase Kirkland, *Industry Comes of Age: Business, Labor, and Public Policy, 1860–1897* (Chicago: Quadrangle Paperback, 1967), 240; M. A. Hildreth to Mayor E. H. Smith, April 17 and June 26, 1893, Box 1, Melvin A. Hildreth Papers, Institute for Regional Studies.

33. Ryan, *Civic Wars*, 100; *Fargo Forum and Daily Republican*, May 8 and November 8, 1895, July 31, 1897, July 6, 1898; Fargo City Council Minutes, July 7, 1899, and June 4, 1900, vol. 5, 501, 618–19.

34. Eric H. Monkonnen, *Police in Urban America, 1860–1920* (Cambridge: Cambridge University Press, 1981), 10–11, 49, 55–56, 62, 86–87, 105–6, and *The Dangerous Class: Crime and Poverty in Columbus, Ohio, 1860–1885* (Cambridge: Harvard University Press, 1975), 4–5, 164–65; Teaford, *The Unheraled Triumph*, 166–67, 170, and 276.

35. *Moorhead Weekly News*, May 5, 1898; Fargo City Council Minutes, April 21, May 4, October 5, November 2, December 7, 1891, January 4, February 1, October 3, 1892, vol. 3, 349, 355, 434–35, 454, 462, 469, September 5, 1893, January 8, 1894, vol. 4, 114, 167, 189; *Fargo Daily Argus*, September 20, 1892; *Fargo Forum*, November 1, 1894. The Fargo and Moorhead police departments mirrored national trends noted by two urban historians: Monkkonen, *America Becomes Urban*, 93–95, 98–103, 109–10, argues that the police modeled service. They were visible, accessible, and empowered to regulate activities ranging from public health to corralling stray livestock. These became public goods provided regularly without fees. Schlesinger, *Rise of the City*, 116–17, suggests that cities combated crime by divorcing the police from corrupt politics

and by improved technology. Yale locks, better constructed vaults and safes, electrically lighted streets, burglar alarms, and police call boxes enhanced security.

36. Moorhead City Council Minutes, February 10, March 7 and 8, April 4, 1892, 176, 178, 180–81, and 187; *Moorhead Weekly News,* April 7 and 14, May 12, 1892, October 4, 1894, and December 7, 1899.

37. *Moorhead Weekly News,* June 8 and 15, 1893; Norene A. Roberts, *Fargo Heritage* (Fargo: Heritage Society, 1983), 11; David Grant, "The Fargo Fire of 1893 Revisited," *Red River Valley Historian* 2 (spring–summer 1969): 45–46; Albro Martin, *James J. Hill and the Opening of the Northwest* (New York: Oxford University Press, 1976), 397; *Fargo Forum,* June 14 and October 31, 1893; Fargo City Council Minutes, June 8 and July 5, 1893, June 4, 1894, vol. 4, 52–53, 83, 225.

38. S. G. Comstock to J. J. Hill, June 8, 1893, General Correspondence, James J. Hill Papers, James J. Hill Library, St. Paul; M. A. Hildreth to C. L. Hildreth, June 10, 1893, Box 1, Hildreth Papers; Henry A. Bruns in *Moorhead Weekly News,* June 15, 1893; Grant, "The Fargo Fire of 1893 Revisited," 47. *Forum* editor A. W. Edwards, quoted in Moline, *The Forum,* 58–59.

39. Roberts, *Fargo Heritage,* 12; Grant, "The Fargo Fire of 1893 Revisited," 47; Roy Johnson Index Fargo City Council Minutes, June 8, 1893, and November 4, 1895, 5–6; *Fargo Forum and Daily Republican,* June 14 and August 2, 1893, November 17, 1894, September 30, 1896, and January 1, 1898.

40. *Fargo Forum and Daily Republican,* May 9 and June 7, 1894, June 7, 1898, April 18, June 3, 7, and 9, 1899, June 7, 1900; Fargo City Council Minutes, April 17, 1899, and January 2, 1900, vol. 5, 454, 572–73.

41. Mark Peihl, "A Century of Flooding," *CCHS Newsletter* 20 (March/April 1997): 5; *Fargo Forum and Daily Republican,* April 1, 2, 5, and 6, 1897.

42. *Fargo Forum and Daily Republican,* April 7, 8, 16, and 20, May 4, 1897, and February 8, 1898; Angela Boleyn, *Quarter Sections and Wide Horizons* (Bismarck: North Dakota State Library, 1978), 282; Fargo City Council Minutes, April 19, 1897, vol. 5, 117.

43. Fargo City Council Minutes, April 5, 1897, vol. 5, 103; *Fargo Forum and Daily Republican,* April 6, 8, 9, and 14, 1897.

44. Fargo City Council Minutes, April 20, 1897, vol. 5, 122; *Fargo Forum and Daily Republican,* April 9, 13, 15, 16, 20, and 21, 1897.

45. *Fargo Forum and Daily Republican,* May 19, November 19, and December 24, 1896, August 17 and 19, 1897, and September 22, 1900; *Moorhead Weekly News,* March 2, 1893.

46. *Moorhead Weekly News,* February 1, 1894, March 14, 1895, and December 20, 1900; Justius Probstfield to R. M. Probstfield, March 2, 1893, Box 1, Probstfield Papers, Northwest Minnesota Historical Center, Minnesota State University Moorhead.

47. *Moorhead Weekly News,* March 21, 1895; *Fargo Forum and Daily Republican,* February 18 and 25, March 4, 1896.

48. Monkkonen, *America Becomes Urban,* 119; *Fargo Forum and Daily Republican,* February 18 and 21, March 7, 10, and 18, 1896; *Moorhead Weekly News,* February 20, March 12 and 19, April 2, 9, 16, 23, and 30, November 5, 1896; Moorhead City Council Minutes, March 20, 1896, 182–83, and March 31, 1896, 185.

49. Henry Johnson, *The Other Side of Main Street: A History Teacher from Sauk Centre* (New York: Columbia University Press, 1943), 121–22; *Fargo Forum and Daily Republican,* March 18, 1897, and February 15, 1898; *Moorhead Weekly News,* February 17, 1898.

50. Johnson, *The Other Side of Main Street,* 129–30; *Moorhead Weekly News,* March 24 and May 5, 1898, March 16 and 30, 1899.

51. *Moorhead Weekly News,* February 8, March 18, 22, and 29, July 5, August 9, September 13, October 4, November 15 and 29, December 6 and 13, 1900; *Fargo Forum and Daily Republican,* November 16, 1900.

52. *A Century Together,* 163; *Moorhead Weekly News,* January 18, March 15 and 29, May 24, 1900. Teaford, *The Unheralded Triumph,* 43–47, describes the late-nineteenth-century trend toward increased mayoral powers of veto, appointment, and removal.

53. Elwyn B. Robinson, *History of North Dakota* (Lincoln: University of Nebraska Press, 1966), 199, 208, 230–31; Robert P. Wilkins and Wynona Huchette Wilkins, *North Dakota: A Bicentennial History* (New York: W. W. Norton, 1977), 107–8; Fargo Mayoral Elections, 1875–1941. According to John Bye, Ball resigned on March 24, 1890, and the council elected Republican Martin Hector his replacement.

54. Fargo Mayoral Elections, 1875–1941; *Fargo Forum and Daily Republican,* April 20, 1898. On mayoral and council power, see Teaford, *The Unheralded Triumph,* 16–17, 43–47. By 1900, aldermen's powers in large cities had declined to that of ward advocate as executive departments replaced council committees. Yet councils retained their significant role in determining policy in smaller cities like Moorhead and Fargo.

55. "Mayor W. F. Ball," *Record* 1 (May 1895): 33; *Fargo Daily Argus,* April 6, 1891; *Fargo Forum and Daily Republican,* March 10, 13, and 28, April 13 and 18, May 8 and 10, 1894; Fargo City Council Minutes, April 17, 1894, vol. 4, 208.

56. *Fargo Daily Argus,* February 23, March 29, April 4 and 5, 1892; *Fargo Forum,* March 1, 1894; M. A. Hildreth to W. L. Willard, May 5, 1894, Box 2, Hildreth Papers.

57. *Fargo Forum and Daily Republican,* January 16, February 5, 11, and 25, March 16 and 17, April 7, 1896.

58. *Hon. J. A. Johnson: A Partial Copy of His Letters, Travels, and Addresses,* ed. Alice E. Chester and Laura Johnson (Fargo: Privately printed, 1908), 3–4, 9; *Fargo Forum and Daily Republican,* April 22, 29, and 30, May 1, June 26, July 1 and 21, 1896, March 19, May 27 and 31, July 7, October 5 and 19, 1897, May 5, 1898.

59. *Fargo Forum and Daily Republican,* October 20, 1891, September 4, December 28 and 31, 1896, April 21, July 12, 13, and 30, August 18, October 5 and 19, 1897, April 5, and November 10, 1898. By securing uniform municipal legislation in North Dakota and joining the National League of Municipalities, Mayor Johnson participated in discussions about professional public administration and the home-rule crusade. On civic efficiency, home rule, and the special state legislation it replaced, see Teaford, *The Unheralded Triumph,* 61–62, 84–85, 94, 98, 102, and 104.

60. *Record* 3 (October 1897): 86; Ole Berg, Conrad S. Greene, and others to O. G. Barnes, February 17, 1898, O. G. Barnes Papers, Box 2, Institute for Regional Studies; *Fargo Forum and Daily Republican,* October 15, 1897, January 18, March 12, 14, 15, and 16, 1898.

61. *Fargo Forum and Daily Republican,* March 23, 24, 31, April 1, 2, and 5, 1898.

62. *Fargo Forum and Daily Republican,* April 20 and August 9, 1898, April 11, May 3, November 18 and 21, December 13, 1899; Fargo City Council Minutes, September 5, 1898, April 3 and November 6, 1899, vol. 5, 386, 449, and 551.

63. *Fargo Forum and Daily Republican,* January 1, March 8, 16, 23, 27, and 29, April 3, 1900.

64. *A Century Together,* 52, 167; Roy Johnson Index to Fargo City Council Minutes, April 5,

1875, and April 22, 1882, 23; *Fargo Daily Republican,* August 10 and September 5, 1882; Monk-konen, *America Becomes Urban,* 99–100, 109–10, and *Police in Urban America,* 147–49, 155–56, and 159–61.

65. Roy Johnson Index Fargo City Council Minutes, May 12, 1875, and January 7, 1879, 24; Moorhead City Council Minutes, August 1, 1876, 44; June 12, 1878, 82; June 2, 1879, 105; May 2, 1881, 8; Fargo City Council Minutes, May 12 and 13, 1875, January 7, 1879, vol. 1, 6–8, 124; August 6, 1883, June 2, 1884, July 2 and November 22, 1888, vol. 3, 66–72, 163–67, 558, and 599; *Fargo Times,* March 22, 1879; *Fargo Daily Republican,* August 21, October 23, 1882; *Fargo Sunday Argus,* March 18, 1883.

66. Roy Johnson Index Fargo City Council Minutes, November 6, 1893, 24; Fargo City Council Minutes, August 21, 1893, vol. 4, 104; *Fargo Forum,* October 24, 1893, July 1, November 12, and December 3, 1895; Moorhead City Council Minutes, May 22 and August 10, 1906, 513 and 538, March 21, 1910, 210–11; Moll, "Moorhead, MN," 57.

67. *Red River Gazette,* May 1, 1873; *Red River Star,* April 10, 1875; Moorhead City Council Minutes, March 22 and April 18, 1881, 2 and 5; *Fargo Sunday Argus,* March 5, 1882; *Moorhead Weekly News,* April 12, 1888; *Fargo Express,* June 4 and July 2, 1874; Fargo City Council Minutes, May 12, 1875, vol. 1, 7, and May 3, 1880, vol. 2, 18; *Fargo Times,* June 21, 1879.

68. Kirkland, *Industry Comes of Age,* 241; Fargo City Council Minutes, May 2, 18, and 25, June 14 and 21, 1881, vol. 2, 140, 146, 148, 153–54, 156; April 26 and May 7, 1883, vol. 3, 19, 23–24; May 14, 1895, vol. 5, 327–28; Roy Johnson Index Fargo City Council Minutes, April 26 and July 16, 1883, May 14 and July 24, 1895, 24–26; *Fargo Daily Republican,* May 9, 16, 18, and 19, 1882; *Fargo Daily Argus,* May 13 and 20, 1884; *Fargo Sunday Argus,* May 15, 1881. *Moorhead Weekly News* August 1, 1895; *Fargo Forum and Daily Republican,* April 19, 1894, May 8, 9, and 15, August 14, September 14, 1895, and June 15, 1896.

69. *Fargo Forum and Daily Republican,* November 3 and 19, 1896, March 7 and 8, June 6, and July 6, 1898; Fargo City Council Minutes, September 6 and December 5, 1898, May 1 and 8, June 19, 1899, June 18, 1900, vol. 5, 422, 464, 469, 488, 623; Roy Johnson Index Fargo City Council Minutes, September 17, 1900, January 2, May 7, and July 9, 1906, 26–27; Teaford, *The Unheralded Triumph,* 227–28, 234; Danbom, *Going It Alone,* 88.

70. *Moorhead Weekly News,* April 19, May 10, 24, 31, June 7, August 9, September 20, 1894, July 5, 1894, April 9, 1896; Moorhead City Council Minutes, April 25, May 7, and July 2, 1894, 11–12, 14, 17, 26, May 6, 1895, 100, and May 16, 1917, 55; *A Century Together,* 165.

71. *Fargo Express,* March 12, 1874; *Second Annual Report of the Chamber of Commerce of Fargo, North Dakota, 1880–1881* (Fargo: Daily Argus, 1881), 30; *Fargo Sunday Argus,* May 22, 1881, May 27, 1883, and May 1, 1887. Jennie Burns Angell's recollection of Pollock is from Boleyn, *Quarter Sections and Wide Horizons,* 348. *Clay County Advocate,* November 23, 1878; Moorhead City Council Minutes, April 4, 1887, 419; *Moorhead Weekly News,* April 7, 1887, and April 13, 1893.

72. Martin V. Melosi, *The Sanitary City: Urban Infrastructure in America from Colonial Times to the Present* (Baltimore: Johns Hopkins University Press, 2000), 12–13, 39, 41–42, 58, 103–4, and 106–7.

73. *Red River Star,* June 14, 1873, August 29, 1874, and April 29, 1876; Moorhead City Council Minutes, May 19, 1875, 9; *Fargo Times,* March 29, 1879; *Fargo Daily Republican,* February 13, March 6, May 25, and July 25, 1882; Fargo City Council Minutes, February 13, 1882, vol. 2, 202–4 and June 16, 1883, vol. 3, 48–49; *Moorhead Weekly News,* July 25, 1889. On sanitary problems

and the difficulties of enforcing health ordinances in frontier cities, see Larsen and Cottrell, *The Gate City*, 101–4, 109–13.

74. Teaford, *The Unheralded Triumph*, 125 and 150; *Red River Star*, July 5, 1873; Roy Johnson Index Fargo City Council Minutes, May 6, 1880, November 24, 1881, May 1, 1882, February 5 and December 3, 1883, 12–13; *A Century Together*, 196; *Fargo Times*, July 22 and 29, 1880; Fargo City Council Minutes, November 27, 1881, and February 5, 1883, vol. 2, 186, 320; *Fargo Forum*, April 4, 1893, and May 11, 1894.

75. Martin V. Melosi, *Garbage in the Cities: Refuse, Reform, and the Environment, 1880–1980* (College Station: Texas A&M University Press, 1981), 21–22, 30, 49–50, 104, 110, and 112; Fargo City Council Minutes, May 5, 1886, vol. 3, 294, and July 6, 1891, vol. 4, 405; *Fargo Daily Argus*, July 7, 1891, and June 21, 1892; Moorhead City Council Minutes, May 4, 1896, 195, March 4, 1901, 147, March 23, 1903, 298, May 16, 1906, 505, and May 6, 1913, 394–95.

76. *Fargo Forum and Daily Republican*, February 2 and March 14, 1894, January 17, 1896, March 4 and 12, November 11 and 15, 1897; Moorhead City Council Minutes, April 4, 1898, 449, March 24, 1901, 153, and April 17, 1902, 234; *Moorhead Weekly News*, July 7, 1898, August 23 and September 27, 1900; Melosi, *Sanitary City*, 13.

77. Moorhead City Council Minutes, December 4, 1905, 473, May 16, 1906, 505, March 9 and 23, 1908, 32–33 and 40; Roy Johnson Index Fargo City Council Minutes, November 20 and December 4, 1905, May 7 and July 2, 1906, 13.

78. Teaford, *The Unheralded Triumph*, 246 and 250; Mark Peihl, "A Sobering Look at 19th Century Life," *CCHS Newsletter* 22 (March/April 1999): 8–10; U.S. Bureau of the Census, *Census Reports*, vol. 3, *Twelfth Census of the United States Taken in Year 1900—Vital Statistics*, Part I, *Analysis and Rate Tables* (Washington: U.S. Census Office, 1902), lxxix–lxxxii.

79. Teaford, *The Unheralded Triumph*, 218–19 and 226; Sam Bass Warner Jr., *The Private City: Philadelphia in Three Periods of Growth* (Philadelphia: University of Pennsylvania Press, 1968), 99–100, 108–11; Moorhead City Council Minutes, July 18 and August 20, 1878, 84; Turner and Semling, *History of Clay and Norman Counties*, 1:269; Fargo City Council Minutes, October 7, 1878, vol. 1, 115, November 7, 1881, August 7 and September 14, 1882, and March 5, 1883, vol. 2, 181, 275–76, 289, and 326; *Fargo Sunday Argus*, January 28, 1883; *Fargo Daily Republican*, September 29, 1882. On storm sewers, see Thomas J. Schlereth, *Victorian America: Transformation in Everyday Life, 1876–1915* (New York: Harper Perennial, 1991), 112, and on sewer systems, see Melosi, *Sanitary City*, 90–92, 99, 149, 153, 162–64 and 172–73.

80. M. A. Hildreth to Mayor E. H. Smith, April 17, 1893, Box 1, Hildreth Papers; *Fargo Forum and Daily Republican*, March 5 and October 25, 1895; Fargo City Council Minutes, May 1, June 19, July 7, 1899, vol. 5, 464, 490–91, 501, and October 27, 1900, vol. 5, 32.

81. *A Century Together*, 169; *Fargo Times*, April 12, 1879, January 8, February 26, March 25, April 8 and 22, June 17, October 7, and December 21, 1880; Fargo City Council Minutes, August 6, 1880, vol. 2, 93; *Second Annual Report of the Chamber of Commerce of Fargo, North Dakota*, 40; *Fargo Sunday Argus*, October 9, 1881, and August 26, 1883. On the growth of American city water systems, see Melosi, *Sanitary City*, 30, 39, 56–57, 73–75, and 88–89. Teaford, *The Unheralded Triumph*, 220–23, sees U.S. water systems as technologically superior in supplying greater quantities of water than European cities for the personal comforts of bathtubs and flush toilets.

82. Fargo City Council Minutes, March 14 and June 6, 1881, May 2, 1882, vol. 2, 152, 244, and 246, September 14, 1885, vol. 3, 260, and May 24 and June 25, 1890, vol. 4, 208 and 220; Roy

Johnson Index Fargo City Council Minutes, September 14, 1885, June 8 and October 4, 1886, June 7 and July 11, 1887, June 23, September 23, and October 1, 1890, 28–29; *Fargo Daily Republican*, May 19 and July 12, 1882; *Fargo Daily Argus*, September 9, 1885. Private water systems served a useful function initially, but high rates, bad service, and scarce capital doomed them, according to Nelson Manfred Blake, *Water for the Cities: A History of the Urban Water Supply Problem in the United States* (Syracuse, N.Y.: Syracuse University Press, 1956), 77.

83. Moorhead City Council Minutes, July 19 and August 14, 1880, 129 and 133, August 22, 1881, 22; *Moorhead Weekly News*, November 9, 1882, and June 7, 1888; Fredericks, "Early History of Moorhead," 17; Peihl, "Moorhead's 1880s (Un)Well," 5–6, 8.

84. Kirkland, *Industry Comes of Age*, 242–43, 252–53; Melosi, *Sanitary City*, 120–21; *Moorhead Weekly News*, March 1, 1894; E. F. Ladd to C. H. Parsitt, April 10, 1895, Box 1, Folder 3, Edwin Fremont Ladd Family Papers, Institute for Regional Studies; *Fargo Daily Argus*, September 16, 1890; Fargo City Council Minutes, October 14, 1891, vol. 3, 437; Roy Johnson Index Fargo City Council Minutes, January 5, 1891, May 8, 1891, April 4, 1898, March 18, 1903, September 5, 1904, and December 3, 1906, 29–30; *Fargo Forum and Daily Republican*, September 25 and 26, 1895, February 5, 1896, April 5 and August 20, 1898; "Fargo City Water Works," *Record* 3 (December 1897): iii. Teaford, *The Unheralded Triumph*, 226, admits United States backwardness in water filtration. Water volume made it costly and water from rural reservoirs made it unnecessary.

85. Moorhead City Council Minutes, December 5, 1892, 270–71, 273, February 3, 1896, 171–73, and January 20, 1913, 375; *Moorhead Weekly News*, April 12, 1894, January 23, 1896, and July 19, 1900; Turner and Semling, *History of Clay and Norman Counties*, 1:270; *A Century Together*, 169–70.

86. *Red River Gazette*, October 10, 1872, and January 16, 1873; Teaford, *The Unheralded Triumph*, 162–63; Amy S. Greenberg, *Cause for Alarm: The Volunteer Fire Department in the Nineteenth-Century City* (Princeton, N.J.: Princeton University Press, 1998), 162; Fredericks, "Early History of Moorhead," 67–68, 72; *A Century Together*, 165; *Clay County Advocate*, October 5, 1878; *Daily Argonaut*, January 11, 18, and 28, 1882; Moorhead City Council Minutes, August 14, September 15, and October 16, 1882, 73, 80, 85, and February 10, 1883, 104–5; *Moorhead Weekly News*, September 7, 1882.

87. *A Century Together*, 53; Roy Johnson Index Fargo City Council Minutes, April 15, 1875, November 19, 1877, January 22, 1880, November 26 and December 13, 1883, February 13, 1884, February 2, 1885, February 6, 1888, and March 4, 1889, 4–5; Fargo City Council Minutes, November 13 and 19, December 10, 1877, vol. 1, 81, 83, and 87, March 6, 1882, vol. 2, 39, and November 26, 1883, vol. 3, 117; *Fargo Times*, January 29, 1880; *Fargo Daily Republican*, July 28 and September 14, 1882; *Fargo Sunday Argus*, February 4, 1883; Greenberg, *Cause for Alarm*, 9 and 34.

88. *Fargo Daily Argus*, January 15, 1884; *Fargo Daily Republican*, January 2, February 14, September 14, October 24 and 25, and December 27, 1882; Greenberg, *Cause for Alarm*, 9, 20, 22, 25, 29, 34, 37.

89. Roy Johnson Index Fargo City Council Minutes, June 8, 1893, September 3, 1900, January 12 and November 19, 1903, January 4 and July 18, 1904, 5–6; *Fargo Forum and Daily Republican*, April 19, 1898; Fargo City Council Minutes, May 1, 1899, vol. 1, 462; Moorhead City Council Minutes, May 4, 1896, 195 and 201, February 24, 1902, 229, and May 7, 1906, 501.

90. *A Century Together*, 53; Turner and Semling, *History of Clay and Norman Counties*, 1:269;

Fargo Forum and Daily Republican, June 11, 1894, January 17, June 11, and December 6, 1895, January 30, June 23, August 18, and December 1, 1896, January 22, 1897, and April 11, 1898; *Fargo Sunday Argus,* February 16 and March 2, 1890; *Fargo Daily Argus,* October 20, 1891; Fargo City Council Minutes, October 14, 1891, vol. 3, 439; Greenberg, *Cause for Alarm,* 43–44 and 59–60.

91. Kirkland, *Industry Comes of Age,* 243–44, 252–53; Teaford, *The Unheralded Triumph,* 229.

92. *Moorhead Advocate,* January 5, 1878; Roy Johnson Index Fargo City Council Minutes, December 5, 1879, June 14 and November 7, 1881, October 1 and 5, 1883, January 13, June 8, October 10, 1886, March 29 and July 6, 1887, 2–3; Fargo City Council Minutes, November 7, 1881, vol. 2, 180, and September 7, 1885, vol. 3, 257; *Fargo Daily Republican,* January 9, February 4 and 13, August 21, and September 20, 1882; R. E. Fleming to Brush Electric Co., April 2, 1882, Box 1, Folder 2, Rufus E. Fleming Papers, Institute for Regional Studies; *Fargo Daily Argus,* August 12, 1885; *Fargo Sunday Argus,* July 15, 1888.

93. Fargo City Council Minutes, April 30, 1888, vol. 3, 490–92, May 8 and 20, July 1, 1889, March 10 and 15, 1890, August 5, 1895, vol. 4, 55, 59, 157–59, 161–63, 370–71, and July 5, 1898, vol. 5, 364; Roy Johnson Index City Council Minutes, May 7, 1888, February 4, March 25, and September 9, 1889, July 7 and August 19, 1890, and March 7, 1892, November 28, 1898, April 27, May 9, and July 1, 1901, August 14, 1902, 3–4; *Fargo Forum and Daily Republican,* August 6 and October 15, 1895, November 22, 1898.

94. *A Century Together,* 168; Turner and Semling, *History of Clay and Norman Counties,* 1:270; Moorhead City Council Minutes, October 23 and December 4, 1882, 87 and 92, March 3, 1884, 223, December 7 and 9, 1885, 352 and 356; *Moorhead Weekly News,* December 7, 1882, February 8, 1883, March 6 and 13, 1884, December 17, 1885.

95. Moorhead City Council Minutes October 5, 1891, 143–45, April 3, 1893, 306, April 14 and May 6, 1895, 94, February 3, 1896, 170–71; *Moorhead Weekly News,* March 3, 1892, November 7, 1895, and May 7, 1896.

96. *Moorhead Weekly News,* May 5 and June 30, 1898, March 16, October 12 and 19, 1899; Moorhead City Council Minutes, September 18 and October 6, 1899, 10, 19.

97. [Sister?] to Charles Probstfield, August 22, 1898, Box 1, Probstfield Papers; *Moorhead Weekly News,* October 12 and 19, 1899, February 8, 1900.

98. Mark Peihl, "Fargo and Moorhead Electric Street Railway: 1904–1937," *CCHS Newsletter,* 17 (November/December 1994): 7–9; Roy Johnson Index Fargo City Council Minutes, November 1, 1880, October 14, 1886, October 19, 1891, June 6, 1898, June 11, 1902, 8–11; *Fargo Times,* November 4, 1880; *Fargo Daily Republican,* April 20, June 19 and September 13, 1882; Fargo City Council Minutes, May 5, 1884, vol. 3, 155; *Daily Argonaut,* February 13, 1882; *Moorhead Weekly News,* March 13, 1884; Moorhead City Council Minutes, October 22, 1891, 153–59.

99. Kirkland, *Industry Come of Age,* 244–45, 253; Teaford, *The Unheralded Triumph,* 240; Kenneth T. Jackson, *Crabgrass Frontier: The Suburbanization of the United States* (New York: Oxford University Press, 1985), 111; Peihl, "Fargo and Moorhead Electric Street Railway," 7–10, 12; Roy Johnson Index Fargo City Council Minutes, June 11, 1902, October 15, 1903, September 12, 1904, 11; *A Century Together,* 165.

100. Peihl, "Fargo and Moorhead Electric Street Railway," 8–10; Moorhead City Council Minutes, May 5, 1902, 236, March 18, 1903, 298, October 5 and November 10, 1904, 388, 394, May 6, 1912, 339.

101. *Fargo Sunday Argus,* November 18, 1883; Schlereth, *Victorian America,* 115–16; Fargo

City Council Minutes, January 3, 1881, and May 5, 1882, vol. 2, 110, 241–42; Roy Johnson Index Fargo City Council Minutes, March 6, 1905, 28; Moorhead City Council Minutes, October 7, 1912, 361. For the uneven achievements of American municipal governments, see Teaford, *The Unheralded Triumph*, 251, 262, 269–70, 281–82, and Warner, *The Private City*, 202, 204–5.

CONCLUSION

1. Elwyn B. Robinson, "The Themes of North Dakota History," *North Dakota History* 26 (winter 1959): 6–9, 14–15; David B. Danbom, "North Dakota: The Most Midwestern State," in *Heartland: Comparative Histories of the Midwestern States,* ed. James H. Madison (Bloomington: Indiana University Press, 1988), 109–10. On the factors limiting Fargo's growth, see Lawrence H. Larsen and Roger T. Johnson, "Obstacles to Urbanization on the Northern Great Plains of the United States," *North Dakota History* 50 (summer 1983): 17–20; Lawrence H. Larsen, *The Urban West at the End of the Frontier* (Lawrence: Regents Press of Kansas, 1978), 9–10, 40, 42–43, 100–3, 116; Lawrence H. Larsen and Barbara J. Cottrell, *The Gate City: A History of Omaha,* enlarged ed. (Lincoln: University of Nebraska Press, 1997), 31–32, 69–71, 79f. On population of Great Plains states, see Richard White, *"It's Your Misfortune and None of My Own": A History of the American West* (Norman: University of Oklahoma Press, 1991), 188. In 1900, Kansas had 1,470,495 people, Nebraska 1,066,300, and North Dakota 319,136.

2. Thomas White Harvey, "The Making of Railroad Towns in Minnesota's Red River Valley" (master's thesis, Pennsylvania State University, 1982), 191–94, 222; *The WPA Guide to 1930s North Dakota,* new introduction by Gerald G. Newborg and Marcia Britton Wolter (Bismarck: State Historical Society of North Dakota, 1990), 129–30, 137; Elwyn B. Robinson, *History of North Dakota* (Lincoln: University of Nebraska Press, 1966), 378; David B. Danbom, "Postscript," in Elwyn B. Robinson, *History of North Dakota* (Fargo: Institute for Regional Studies—North Dakota State University, 1995), 585 and 589–90.

3. Sam Bass Warner Jr., *The Private City: Philadelphia in Three Periods of Growth* (Philadelphia: University of Pennsylvania Press, 1968), 3–4, 111, 117–18, 213–14.

4. Ibid., 100, 108–11; Larsen, *Urban West,* xi, 19, 120.

5. Robinson, *History of North Dakota* (1966), 230–31, 257, 260; Henry Johnson, *The Other Side of Main Street: A History Teacher from Sauk Centre* (New York: Columbia University Press, 1943), 133–34. For progressives as "evangelistic modernizers," see John Whiteclay Chambers II, *The Tyranny of Change: America in the Progressive Era, 1900–1917* (New York: St. Martin's Press, 1980), 112.

6. Robert P. Wilkins, "Alexander McKenzie and the Politics of Bossism," in *The North Dakota Political Tradition,* ed. Thomas W. Howard (Ames: Iowa State University Press, 1981), 23, 25, 28, 33–34, 38–39; Charles N. Glaab, "John Burke and the Progressive Revolt," in Howard, *The North Dakota Political Tradition,* 41, 43, 45, 48, 50–51, 59, 61; Robinson, *History of North Dakota* (1966), 258–61; Carl H. Chrislock, *The Progressive Era in Minnesota, 1899–1918* (St. Paul: Minnesota Historical Society Press, 1971), 31–32, 35–36, 60, 86–88, 200; Robert H. Wiebe, *The Search for Order* (New York: Hill and Wang, 1967), 292–302. The literature on progressivism is vast and the issues are complex. On tensions between grassroots participation and progressive emphasis on efficiency, expertise and order, see Samuel P. Hays, *Conservation and the Gospel of Efficiency: The Progressive Conservation Movement, 1890–1920* (New York: Atheneum, 1969), preface,

265–66, 276. On moral reform of 1890s municipal politics, see Paul Boyer, *Urban Masses and Moral Order in America, 1820–1920* (Cambridge: Harvard University Press, 1978), 162, 168–74, 220–21, 280–82.

7. J. A. Johnson to A. O. Thomas, May 15, 1885, and to A. E. Wood, June 5 and 10, 1885, M491, Reel One, John Augustus Johnson Papers, Minnesota Historical Society, St. Paul.

8. *Hon. J. A. Johnson: A Partial Copy of His Letters, Travels and Addresses,* ed. Alice E. Chester and Laura A. Johnson (Fargo: Privately printed, 1908), 5–6, 107–9, 120–22, 167–68; Edward Chase Kirkland, *Industry Comes of Age: Business, Labor and Public Policy, 1860–1897* (Chicago: Quadrangle Paperback, 1967), 249–50; *Fargo Argus,* August 3, 1898; J. A. Johnson to SU, March 7, 1898, M491, Reel One, John Augustus Johnson Papers; Roy Johnson Index Fargo City Council Minutes, January 11 and October 19, 1897, 10, Institute for Regional Studies, North Dakota State University, Fargo.

9. Mayor J. A. Johnson, "Saloon Suppression Produces Business Prosperity" (1900); J. A. Johnson to M. A. Hildreth and to *Fargo Forum,* May 9, 1903; clippings from *Fargo Forum,* March 19, 1902, May 9 and August 19, 1903. M491, Reel One, John Augustus Johnson Papers.

10. Chester and Johnson, *Hon. J. A. Johnson,* 6–8, 129–31, 202–4; *Fargo Forum,* April 5 and May 21, 1904, April 18 and September 25, 1906, January 17 and March 22, 1907; *Grand Forks Evening Press,* July 20, 1904; *Fargo Morning Call and Daily Argus,* April 3, May 4 and 22, and August 14, 1906.

11. *Moorhead Weekly News,* February 28, 1895; Johnson, *The Other Side of Main Street,* 123–28.

12. Johnson, *The Other Side of Main Street,* 127–28, 130, 136–39.

13. Moorhead City Council Minutes, May 22 and December 4, 1911, 284 and 312, May 6, September 9, December 9, 1913, 395–96, 424, and 437, January 6, 1914, 439. Women's gendered notion of social justice and good government is summarized by Thomas Winter, "Gender and Urban Development in the 'City of Big Shoulders,' 1871–1933," *Reviews in American History* 31 (December 2003): 564–67.

14. Kenneth Fox, *Better City Government: Innovation in American Urban Politics, 1850–1937* (Philadelphia: Temple University Press, 1977), ix, xiv–xix, 4–5, 21–22, 50–51, 53–54, 60–64, 121, 123, and 180–81.

15. Erdrich quoted in Carl Abbott, *The Metropolitan Frontier: Cities in the Modern American West* (Tucson: University of Arizona Press, 1993), 48 and 178.

16. On character, see Danbom, "Postscript," 585 and 592. Robinson concluded his classic *History of North Dakota* in 1966 with a chapter titled "The Character of a People." He suggested that the North Dakota frontier had provided abundant opportunities for self-improvement through the work ethic and fostered greater respect for women, more democratic ideas, and disregard for class distinctions. It also created feelings of inferiority as "country cousins" that spurred people to success and feelings of loyalty to their local communities and state.

Index

CARROLL ENGELHARDT is professor emeritus of history at Concordia College in Moorhead, Minnesota. He is the author of *On Firm Foundation Grounded: The First Century of Concordia College, 1891–1991*, as well as several articles on the history of public education.